Microsoft

MCSA/MCSE
Self-Paced Training Kit

Implementing and Administering
SECURITY
in a Microsoft
WINDOWS 2000
NETWORK

Exam 70-214

Microsoft Corporation with
Matthew Strebe, MCSE

PUBLISHED BY
Microsoft Press
A Division of Microsoft Corporation
One Microsoft Way
Redmond, Washington 98052-6399

Library of Congress Cataloging-in-Publication Data
MCSA/MCSE Self-Paced Training Kit. Implementing and Administering Security in a
    Microsoft Windows 2000 Network: Exam 70-214 / Microsoft Corporation.
        p. cm.
    Includes index.
    ISBN 0-7356-1878-X
    1. Electronic data processing personnel--Certification.   2. Microsoft
software--Examinations--Study guides.   3. Computer networks--Examinations--Study
guides.   I. Microsoft Corporation.

QA76.3.M326575   2003
005.8--dc21   2002044872

Printed and bound in the United States of America.

1 2 3 4 5 6 7 8 9   QWT   8 7 6 5 4 3

Distributed in Canada by H.B. Fenn and Company Ltd.

A CIP catalogue record for this book is available from the British Library.

Microsoft Press books are available through booksellers and distributors worldwide. For further information about international editions, contact your local Microsoft Corporation office or contact Microsoft Press International directly at fax (425) 936-7329. Visit our Web site at www.microsoft.com/mspress. Send comments to *tkinput@microsoft.com*.

Active Directory, ActiveX, Encarta, Great Plains Software, Microsoft, Microsoft Press, MS-DOS, NetMeeting, Outlook, Visual Studio, Windows, and Windows NT are either registered trademarks or trademarks of Microsoft Corporation or Great Plains Software, Inc., in the United States and/or other countries. Other product and company names mentioned herein may be the trademarks of their respective owners.

The example companies, organizations, products, domain names, e-mail addresses, logos, people, places, and events depicted herein are fictitious. No association with any real company, organization, product, domain name, e-mail address, logo, person, place, or event is intended or should be inferred.

For Microsoft Press:
Acquisitions Editor: Kathy Harding
Project Editor: Karen Szall

For Studioserv:
Project Manager: Steve Sagman
Technical Editor: Jack Beaudry
Copyeditor: Gail Taylor
Desktop Publisher: Sharon Bell
Indexer: Julie Kawabata

Body Part No. X08-95191

Contents

About This Book

Welcome to the *MCSA/MCSE Self-Paced Training Kit: Implementing and Administering Security in a Microsoft Windows 2000 Network, Exam 70-214.* This book provides in-depth and detailed information about the major security services in Microsoft Windows 2000 networks, including securing desktops and servers using Group Policy, configuring and managing certificates and certificate authorities, implementing encrypted network connections using IPSec, properly securing public Internet servers and services, and keeping your systems up to date automatically.

Note   For more information about becoming a Microsoft Certified Systems Administrator (MCSA) or Microsoft Certified Systems Engineer (MCSE), see the section titled "The Microsoft Certified Professional Program" later in this introduction.

Each chapter in this book is divided into lessons. Most lessons include hands-on procedures that allow you to practice or demonstrate a particular concept or skill. Each lesson ends with a set of review questions to test your knowledge of the lesson material and a short summary of the major points covered in the lesson.

The "Getting Started" section of this introduction provides important setup instructions that describe the hardware and software requirements to complete the procedures in this course. It also provides information about the networking configuration necessary to complete some of the hands-on procedures. Read through this section thoroughly before you start the lessons.

Intended Audience

This book was developed for information technology (IT) professionals who need to design, plan, implement and support a Microsoft Windows 2000 network infrastructure or who plan to take the related Microsoft Certified Professional exam 70-214, *Implementing and Administering Security in a Microsoft Windows 2000 Network.* To use this book, you should understand basic Windows 2000 installation and configuration, as well as Active Directory installation and basic concepts.

Prerequisites

This training kit requires that students meet the following prerequisites:

- Certified as a Microsoft Certified Professional (MCP) in Windows 2000 Professional or Windows 2000 Server
- Experienced installing and configuring Active Directory directory service
- One year experience using Windows 2000

Reference Materials

You might find the following reference materials useful:

- *Microsoft Windows 2000 Server Resource Kit* (Microsoft Press, 2002)
- Windows 2000 On-Line Help
- Microsoft Technet at *http://www.microsoft.com/technet*

About The CD-ROMs

For your use, this book includes a Supplemental Course Materials CD-ROM. This CD-ROM contains:

- An electronic version (eBook) of this training kit.
- An eBook of the *Microsoft Encyclopedia of Networking, Second Edition.*
- A practice test made up of sample exam questions. Use these questions to assess your understanding of the concepts presented in this book.

A second CD-ROM contains a 120-day evaluation edition of Microsoft Windows 2000 Server.

Caution   The 120-day Evaluation Edition provided with this training is not the full retail product and is provided only for the purposes of training and evaluation. Microsoft Technical Support does not support this evaluation edition.

For additional support information regarding this book and the CD-ROM (including answers to commonly asked questions about installation and use), visit the Microsoft Press Technical Support Web site at *http://www.microsoft.com/mspress/support/.* You can also email tkinput@microsoft.com or send a letter to Microsoft Press, Attention: Microsoft Press Technical Support, One Microsoft Way, Redmond, WA 98052-6399.

Features of This Book

Each chapter contains sections that are designed to help you get the most educational value from the chapter:

- Each chapter opens with a "Before You Begin" section, which prepares you for completing the chapter.
- The chapters are then divided into lessons. Whenever possible, lessons contain practices with exercises that give you an opportunity to use the skills being presented or explore the part of the application being described.

  All exercises offer step-by-step procedures that are identified with a bullet symbol like the one to the left of this paragraph.
- At the end of each lesson is the "Review" section that you can use to test what you have learned.
- The review is followed by the "Summary" section, which identifies the key concepts from the lesson.

Appendix A, "Questions and Answers," contains all of the questions asked in each chapter and the corresponding answers.

Notes

Several types of Notes appear throughout the lessons.

- Notes marked **Tip** contain explanations of possible results or alternative methods for performing tasks.
- Notes marked **Important** contain information that is essential to completing a task.
- Notes marked **Note** contain supplemental information.
- Notes marked **Caution** contain warnings about possible loss of data.
- Notes marked **More info** contain references to other sources of information.
- Notes marked **Planning** contain hints and useful information that should help you plan the implementation.

Conventions

The following conventions are used throughout this book.

Notational Conventions

- Characters or commands that you type appear in **bold** type.
- *Italic* is used for book titles and for emphasis of terms.

- Names of files and folders appear in initial capital letters, except when you are to type them directly. Unless otherwise indicated, you can use lowercase letters when you type a file name in a dialog box or at a command prompt.

- File name extensions, when they appear without a file name, are in lowercase letters.

- Acronyms appear in all uppercase letters.

- Monospace type represents code samples, examples of screen text, or entries that you might type at a command prompt or in initialization files.

- Icons represent specific sections in the book as follows:

Icon	Skill Being Measured
	A hands-on exercise. You should perform the exercise to give yourself an opportunity to use the skills being presented in the lesson.
	Lesson review questions. These questions at the end of each lesson allow you to test what you have learned in the lessons. You will find the answers to the review questions in the Questions and Answers appendix at the end of the book.

Keyboard Conventions

- A plus sign (+) between two key names means that you must press those keys at the same time. For example, "Press ALT+TAB" means that you hold down Alt while you press Tab.

- A comma (,) between two or more key names means that you must press each of the keys consecutively, not together. For example, "Press ALT, F, X" means that you press and release each key in sequence. "Press ALT+W, L" means that you first press Alt and W at the same time, and then release them and press L.

- You can choose menu commands with the keyboard. Press the ALT key to activate the menu bar, and then sequentially press the keys that correspond to the highlighted or underlined letter of the menu name and the command name. For some commands, you can also press a key combination listed in the menu.

- You can select or clear check boxes or option buttons in dialog boxes with the keyboard. Press the ALT key, and then press the key that corresponds to the underlined letter of the option name. Or you can press TAB until the option is highlighted, and then press the spacebar to select or clear the check box or option button.

- You can cancel the display of a dialog box by pressing the ESC key.

Chapter and Appendix Overview

This self-paced training course combines notes, hands-on procedures, and review questions to teach you about security issues in a Windows 2000 network. It is designed to be completed from beginning to end, but you can choose a customized track and complete only the sections that interest you. If you choose the customized track option, see the "Before You Begin" section in each chapter. Any hands-on procedures that require preliminary work from preceding chapters refer to the appropriate chapters.

The book is divided into the following sections and chapters:

- The "About This Book" section contains a self-paced training overview and introduces the components of this training kit. Read this section thoroughly to get the greatest educational value from this self-paced training and to plan which lessons you will complete.
- Chapter 1, "Group Policy," describes Windows 2000 tools for managing Group Policy and introduces basic security concepts.
- Chapter 2, "User Accounts and Security Groups," looks at how users and groups can be used to manage security on local computers and domains.
- Chapter 3, "Restricting Accounts, Users, and Groups," introduces the permission system used on the NTFS file system and for registry objects, and describes how to manage permissions, auditing, and Active Directory security.
- Chapter 4, "Account-Based Security," covers the security template features of Active directory and how to manage, deploy, and troubleshoot templates.
- Chapter 5, "Certificate Authorities," introduces Certificate Services and describes how to install and maintain a certificate authority.
- Chapter 6, "Managing a Public Key Infrastructure," describes how to issue, renew, and revoke certificates, deploy and publish certificates, and troubleshoot certificate issues.
- Chapter 7, "Increasing Authentication Security," covers Windows 2000 methods of authenticating clients running diverse operating systems, the Kerberos authentication system, and configuring trusts between networks.
- Chapter 8, "IP Security," describes how to configure IP Security (IPSec) authentication and encryption, deploy IPSec certificates, and troubleshoot IP Security.
- Chapter 9, "Remote Access and VPN," covers the Windows 2000 Routing and Remote Access Service. It describes how to configure basic RRAS security, manage authentication and client settings, and configure virtual private network (VPN) protocols.
- Chapter 10, "Wireless Security," describes how to configure and secure wireless networks using the WEP and 802.1x standards and how to configure wireless clients for maximum security.

- Chapter 11, "Public Application Server Security," describes Microsoft ISA server and how it can be used to secure public servers, and specific security considerations for Microsoft SQL Server and Microsoft Exchange servers.

- Chapter 12, "Web Service Security," covers IIS (Internet Information Services), the Web server component of Windows 2000. It describes how to configure IIS authentication methods and SSL encryption for secure sites.

- Chapter 13, "Event Monitoring and Intrusion Detection," looks at how auditing and event logs can help you detect intruders and provide a chain of evidence, along with methods of recovering from and preventing network intrusion.

- Chapter 14, "Software Maintenance," describes the Windows 2000 mechanisms for incremental updates, including service packs and hotfixes, and introduces tools for deploying updates across the enterprise.

- Appendix A, "Questions and Answers," lists all of the review questions from the book, showing the page number for each question and the suggested answer.

- The glossary provides definitions for many of the terms and concepts presented in this training kit.

Where to Find Specific Skills in This Book

The following tables provide a list of the skills measured on certification exam 70-214, *Implementing and Administering Security in a Microsoft Windows 2000 Network*. The table provides the skill, and where in this book you will find the lesson relating to that skill.

Note   Exam skills are subject to change without prior notice and at the sole discretion of Microsoft.

Implementing, Managing, and Troubleshooting Baseline Security

Skill Being Measured	Location in Book
Configure security templates. ■ Configure registry and file system permissions. ■ Configure account policies. ■ Configure audit policies. ■ Configure user rights assignment. ■ Configure security options. ■ Configure system services. ■ Configure restricted groups. ■ Configure event logs.	Chapter 4 (all lessons)
Deploy security templates. Deployment methods include using Group Policy and scripting.	Chapter 3, Lesson 4
Troubleshoot security template problems. Considerations include Group Policy, upgraded operating systems, and mixed client-computer operating systems.	Chapter 4, Lesson 4
Configure additional security based on computer roles. Computer roles include Microsoft SQL Server computer, Microsoft Exchange Server computer, domain controller, Internet Access Service (IAS) server, Internet Information Services (IIS) server, and mobile client computer.	Chapter 11 and throughout other chapters
Configure additional security for client-computer operating systems by using Group Policy.	Chapter 1, Lesson 2

Implementing, Managing, and Troubleshooting Service Packs and Security Updates

Skill Being Measured	Location in Book
Determine the current status of service packs and security updates. Tools include MBSA and HFNetChk.	Chapter 14, Lesson 1
Install service packs and security updates. Considerations include slipstreaming and using Remote Installation Services (RIS), custom scripts, and isolated networks.	Chapter 14, Lesson 1
Manage service packs and security updates. Considerations include server computers and remote client computers. Tools include Microsoft Software Update Service, Automatic Updates, and SMS.	Chapter 14, Lesson 2
Troubleshoot the deployment of service packs and security updates. Typical issues include third-party application compatibility, permissions, and version conflicts.	Chapter 14

Implementing, Managing, and Troubleshooting Secure Communication Channels

Skill Being Measured	Location in Book
Configure IPSec to secure communication between networks and hosts. Hosts include domain controllers, Internet Web servers, databases, e-mail servers, and client computers. ■ Configure IPSec authentication. ■ Configure appropriate encryption levels. ■ Configure the appropriate IPSec protocol, including AH and ESP. ■ Deploy and manage IPSec certificates. Considerations include renewing certificates.	Chapter 8, Lesson 1
Troubleshoot IPSec. Issues include IPSec rule configurations, firewall configurations, routers, and authentication.	Chapter 8, Lesson 3
Implement security for wireless networks. ■ Configure public and private wireless LANs. ■ Configure wireless encryption levels, including WEP and 802.1x.	Chapter 10, Lessons 1 and 2
■ Configure wireless network connections settings on client computers. Client-computer operating systems are Windows 2000 Professional and Windows XP Professional.	Chapter 10, Lesson 3
Configure Server Message Block (SMB) signing to support packet authentication and integrity.	Chapter 8, Lesson 1

Skill Being Measured	Location in Book
Deploy and manage SSL certificates. Considerations include renewing certificates and obtaining self-issued certificates versus public-issued certificates. ■ Obtain public and private certificates. ■ Install certificates for SSL. ■ Renew certificates.	Chapter 12, Lesson 3
Configure SSL to secure communication channels. Communication channels include: ■ Client computer to Web server ■ Web server to SQL Server computer ■ Client computer to Active Directory domain controller ■ E-mail server to client computer	Chapter 12, Lesson 3 Chapter 11, Lessons 2 and 3

Configuring, Managing, and Troubleshooting Authentication and Remote Access Security

Skill Being Measured	Location in Book
Configure and troubleshoot authentication. ■ Configure authentication protocols to support mixed Windows client-computer environments. ■ Configure the interoperability of Kerberos authentication with UNIX computers. ■ Configure authentication for extranet scenarios. ■ Configure trust relationships. ■ Configure authentication for members of non-trusted domain authentication.	Chapter 7 and Chapter 2
Configure and troubleshoot authentication for Web users. Authentication types include Basic, Integrated Windows, anonymous, digest, and client certificate mapping.	Chapter 12, Lesson 2
Configure authentication for secure remote access. Authentication types include PAP, CHAP, MS-CHAP, MS-CHAP v2, EAP-MD5, EAP-TLS, and Multi-factor authentication with smart cards and EAP.	Chapter 9, Lesson 2
Configure and troubleshoot virtual private network (VPN) protocols. Considerations include: ■ Internet service provider (ISP) ■ Client-computer operating system ■ Network Address Translation (NAT) devices ■ Routing and Remote Access server ■ Firewall server	Chapter 9, Lesson 4
Manage client-computer configuration for remote access security. Tools include remote access policy and Connection Manager Administration Kit.	Chapter 9, Lesson 3

Implementing and Managing a Public Key Infrastructure (PKI) and Encrypting File System (EFS)

Skill Being Measured	Location in Book
Install and configure Certificate Authority (CA) hierarchies. Considerations include enterprise, standalone, and third-party CAs. ■ Install and configure the root, intermediate, and issuing CA. Considerations include renewals and hierarchy. ■ Configure certificate templates. Considerations include LDAP queries, HTTP queries, and third-party CAs. ■ Configure the publication of Certificate Revocation Lists (CRLs). ■ Configure public key Group Policy. ■ Configure certificate renewal and enrollment. ■ Deploy certificates to users, computers, and CAs.	Chapter 5, Lessons 1 and 2
Manage Certificate Authorities (CAs). Considerations include enterprise, stand-alone, and third-party CAs. ■ Enroll and renew certificates. ■ Revoke certificates. ■ Manage and troubleshoot Certificate Revocation Lists (CRLs). Considerations include publishing the CRL. ■ Back up and restore the CA.	Chapter 5, Lesson 3
Manage client-computer and server certificates. Considerations include SMIME, EFS, exporting, and storage. ■ Publish certificates through Active Directory. ■ Issue certificates using MMC, Web enrollment, programmatic, or auto enrollment using Windows XP. ■ Recover KMS-issued keys.	Chapter 6, Lessons 1 and 2 Chapter 5, Lesson 3
Manage and troubleshoot EFS. Considerations include domain members, workgroup members, and client-computer operating systems.	Chapter 6

Monitoring and Responding to Security Incidents

Skill Being Measured	Location in Book
Configure and manage auditing. Considerations include Windows Events, Internet Information Services (IIS), firewall log files, Network Monitor Log, and RAS log files. ■ Manage audit log retention. ■ Manage distributed audit logs by using EventComb.	Chapter 13, Lesson 1
Analyze security events. Considerations include reviewing logs and events.	Chapter 13, Lesson 2
Respond to security incidents including hackers, viruses, denial-of-service (DoS) attacks, natural disasters, and maintaining chains of evidence.	Chapter 13, Lesson 3
■ Isolate and contain the incident. Considerations include preserving the chain of evidence. ■ Implement counter measures. ■ Restore services.	

Getting Started

This self-paced training kit contains hands-on procedures to help you learn securing your Windows 2000 network infrastructure. To complete some of these procedures, you must have as many as four computers networked together or connected to a larger network. All computers must be capable of running Windows 2000 Server and meeting its minimum hardware requirements.

These exercises have been tested using virtual machine software. You can consider using virtual machine software to reduce the number of physical computers required to complete the exercises in this book.

Caution   The exercises in this book require you to make changes to your servers. This might cause undesirable results if you are connected to a larger network. You should not perform any of these exercises on production computers without testing them first and adapting them to your network configuration. Check with your network administrator before attempting these exercises.

Hardware Requirements

To complete all of the exercises in this training kit, each computer must have the following minimum configuration. All hardware should be on the Microsoft Windows 2000 Hardware Compatibility List.

- Intel Pentium II or later processor.
- 128 MB RAM
- 2 GB hard disk drive
- 100 Mbps network interface adapter
- CD-ROM drive
- Microsoft Mouse or compatible pointing device
- An Apple Macintosh computer that meets the minimum requirements for OS X 10.1.
- An 802.1x compliant Wireless Access Point such as the Intel Pro 5000 802.11a WAP.
- A wireless network adapter compatible with your WAP.

Software Requirements

The following software is required to complete the procedures in this course.

- Windows 2000 Server
- Windows 2000 Professional

The following software is required to complete specific exercises that cover security issues specific to the software. If you do not have the software to complete an exercise, you should read the material to be familiar with the concepts presented.

- Windows 98
- Apple Macintosh OS X 10.1 or later
- Microsoft ISA Server
- Microsoft SQL 2000 Server
- Microsoft Exchange 2000 Server
- A 120-day evaluation copy of Microsoft Windows 2000 Server is included on the CD-ROMs in this training kit. Evaluation versions of the remaining required software are available for download from *http://www.microsoft.com*.

Caution   The 120-day Evaluation Edition provided with this training is not the full retail product and is provided only for the purposes of training and evaluation. Microsoft Technical Support does not support this evaluation edition. For additional support information regarding this book and the CD-ROMs (including answers to commonly asked questions about installation and use), visit the Microsoft Press Technical Support Web site at *http://www.microsoft.com/mspress/support/*. You can also email TKINPUT@MICROSOFT.COM, or send a letter to Microsoft Press, Attn: Microsoft Press Technical Support, One Microsoft Way, Redmond, WA 98502-6399.

Setup Instructions

Set up your computer according to the manufacturer's instructions.

For the exercises that require networked computers, you need to make sure the computers can communicate with each other.

- The first computer will be configured as a primary domain controller (PDC), and will be assigned the computer account name dc01 and the domain name domain.fabrikam.com. This computer will act as a domain controller, enterprise root Certificate Authority and DNS server for domain.fabrikam.com.
- The second computer will act as a client workstation in the domain for most of the procedures in this course.
- The third computer will act as a certificate authority, SQL Server, as a Web server, and as an Exchange server for procedures throughout this book.
- The fourth computer will act as an Internet firewall for procedures in Chapter 11.

Caution   If your computers are part of a larger network, you *must* verify with your network administrator that the computer names, domain name, IP addresses, and other information used in setting up Windows 2000 as described in Chapter 1 and throughout this book do not conflict with network operations. If they conflict, ask your network administrator to provide alternative values and use those values throughout all of the exercise in this book.

The eBooks

The CD-ROM also includes an electronic version of this Training Kit and an electronic version of the *Microsoft Encyclopedia of Networking, Second Edition*. To view these eBooks, you need Microsoft Internet Explorer 5.01 or later and the corresponding HTML Help components on your system. For your convenience, Internet Explorer 6 has been included on the CD-ROM.

▶ **To use the eBooks**

1. Insert the Supplemental Course Materials CD-ROM into your CD-ROM drive.

   Note If AutoRun is disabled on your machine, run StartCD.exe in the root folder of the CD-ROM.

2. Click Training Kit eBook on the user interface menu and follow the prompts. (To install the Encyclopedia of Networking, click Encyclopedia eBook and follow the prompts.)

   Note You must have the Supplemental Course Materials CD-ROM inserted in your CD-ROM drive to view the eBooks.

The Practice Test

The CD-ROM includes an electronic assessment tool that generates multiple practice tests with automated scoring and answer feedback.

▶ **To install the sample exam questions on your hard disk drive**

1. Insert the Supplemental Course Materials CD into your CD-ROM drive.

   Note If AutoRun is disabled on your machine, run StartCD.exe in the root directory of the CD or refer to the Readme.txt file on the CD.

2. Click Practice Test on the user interface menu and follow the prompts.

The Microsoft Certified Professional Program

The Microsoft Certified Professional (MCP) program provides the best method to prove your command of current Microsoft products and technologies. Microsoft, an industry leader in certification, is on the forefront of testing methodology. The exams and corresponding certifications are developed to validate your mastery of critical competencies as you design and develop, or implement and support, solutions with Microsoft products and technologies. Computer professionals who become Microsoft certified are recognized as experts and are sought after industry-wide.

The Microsoft Certified Professional program offers multiple certifications, based on specific areas of technical expertise, including:

■ *Microsoft Certified Professional (MCP).* Demonstrated in-depth knowledge of at least one Microsoft Windows operating system or architecturally significant platform. An MCP is qualified to implement a Microsoft product or technology as part of a business solution for an organization.

■ *Microsoft Certified Systems Engineer (MCSE)*. Qualified to effectively analyze the business requirements, and design and implement the infrastructure for business solutions based on the Microsoft Windows and Microsoft .NET Server operating system and Microsoft Servers software.

■ *Microsoft Certified Systems Administrator (MCSA)*. Individuals with the skills to manage and troubleshoot existing network and system environments based on the Microsoft Windows and Microsoft .NET Server operating systems.

■ *Microsoft Certified Database Administrator (MCDBA)*. Individuals who design, implement, and administer Microsoft SQL Server databases.

■ *Microsoft Certified Solution Developer (MCSD)*. Professional developers qualified to analyze, design, and develop enterprise business solutions with Microsoft development tools and technologies including the Microsoft .NET Framework.

■ *Microsoft Certified Application Developer (MCAD)*. Professional developers qualified to develop, test, deploy, and maintain powerful applications using Microsoft tools and technologies including Microsoft Visual Studio .NET and XML Web services.

■ *Microsoft Certified Trainer (MCT)*. Instructionally and technically qualified to deliver Microsoft Official Curriculum through a Microsoft Certified Technical Education Center (CTEC).

Microsoft Certification Benefits

Microsoft certification, one of the most comprehensive certification programs available for assessing and maintaining software-related skills, is a valuable measure of an individual's knowledge and expertise. Microsoft certification is awarded to individuals who have successfully demonstrated their ability to perform specific tasks and implement solutions with Microsoft products. Certification brings a variety of benefits: to the individual, and to employers and organizations.

Microsoft Certification Benefits for Individuals

As a Microsoft Certified Professional, you receive many benefits:

■ Industry recognition of your knowledge and proficiency with Microsoft products and technologies.

■ A Microsoft Developer Network subscription. MCPs receive rebates or discounts on a one-year subscription to the Microsoft Developer Network (*msdn.microsoft.com/subscriptions/*) during the first year of certification. (Fulfillment details will vary, depending on your location; please see your Welcome Kit.)

- Access to technical and product information direct from Microsoft through a secured area of the MCP Web site (go to *http://www.microsoft.com/traincert/ mcp/mcpsecure.asp/*).

- Access to exclusive discounts on products and services from selected companies. Individuals who are currently certified can learn more about exclusive discounts by visiting the MCP secured Web site (go to *www.microsoft.com/traincert/mcp/ mcpsecure.asp/* and select the "Other Benefits" link).

- MCP logo, certificate, transcript, wallet card, and lapel pin to identify you as a Microsoft Certified Professional (MCP) to colleagues and clients. Electronic files of logos and transcript may be downloaded from the MCP secured Web site (go to *http://www.microsoft.com/traincert/mcp/mcpsecure.asp/*) upon certification.

- Invitations to Microsoft conferences, technical training sessions, and special events.

- Free access to *Microsoft Certified Professional Magazine Online*, a career and professional development magazine. Secured content on the *Microsoft Certified Professional Magazine Online* Web site includes the current issue (available only to MCPs), additional online-only content and columns, an MCP-only database, and regular chats with Microsoft and other technical experts.

- Discount on membership to PASS (for MCPs only), the Professional Association for SQL Server. In addition to playing a key role in the only worldwide, user-run SQL Server user group endorsed by Microsoft, members enjoy unique access to a world of educational opportunities (go to *http://www.microsoft.com/traincert/ mcp/mcpsecure.asp/*).

An additional benefit is received by Microsoft Certified System Engineers (MCSEs):

- A 50 percent rebate or discount on a one-year subscription to *TechNet* or *TechNet Plus* during the first year of certification. (Fulfillment details will vary, depending on your location. Please see your Welcome Kit.) A *TechNet* subscription provides MCSEs with a portable IT survival kit that is updated monthly. It includes the complete Microsoft Knowledge Base as well as service packs and kits.

An additional benefit is received by Microsoft Certified System Database Administrators (MCDBAs):

- A 50 percent rebate or discount on a one-year subscription to TechNet or TechNet Plus during the first year of certification. (Fulfillment details will vary, depending on your location. Please see your Welcome Kit.) A *TechNet* subscription provides MCSEs with a portable IT survival kit that is updated monthly. It includes the complete Microsoft Knowledge Base as well as service packs and kits.

- A one-year subscription to *SQL Server Magazine*. Written by industry experts, the magazine contains technical and how-to tips and advice—a must for anyone working with SQL Server.

A list of benefits for Microsoft Certified Trainers (MCTs) can be found at *www.microsoft.com/traincert/mcp/mct/benefits.asp/*.

Microsoft Certification Benefits for Employers and Organizations

Through certification, computer professionals can maximize the return on investment in Microsoft technology. Research shows that Microsoft certification provides organizations with:

- Excellent return on training and certification investments by providing a standard method of determining training needs and measuring results.
- Increased customer satisfaction and decreased support costs through improved service, increased productivity and greater technical self-sufficiency.
- Reliable benchmark for hiring, promoting and career planning.
- Recognition and rewards for productive employees by validating their expertise.
- Retraining options for existing employees so they can work effectively with new technologies.
- Assurance of quality when outsourcing computer services.

Requirements for Becoming a Microsoft Certified Professional

The certification requirements differ for each certification and are specific to the products and job functions addressed by the certification.

To become a Microsoft Certified Professional, you must pass rigorous certification exams that provide a valid and reliable measure of technical proficiency and expertise. These exams are designed to test your expertise and ability to perform a role or task with a product, and are developed with the input of professionals in the industry. Questions in the exams reflect how Microsoft products are used in actual organizations, giving them "real-world" relevance.

- Microsoft Certified Product (MCPs) candidates are required to pass one current Microsoft certification exam. Candidates may pass additional Microsoft certification exams to further qualify their skills with other Microsoft products, development tools, or desktop applications.
- Microsoft Certified Systems Engineers (MCSEs) are required to pass five core exams and two elective exams.
- Microsoft Certified Systems Administrators (MCSAs) are required to pass three core exams and one elective exam that provide a valid and reliable measure of technical proficiency and expertise.

- Microsoft Certified Database Administrators (MCDBAs) are required to pass three core exams and one elective exam that measure of technical proficiency and expertise.
- Microsoft Certified Application Developers (MCADs) are reqired to pass two core exams and one elective exam in an area of specialization.
- Microsoft Certified Solution Developers (MCSDs) are required to pass three core exams and one elective exam. (MCSD for Microsoft .NET candidates are required to pass four core exams and one elective.)
- Microsoft Certified Trainers (MCTs) are required to meet instructional and technical requirements specific to each Microsoft Official Curriculum course they are certified to deliver. The MCT program requires on-going training to meet the requirements for the annual renewal of certification. For more information about becoming a Microsoft Certified Trainer, visit *http:// www.microsoft.com/traincert/mcp/mct/* or contact a regional service center near you.

Technical Training for Computer Professionals

Technical training is available in a variety of ways, with instructor-led classes, online instruction, or self-paced training available at thousands of locations worldwide.

Self-Paced Training

For motivated learners who are ready for the challenge, self-paced instruction is the most flexible, cost-effective way to increase your knowledge and skills.

A full-line of self-paced print and computer-based training materials is available direct from the source—Microsoft Press. Microsoft Official Curriculum courseware kits from Microsoft Press are designed for advanced computer system professionals and are available from Microsoft Press and the Microsoft Developer Division. Self-paced training kits from Microsoft Press feature print-based instructional materials, along with CD-ROM based product software, multimedia presentations, lab exercises, and practice files.

Microsoft Certified Technical Education Centers

Microsoft Certified Technical Education Centers (CTECs) are the best source for instructor-led training that can help you prepare to become a Microsoft Certified Professional. The Microsoft CTEC program is a worldwide network of qualified technical training organizations that provide authorized delivery of Microsoft Official Curriculum courses by Microsoft Certified Trainers to computer professionals.

For a listing of CTEC locations in the United States and Canada, visit the Web site at *http://www.microsoft.com/traincert/ctec/*.

Technical Support

Every effort has been made to ensure the accuracy of this book and the contents of the companion disc. If you have comments, questions, or ideas regarding this book or the companion disc, please send them to Microsoft Press using either of the following methods:

E-mail

TKINPUT@MICROSOFT.COM

Postal Mail

Microsoft Press
Attn: MCSA/MCSE Training Kit: Implementing and Administering Security
in a Microsoft Windows 2000 Network Editor
One Microsoft Way
Redmond, WA 98052-6399

For additional support information regarding this book and the CD-ROM (including corrections and answers to commonly asked questions about installation and use), visit the Microsoft Press Technical Support Web site at *http://www.microsoft.com/ mspress/support/*. To connect directly to the Microsoft Press Knowledge Base and enter a query, visit *http://www.microsoft.com/mspress/support/search.asp*. For support information regarding Microsoft software, please connect to *http://support.microsoft.com/*.

Evaluation Edition Software Support

The 120-day Evaluation Edition provided with this training is not the full retail product and is provided only for the purposes of training and evaluation. Microsoft and Microsoft Technical Support do not support this evaluation edition.

Caution   The Evaluation Edition of Microsoft Windows 2000 Server included with this book should not be used on a primary work computer. The evaluation edition is unsupported. For online support information relating to the full version of Windows 2000 Server that *might* also apply to the Evaluation Edition, you can connect to *http://support.microsoft.com/*

Information about any issues relating to the use of this evaluation edition with this training kit is posted to the Support section of the Microsoft Press Web site (*www.microsoft.com/mspress/support/*).

For information about ordering the full version of any Microsoft software, please call Microsoft Sales at (800) 426-9400 or visit *http://www.microsoft.com*.

C H A P T E R   1

Group Policy

About This Chapter

Group Policy is the primary configuration management tool for Microsoft Windows networks. *Configuration management* establishes how users work with client computers and servers in a network; it determines which software is available to users, how desktops look, and what operating system features are enabled. Without a centralized configuration management tool like Group Policy, configuring clients and client-side security settings on each computer in a large network would take a very long time.

Because Group Policy controls how desktop computers work and determines which software is available to users, you can use it as a security mechanism. Group Policy can restrict dangerous operating system features to prevent well-meaning users from accidentally damaging their computers' configurations. It can also limit access to configuration tools and software that malicious users can use to hack into other computers and carry out a wide variety of attacks. However, because Group Policy is primarily a central configuration management tool rather than a security feature, administrators need to be aware of its security limitations. These limitations are covered in Lesson 5 of this chapter.

This chapter explains in detail what Group Policy is and how it works. When you understand the capabilities and limitations of Group Policy, you can effectively use Group Policy as both a natural administrative point of control and as a security configuration tool.

Exam Tip   You need to understand how Group Policy is applied in domains and organizational units and how policy is inherited by subordinate organizational units. Be sure you study Group Policy and its application, and practice applying Group Policy to different organizational unit structures to examine its effects.

Before You Begin

To complete this chapter, you must have

- One year of direct work experience with Windows 2000
- Familiarity with Windows 2000 as both a server platform and an end-user operating system
- A test computer configured with Microsoft Windows 2000 Server and Active Directory

Note   The companion CD-ROM contains a 120-day evaluation version of Windows 2000 Server that you can use to complete the exercises in this book.

- Access to a client in the same domain as the Windows 2000 server
- A basic understanding of the Active Directory directory service

Note   The term "Windows" in this book refers only to Windows 2000 and subsequent Microsoft operating systems. Windows NT is similar in many respects but is not specifically covered. Microsoft Windows 3.1, Windows 95, Windows 98, or Windows Me are not covered.

Lesson 1: Active Directory and Group Policy

An *Active Directory* is a hierarchy of domains, which represents major business divisions of thousands of users and computers, and of organizational units (OUs), which model the internal structure of a business unit or medium to small organization. Active Directory also contains a parallel structure of sites, which is used to model the physical locations of an organization and the data connections between them, so that Windows can automatically optimize communication between sites.

Group Policy is a package of settings files, scripts, and installation files that together create a specific computer configuration for a class of users or computers. Using Group Policy, administrators can create, manage, and deploy many different computer configurations to create a consistent work environment for various classes of workers across any number of client computers in an organization.

Group Policy is used to manage administrative and security settings for groups of users and computers based on their memberships in organizational units such as departments, corporate divisions, or security domains, or their locations at specific sites, campuses, or facilities. Additionally, Group Policy is used to configure special requirements for specific computers such as those used as public kiosks.

Group Policy settings are stored in Group Policy Objects (GPOs). These GPOs must be linked to Active Directory containers (domains, organizational units, and sites) to take effect, so it's important to understand the components of Active Directory that relate to Group Policy. This lesson discusses the link between Active Directory and Group Policy, and it walks you through the steps necessary to create a sample Active Directory structure that you can use for the remainder of the exercises in this chapter.

After this lesson, you will be able to

- Create an Active Directory structure that mirrors your organization's structure
- Efficiently map an organization's structure to an Active Directory hierarchy

Estimated lesson time: 10 minutes

Understanding Active Directory Structures

A business's organizational structure creates a natural environment for the deployment of software and the configuration of computers. For example, users within an Accounting OU are likely to require access to the same accounting and financial software applications, while members of an Engineering OU might require access to an entirely different set of applications, such as Computer Aided Design (CAD) and Computer Aided Modeling (CAM) applications. Each group is also highly likely to require access to different network storage areas. You can use Group

Policy to configure and deploy software and control access to network storage for these various users when you have an Active Directory hierarchy that mimics your organizational structure.

Active Directory structures are normally created to mirror an organization's business structure. Departments, divisions, teams, and workgroups are usually modeled as organizational units (OUs), but very large companies might model divisions as domains rather than OUs. Windows 2000 domains can efficiently contain hundreds of thousands of objects, so a single domain can be appropriate for businesses with fewer than 100,000 users. However, domains can also be used to enforce security boundaries between departments in organizations where security is of paramount concern, so the number of domains in organizations can vary widely.

Figure 1.1 shows an example Active Directory structure that models a fictitious business.

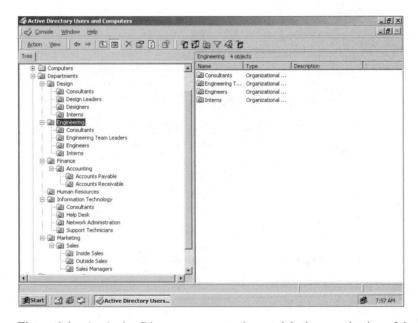

Figure 1.1   An Active Directory structure that models the organization of the business

Active Directory containers are a special type of Active Directory object that can contain other Active Directory objects such as users, computers, and other subordinate Active Directory containers. Domains, OUs, and sites are all Active Directory containers.

Whether divisions are modeled as domains or OUs, the application of Group Policy remains the same. By linking a GPO to an Active Directory container, you can apply its Group Policy settings to all the Active Directory objects within the container. For example, by linking a GPO to a domain, you can apply the configuration and settings enacted by that GPO to all the users and computers within that domain.

More Info   For more detailed information about creating an Active Directory infrastructure for your organization, see the *Microsoft Windows 2000 Server Deployment Planning Guide* (Microsoft Press, 2002).

Practice: Designing an Active Directory Hierarchy

In this practice, you model the organizational structure for Fabrikam, Inc., a medium-sized manufacturing business, by creating an Active Directory hierarchy. This business has multiple departments and different types of users within each department.

Before performing this practice, you should install Windows 2000 Server on a computer and then install Active Directory for a domain called "domain.fabrikam.com." This installation will be used throughout this book to perform exercises.

After you complete this practice, you will have a basic understanding of how an organization's structure can be efficiently mapped to an Active Directory hierarchy, which sets the stage for the deployment of Group Policy.

▶   **To create an OU**

1. Click Start, point to Programs, point to Administrative Tools, and click Active Directory Users And Computers.

2. In the Active Directory Users And Computers tree in the Active Directory Users And Computers management console, expand domain.fabrikam.com.

    The OUs that are subordinate to the domain appear in a list. Initially, these include only default, generic OUs.

3. Right-click domain.fabrikam.com, point to New, and click Organizational Unit.

4. In the Name box, type **Departments** and press ENTER.

An OU named Departments appears in the Active Directory tree under the domain.fabrikam.com domain. At this point, your console should look like Figure 1.2.

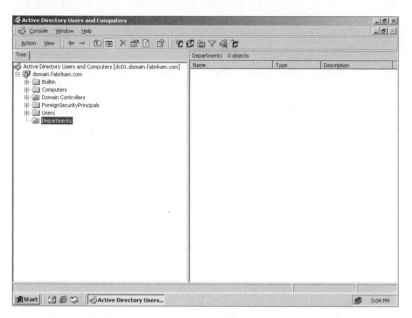

Figure 1.2   The Departments domain created under domain.fabrikam.com

▶ **To create a subordinate OU**

1. Right-click the Departments OU, point to New, and choose New, Organizational Unit.

2. In the Name box, type **Design,** and press ENTER.

A subordinate OU is added under the Departments OU.

▶ **To create an Active Directory hierarchy**

1. Using the steps you followed to create a subordinate OU, create five OUs under the Departments OU. Name them Engineering, Finance, Human Resources, Marketing, and Information Technology.

2. For the Engineering OU, create the following subordinate OUs: Engineering Team Leaders, Engineers, Interns, and Consultants.

3. For the Finance OU, create a subordinate OU named Accounting.

4. For the Accounting OU, create another layer of subordinate OUs. Create two subordinate OUs: Accounts Payable and Accounts Receivable.

5. For the Marketing OU, create the following OU: Sales. Under Sales, create the following subordinate OUs: Sales Managers, Outside Sales, and Inside Sales.

6. For the Information Technology OU, create the following subordinate OUs: Network Administration, Support Technicians, Help Desk, and Consultants.

7. Create OUs under the Design OU named Design Leaders, Designers, Interns, and Consultants.

You now have a domain structure that looks like Figure 1.1. The domain.fabrikam.com domain now contains OUs that model the organization of the business.

Lesson Review

The following questions are intended to reinforce key information in this lesson. If you are unable to answer a question, review the lesson and try the question again. Answers to the questions can be found in the appendix.

1. To what must you link GPOs for them to take effect?

2. What are the types of Active Directory containers?

3. What does an Active Directory hierarchy usually model?

4. What are the two reasons for a business to use more than one domain?

Lesson Summary

■ Active Directory containers normally model the organizational structure of a business.

■ GPOs must be linked to Active Directory containers to take effect.

■ You can use Group Policy to configure and deploy software and control access to network storage for various users.

Lesson 2: Configuring Group Policy

Now that you've modeled the structure of a typical organization using Active Directory, you have classes of users and computers to which you can apply specific computer configurations by creating a Group Policy.

After this lesson, you will be able to

- Create GPOs
- Manage GPOs in Active Directory
- Manage GPOs in the Microsoft Management Console (MMC)
- Filter the application of GPO by security groups
- Delegate administrative authority to GPOs

Estimated lesson time: 30 minutes

Understanding Group Policy

Group Policy is a combination of user interface restrictions and administrative settings that can prevent users from making changes to the computers' configurations or operating the computers in a manner that might violate the organization's security posture. Group Policy can also contain scripts and installation packages to establish a consistent work environment for users.

Group Policy is deployed to users and computers by linking a GPO to Active Directory containers such as sites, domains, OUs, and individual computers. A *GPO* is a directory containing all the files that are required to enact a Group Policy, and is explained in detail in this lesson. When a GPO is linked to an Active Directory container, it applies a Group Policy to all the computers within that container when they are booted and to all users within that container when they log on to a computer, whether or not the computer is also contained within that container.

Using this simple deployment mechanism, Group Policy provides an automated way for administrators to

- Deploy software such as Microsoft Office applications, drivers, and patches.
- Control desktop·configuration such as the programs that are available to users, the look of Microsoft Windows Explorer, the programs that can or cannot be run, and which local drives can be accessed.
- Deploy startup and logon scripts to map network drives and printers and perform other repetitive tasks.
- Manage the options and features of applications like Microsoft Internet Explorer, Microsoft NetMeeting, and third-party applications.

To sum up, Group Policy allows administrators to configure administrative and security settings for classes of users and computers and apply them automatically wherever the computers are located and whenever users log on, irrespective of the computer they use.

Linking Group Policy to Active Directory Containers

Administrators can apply GPOs to Active Directory objects by linking them to an Active Directory domain or OU objects using the Active Directory Users And Computers management console, or by linking them to site objects using the Sites And Services management console. A specific GPO can be linked to any number of Active Directory objects. You can link a GPO to a domain or OU in two ways:

- When you create a GPO from within an Active Directory object's Properties dialog box, the operating system creates a link between the GPO and the Active Directory object.
- In the Active Directory Users And Computers management console, you can manually link a GPO to an Active Directory object on the Group Policy tab in the Properties dialog box for the Active Directory object.

Local Group Policy

Local GPOs are GPOs that are stored directly on client computers rather than downloaded from a domain controller. Because they are stored locally, they are always available, even when the computer has no connection to the network or is not a member of a domain.

When Windows starts, local GPOs are applied first. Local GPOs are normally used to control settings on computers that are not part of a domain or are unable to contact the domain, but they can be used on any computer regardless of its domain membership. After local Group Policy settings are applied, computers that are members of a domain then download GPOs from domain controllers based on the computer's membership in a domain, site, or OU, and apply those settings.

Caution   Because local GPOs are applied first, their settings are frequently overridden by domain Group Policy settings.

Active Directory Group Policy

Every GPO has two components:

- A Computer Configuration portion that is applied before anyone logs on.
- A User Configuration portion that is applied based on the identity of the logged on user.

After Windows applies local Group Policy to computers in a domain when they start, it downloads the Computer Configuration portion of any GPOs from Active

Directory that apply to them. It then applies the Computer Configuration portion of all GPOs before displaying the logon prompt.

When users log on, the process is repeated for the User Configuration portion of the same set of GPOs.

Tip GPOs cannot be applied if the user does not have Read and Apply permissions to the GPO. Because Read and Apply permissions are required, permissions can be used to filter the application of Group Policy based on user membership in a security group. Permissions are the subject of Chapter 4, "Account-Based Security."

Group Policy Application Order

GPOs are applied in the following order by default:

1. Local Group Policy
2. Site-linked Group Policy
3. Domain-linked Group Policy
4. OU-linked Group Policy

Domain and OU GPOs are downloaded and applied in hierarchical order from parent to child within the Active Directory structure. For example, if a computer were located within the Sales OU in the example domain created in Lesson 1, it would download Group Policy settings applied to the domain.fabrikam.com domain, the Marketing OU, and the Sales OU, in that order.

Unless a GPO is specifically set not to allow overrides, Group Policy settings automatically override the same Group Policy settings applied by earlier GPOs. For example, if a Group Policy for the Marketing OU specifies that objects on the desktop should be disabled, but the same Group Policy setting for a GPO linked to the Sales OU specifies that they should be enabled, they will be enabled for a computer in the Sales OU but disabled for a computer within the Marketing OU.

Administrators can change the default order in which GPOs are applied by modifying the settings for the link between the Active Directory object and the GPO (as discussed later in this lesson).

Note So that you can more easily determine the combined effects of GPO settings, it is good practice to construct Group Policy settings that are more specific and more restrictive as you descend through the Active Directory container hierarchy.

Administrators can also modify the application order of GPOs for any Active Directory container. By modifying the application order, administrators can prioritize certain GPOs to ensure that their settings will override other GPOs, or flag a GPO to prevent its settings from being overridden no matter when it is applied.

For example, you might have a GPO that contains critical password policies that you want to have enforced no matter what policies might be set in other GPOs. By prioritizing that GPO, you ensure that it is applied last and that its settings override those contained in other GPOs.

Physical Structure of GPOs

Physically, GPOs are packages of files that are interpreted on the client computers to which the GPO is linked. GPOs are stored as folders and files in the domain controller's SYSVOL share and are automatically replicated among domain controllers.

Group Policy is implemented by a number of distinct components called Group Policy *client-side extensions*. Each extension interprets the specific files stored in the GPO in Active Directory that pertain to it and makes various changes to the client based on the settings contained in the GPO. The various Group Policy client-side extensions manage

- Folder redirection
- Disk quotas
- Scripts
- Security
- Encrypting File System (EFS) recovery
- Application management
- Internet Explorer settings
- Registry settings
- IP security

In addition to these functions, independent software vendors (ISVs) can create additional Group Policy client-side extensions, and Microsoft can release more of these extensions in future versions of Windows.

The various Group Policy client-side extensions account for the wide range of functionality in Group Policy. Group Policy is not just registry settings, or registry settings plus scripts plus installation policies. Group Policy is any type of file contained in a GPO and interpreted by a Group Policy client-side extension. This extensibility of Group Policy is one of its primary advantages, but it also makes Group Policy somewhat complex.

The Group Policy client-side extension that manages registry settings to modify the behavior of the operating system is configured through .adm files, which contain information about registry keys, their available settings, and their location within the Group Policy namespace (the object hierarchy visible in the Group Policy editor). Two .adm files are especially important: Inetres.adm, which controls Internet Explorer registry settings, and System.adm, which controls Windows settings. Conf.adm, which controls NetMeeting configuration, is also included by default. Administrators can create their own .adm files to add functionality to a GPO. These files are stored within each GPO's \ADM folder in SYSVOL. In the case of Local GPOs, .adm files (and all other Group Policy files) are stored within the %SystemRoot%\system32\GroupPolicy folder.

Group Policy folders within a domain controller's SYSVOL directory are named using an automatically generated globally unique identifier (GUID). No two GUIDs are identical. Each GUID is unique among domain controllers anywhere in the world. Therefore, when two organizations and their Active Directories merge, their Group Policy folders won't conflict because they have different identifiers.

Tip   You can determine which folder corresponds to a specific Group Policy by looking at the Group Policy's Properties dialog box. The GUID for a specific policy is displayed, and it matches the name of the folder that contains the GPO in the SYSVOL share.

Logical Structure of GPOs

Every GPO has two components:

- The *Computer Configuration* portion of a GPO is applied to every user of a computer when the computer is booted, and before anyone logs on Use Computer Configuration objects to manage how a computer will behave no matter who is logged on.
- The *User Configuration* portion of a GPO is applied based on the identity of the logged on user, and it applies only to that user. Use User Configuration objects to manage how specific users are allowed to operate computers, regardless of which computer they log on to. If a User Configuration setting conflicts with a Computer Configuration setting, the Computer Configuration setting takes precedence unless the User Configuration policy has been flagged, indicating that it is not to be overridden.

In a GPO's properties, it is good practice to limit the GPO to either Computer Configuration or User Configuration policies and disable the other policy type. This practice will enhance the organization of your Group Policies by separating User Configuration settings from Computer Configuration settings. It will also speed the application of Group Policy because, if a policy contains both sets of settings, it must be loaded twice, and for each load, half of the policy will not apply.

Tip   Splitting GPOs into those that apply to users and those that apply to computers, and disabling the portion that is not necessary, reduces the load time for GPOs.

Computer Configuration and User Configuration policies each have three major divisions:

- The *Software Settings* portion of a configuration contains settings extensions provided primarily by independent software vendors for software installation.
- The *Windows Settings* portion of a configuration contains settings that apply to Windows, as well as startup/shutdown scripts (Computer Configuration) or logon/logoff scripts (User Configuration). The Windows Settings portion of a configuration contains most of the settings that are security specific.
- The *Administrative Templates* portion of a configuration can be extended by administrators using .adm files, and it contains settings that modify the behavior of Internet Explorer, Windows Explorer, and other programs.

Figure 1.3 shows the logical structure of a GPO within a management console.

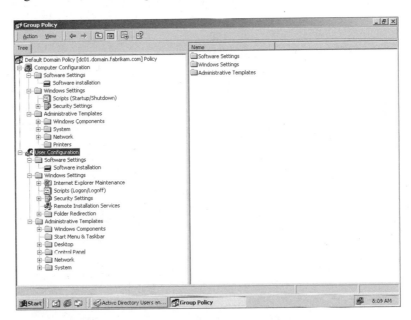

Figure 1.3   The computer and user portions of a GPO

Managing Group Policy

You can manage Group Policy by navigating through Active Directory using either the Active Directory Users And Computers management console or the Active Directory Sites And Services management console. Once you have navigated to the specific Active Directory object to which a Group Policy will apply, you can open the object's Properties dialog box and manage the GPOs that are linked to that object.

Creating GPOs

You can create GPOs on the Group Policy tab of an Active Directory object's Properties dialog box. Click the New button to create a new GPO in the domain controller's SYSVOL, assign it a GUID, and populate it with default administrative templates. You can then click Edit to modify the default Group Policy for the purpose you intend.

Linking GPOs to Active Directory Objects

Each GPO is automatically linked to the Active Directory object from which you created it. If you want to link the same GPO to a different Active Directory object, manually create a link by clicking the Add button on the Group Policy tab in the Properties dialog box for the target Active Directory object, and then, in the Add A Group Policy Object Link dialog box, selecting the appropriate GPO from the list. You can link a single GPO to any number of Active Directory objects.

GPO Settings

There are numerous specific settings you can use to control how a GPO is applied to an Active Directory object. These settings do not modify the GPO itself; they modify the link between the GPO and the Active Directory object to which it applies.

In the Properties dialog box for an Active Directory object, you can change the order in which GPOs are applied to the object by modifying their order in the Group Policy list. GPOs listed lowest are applied first followed by GPOs higher in the list. The GPOs at the bottom of the list have the least effect because they are overridden by the settings in GPOs listed above them. It's important to remember that GPOs at the top of the list have the highest priority and effectiveness. To change the order in which GPOs are applied, select a specific GPO and then use the Up and Down buttons to move it to the position you want.

If you have extremely important Group Policy settings that must be effective no matter where they occur in the Group Policy Application order, you can flag the GPO to allow no overrides from subsequently applied GPOs. This feature is extremely useful for enforcing security within a single GPO. By containing security-related Group Policy settings within a single GPO and setting that GPO to disable policy override, you need not worry about the application order of GPOs or about other GPOs that might apply to a specific Active Directory object. To prevent subsequent GPOs from overriding a GPO, click the Options button on the Group Policy tab of the Active Directory object's Properties dialog box, and select the No Override check box.

To test the effects of a specific policy or to temporarily disable a restriction, you can disable the application of a GPO that is linked to an Active Directory object. To do so, click the Options button on the Group Policy tab of the Active Directory object's Properties dialog box and select the Disabled check box.

By default, GPOs contain both a Computer Configuration portion and a User Configuration portion. To optimize speed and minimize network traffic, you should separate your GPOs into those that affect computer configuration and those that affect user configuration. You can disable the unnecessary portion (either the Computer or the User Configuration settings) of a GPO by clicking the Properties button on the Group Policy tab and selecting the Disable Computer Configuration Settings check box or the Disable User Configuration Settings check box.

Delegating Group Policy Management

In large organizations, administrative control is delegated on a per-domain or per-OU basis. Domains and OUs require somewhat different security and administrative settings. Some security settings are mandated for the entire organization or large parts of it, while other settings might be appropriate only for specific child domains or OUs.

When administrative control is delegated for portions of Active Directory, you must restrict administrators from modifying GPOs that are outside of their authority. Because an administrator must have both Read and Write access to modify a GPO, you can restrict access by changing permissions to remove Write access for GPOs outside an administrator's authority.

Filtering Group Policy Application

Users are normally assigned to a single OU. User policies are also assigned on a per-OU basis. However, some users within the OU, such as power users or subordinate administrators, might require different security settings.

To separate users within an OU so that different GPOs are applied to them, you can either create subordinate OUs, applying the various GPOs to those subordinate OUs rather than to the parent OU, or you can filter the application of a Group Policy setting by using permissions.

A GPO can be applied to a user only if the user has Read and Apply Group Policy permissions to the object. By default, Authenticated Users inherit these rights for all GPOs, so this is not normally an issue.

You can prevent the application of a GPO to a user or group of users by creating a specific Deny Access Control Entry in the Group Policy Object's access control list (ACL). ACLs are used to determine which users can access a specific secured resource such as a file or folder. ACLs are explained in detail in Chapter 4, "Account-Based Security."

Warning   Because users must have Read access to a GPO to apply it, it is possible for a hacker to open a GPO for exclusive read and prevent other user accounts from applying the GPO. Use the auditing features of Windows 2000 described in Chapter 4 to be alerted to this type of activity.

While Group Policy filtering is effective, it is best practice to create additional subordinate OUs and control the assignment of GPOs through links to those additional Active Directory objects. Filters are not obvious in the Active Directory Users And Computers management console, so it can be very difficult to tell when they are in effect. Administrators who rely on filtering frequently have problems troubleshooting the application of Group Policy because there's no way to survey the entire scope of application when filters are in use.

Use Group Policy filtering only in those rare cases when you cannot apply Group Policy the way you want using additional Active Directory container objects and linking, such as when the GPO is far up the Active Directory hierarchy and you do not have administrative rights to move the GPO to a more appropriate location.

Practice: Managing Group Policy

In this practice, you create and manage GPOs. You specify GPO linking and settings that apply to those links, and you practice unlinking and deleting GPOs. Finally, you create a management console from which you can directly manage GPOs irrespective of their position within Active Directory.

Exercise 1: Creating GPOs

Creating a GPO is simple. Open the Active Directory Users And Computers management console to create a GPO that is linked to a domain or an OU, or open the Sites And Services management console to create a GPO that is linked to a site.

Note   These exercises continue the Fabrikam scenario from Lesson 1.

▶   **To create a GPO**

1. Log on to the domain controller as the administrator.
2. Click Start, point to Programs, point to Administrative Tools, and click Active Directory Users And Computers.
3. In the Active Directory Users And Computers tree in the Active Directory Users And Computers management console, right-click domain.fabrikam.com, and choose Properties.

4. In the domain.fabrikam.com Properties dialog box, select the Group Policy tab. The Group Policy tab appears, as shown in Figure 1.4.

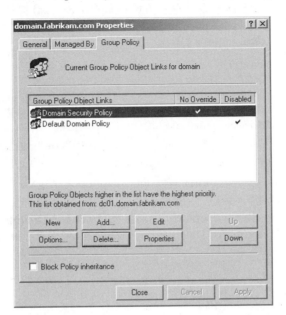

Figure 1.4   The Group Policy Object Links in the Properties dialog box for the domain

5. Click New.
6. Type **Domain Security Group Policy** as the name of the GPO. The object has now been created.
7. Click New.
8. Type **Domain Standard Desktop** as the name of the GPO. Two GPOs have now been created.

    Why would you want to create a separate GPO to manage settings at the same Active Directory level as an existing GPO, rather than simply modifying the existing object?

9. Click Close.

Exercise 2: Specifying GPO Settings

You specify settings for GPOs the same way you create GPOs, from the Active Directory object's Group Policy tab in its Properties dialog box.

▶ **To specify settings for a GPO**

Perform this exercise while logged on to the domain controller as the Administrator.

1. In the Active Directory Users And Computers tree, right-click domain.fabrikam.com, and choose Properties.
2. On the Group Policy tab of the domain.fabrikam.com Properties dialog box, select Domain Security Group Policy in the list of GPOs.
3. Click the Up button to make the Domain Security GPO higher in the list than the Default Domain Policy.
4. Click Options to open the Domain Security Policy Options dialog box, as shown in Figure 1.5.

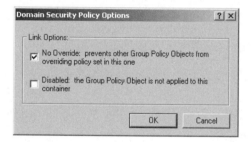

Figure 1.5   The Domain Security Policy Options dialog box

5. Select the No Override check box to prevent subsequent GPOs from overriding the policy settings of the Domain Security GPO, and click OK. This prevents any subsequently applied GPO from overriding your security-related Group Policy settings.
6. Select the Default Domain Policy GPO, and then click the Down button to move the Default Domain Policy below the Domain Standard Desktop GPO.
7. Click Options to open the Domain Security Policy Options dialog box (Figure 1.5).
8. Select the Disabled check box to prevent the Default Domain Policy GPO from being applied to this Active Directory container.
9. In the Confirm Disable message box, click Yes to confirm, and then click OK.

10. Click the Domain Standard Desktop GPO in the list of GPOs, and click Properties. The Domain Standard Desktop Properties dialog box appears, as shown in Figure 1.6.

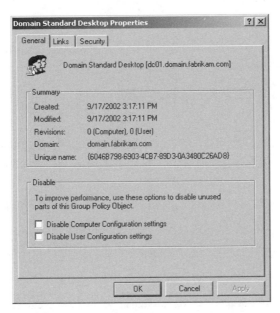

Figure 1.6   The GPO Properties for the Domain Standard Desktop Group Policy

11. Select the Disable Computer Configuration Settings check box because this GPO contains only user settings. Click Yes to confirm, and then click OK.

12. Click Close to close the domain.fabrikam.com Properties dialog box.

Exercise 3: Controlling Administrative Access to GPOs

You can use permissions to control administrative access to Group Policy and delegate administration to subordinate administrators in a large domain. In this exercise, you will remove the permissions of those who are members of the Enterprise Admins group but not members of the Domain Admins group. This will prevent Enterprise Admins from modifying the Domain Security GPO.

▶ **To restrict administrative access to a GPO**

Perform this procedure while logged on to the domain controller as Administrator and running the Active Directory Users And Computers management console.

1. In the Active Directory Users And Computers tree, right-click domain.fabrikam.com and choose Properties.

2. In the domain.fabrikam.com Properties dialog box, click the Group Policy tab.

3. Select the Domain Security Group Policy in the GPO Links list, and click Properties.

4. In the Domain Security Policy Properties dialog box, click the Security tab. The Security tab for the GPO appears, as shown in Figure 1.7.

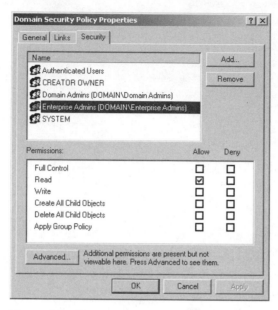

Figure 1.7   You can set permissions to access every GPO uniquely

5. In the list of names, select the Enterprise Admins group.

6. In the Allow column, clear the Write, Create All Child Objects, and Delete All Child Objects permissions.

7. Click OK, and click Close.

Exercise 4: Filtering GPO Application

Sometimes you'll need to prevent the application of Group Policy to users within an OU or domain. You can use permissions to easily accomplish this Group Policy filtering. In this exercise, you will filter the application of the Domain Standard Desktop GPO so that it will not apply to members of the Domain Admins group irrespective of their participation within any OU.

▶ **To prevent a GPO from being applied to members of a security group**

Perform this procedure while logged on to the domain controller as Administrator and running the Active Directory Users And Computers management console.

1. In the Active Directory Users And Computers tree, right-click domain.fabrikam.com, and choose Properties.

2. On the Group Policy tab of the domain.fabrikam.com Properties dialog box, select the Domain Standard Desktop GPO in the GPO list.

3. Click the Properties button.

4. On the Security tab of the Domain Standard Desktop Properties dialog box, select the Domain Admins group.

5. In the Permissions list, select the Apply Group Policy check box in the Deny column, and click OK.

Note   While you would normally also disallow read access, it is not necessary in cases where you only want to filter the application of rather than prevent access to a GPO.

A Security message box informs you that unintended consequences might occur due to group membership and asks if you want to continue.

6. Click Yes in the Security message box, and click OK.

Exercise 5: Linking an Active Directory Object to a GPO

In large organizations, it makes sense to create standard GPOs and apply them to numerous sites, domains, and OUs. You can use Group Policy linking to accomplish this. In this exercise, you link the Domain Standard Desktop GPO to three specific OUs within the domain.fabrikam.com organization.

▶ **To link an Active Directory object to a GPO**

Perform this procedure while logged on to the domain controller as an Administrator.

1. Click Start, point to Programs, point to Administrative Tools, and click Active Directory Users And Computers.

2. In the Active Directory Users And Computers tree in management console, expand domain.fabrikam.com and Departments to show the Design department.

3. Select Design, and click Properties on the toolbar.

4. In the Design Properties dialog box, select the Group Policy tab. The Group Policy tab contains no entries in the Group Policy Object Links list.

5. Click Add. The Add A Group Policy Object Link dialog box appears, as shown in Figure 1.8.

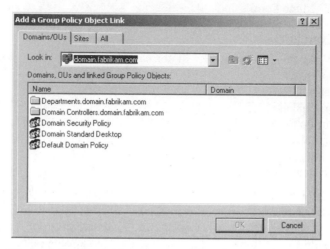

Figure 1.8   The Add A Group Policy Object Link dialog box

6. Click Folder Up twice to browse from the current OU to the domain OU where the Domain Standard Desktop GPO is stored.

7. Double-click the Domain Standard Desktop in the GPO list. This Group Policy Object is now linked to the Design OU.

8. Click OK.

9. Repeat steps 3 through 8 for the Human Resources and Marketing OUs.

Exercise 6: Removing a GPO Link

When you no longer need a GPO to be linked to a specific Active Directory object, you can remove the link between them. In this exercise, you remove the link between the domain.fabrikam.com Active Directory container and the Domain Standard Desktop GPO. After you accomplish this, the Domain Standard Desktop Group Policy will apply only to the OUs that you specified in Exercise 5.

▶ **To remove a GPO link from an Active Directory object**

Perform this procedure while logged on to the domain controller as an Administrator and running the Active Directory Users And Computers management console.

1. In the Active Directory Users And Computers tree, right-click the domain.fabrikam.com domain, and choose Properties.

2. In the domain.fabrikam.com Properties dialog box, select the Group Policy tab.

3. Select the Domain Standard Desktop GPO in the GPO list, and click Delete.

   The Delete Selection dialog box asks if you want to remove only the link or if you also want to delete the GPO.

4. In the Delete Selection dialog box, select Remove The Link From The List.

5. Click OK. The GPO is removed from the list.

6. Click Close.

Exercise 7:   Deleting a GPO

When a GPO is no longer necessary, you can delete it. GPOs can become obsolete because of changes in corporate policy or because you've compiled a condensed set of GPOs from a large set of early, smaller GPOs and you no longer need the original GPOs. In this example, you will delete the Domain Standard Desktop Group Policy because a single desktop standard will not be effective for this organization.

▶ **To delete a GPO**

Perform this procedure while logged on to the domain controller as Administrator while running the Active Directory Users And Computers management console.

1. In the Active Directory Users And Computers tree, expand domain.fabrikam.com and Departments to reveal the Design OU.

2. Right-click the Design OU, and choose Properties.

3. In the Design Properties dialog box, select the Group Policy tab.

4. Select Domain Standard Desktop in the GPO list, and click Delete.

5. In the Delete Selection dialog box, select Remove The Link And Delete The Group Policy Object Permanently.

6. Click OK, and click Yes to confirm.

7. Click Close.

8. Right-click the Marketing OU, and choose Properties.

9. In the Marketing Properties dialog box, select the Group Policy tab.

   Notice that the Domain Standard Desktop GPO that was linked to this OU no longer appears in the OU list because it has been deleted.

10. Click Close, and then close the Active Directory Users And Computers management console.

Exercise 8: Creating a Group Policy Management Console

In large organizations in which GPOs are frequently linked to numerous Active Directory objects, it is more convenient to manage GPOs separately from the Active Directory objects to which they are linked.

You can use the Group Policy snap-in and the Microsoft Management Console (MMC) to create a management console that allows you to manage all of your GPOs in one place. Or you can create numerous management consoles that allow various administrators to manage the GPOs that apply to their domains or OUs.

▶ **To create a convenient Group Policy management console**

Perform this procedure while logged on to the domain controller as Administrator.

1. Click Start, click Run, type **mmc,** and press ENTER to open an empty management console.
2. From the Console menu, choose Add/Remove Snap-In.
3. In the Add/Remove Snap-ins dialog box, click Add.

   The Add Standalone Snap-in dialog box appears, as shown in Figure 1.9. In this dialog box, you can create custom management consoles containing all of your custom created GPOs.

Figure 1.9   The Add Standalone Snap-in dialog box

4. Double-click the Group Policy Snap-in to open the Select Group Policy Object Wizard.

5. In the Select Group Policy Object dialog box, click Browse.

6. In the Browse For A Group Policy Object dialog box, select Domain Security Group Policy in the list, and click OK. The Select Group Policy Object Wizard should now match Figure 1.10.

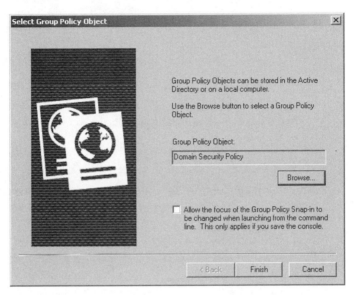

Figure 1.10   The Select Group Policy Object Wizard

7. Click Finish.

8. Repeat steps 3 through 7 for the Domain Default Policy.

9. Click Close, and then click OK.

10. Click Save on the toolbar.

11. Type **Group Policies** as the name of this Group Policy Console, and click Save.

12. Close the management console.

A Group Policies.mmc console now appears in the Administrative Tools folder in the Start menu. In this console you can directly modify Group Policy settings.

Lesson Review

The following questions are intended to reinforce key information in this lesson. If you are unable to answer a question, review the lesson and try the question again. Answers to the questions can be found in the appendix.

1. From what management tool can you create GPOs?

2. When you create a GPO, what is automatically created along with it?

3. What is the default application order for GPOs?

4. Group Policy is implemented by distinct components called what?

Lesson Summary

- You use Group Policy to manage a large group of computers and users as a class.
- Group Policy allows administrators to control client configuration based on policy documents stored on domain controllers and linked to Active Directory.
- The GPOs you create using the Active Directory management consoles are automatically linked to the Active Directory object from which they are created. GPOs can be linked to any number of other Active Directory objects.
- You can create a separate management console to manage GPOs separately from Active Directory.

Lesson 3: Configuring Client Computer Security Policy

Group Policy contains configuration and security settings that you can use to control the behavior, security, and appearance of Windows Explorer as well as a computer's network configuration. Using Group Policy, you can accomplish these tasks to standardize and restrict access to many of the features of Windows Explorer:

- Restrict access to desktop icons.
- Limit the programs that a user can run.
- Hide drive icons in My Computer and in the Open and Save dialog boxes.
- Restrict features of Active Desktop.
- Remove features of Windows that are unnecessary for your organization.
- Create startup/shutdown and logon/logoff scripts that create a standard network environment.
- Manage offline documents and content.

After this lesson, you will be able to

- Configure Group Policy to tailor the user experience for various classes of workers
- Restrict access to management tools
- Restrict access to Internet Explorer configuration

Estimated lesson time: 20 minutes

Using Client-Side Group Policy Configuration

Group Policy is most appropriately used to prevent users from accidentally reconfiguring and interfering with the operation of their computers. While avoiding user downtime is important in an environment where single-user computers are common, it is critical in an environment where multi-user servers such as Terminal Services servers are used. In these environments, desktop and application settings directly affect everyone who uses the terminal server.

Tip   You access most configuration tools in Windows through the Microsoft Management Console (MMC). Restricting access to the MMC is critical to preventing users from making administrative changes to their computers. Group Policy can also be used to control access to the MMC.

In most enterprises, workers typically use a relatively small set of programs, defined by the kind of work they perform. For example, an administrative assistant might use Microsoft Outlook and Microsoft Word extensively, but have no need for Microsoft Excel or other programs. An accountant might require access to the Great Plains Software database client, Excel, and Internet Explorer on a regular basis, use Outlook and Word infrequently, and not use any other programs. An assembly-line worker might need only a Microsoft Access client for a SQL Server data collection application.

By far the most important security feature of Group Policy is its ability to restrict the number of programs that are available to a group as required by their jobs. Group Policy implements this restriction by matching the name of the application against an allowed list. This absolutely prevents the vast majority of security breaches that a user might cause either maliciously or accidentally. However, restricting access to certain programs does not prevent a user from downloading a similar program and running it to obtain the same functionality.

Important   A clever hacker will rename an executable to have the same name as a program that he knows is allowed. You must use NTFS file system permissions to prevent this workaround.

It is absolutely crucial that you test Group Policy application whenever you create or modify GPOs, or when you suspect that your GPO is not completely effective. The easiest way to test GPOs is to create a test user account within the OU in question, so that the test user is a peer to the types of user accounts that the Group Policy is intended to control. Once you've created this test user, you can log on to your computer using the test user account to test the GPO.

Configuring Group Policy by Type of Worker

Group Policy is frequently used to create separate desktop configurations for different types of workers. Consider the difference between the requirements of knowledge workers and task workers.

- *Knowledge workers* require the ability to run multiple Office programs, create and manage documents of different types, and access various network shares. This configuration matches the way that most business computers are configured today. Beyond typical access to applications and shared information, knowledge workers need somewhere to store the documents that they create; documents are often stored on a share located on a network file server. However, knowledge workers do not need to be able to reconfigure their computers and benefit from a streamlined desktop without unnecessary distractions.

- *Task workers* perform the same task routinely and have need for only a few programs. These workers find it most convenient if the programs they need to use are conveniently available without distraction. Security for these clients can be dramatically improved by restricting the programs they are allowed to run to the set of applications they are known to use. This type of restriction is the most important security feature allowed by Group Policy because it eliminates the ability of users to run programs that provide unauthorized access. This prevents nearly all types of hacking originating from clients.

Because task workers in many cases run database clients that do not require access to the local or remote file system, you can eliminate all drive mappings and allow only the database client required by the worker. This turns the client into a single-function kiosk, which is the most secure configuration possible. You could even use a Group Policy setting to enable a custom user interface that offers only the one program required by the task worker. In such an environment, making Windows Explorer unavailable and disabling the Task Manager would prevent the computer from being used to run any other program.

Configuring Internet Explorer Using Group Policy

Just as you can use Group Policy to control the behavior of most components of Windows, you can use it to control the behavior of Internet Explorer. Group Policy restrictions for Internet Explorer are contained in two places in the Group Policy namespace:

- \User Configuration\Windows Settings\Internet Explorer Maintenance
- \User Configuration\Administrative Templates\Windows Components\Internet Explorer

The Internet Explorer Maintenance settings control home page and other URLs, Security Zone settings, content rating settings, and other such "pre-deployment" settings, similar to those that can be configured with the Internet Explorer Administration Kit.

The Internet Explorer settings allow you to disable components of the Internet Explorer user interface, such as menu items, Properties dialog boxes, and options.

Controlling Internet Explorer Settings

To truly secure the Web browsing experience, you must use Group Policy to direct your internal users through a proxy server such as Microsoft Internet Security Accelerator that is capable of checking the HTTP protocol for errors and restricting access to sites that are dangerous. The primary security purpose of controlling Internet Explorer settings is to prevent users from bypassing the proxy server to browse the Web directly.

For organizations whose security policy does not require a proxy server, you can control Internet Explorer security settings to prevent users from changing security zone restrictions that could enable dangerous content like ActiveX controls from Web sites that you don't trust.

Finally, controlling Internet Explorer settings is a convenient way to create a uniform browsing experience for users and maintain consistent home and support pages throughout an organization, facility, or department.

Limitations of Group Policy

When you configure Internet Explorer security using Group Policy, bear in mind that most of the settings are user interface restrictions that do not truly disable a particular type of functionality. If a user finds some other interface or downloads some program, script, or registry file that is capable of making a change to Internet Explorer settings, your Group Policy could be overridden by these changes. Hackers trade these sorts of scripts over the Internet.

For example, in the Group Policy namespace \User Configuration\Administrative Templates\Windows Components\Internet Explorer, the \Browser menus\Tools menu option Disable Internet Options might seem like an easy way to disable access to the Internet Explorer Internet Options dialog box. However, a knowledge-able user can get to these settings in Control Panel even if the browser menu item is disabled. In this specific case, use the Internet Explorer\Internet Control Panel options to disable each tab of the Internet Options Control Panel so that Control Panel is not available in either case.

The Internet Explorer Internet Options case is a classic example of why interface-based security restrictions of the sort implemented by GPOs are "surface" security restrictions rather than the "deep" security restrictions provided by ACLs for the file system and Active Directory. Surface interface-based restrictions don't remove a program's functionality; they just remove the ability of a user to invoke the functionality. If the user is clever enough to find a way around the restrictions, the code still exists and is available to thwart your security settings. Getting around Group Policy restrictions is frequently achieved by writing scripts that interact directly with a program's configuration API, for example.

For this reason, you must rigorously test both the correct application of Group Policy and all the methods you can think of to circumvent a specific policy setting to be certain that your policy settings are effective. When you test Group Policy settings, try different methods to accomplish the same configuration change to make sure that the Group Policy option covers all the possibilities.

Table 1.1 lists Internet Explorer configurations that are especially important to security.

Table 1.1   Internet Explorer Configurations to Disable for Security

Disable these features:	Search Customization Settings
	Internet Connection Wizard
	Reset Web Settings feature
	Importing and exporting of favorite links
Disable these capabilities:	Changing Advanced page settings
	Changing home page settings
	Changing proxy settings
	Changing ratings settings
	Changing certificate settings
	Saving passwords through AutoComplete
	Changing messaging settings
	Changing default browser check
In the Internet Control Panel, disable these pages:	General page
	Security page
	Content page
	Connections page
	Programs page
	Advanced page

Practice: Configuring Group Policy for Clients

In this practice, you configure two different Group Policies for different types of workers. You also restrict access to the MMC and prevent users from reconfiguring Internet Explorer.

Exercise 1: Configuring a Computer for Knowledge Workers

To create a Group Policy that's appropriate for knowledge workers, you enable numerous configuration settings within the \User Configuration\Administrative Templates\Windows Components namespace.

Note   Perform this exercise while logged on to the domain controller as Administrator.

► **To create a GPO for knowledge workers**

1. Open Active Directory Users And Computers.
2. Expand the domain.fabrikam.com domain and the Departments OU.
3. Right-click the Engineering OU, and choose Properties.
4. In the Engineering Properties dialog box, select the Group Policy tab, and click New.
5. Type **Engineering Desktop Settings** as the name for the GPO.

► **To remove access to configuration icons**

1. On the Group Policy tab, select Engineering Desktop Settings, and click Edit. The Group Policy editor appears, as shown in Figure 1.11.

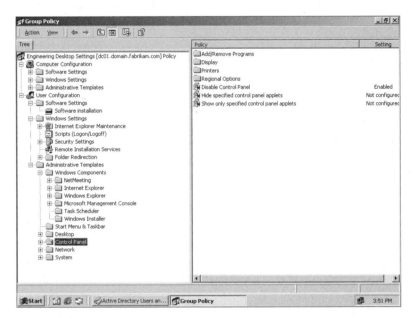

Figure 1.11   The Group Policy editor

2. Under User Configuration in the tree in the Group Policy window, expand Administrative Templates, and then expand the Windows Components.
3. Click the Control Panel node in the GPO namespace.
4. Double-click Disable Control Panel.

5. In the Disable Control Panel Properties dialog box, select Enabled, and click OK.
6. In the tree under Administrative Templates, select Desktop.
7. Double-click Hide My Network Places Icon On Desktop.
8. In the Hide My Network Places Icon On Desktop dialog box, select Enabled, and click OK.

▶ **To restrict access to dangerous executables**

1. In the tree under Administrative Templates, select System.
2. Double-click Disable Registry Editing Tools.
3. In the Disable Registry Editing Tools dialog box, select Enabled, and click OK.
4. Double-click Disable The Command Prompt.
5. In the Disable The Command Prompt dialog box, select Enabled, and click OK.
6. In the tree, expand System, and select Logon/Logoff.
7. Double-click Disable Task Manager.
8. In the Disable Task Manager dialog box, select Enabled, and click OK.

▶ **To modify the Start menu settings**

1. In the tree, select Start Menu & Taskbar.
2. Double-click Disable Programs On Settings Menu.
3. In the Disable Programs On Settings Menu dialog box, select Enabled, and click OK.
4. Double-click Disable And Remove Links To Windows Update.
5. In the Disable And Remove Links To Windows Update dialog box, select Enabled, and click OK.
6. Double-click Add Logoff On The Start Menu.
7. In the Add Logoff On The Start Menu dialog box, select Enabled, and click OK.

▶ **To restrict access to local hard disk drives**

1. In the tree under Windows Components, select Windows Explorer in the GPO namespace.
2. Double-click Hide These Specified Drives In My Computer.

3. In the Hide These Specified Drives In My Computer dialog box, select Enabled, select Restrict A, B, C, and D Drives Only from the list, and click OK.

4. Double-click Prevent Access To Drives From My Computer.

5. In the Prevent Access To Drives From My Computer dialog box, select Enabled, select Restrict A, B, C, and D Drives Only from the list, and click OK.

6. Close the GPO.

Exercise 2: Using Scripts to Create a Consistent Environment

The Group Policy created in the previous exercise is not yet complete. You have removed local drives to prevent a worker from accidentally storing files locally rather than on a server, but you've provided no mechanism for users to create their own drive mappings to the server, nor have you created any mappings. To complete this Group Policy, you need to create a logon script that maps a network drive to a server so that the user has a place to store documents.

First, you need to create a shared folder on the server to provide a place for user documents to be stored. You then create a logon script associated with a GPO to map a network drive. You might find that a network drive you want to use for a persistent drive mapping already exists in the user's profile or has been mapped by a previously applied GPO. To ensure that your mapping takes precedence over any pre-existing mapping, first delete any mappings pertaining to the drive letter, and then create your own.

▶ **To create a shared folder on the server**

1. On the desktop, double-click My Computer.

2. In My Computer, double-click the C drive.

3. On the File menu, point to New, and choose Folder. A new folder appears on the desktop.

4. Name the folder **Company**.

5. Right-click the Company folder, and click Sharing.

   The Company Properties dialog box appears with the Sharing tab visible, as shown in Figure 1.12. Sharing a folder makes its contents accessible over the network.

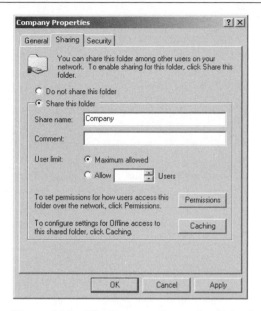

Figure 1.12   The Company Properties dialog box

6. In the Company Properties dialog box, select Share This Folder, and click OK.

7. Close all the windows on the desktop.

▶ **To create the logon script**

1. Open Active Directory Users And Computers.

2. In Active Directory Users And Computers management console, expand domain.fabrikam.com and the Departments OU.

3. Right-click the Engineering OU, and choose Properties.

4. On the Group Policy tab of the Engineering Properties dialog box, select the Engineering Desktop Settings GPO.

5. Click Edit.

6. In the Group Policy editor, expand the User Configuration\Windows Settings node in the GPO namespace.

7. Click Scripts (Logon/Logoff).

8. Double-click Logon.

   The Logon Properties dialog box appears, as shown in Figure 1.13, allowing you to link logon scripts to a GPO.

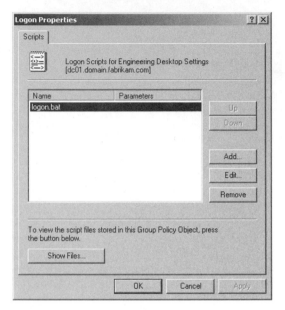

Figure 1.13   The Logon Properties dialog box

9. Click Add. The Add A Script dialog box asks for a Script Name and optional parameters.

10. Click Browse to open a file browser.

11. Right-click in the file list window, point to New, and click Text Document.

12. Type **Logon.bat** to rename the New Text Document.txt file.

    A dialog box asks if you really want to change the file's extension.

13. Click Yes to change the type of the file.

▶ **To edit the logon script**

1. Right-click Logon.bat, and click Edit.

   Microsoft Notepad launches and Logon.bat is opened for editing. The file is empty.

2. Type **net use z: /delete,** and press ENTER to start a new line.

3. Type **net use z: \\dc01\Company** as the second line of the batch file. If your server is not named dc01, replace dc01 with the name of your server.

4. Close Notepad.

5. Click Yes to save the changes.

6. In the Browse dialog box, click Open.

7. Click OK. The text file you've just created is now associated with the GPO as a logon script.

8. Click OK, and then close the GPO.

9. Click OK to close the Engineering Properties dialog box.

10. Close the Active Directory Users And Computers management console.

Exercise 3: Configuring a Computer for Task Workers

This policy builds on the knowledge worker policy because it is applied to an OU that is subordinate to the knowledge worker policy. It is important to remember that the task worker policy is not complete by itself and requires some of the restrictions provided in the knowledge worker Group Policy to remain secure.

In this exercise, the task worker requires access to Microsoft WordPad, a Windows accessory that creates and manages documents. You will enable the following Group Policy settings within the \User Configuration\Administrative Templates node:

- \Desktop\Hide all icons
- \Start Menu & Taskbar\Disable and remove shutdown
- \Start Menu & Taskbar\Remove Search
- \Start Menu & Taskbar\Remove Run
- \Start Menu & Taskbar\Remove Help
- \Start Menu & Taskbar\Remove Favorites
- \Start Menu & Taskbar\Remove Documents
- \Start Menu & Taskbar\Disable changes to Taskbar and Start Menu Settings
- \System\Run only allows Windows applications: wordpad.exe

Note   Perform this exercise while logged on to the domain controller as Administrator.

▶ **To create a GPO for a restricted desktop appropriate for a task worker**

1. Open Active Directory Users And Computers.

2. In the tree in the Active Directory Users And Computers management console, expand Departments, and select the Engineering OU.

3. Right-click the OU, and click Properties.

4. In the Engineering Properties dialog box, click the Group Policy tab.

5. Click New. A new GPO object appears in the GPO list.

6. Type **Intern Restrictions** as the name for the GPO.

▶   **To configure the GPO settings**

1. Click Edit to open the Group Policy editor.

2. In the tree, expand the GPO's User Configuration node, and then expand the Administrative Templates node.

3. Expand the Windows Components node.

4. Click Desktop in the GPO namespace.

5. Double-click Hide All Icons On Desktop.

6. In the Hide All Icons On Desktop dialog box, select Enabled, and click OK.

7. Click Start Menu & Taskbar in the GPO namespace.

8. Double-click Disable And Remove The Shut Down Command.

9. In the dialog box, select Enabled, and click OK.

10. Double-click Remove Search Menu From Start Menu.

11. In the dialog box, select Enabled, and click OK.

12. Double-click Remove Run Menu From Start Menu.

13. In the dialog box, select Enabled, and click OK.

14. Double-click Remove Help Menu From Start Menu.

15. In the dialog box, select Enabled, and click OK.

16. Double-click Remove Favorites Menu From Start Menu.

17. In the dialog box, select Enabled, and click OK.

18. Double-click Remove Documents Menu From Start Menu.

19. In the dialog box, select Enabled, and click OK.

20. Double-click Disable Changes To Taskbar And Start Menu Settings.

21. In the dialog box, select Enabled, and click OK.

▶ **To allow only specific executables to be launched**

1. Click System in the GPO namespace.

2. Double-click Run Only Allowed Windows Applications to open the Properties dialog box, as shown in Figure 1.14.

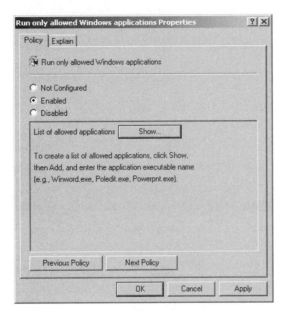

Figure 1.14   The Run Only Allowed Windows Applications policy setting is very important for security

3. Select Enabled, and click Show.

4. When the Allowed Applications dialog box appears, click Add.

5. Type **wordpad.exe,** click OK, and then click OK again.

6. Close the Group Policy editor.

7. Click Close, and then close the Active Directory Users And Computers management console.

Exercise 4: Configuring MMC Client Security

In this exercise, you create a domain-wide MMC restriction that applies to all members of the domain, and then you create a filter to prevent the MMC restriction from affecting domain administrators.

▶ **To prevent users from using the MMC to configure their computers**

1. Create a policy called MMC Restrictions in the fabrikam.com domain Group Policy editor.

   Use the previous exercise to refresh your memory about how to do this, if necessary.

2. Click Edit to open the Group Policy editor.

3. Expand User Configuration, Administrative Templates, and Windows Components, and select Microsoft Management Console.

4. Double-click Restrict The User From Entering Author Mode.

5. In the dialog box, select Enabled, and click OK.

6. Double-click Restrict Users To The Explicitly Permitted List Of Snap-ins.

7. In the dialog box, select Enabled, and click OK.

8. Close the GPO.

9. Click Properties to open the MMC Restrictions Properties dialog box.

10. On the Security tab of the dialog box, select Domain Admins.

11. Select the Apply Group Policy check box in the Deny column, and click OK.

    A Security message box asks if you want to continue.

12. Click Yes and close the domain.fabrikam.com Properties window and the Active Directory Users And Computers management console.

Exercise 5: Configuring Internet Explorer Security

In this exercise, you configure Internet Explorer to eliminate the user's ability to make changes to a configuration.

Note Perform this exercise while logged on to the domain controller as an Administrator.

▶ **To configure Internet Explorer settings in a GPO**

1. Open the Engineering Desktop Settings GPO.

2. Expand User Configuration, Windows Settings, and Internet Explorer Maintenance.

3. Click Browser User Interface, and then double-click Browser Title.

4. In the Browser Title dialog box, select the Customize Title Bars check box.

5. In the Title Bar Text box, type **Fabrikam**, and click OK.

6. In the GPO tree, click URLs.

7. Double-click Important URLs.

8. In the Important URLs dialog box, select the Customize Home Page URL check box, and in the Home Page URL box, type **http://www.fabrikam.com**.

9. Select the Customize Search Bar URL check box, and in the Search Bar URL box, type **http://www.msn.com**.

10. Select the Customize Online Support Page URL check box, and in the Online Support Page URL box, type **http://support.microsoft.com**.

11. Click OK.

▶ **To establish Internet Explorer Zone restrictions**

1. In the GPO tree, click the Security node under Internet Explorer Maintenance.

2. Double-click Security Zones And Content Ratings.

3. In the Security Zones And Content Ratings dialog box, select Import The Current Security Zones Settings.

4. Click Modify Settings. The Security dialog box appears, as shown in Figure 1.15.

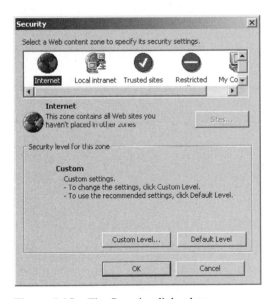

Figure 1.15   The Security dialog box

5. Select Internet, and click Custom Level.

   The Security Settings dialog box appears, as shown in Figure 1.16. Use this dialog box to customize the various security levels.

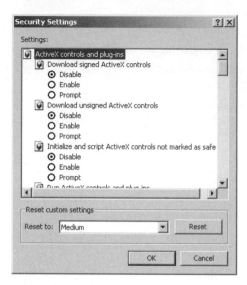

Figure 1.16   The Internet Explorer Security Settings dialog box

6. Select High in the Reset To list, click Reset, click Yes to confirm, and click OK.

7. Click OK to close the Security Settings dialog box.

8. Click OK to close the Security Zones And Content Ratings dialog box.

▶ **To prevent users from changing Internet Explorer settings**

1. In the GPO tree, expand User Configuration, Administrative Templates, and Windows Components.

2. Click Internet Explorer.

3. Double-click Disable Changing Proxy Settings.

4. In the dialog box, select Enabled, and click OK.

5. Double-click Disable Internet Connection Wizard.

6. In the dialog box, select Enabled, and click OK.

7. In the GPO tree, expand Internet, and click Internet Control Panel.

8. Double-click Disable The General Page.

9. In the dialog box, select Enabled, and click OK.

10. Double-click Disable The Security Page.

11. In the dialog box, select Enabled, and click OK.

12. Double-click Disable The Content Page.

13. In the dialog box, select Enabled, and click OK.

14. Double-click Disable The Connections Page.

15. In the dialog box, select Enabled, and click OK.

16. Double-click Disable The Programs Page.

17. In the dialog box, select Enabled, and click OK.

18. Double-click Disable The Advanced Page dialog box.

19. In the dialog box, select Enabled, and click OK.

20. Close the Group Policy configuration editor.

Lesson Review

The following questions are intended to reinforce key information in this lesson. If you are unable to answer a question, review the lesson and try the question again. Answers to the questions can be found in the appendix.

1. What is the most important security feature of Group Policy?

2. What is the easiest way to test how Group Policy will affect a class of users?

3. What security component is required to truly secure users and computers from potentially harmful Internet content?

4. What should users be restricted from using to prevent them from mis-configuring their computers?

5. Why would you delete drive mappings prior to establishing them in a logon script?

Lesson Summary

- The primary purpose of Group Policy is to secure, control, and standardize the configuration of a large group of client computers and user accounts.

- Group Policy should be tailored to classes of workers so that applications can be restricted to the narrowest possible set for any individual worker.

- Testing the application of Group Policy using a test account is critical to understanding the ultimate effects of Group Policy in any specific instance.

- Group Policy restrictions disable access to User Interface features; they do not necessarily restrict access by third-party programs or scripts to the features that they control.

Lesson 4: Troubleshooting Group Policy Application

Testing the application of Group Policy is crucial to understanding the effects on users in any specific implementation. The combination of multiple overriding GPOs on a user or computer can create a myriad of possible outcomes even when Group Policy is operating correctly.

The proper operation of Group Policy mechanisms depends on numerous inter-dependent operating system features, all of which must be configured correctly to guarantee the proper operation of Group Policy. For this reason, you must under-stand how to troubleshoot the application of Group Policy to determine why unexpected or unintentional results have occurred.

After you complete this lesson, you will be able to

- Determine why Group Policy application problems can occur
- Test for proper connectivity to domain controllers
- Test the proper configuration of Domain Name System (DNS) settings
- Enable verbose Group Policy logging for troubleshooting purposes
- Use troubleshooting tools to find configuration errors on clients and servers

Estimated lesson time: 30 minutes

Understanding Typical Group Policy Application Problems

Users encounter a number of relatively routine problems when working with Group Policy. Typical problems with Group Policy application include

- Unexpected or unintended results
- Incomplete application of policy
- Lack of policy application

In a properly functioning network, these problems typically occur because multiple GPOs are being applied and it's not always obvious which policy has priority for a specific setting. Other possible causes are a client computer that can't resolve the name of a domain controller or that doesn't have proper access to a GPO or SYSVOL share. Typical solutions to Group Policy problems include verifying that

- The client has properly configured DNS settings and can resolve the domain controller.
- The user or computer account is actually contained within the Active Directory container that is linked to the GPO.

- A previously applied policy is not set to No Override.
- The user has Read and Apply permissions for the GPO.

The Effect of DNS Resolution on Group Policy

Group Policy cannot be correctly applied unless a client can resolve the name of the domain controller responsible for storing the Group Policy. Even if the host name can be resolved from the client, because of the way DNS works, the Group Policy client-side extensions might not be able to resolve the server name.

When a computer attempts to resolve a host name, such as dc01.domain.fabrikam.com, the name of the host is known to the client and can be sent to the DNS server to determine the IP address. However, when a client looks for a domain controller without knowing its name, it sends a special type of DNS lookup called a Service (SRV) record lookup. In an SRV record lookup, DNS returns to the client the name of the domain controller, and the client repeats the request for the server's IP address once it knows the server's host name. The practical result of this process is that, while you might be able to resolve a domain controller's name from a specific client, Group Policy cannot be applied unless a valid SRV record exists on the client's DNS server that will return the appropriate domain controller's name to the client.

For this reason, clients cannot apply Group Policy unless domain controllers have proper SRV records in the DNS service. This is usually not a problem when dynamic DNS is in use, because these records are automatically created when hosts are promoted to domain controllers, but in environments where static or non-Active Directory integrated DNS is in use, keeping these records up to date can be a constant hassle.

Tip   If you run a mixed Windows-UNIX network, it's easier to use Windows to provide DNS service. UNIX clients can resolve against Windows servers easily, and Windows DNS can be integrated with Active Directory so that the complex records required for proper domain operation are automatically created.

Esoteric Problems with Group Policy Application

Because of the complexity of Group Policy operations, larger networks are likely to experience problems due to replication of GPOs. Also, more complex Active Directory structures can take significantly more time to analyze when an attempt is made to determine which specific GPO contains a particular setting. Finally, sites in the process of migrating from a Microsoft Windows NT 4 domain structure to Active Directory might find that Windows NT 4 system policy has unexpected results when used with Group Policy. Esoteric problems with Group Policy include

- Changes to Group Policy work locally, but do not work at other sites or in other domains.

- Replication of GPOs can be much slower than anticipated.
- Some portions of Group Policy have been applied, but others have not.

Numerous domain controller configuration problems can interfere with the proper application of Group Policy. However, most of these problems will also affect other areas of domain controller operation, so it should be somewhat obvious if a domain controller is not functioning properly.

When a client computer applies Group Policy, the various Group Policy client-side extensions write their results to the file %systemroot%\Debug\UserMode \User-env.log. Reading this file can usually point you to the problem that is occurring, especially if the problem is related to resource access permissions or DNS lookup failure.

Solving esoteric Group Policy application problems is not necessarily more difficult than solving simple problems, once you know all of the symptoms. You can solve most esoteric Group Policy problems by checking a few additional configurations. To solve esoteric problems, you must

- Confirm that replication is occurring correctly and that the Group Policy is the same across domain controllers.
- Ensure than individual GPOs are kept small so that they replicate quickly among sites.
- Ensure that the user has Read and Apply permissions for the GPO (in other words, ensure that the GPO is not being filtered) using Userenv.log.
- Verify that Windows isn't attempting to apply Windows NT 4 policy to the client.
- Reboot the computer and log on again to ensure that all types of Group Policy extensions have been refreshed.

Understanding Windows NT 4 Domain Migration Issues

Several side effects can occur in Group Policy application for networks that are in the midst of a migration from Windows NT 4 domains to Windows 2000 domains. The following list identifies the specific effects of Windows NT 4 users and client computers on the application of Group Policy in a Windows 2000 domain:

- If the computer is running Windows NT 4, it receives Windows NT 4–style system policy rather than the Windows 2000–style Computer Configuration portion of Group Policy, irrespective of how the computer's account is managed.
- If Windows NT 4–based domain controllers manage a user account, that user account receives Windows NT 4–style system policy rather than the Windows 2000–style User Configuration portion of a GPO, regardless of the client operating system.

- If Active Directory manages the user account, the user receives the User Configuration portion of a GPO no matter which operating system is installed on the client computer. This means that Windows NT 4 clients receive the User Configuration portion of a GPO when an Active Directory account logs on, and that Windows 2000 clients receive system policy when accounts managed by Windows NT 4 domain controllers log on.

Tip   To avoid problems with various types of policy affecting client computers, upgrade all user accounts to Active Directory as quickly as possible by upgrading resource domains to Windows 2000. Update Windows NT backup domain controllers to Windows 2000 as quickly as possible after that. Don't upgrade Windows NT clients to Windows 2000 until all domain controllers are running Windows 2000 Server.

Remember that Windows NT 4–compatible system policy permanently tattoos the registry of Windows NT computers. When accounts (machine accounts or user accounts) are moved to Active Directory, or when computers are upgraded from Windows NT 4 to Windows 2000, unwanted residual registry settings might remain from the application of system policy. Use Regini.exe to clean the registry of the computer that has residual system policy problems. Better yet, perform clean installations of Windows 2000 rather than upgrade Windows NT computers.

Anticipating Problems Relating to Windows NT 4 Trust Relationships

Trust relationships control the way that users can access resources in remote domains. When a trust relationship exists between two domains, users in the trusted domain can access resources in the trusting domain without having to log on to the trusting domain.

When you upgrade multiple domains from Windows NT to Windows 2000, trust relationships are not automatically upgraded, which can occasionally cause Group Policy application problems. After upgrading both domains to Windows 2000, break and reestablish trust relationships to ensure that they operate as expected.

Practice: Troubleshooting the Application of Group Policy

In this practice, you troubleshoot the application of Group Policy by enabling user environment logging on the client side, by running Dcdiag.exe to check for the proper configuration of the domain controller, and by running Netdiag.exe to check for the proper connectivity between the client and the domain controller.

Exercise 1: Enabling User Environment Debug Logging in Windows 2000

Windows 2000 logs the application of Group Policy to a file in the %systemroot% \debug\UserMode\userenv.log. By default, this file does not contain much information, but you can record and display more information by enabling verbose logging. Verbose logging tells the client-side extensions to log every message they generate, which provides quite a bit of information about how policy is being applied. Knowing the details about how policy is being applied will help you discover what is going wrong when problems occur, because the error messages will show up in the log file.

▶ **To enable verbose logging in Windows 2000 on the client side**

1. On the client where you suspect that a Group Policy application problem is occurring, log on as an administrator.
2. Click Start, and click Run.
3. Type **Regedit,** and press ENTER.
4. In the Registry Editor, expand HKEY_LOCAL_MACHINE\Software \Microsoft\Windows NT\Current Version\WinLogon.
5. Click Edit, point to New, and click DWORD Value.
6. Type **UserEnvDebugLevel**.
7. Double-click UserEnvDebugLevel.
8. In the Edit DWORD Value dialog box, type **10002** in the box and ensure that Hexidecimal is selected.
9. Click OK, close the Registry Editor, and log off.

▶ **To interpret the Group Policy application log**

1. Log on as a test user to whom the Group Policy should apply.
2. Wait for about one minute for the system to finish accessing the hard disk drive, and then log off.
3. Log on as an administrator.
4. Open C:\WINNT\Debug.
5. Double-click UserEnv.log.
6. If an Open With dialog box appears, click Notepad, and click OK. Notepad displays the log file as a text document.
7. Browse through the log file. The last entry is the most recent (administrative) logon, so you are interested in the section prior to that. A considerable amount of information applies to each logon, so scroll back far enough to see the initial boot log entry to be sure that you're interpreting the correct result set.

Exercise 2: Verifying Domain Controller Configuration

You can use the Dcdiag.exe program to determine what is wrong with a domain controller or to verify that it is operating properly and that the problem is most likely on the client side.

▶ **To determine whether a domain controller is properly configured**

1. Log on to the domain controller you want to test as the administrator.
2. If the Windows 2000 support tools are not installed, install them from the Windows 2000 Server CD. The tools are located in the \Support\Tools folder.
3. Open a command prompt.
4. Type **dcdiag /v >dcdiag.log**. The command prompt will pause for about one minute.
5. Type **notepad dcdiag.log**. Notepad displays the results of the diagnostic in a text document.
6. Scroll through the contents of the log file looking for error messages or test sequences that failed. These will indicate what is wrong and guide your troubleshooting efforts.

Exercise 3: Verifying Client Connectivity

You can use the Netdiag.exe program to determine whether proper name resolution is in place between a client and a domain controller.

▶ **To check for proper name resolution between a client and a domain controller**

1. Log on to the client you want to test as an administrator.
2. Insert the Windows 2000 Server CD in the computer's CD-ROM drive.
3. Open the \Support\Tools folder.
4. Double-click the Deploy.cab file. The contents of the Deploy.cab file appear.
5. Double-click the Netdiag.exe file. A dialog box asks where you want to extract the file to.
6. Select a path on the client computer's local hard disk (for example: C:\Winnt\Temp).
7. Open a command prompt.
8. Change the directory to the location where you extracted Netdiag.exe.
9. Type **netdiag /v >diagnose.log**. The command prompt will pause for about one minute.
10. Type **notepad diagnose.log**. Notepad displays the diagnostic log file in a text document.
11. Browse through the output, scroll down to the line: "DC discovery test:" and ensure that it says Passed. If not, use the output of the log to discover which tests failed and which parameters need to be corrected.

Lesson Review

The following questions are intended to reinforce key information in this lesson. If you are unable to answer a question, review the lesson and try the question again. Answers to the questions can be found in the appendix.

1. To which file does Windows log Group Policy application errors?

2. If a new Windows 2000 client computer can log on to the local domain controller, but no Group Policy is applied for the machine or user configurations, what is the most likely problem?

3. If you log on to a Windows 2000 domain from a Windows NT 4 computer using a user account managed by Active Directory, how will Group Policy be applied?

Lesson Summary

- Group Policy is a complex group of services and is highly dependent on the proper operation of many network services. Incorrect configuration of any of these services can cause problems for Group Policy application.
- Because Group Policy is designed to be applied in layers, it is not always obvious which GPO contains a particular setting.
- DNS must be operating correctly and properly configured on the client for GPOs to be downloaded. Users must have permission to read and apply GPOs for the GPOs to take effect.
- You can use the Dcdiag.exe support tool to determine whether or not a domain controller is operating correctly. You can use the Netdiag.exe tool to determine whether a client computer is configured correctly.

Lesson 5: Security Limitations

As with any network service, hackers and malicious users can interfere with the application of Group Policy. Also, once Group Policy is applied, it can be circumvented by numerous means because Group Policy is designed to prevent access to user interface features, not to secure base operating system resources.

After you complete this lesson, you will be able to

- Identify ways that hackers and malicious users might circumvent the application of Group Policy
- Identify ways that users might circumvent Group Policy restrictions that have been applied

Estimated lesson time: 10 minutes

Understanding the Role of Group Policy in Network Security

Controlling network configuration is critical to security. When users can configure network settings, they can circumvent new Group Policy completely.

Users can circumvent the application of new Group Policy settings by preventing a client from contacting a domain controller. This can be as simple as unplugging the network cable from the computer and then logging on with a cached profile, for example. When the computer is reconnected, it will have access to the network, but without the new Group Policy settings in place.

Group Policy settings will be applied at the next periodic refresh interval, but that won't occur for at least 90 minutes. Other methods of preventing Group Policy from being applied include changing or interfering with the DNS services necessary to resolve the Group Policy servers, or interfering with the servers themselves.

If users are allowed to configure their own new computers out of the box, they can prevent the application of Group Policy entirely by setting their DNS settings to a public DNS server rather than to the domain DNS servers. They will still be able to join the domain and log on as long as there is a domain controller within their Ethernet broadcast area (the local area network), but the Group Policy client will not be able to determine the address of the domain controller to download GPOs to the client. This will prevent the application of Group Policy, and since the computer is new, it won't have cached settings in place. Do not allow users to configure their own new computers without verifying their DNS settings.

Another way a user can prevent the application of Group Policy is to browse to the server's SYSVOL share, and then open the various Group Policy files in Read-Exclusive mode. The attacker can then log on to another workstation, which prevents the Group Policy settings from being applied to the subsequent logon. This is an esoteric attack that works because of a special type of Read access called Exclusive mode, which prevents other users from opening a file. This mode is intended to prevent other users on the network from opening a document that is already in use and accidentally corrupting it. But because these Group Policy files cannot be read, and users must have Read access to GPOs to download them, the system behaves as if the user does not have Read access to the GPO, and so filters it from being applied to subsequent users.

When you work with Group Policy, it is crucial to remember that Group Policy restrictions are merely surface user interface restrictions that do not remove functionality from the computer or even from the user. For example, while it is possible to remove drive icons from the My Computer window, you can still access those drives through the Search function, from earlier applications, and from the command prompt. Drives also available to scripts or applications written by independent software vendors. For this reason, be certain to test your Group Policy applications against all possible methods of access.

Practice: Circumventing the Security Limitations of Group Policy

In this practice, you go through a small number of steps that allow you to circumvent restrictions put in place by Group Policy, even on a highly restricted machine. This demonstrates that while Group Policy can obscure operating system functionality from users, it is not a true security mechanism in its own right and should not be relied on as the sole means of establishing security on a client computer. File system permissions remain the most important security tool an administrator can use to prevent the exploitation of a client computer.

No matter how well you secure a client computer with Group Policy, if the computer remains useful, it will be subject to user circumvention. For example, even if you've disabled access to local drives, disabled access to desktop icons, and disabled the command prompt, a user can use the following attack to get around all of these restrictions.

This attack works because the command prompt restriction is based on the name of the executable program. Because an earlier version of Cmd.exe called Command.com exists on all Windows computers by default, a user can create a batch file that calls that alternate command prompt to gain command-prompt functionality. From the command line, nearly any administrative function can be performed to further circumvent Group Policy security restrictions. For example, a user could use the ftp program to download an alternative program to edit the registry.

Even when this flaw is patched, other similar flaws will always exist because Group Policy does not truly secure client computers, it only obscures access to functionality through a myriad of configurable settings. It is crucial that security administrators understand the real limitations of Group Policy so that they can plan for events in which Group Policy cannot effectively control user behavior. By circumventing Group Policy, a user can gain wide control on any client computer and create documents anywhere on the network.

▶ **To circumvent Group Policy**

1. Open Notepad. If Notepad is not available, open Word or any other word processing or text editing program.
2. In a new document, type **command**.
3. From the File menu, choose Save As.
4. If a restricted feature dialog box opens, click OK to dismiss it. It will not interfere with saving the document.
5. Select a location where you have Write access, such as a shared folder or your home directory.
6. In the Show Files Of Type list, select All Files.
7. In the Document Name box, type **hack.bat,** and click Save.
8. From the File menu, choose Open.
9. In the Files Of Type list, select All Files.
10. Right-click the Hack.bat file.

    Notice that nothing happens.
11. In the Open File dialog box, click View As, and click Thumbnails.
12. Right-click the thumbnail view of Hack.bat.

    Notice that this time, a shortcut menu appears.
13. Click Open.

    Windows launches the file, executing the command within the batch file, which launches Command.com. A command prompt appears.

    You can use this command prompt to launch programs, copy files, map network drives, or perform other administrative functions that are not limited by NTFS or share permissions. For example, you could type **subst s: c:** to create an S drive alias for the C drive that will then show up in Windows Explorer.

Lesson Review

The following questions are intended to reinforce key information in this lesson. If you are unable to answer a question, review the lesson and try the question again. Answers to the questions can be found in the appendix.

1. What are some of the ways that users could interfere with the application of Group Policy on their computers?

2. If you disable access to the C drive in a Group Policy, what methods might a user use to regain access to it?

3. If you limit a client computer to running just a single program, how might a hacker run the program of their choice?

Lesson Summary

- Users can circumvent the application of new Group Policy settings by preventing their clients from contacting a domain controller. Hackers might interfere with DNS services or servers to prevent the application of Group Policy.

- Group Policy restrictions are merely surface restrictions that do not remove the functionality from the computer or user. They merely remove the normal method of access to it.

- Group Policy must be supplemented by file system permissions and pervasive network security to remain effective as a security mechanism.

C H A P T E R 2

User Accounts and Security Groups

About This Chapter

Security in the Microsoft Windows 2000 operating system is based on *user authentication*, the process of determining the identity of the person accessing the computer. Once the operating system has identified the user, it can enforce security restrictions based on the user's identity by applying rules, rights, and permissions.

A *user account* contains the information that identifies a user. *Security groups* allow you to combine any number of users who have similar security requirements into a single security group account and manage security for them as a unit.

Also covered in this chapter are *security templates,* which establish a level of security across the network. This chapter discusses what you need to know to manage and deploy security templates and provides information about troubleshooting common problems.

Exam Tip   Understanding how to use security groups for users who require similar access to secure resources is crucial to effective administration and to passing the exam. Make sure you understand how to use permissions and security groups to both grant and restrict access to resources.

Before You Begin

To complete this chapter, you must have

- A test computer configured with Microsoft Windows 2000 Server and with Active Directory installed
- A test computer running Microsoft Windows 2000 Professional and joined to the server's domain

---

Tip   You can use Windows XP Professional in these exercises if you enable the Classic Start Menus on the Start Menu tab of the Taskbar And Start Menu Properties window.

Lesson 1: Creating Local User Accounts and Security Groups

A fundamental component of Windows security is the user account. A *user account* identifies the person using the computer to the operating system so that it can apply appropriate authorization to access resources. Using another fundamental component, security groups, you can manage users with similar security requirements. This lesson discusses local user accounts and security groups on workstations and member servers. *Member servers* are servers that are members of a domain but not domain controllers.

After this lesson, you will be able to

- Create and manage local user accounts
- Create and manage local security groups

Estimated lesson time: 30 minutes

Managing User Accounts

While logging on to a computer running Windows, a user must provide credentials (Figure 2.1), such as a user account name and password, that prove the user is authorized to access the system. Windows can also be configured to use smart cards or other types of authentication, but passwords are the default and most common form of authentication.

Windows provides two types of user accounts: local accounts and domain accounts. If you log on to a computer using a *local account*, you have access to that computer only. If you log on to a computer using a *domain account*, you have access not only to that computer, but also to network resources throughout the domain. Local accounts are stored on all Windows computers except domain controllers, and domain accounts are stored in Active Directory on domain controllers so they can be used on any computer that is a member of the domain.

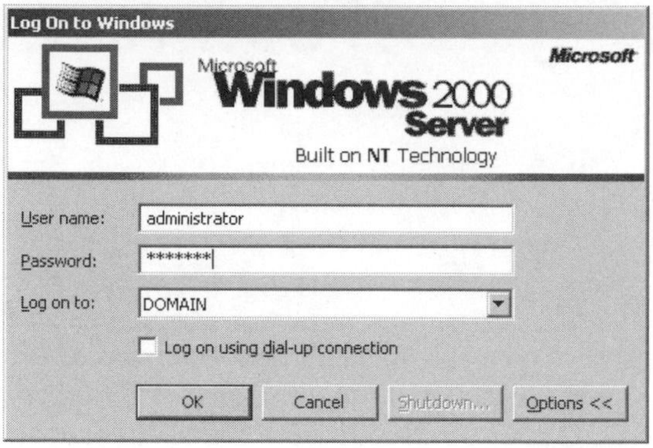

Figure 2.1 The Microsoft Windows 2000 logon prompt

Important Joining a computer to a domain does not disable its local system accounts. Each computer has a default administrator account that can still be used to gain access to the system irrespective of its membership in a domain. Always secure the local computer administrator account with a strong password to prevent anyone from using it to exploit the computer. If computer users need administrative privileges on their own machines, create a domain account for this purpose and make that account a member of their local computer's administrators group.

Computers that are members of a domain should have the fewest possible numbers of local user accounts and security groups because it is very difficult to manage local user accounts individually on every machine in a domain. In a domain, control security using domain user accounts and groups rather than local user accounts.

To the system, a user account is represented not by its name but by its security identifier (SID). A SID uniquely identifies a *security principal* throughout the system. A security principal is any Active Directory object, such as a user account, a computer account, or a security group, that can be assigned permissions and rights.

Because user accounts are represented not by names in the system but by SIDs, a user account remains unchanged even when it is renamed. However, a newly created account with the same name as a deleted account will have a different SID, and will not have access to the same resources as its predecessor.

SIDs are globally unique and are never reused; no two user accounts anywhere in the world can have the same security identifier. The operating system guarantees this by including the computer's SID with each local user account SID, and by choosing computer SIDs randomly from a pool of numbers so large that it's practically impossible for any two to be the same. This means that no account from one computer will be able to log on to another computer, eliminating a serious security problem that affects other operating systems.

Note   When attached to a domain, Windows XP Professional requires password authentication. However, for local access, the Windows XP operating system does not require password authentication by default. Users must still log on by asserting their identities, and all local Windows security mechanisms are in effect as they are described in this chapter. The only difference between providing a password and clicking an account icon is that by clicking an icon, users are trusted to identify themselves correctly (rather than proving their identity with a password) in environments where user level security is not a concern, such as a home environment where two or more family members share a computer. Account holders can set a password to protect their local accounts.

SIDs are used by the system to determine which security principals, such as user accounts and security groups, have access to specific secured resources. A structure in every secured resource, called an access control list (ACL), contains an entry for every security principal that is allowed to access the resource. If a user has access to a secure resource, the user account's SID, or the SID of a group the user belongs to, appears in the secured resource's ACL as an *access control entry* (ACE). The ACE contains the SID of the allowed security principal along with the type of access allowed, such as Read access or Change access. ACLs are discussed in detail in Chapter 4, "Account-Based Security."

Figure 2.2 shows the ACL for a folder named Departments. The SIDs of user accounts are displayed as the name of the account unless the account has been deleted, in which case the actual SID number is displayed.

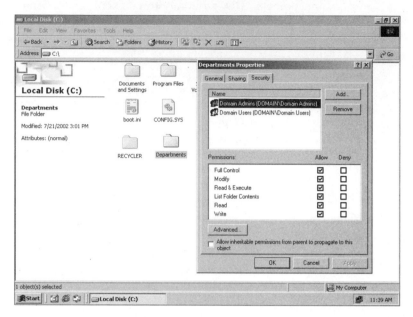

Figure 2.2   The access control list for the Departments folder

Managing Security Groups

If every user account's individual SID were used to indicate access to a specific resource, the ACL of that resource would become unmanageably large as the number of users increased. In such a system, the folder's ACL would need to have 10,000 entries if 10,000 users required access to the folder. On a network with just a few thousand users, the time required to check permissions would eclipse all other functions performed by the operating system. Using security groups prevents this problem by dramatically reducing the number of SIDs listed in ACLs.

Optimizing Security Checking

To optimize security checking for the machine and make administration more convenient, users with the same security requirements can be combined into security groups. A security group has its own unique SID, so it can be used to specify permissions for a resource.

After you've made a user account a member of a security group, the security group's SID is placed in the user's *access token* when the user logs on. An *access token* represents the complete credentials of the logged on user. When the user attempts to access a secured resource, the user's access token contains the security group's SID, which matches the SID in the ACL for that resource, so the system allows the user access to anything the group can access. Access tokens are described in detail later in this lesson.

Essentially, when users are combined into security groups, Windows has to search through security groups only when a user logs on to gather all the SIDs to create the user's access token. When the user is logged on, there's no further need to check group access. Another benefit of using security groups is that ACLs can be much smaller because they need to contain only the SIDs of security groups, rather than those of individual users.

Administering Groups

Create a security group whenever a unique combination of security requirements applies to a number of users. Any time a folder should be secured for a unique set of users, create a security group, secure the folder using the security group, and add those users who need access to the folder to the group.

For example, if a working group of engineers embarks on a new project that is sensitive and requires secure handling, create a security group that contains the members of the working group, and create a folder on a server that has its NTFS file system permissions set to allow access only to that security group.

Security groups frequently mirror the structure of departments, working groups, teams, and corollary duties in an organization, and they are usually created ad hoc to fulfill an immediate security need.

More Info   Information about how to effectively use permissions is contained in Chapter 4, "Account-Based Security."

User accounts can be members of any number of security groups, so there's no need to limit your use of them. For example, a financial controller might be a member of the Controller, Bookkeeping, Accounts Payable, Accounts Receivable, and Accountant groups. In this way, the financial controller has access to all the resources to which these groups have access.

Authenticating a User on a Local Computer

A user who attempts to use a Windows 2000 computer must authenticate with the computer, usually by providing the user account name and password that are stored with that user account. Windows checks the information provided against the user account database to see if the password matches. If the password matches, the user is presumed to be the person for whom the account was established, and access to the computer is allowed. Other authentication methods are supported by Windows, such as biometric authentication or smart card authentication, but password authentication is the default and most widely used method.

More Info   Chapter 6, "Managing a Public Key Infrastructure," and Chapter 7, "Increasing Authentication Security," contain more information about alternative authentication methods.

Local Logon Process

As Windows 2000 starts, its final task is to start the Winlogon component of the Local Security Authority (LSA). The *Local Security Authority* is the process in Windows that is responsible for enforcing authorization in Windows. The LSA performs nearly all security-related functions, including logging on users and creating access tokens, accessing security accounts databases, and checking permissions on secured resources.

Note   The LSA process constantly runs in the background on all Windows computers, and it appears in Task Manager as Lsass.exe.

The Winlogon component of the LSA is responsible for displaying the familiar logon dialog box in Windows (Figure 2.1), which collects the user's account name and password. The LSA uses that information to query the *Security Accounts Manager* (SAM), a secure database of user accounts stored in the registry, to check the password and, if it matches, to retrieve the user's SID and the SIDs of all the groups to which the user belongs. The LSA combines these SIDs to form an access token. The LSA then starts the user's shell program (usually Microsoft Windows Explorer) and passes the access token to the shell program.

When any program starts another program, it passes the access token that it inherited to the program it launches. In this way, every application executes with the credentials of the user who originally logged on, and every application is said to run in that user's security context.

Figure 2.3 shows the local authentication process.

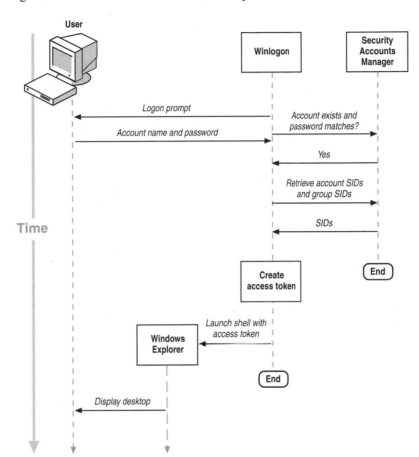

Figure 2.3 The local logon process

The interactive logon process works like this:

1. Winlogon service of the Local Security Authority collects the user name and password.
2. LSA queries the SAM to verify the user name and password.
3. LSA creates an access token based on the user account SID and security group SIDs.
4. The access token is passed to subsequent processes, which is Windows Explorer unless the default has been changed by Group Policy. The user is now logged on.

Local Resource Access

When a program requires access to a secured resource, such as a file, it provides its access token (which is the access token of the user who originally logged on) to the security reference monitor component of the LSA. The security reference monitor compares the SIDs contained in the access token to the SIDs contained in the secure resource's ACL and allows access only if a match is found between the SIDs and the type of access requested. ACLs and resource access are described in greater detail in Chapter 4, "Account-Based Security."

Local Built-In Groups

Windows 2000 provides a set of built-in local groups. *Built-in groups* are groups that have been predefined with specific user rights, and are used to secure the base operating system. By making user accounts members of these built-in groups, as shown in Table 2.1, you can easily define the roles and rights of a user.

Table 2.1   Built-In Local Groups

Group	Use
Administrators	Users who have full administrative access to the computer. The built-in administrator account is a member of this group. The Domain Admins group is made a member of this group if the machine is joined to a domain.
Backup Operators	Users who have the ability to back up and restore files to the computer irrespective of the security permissions on those files. They do not have any other administrative rights.
Guests	Members whose use is limited to specifically assigned secured resources for occasional use. Guests cannot make permanent changes to their desktop settings. The built-in guest account is a member of this group by default, and the Domain Guests group is added to Guests if the machine belongs to a domain.
Power Users	User accounts with the elevated user rights to modify accounts and create shares.
Replicator	A user account with the right to replicate files in a domain.
Users	Standard users. All user accounts are added to this group by default, and domain users are added to this group if the computer is a member of a domain.

System Groups

System groups are local groups that do not have administrator-definable lists of members. The system automatically places users in these groups whenever their usage meets the purpose of the group. Table 2.2 lists the system groups and describes the groups' members.

Table 2.2   System Groups for a Local Computer

System group	Use
Everyone	All user accounts that access the computer, including anonymous users and users who have not specifically logged on (if the Guest account is enabled)
Authenticated Users	All user accounts that have successfully authenticated on the local machine and the Active Directory (if the machine is part of a domain)
Creator Owner	The user account that owns a specific secured resource
Network	Any account that logged on to the computer through the server service
Interactive	Users who have logged on locally or through Terminal Services
Anonymous Logon	Users who have enough access to determine which shares are available without logging on
Dialup	Users who have logged on through a Routing and Remote Access Service (RRAS) dial-up session

The most commonly used system group is the Everyone group. When an NTFS disk is formatted, the permissions on the root directory are set to allow the Everyone group Full Control permission to access it, and these permissions are automatically inherited by files and folders placed in the volume. For this reason, the Everyone group appears in many ACLs throughout most systems.

It is always a security mistake to allow the Everyone group Full Control permission to persist on the root of a new NTFS volume, except on the root of the C drive or where page files exist because Windows recreates the page file at every logon, and permissions in the containing folder affect this process. At the very least, permissions for volumes without page files should be changed to remove the Everyone Group ACE and allow the Authenticated Users group to have Full Control. The Everyone system group includes users who may not have provided credentials to the system, and that is essentially the same as having no security set at all.

Tip   Remember to change the root permissions of newly formatted volumes right after you format them to ensure that files and folders moved onto the volume inherit secure permissions.

Workgroup Background Authentication

Although local accounts do not have credentials on other machines, you can make accessing a remote computer seamless when using local system accounts.

Windows 2000 automatically negotiates credentials with another computer when you attempt to access a resource on that computer, sending your account credentials to the remote machine.

- If a local account exists on the remote machine with the same account name and password as the account you are using on your computer, the remote computer will use the logon name and password to generate a session and an access token without prompting for credentials.
- If the machine has an account with the same name but a different password, it will deny access.

Tip Users can also specify that they want to provide credentials to access a machine when they've been denied access because an account with the same name but a different password exists.

- If no matching account exists, the remote machine will prompt for credentials.

Although the automatic logon function can seem like domain authentication, it is inherently different. *Domain authentication* transmits the SIDs for the logged on user's domain account and global security groups (which are explained later in this lesson) between the computers involved, while *workgroup background authentication* passes credentials by account name.

Workgroup background authentication requires accounts to be configured independently on all local computers. Furthermore, passwords are not automatically synchronized when they are changed on any one computer. In effect, access is allowed, but under the security context of the machine's own local account of the same name, rather than by trusting the same domain account that the originating computer trusts. Because two different local accounts are in use (one on each machine), various security settings and policies could be different between the machines. For example, the user account may be an administrator on one machine, but only a typical user account on the other machine.

Another major effect is that the SIDs for the same name accounts are different, and these differences can have unexpected side effects. For example, if you secure a file on an NTFS formatted removable media device using a local system account on one machine, that file is not available to a user account with the same name and password on a different machine, because the SIDs for the two accounts are different. If you perform the same operation on two computers that are members of the same domain using domain accounts, the file is available, because the SID of the domain account used on both computers is the same. NTFS permissions and ACLs are discussed in detail in the next lesson.

Practice: Creating User Accounts and Security Groups

In this practice, you create user and group accounts on a local workstation.

Exercise 1: Managing User Accounts on a Local Computer

In this exercise, you create a number of user accounts for a computer that will be used by multiple users before it is joined to a domain. After creating the accounts, you will delete one account and disable another. The purpose of this exercise is to highlight the difference between local system accounts and the domain accounts that will be covered in the next lesson. In practice, you will rarely use local system accounts in a corporate environment. You will be performing this exercise on a Windows 2000 Professional computer.

▶   **To create a user account**

1. Right-click My Computer, and click Manage. The Computer Management console appears.
2. In the MMC console, expand System Tools, expand Local Users And Groups, and click the Users folder.
3. Right-click the Users folder, and click New User. The New User dialog box appears, as shown in Figure 2.4.

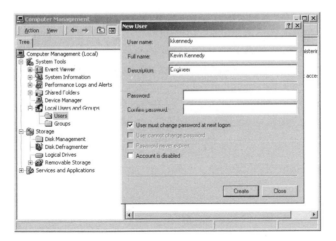

Figure 2.4   Creating a local user account

4. Type **kkennedy** into the User Name box (first initial plus last name).

5. Type **Kevin Kennedy** in the Full Name box.

6. Type **Engineer** in the Description box.

7. Type the same randomly selected password in the Password box and in the Confirm Password box.

8. Clear the User Must Change Password At Next Logon check box.

9. Click Create. The new user account is created with the default settings.

▶ **To populate a computer with user accounts**

1. Using the procedure to create a user account, create local user accounts for the following users:

   ■ Kevin Kennedy

   ■ Friske, Karen

   ■ Frum, John

   ■ Funk, Don

   ■ Gage, Bob

   ■ Galvin, Janice

   ■ Ganio, Jon

   ■ Gehring, Darren

2. Click Close to close the New User dialog box after creating the accounts.

▶ **To delete a local user account**

1. In the Users folder, right-click the account named dgehring, and click Delete. A security warning appears.

2. Read the warning that you cannot recreate the account by using the same account name, and click Yes. Notice that the account has been removed from the user list.

Warning   It is especially important not to leave unused accounts on local computers, because local accounts are frequently forgotten once a machine is joined to a domain. This leaves an active account that hackers could potentially exploit without anyone noticing.

► **To disable a local user account**

1. In the Users folder, right-click the account named kkennedy, and click Properties. The Properties dialog box appears as shown in Figure 2.5.

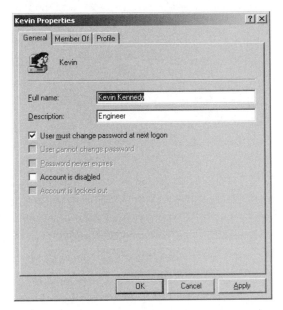

Figure 2.5   The Properties dialog box

2. Select the Account Is Disabled check box, and click OK. Notice that the account now appears with a red icon indicating that the account is disabled.

Exercise 2: Managing Security Groups on a Local Computer

In this exercise, you create two local groups, and then delete one of them.

► **To create local groups**

1. Log on to a Windows 2000 Professional computer as the Administrator.
2. Right-click My Computer, and click Manage. The Computer Management console appears.
3. Expand System Tools, and select the Local Users And Groups folder.
4. Right-click the Groups folder, and click New Group. The New Group dialog box appears
5. In the New Group dialog box, type **Engineers** as the name of the security group.

6. Click Add.

   A list of users appears in the Select Users Or Groups dialog box.

7. Click bgage, dfunk, jfrum, jgalvin, jganio, and kfriske to add them to the group.

8. Click OK to close the Add Users window, and then click Create to create the group.

   The New Group dialog box remains open but is empty after a group is created.

9. Type **CAD Users** as the name of a second new security group.

10. Click Add. The Add Users Or Groups dialog box appears.

11. Select bgage and defunk to add them to the group.

12. Click OK, and click Create.

13. Click Close to close the New Group dialog box.

► **To delete local groups**

1. In the Users folder, right-click the CAD Users group, and click Delete. A Local Users And Groups delete confirmation dialog box appears.

2. Click Yes to confirm that you want to delete the CAD Users group. The group is deleted.

3. Close the management console.

Lesson Review

The following questions are intended to reinforce key information in this lesson. If you are unable to answer a question, review the lesson and try the question again. Answers to the questions can be found in the appendix.

1. If a user account has been deleted, can you restore it by creating a user with the same name? Why or why not?

2. What happens to local accounts when a computer is joined to a domain?

3. What is the difference between workgroup background authentication and domain authentication when a user accesses a resource on a remote computer?

Lesson Summary

- Windows authorizes access to secure resources by authenticating users before they can use the computer. User accounts with unique security identifiers represent the people who operate a computer. You can secure resources by specifying exactly which actions are permitted for which users by adding ACEs to the ACL for a secure resource.

- Local computer accounts are used to manage access to individual workstations and servers. Local computer accounts do not exist on domain controllers because they are replaced by the Active Directory service.

- User accounts can be members of security groups. Security groups also have unique security identifiers and can be used to secure resources wherever a user account could be used.

- Security groups should be created whenever a unique combination of security requirements appears. User accounts can be members of any number of security groups.

Lesson 2: Working with Active Directory Domain Accounts and Security Groups

A *domain* is a group of computers that share the same database of security accounts. In Windows 2000, *domain user accounts* are stored in the Active Directory directory service on domain controllers, along with domain security groups, computer accounts, and numerous other security objects such as Group Policy Objects and sites. Domains allow administrators to manage user accounts and security groups centrally for all computers that are members of the domain. User accounts in the domain are valid on all computers that are members of the domain and need not be established individually on each computer. This lesson will teach you how to manage and administer domain user accounts and domain security groups for optimal use in large environments.

After this lesson, you will be able to

- Create and manage domain user accounts
- Create and manage domain security groups
- Select the correct type of domain security group for a specific purpose

Estimated lesson time: 30 minutes

Working with Domains

Domains are the mechanism within the Microsoft Windows 2000 operating system for achieving Single Sign On (SSO) functionality throughout a network. Single Sign On means that an individual can use a single account name and password on every computer throughout a network (although including computers running non-Microsoft operating systems in an SSO environment requires third-party software). By creating a domain and joining workstations to it, you are telling workstations to trust the accounts stored on domain controllers as if they were local accounts on the computer.

When multiple domains are created in the same Active Directory service, the domains automatically trust each other's user accounts. Therefore, security principals from one domain may be included in the ACLs and security groups of the trusting domain. This is called a *trust relationship*, and you can explicitly change the trust relationships that are automatically created to determine exactly how accounts can be used in other domains.

Like local accounts, domain user accounts and security groups are represented internally by SIDs. Domain SIDs are constructed in exactly the same way as local

SIDs are constructed, except that the Active Directory service stores user account data instead of the SAM.

Authenticating Domain User Accounts

Domain user accounts are stored in the Active Directory database. When a client is a member of a domain and a user attempts to log on using a domain user account, the Winlogon process on the local machine sends the user's name and encrypted password for authentication to the Active Directory authentication server. The Active Directory authentication server checks the credentials against those stored in the Active Directory database and, if they match, sends back a Kerberos ticket containing the user's SID and domain group SIDs, so that the local computer can create an access token for the user. Kerberos tickets are explained in the next section.

Only computers that are members of the domain or a trusted domain can authenticate in the domain. Domain client computers have *computer accounts* stored in the Active Directory that also have computer names, secret keys (like passwords that are automatically created by the system), and SIDs. A computer that is not a member of a domain cannot directly authenticate with a domain controller because it does not have a computer account in the domain. When you join a computer to a domain, the domain controller automatically creates the computer's account. The domain controller and the computer negotiate to create the SID and the computer account's password automatically when the computer account is created.

Domain controllers themselves do not have local user accounts or local groups. The SAM is disabled when Active Directory is installed on a domain controller. Therefore, only Active Directory domain account holders can log on to a domain controller.

Kerberos

Understanding logon authentication in Windows 2000 requires an understanding of Kerberos. *Kerberos* is an authentication service developed at the Massachusetts Institute of Technology (MIT) for use in multi-vendor distributed networks of any size. Kerberos works very similarly to many manual authorization methods you may already be familiar with. For example, to gain access to a county fair, it is common to pay a fee at the gate for an all-day pass. You can then take your day pass to a ticket booth to receive tickets for a specific attraction, such as a Ferris wheel. Once you have your ride-specific tickets, you can provide them to the operator to gain access to the ride.

In Kerberos, the all-day pass is called a ticket-granting ticket (TGT), and it is provided to you when you log on to the domain by the Active Directory authentication service (the front gate). A TGT is valid for a specific period of time, usually eight hours. The attraction-specific tickets are called session tickets (or just tickets), and they are presented to you by the ticket-granting service (the ticket booth) on the domain controller whenever you request access to a specific service on a server. The servers themselves allow access if the session tickets are valid, and these tickets expire very rapidly, usually within five minutes. In Windows 2000, both the authentication service (AS) and the ticket-granting service (TGS) functions of the Kerberos Key Distribution Center (KDC) are run on domain controllers, so KDC is simply the Kerberos term for a domain controller. Figure 2.6 shows the Kerberos logon process.

Note   In UNIX and Kerberos documentation, you'll see the term "realm" used to describe a domain. The terms are synonymous.

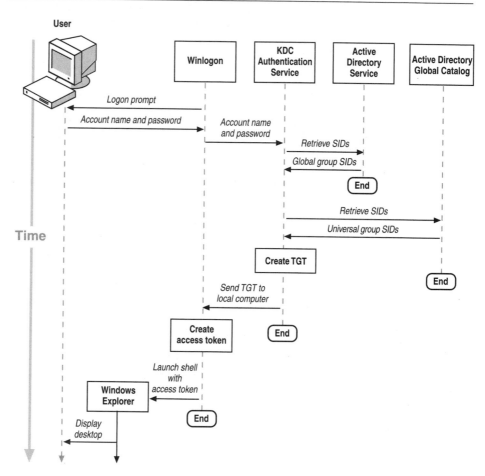

Figure 2.6   The Kerberos domain logon process

Now that you have an overview of the process, the specific details will make sense. Kerberos uses secret key encryption to prove the identity of valid client computers. Client computers must have been joined to the domain through a trusted process during which a secret key can be exchanged. In Windows 2000, this key exchange occurs automatically when a client computer is joined to the domain:

1. The client uses its secret key to encrypt the credentials of the user who is logging on. Because the server can decrypt them, it knows that the client computer that transmitted them is a member of the domain. The domain controller then compares the user's credentials to the information stored in the Active Directory. If they match, the user must have known the account holder's password and is assumed to be the account holder.

2. Once the KDC (the domain controller) has authenticated the user, it generates a ticket-granting ticket, which is essentially a ticket that proves to any computer in the domain that the user has already logged on. The TGT is encrypted using a secret key known only to the KDC, so its contents are not susceptible to compromise even by the client computer that holds it.

3. When a user needs to access a service on any server throughout the domain, the client computer sends its TGT to the TGS, which is also running on the KDC, and requests a ticket for the service in question. The TGS inspects the TGT, determines whether it is valid, and sends the client computer a service-specific session ticket that can be decrypted only by the destination server (and not by the client).

4. The client computer then presents this session ticket to the destination server, which is able to decrypt it because it was encrypted by the KDC using a secret key known only to the two servers. Because the client has a valid session ticket, the server trusts that it received the ticket from the KDC that it trusts, so trust is conferred upon the client, and access is granted to the service.

This process is shown in Figure 2.7.

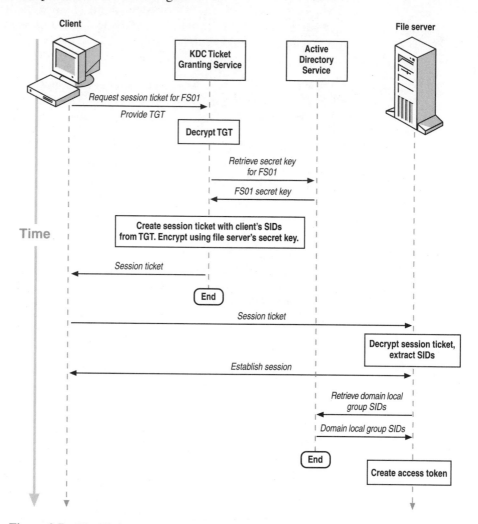

Figure 2.7   The Kerberos resource access process

Because Kerberos tickets are encrypted with a number derived from the current time, they can be decrypted only for a short period, five minutes by default.

Important   Servers must be time synchronized within a domain because a difference of more than five minutes between the KDC and a server will cause tickets to expire and prevent users from accessing services on that server. Limiting the decryption time to short periods also prevents replay attacks where a hacker could sniff the contents of a session, decrypt a ticket, copy the ticket's contents, and then re-use it to gain access to a server.

Domain Transitive Trust

Kerberos also provides the ability for clients who are trusted in one domain to be trusted in another domain. When a user requests a session ticket from its KDC for a server in a foreign domain, the KDC sends a request for a session ticket to the remote KDC as if it were the client. The remote KDC will validate the local KDC's TGT and provide an encrypted session ticket. Because the session ticket is encrypted using the destination server's private key and not the local KDC's private key, the local KDC can provide that ticket to its client, and the client can provide the session ticket directly to the foreign server to gain access to it.

This process works no matter how many domains the trust has to transit. Each KDC in the trust hierarchy receives the request for a service ticket, mimics a client, and passes that request to the next server up. This process continues indefinitely until the KDC that is local to the target server, which creates the valid session ticket, is reached. That ticket is passed back from KDC to KDC until it reaches the KDC that is local to the client computer. That final KDC then passes the session ticket to the client computer, which can then contact the destination server directly using the session ticket. Authentication goes through each intermediate KDC, but once the client computer has been authenticated, access is direct. When the client computer has a valid session key, it contacts the destination server directly and begins to access resources.

These mechanisms are created and handled completely by the operating system. When a domain is added to Active Directory, Windows performs the exchange of cryptographic keys that is required for the two domains to trust one another. When client computers are added to a domain, Windows handles the exchange of cryptographic keys that allows the client computers to prove their participation in the domain to the KDC.

Planning   Administrators need not worry about the underlying mechanism of Kerberos, beyond understanding how it works and understanding that time synchronization is crucial to its operation.

Domain Logon Process

The specific sequence of events in a domain interactive log on is as follows:

1. The Winlogon service of the LSA collects the user name and password.
2. The client's LSA transmits the password name and encrypted password to the Active Directory KDC authentication service, which is integrated into the domain controller's LSA..
3. KDC queries Active Directory for the user's SID and the SIDs of domain groups to which the user belongs. KDC also queries the Global Catalog server in the domain for a list of universal security group SIDs to which the user belongs.

4. KDC AS creates a ticket-granting ticket (TGT) and embeds all the SIDs that apply to the user in the TGT.
5. KDC AS returns the TGT to the client computer's LSA.
6. LSA creates an access token containing all the user's SIDs.
7. LSA launches the local shell and passes the access token to it.

Domain Resource Access

When a client computer connects to a resource server and requests a resource, the client computer first contacts the KDC for the domain and retrieves a session ticket. The client then provides the session ticket to the resource server, which contains all the SIDs that apply to the user in that domain.

The server service for the resource server then constructs an access token to represent the user to local processes. The LSA on the resource server constructs the access token using the authentication data (the list of SIDs) contained in the session ticket, and any additional SIDs that the user is entitled to because of membership in a security group that is local to the domain and not present in Active Directory. The access token will then contain the complete credentials of the logged on user. After the access token has been created, it is associated with the user's session in the server service, and the user can then access resources within the user's own security context on the resource server.

Note   Access tokens never travel over the network—only encrypted session tickets containing the user's SIDs do. This ensures that access tokens themselves cannot be introduced to a computer by any means—servers only generate them, they do not accept them from any source. This prevents the spoofing (or forging) of access tokens to circumvent security.

The resource server trusts the SIDs contained in the session ticket because it assumes that the session ticket cannot be forged and that it came from a domain controller that the resource server trusts. This trust is implicit because the resource server and the domain controller negotiated the secret key that was used to encrypt the session ticket—if the server can decrypt it, it must have been encrypted by a domain controller that knew the correct key.

When a user connects to a resource server and requests resources on it, the service that provides the resource can check the user's credentials and verify the user's permission to access the service. The process works like this:

1. The client computer sends its TGT with a service request to the KDC.
2. The KDC validates the TGT (by decrypting it) and copies the user's SID and all universal and global group SIDs into a new session key.

3. If the client computer is in a different domain than the KDC is (because the ticket has been forwarded through the trust mechanism), the KDC queries its own Active Directory to find additional domain local group SIDs that might apply to the client and adds them to the session ticket.

4. The KDC encrypts the session ticket using the resource server's key. The session ticket is transmitted back to the client computer.

5. The client receives the session ticket but cannot decrypt it because it's encrypted with the target server's key. Because the ticket is encrypted, users on the client computer cannot elevate their own privileges by adding SIDs to a ticket.

6. The client computer forwards the session ticket to the resource server along with the specific service request.

7. The resource server LSA decrypts the session ticket, extracts the list of SIDs, and creates an access token for the client's use locally.

8. The resource server creates a service session using the access token created from the session ticket. The session is security-limited to the client's allowed list of SIDs. Any sessions or processes subsequently created will inherit the client's access token and be similarly limited.

Using Domain Security Groups Effectively

Domain security groups are much like local security groups, except that they apply to all computers throughout the domain. They are based on the same theory and have the same effects.

Note   Irrespective of the Active Directory domains or organizational units into which you place domain security groups, they are valid for the entire domain. For example, a security group created inside the Engineering Team Leaders organizational unit (OU) can contain security principals from any part of the domain and can be used to secure resources on computers that are not members of the OU. The only reason for creating security groups within OUs is to keep objects of similar purpose grouped together in the user interface.

Global security groups in a domain can also be members of other domain and local security groups. When a security group is a member of another security group, it inherits access to the parent security group's resources in the same way that a member user account inherits access. Local groups cannot be members of other groups.

Using Security Groups to Set Permissions

As with local groups, only security groups should appear in the ACLs of secured resources. Users change far more often than you should change ACLs. When you use individual user accounts in ACLs, you must change ACLs frequently, which is a disk- and processor-intensive operation. By using security groups, you need only change ACLs when major reorganizations occur, which is quite rare.

Planning   Avoid placing user accounts in ACLs, even if a specific ACE applies only to a single user. It is still preferable to create a security group to secure a resource for a single user because, if for some reason you need administrative access to the object, you can place your own account in the group to obtain access rather than changing the secured object's ACL.

Changing permissions within an ACL widely on a single computer is burdensome; in domains with millions of files and tens of thousands of folders, it's practically impossible. Adding an account to a security group is simple and does not get more difficult as a domain or organization grows. Administrators who set permissions using individual user accounts will quickly find orphaned SID numbers in ACL displays, as user accounts are deleted and their older and useless ACEs remain behind.

Creating Effective Domain Security Groups

The proper use of security groups in large environments should be divided into two distinct categories: user groups and resource groups.

- A *user group* is used to combine users into a single security identifier—it is the typical way that security groups have always been used. For example, you would put all the engineers in a company into a security group called Engineers.
- A *resource group* is a group that is used to apply permissions to secured objects. These security groups should mimic the names of the objects that they secure. For example, a folder called Customer Profile Data might be secured by a resource group called Customer Profile Data Users.

After you have categorized your security groups, you can apply permissions to users by making user groups members of resource groups. If you place the Engineers group in the Customer Profile Data Users group, all members of Engineers will inherit the necessary SIDs to access those files.

By splitting security groups into user and resource groups, you can manage permissions more efficiently because you won't be tempted to try to force fit an existing group of users to a new resource. For example, you might apply an existing group called Accountants to the Accounts Receivables folder because it already exists. However, if you are in the habit of creating a resource security group like Accounts Receivables Users whenever a new need appears, you will be more likely to properly apply the correct users and thereby minimize the potential for unauthorized use.

Tip   In smaller environments with a single domain, creating separate user and resource groups does not increase efficiency, but it is good practice for future growth and is not significantly less efficient.

Optimizing Groups in Large Organizations

Domain security groups have four contexts, depending on where (and whether) they are stored in the Active Directory database:

- Local groups are not stored in the Active Directory database, but exist on member servers and workstations in the domain. Local groups can contain any other type of group, but they specify access to resources on the local machine only. Active Directories running in mixed mode treat the local groups of domain controllers as domain groups and do not have true domain local groups.

- Domain local groups are specific to a domain in the Active Directory tree. Domain groups cannot contain local groups, and they provide access to resources within the domain only. Domain local groups replace server-based local groups when an Active Directory is switched from a mixed Windows NT and Windows 2000 domain to a native Windows 2000 domain that contains only Windows 2000 domain controllers. Domain local groups are not propagated in a user's session ticket.

More Info   For more information about upgrading from mixed to native mode, see the *Microsoft Windows 2000 Server Resource Kit* (Microsoft Press, 2002).

- Global groups are specific to a single domain in the Active Directory as well, and can contain only user accounts and resources within their own domain. Unlike domain local groups, they are added to a user's session ticket at log on.

- Universal groups are maintained at the Active Directory forest level and are available to all trees within the Active Directory. An Active Directory forest is the structure that contains Active Directory trees, which are Active Directory structures that contains related domains. Domains in a tree automatically trust one another, and trees in a forest automatically trust one another. Universal groups can contain any security principal in Active Directory from any domain, and can be used throughout the forest to create permissions that should apply across multiple trees and domains.

The primary reason that so many scopes of security groups exist is to make Active Directory replication efficient. In a single domain network that has no trust relationships established with other domains, security group scope is irrelevant because there are no scopes beyond the domain—the choice of using a domain local group, a global group, or a universal group has no difference in effect.

Planning   Small businesses should use universal groups routinely so that, as they grow, familiar groups will be available to all domains when those domains are spun off. Larger businesses should use universal groups for security that pervades the entire organization, and global groups for teams and working groups that are local to the domain.

In large networks, making security groups efficient is a key problem. Remember that when a user logs on, the groups that the user is a member of are added to that user's access token. When a user is a member of groups in other domains, the network traffic required to move domain memberships around can become significant. The different group scopes exist to make this process efficient.

Domain local groups and global groups are similar in scope: the group SID (but not its members) is propagated to the Global Catalog, and both group types can contain only security principals from their own domains. There is one key difference between them: global groups are contained in session tickets while domain local groups are not.

- Global group SIDs are added to a user's access token at the time that the user logs on to the domain and are propagated through session tickets irrespective of the resource being accessed.
- Domain local groups are added only to access tokens that are created when resources are accessed on servers within the local domain—in other words, when a user accesses a server in a resource domain, the server will add SIDs that apply to the user from its own domain as well as adding the SIDs contained in the user's session ticket.

Refer to Figures 2.6 and 2.7 to see precisely where in the logon process these two different types of groups are accessed.

Because global groups are contained in session tickets while domain local groups are not, a natural division of labor between them emerges.

- User accounts should always be placed in global groups because they will carry this membership with them in their session tickets. Global groups can be thought of as "groups of users."
- Resources like shared files and printers should be secured using domain local groups, because they never move among domains—their position is fixed. Domain local groups can be thought of as "resource groups," the groups you use when you're adding permissions to resources.

When users need access to resources in a local domain, you can give the global group to which the user belongs access to the resource by placing it in the domain local group. This methodology can dramatically reduce the number of SIDs floating around your network in session tickets, which will speed domain logon and resource access in extremely large networks.

Practice: Creating User Accounts and Security Groups

In this practice, you create user and group accounts in Active Directory.

Exercise 1: Managing Domain User Accounts in Active Directory

In this exercise, you practice managing domain user accounts. You populate Active Directory with multiple user accounts. When this is accomplished, you then move, disable, and delete domain user accounts.

Perform this exercise while logged on to the domain controller as Administrator.

▶ **To create a user inside an OU in Active Directory**

1. Click Start, point to Programs, point to Administrative Tools, and click Active Directory Users And Computers.

    The Active Directory Users And Computers management console appears.

2. Expand the Departments and Engineering OUs you created in Chapter 1.

3. Click Engineering Team Leaders, and click New User on the toolbar. The New Object dialog box appears as shown in Figure 2.8.

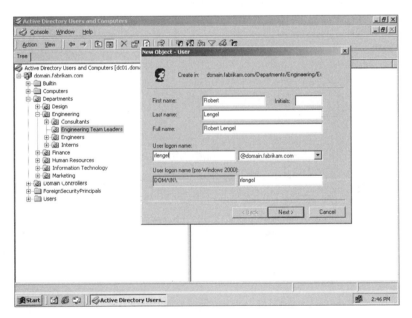

Figure 2.8   The New Object dialog box

4. Type **Robert** in the First Name box.

5. Type **Lengel** in the Last Name box.

6. Type **rlengel** in the User Logon Name box.

7. Click Next. The password properties panel appears.

8. Type the same random password in the Password and Confirm Password boxes.

9. Select the User Must Change Password At Next Logon check box.

10. Click Next, review the summary of your input, and click Finish to add the user.

▶ **To populate Active Directory with user accounts**

Using the following list of OUs, create domain user accounts in the specified OU for the user names appearing after them. Create user names based on the first initial plus last name method. Assign a random password to each user.

- Designers: Syed Abbas, Kim Abercrombie, Humberto Acevedo.
- Design Leaders: Pilar Ackerman.
- Engineers: Jay Adams, Terry Adams, Francois Ajenstat.
- Engineering Team Leaders: Kim Akers, Amy E. Alberts., Robert Lengel.
- Accounts Payable: Gregory F. Alderson.
- Accounts Receivable: Michelle Alexander.
- Accounting: Sean P. Alexander, Michael Allen.
- Finance: Gary E. Altman.
- Human Resources: Nancy Anderson.
- Help Desk: Pamela Ansman-Wolfe.
- Network Administration: Karen Archer.
- Support Technicians: Zainal Arifin, John Arthur.
- Sales Managers: Chris Ashton.

▶ **To move a domain user account**

1. In the Active Directory Users And Computers management console, expand Departments, Information Technology, and then Support Technicians OU.

2. Right-click the Zainal Arifin user account, and choose Move.

3. In the Move dialog box, expand Departments, Information Technology, and select Network Administration.

4. Click OK. User Zainal Arifin is now located in the Network Administration OU.

▶ **To disable a domain user account**

1. In the Active Directory Users And Computers management console, expand Departments, Engineering, and then the Engineers OU.

2. Right-click the Francois Ajenstat user account, and click Disable Account. A message box announces that the account has been disabled.

3. Click OK to acknowledge the message.

   A red X now appears over the user account's icon.

▶ **To delete a domain user account**

1. In the Active Directory Users And Computers management console, click Departments, Engineering, and then Engineers OU.

2. Right-click the Francois Ajenstat user account, and click Delete. A delete confirmation message box appears.

3. Click Yes to confirm that the account should be deleted.

   The account disappears from the list of user accounts.

Exercise 2: Managing Domain Security Groups

In this exercise, you create a domain security group and then add members to the group. Finally, you delete a domain security group.

Perform this exercise while logged on to the domain controller as Administrator.

▶ **To create a domain security group**

1. Open the Active Directory Users And Computers management console.

2. Expand domain.fabrikam.com, and expand Departments.

3. Click Engineering, and click New Group on the toolbar. The New Object dialog box appears.

4. Type **Engineering CAD Files Users** in the Group Name box, as shown in Figure 2.9.

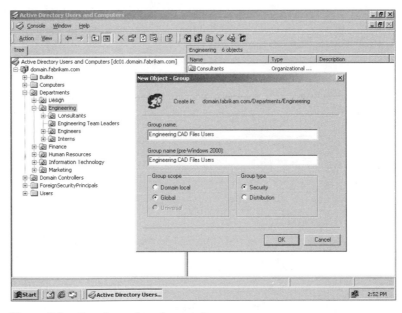

Figure 2.9   Creating a domain security group

5. Click OK to accept the default Global group and Security group options.

   The Engineering CAD Files Users group now exists in Active Directory.

▶ **To add members to a domain security group**

1. Double-click the Engineering CAD Files Users group. The Engineering CAD Files Users Properties dialog box appears.

2. In the dialog box, click the Members tab, and click Add.

   A list of domain users and groups appears.

3. Select Robert Lengel from the list of users, as shown in Figure 2.10, and click OK.

   User account rlengel is now a member of the Engineering CAD Files Users group.

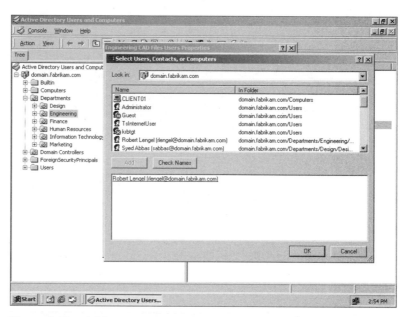

Figure 2.10   Adding a member to a group

Tip   You can use SHIFT+CTRL to select multiple user accounts and add them all to the group at the same time.

▶ **To delete a domain security group**

1. Right-click the Engineering CAD Files Users security group and click Delete. A delete confirmation dialog box appears.

2. Click Yes to confirm.

   The security group is now deleted.

Lesson Review

The following questions are intended to reinforce key information in this lesson. If you are unable to answer a question, review the lesson and try the question again. Answers to the questions can be found in the appendix.

1. What is the difference between a global group and a domain local group?

2. Are access tokens ever transmitted across the network?

3. What are universal groups?

4. What is the purpose of separating groups into user groups and resource groups, when you can use the same groups for both purposes?

Lesson Summary

- The domain logon process is similar to the local logon process, except that user account and security identifier information comes from the Active Directory service on domain controllers rather than from the SAM on the local machine.

- Membership in a domain is actually a one-way trust relationship. Clients trust domain controllers and allow the accounts stored in domain controllers to log on locally to the client computer. This trust is created automatically when the client computer is joined to the domain and can be revoked only by removing the client from the domain.

- Client computers and member servers have local user and security accounts. Domain controllers do not have local accounts, which are replaced by Active Directory accounts when Active Directory is installed.

- Kerberos is the mechanism used to manage trust between clients and servers in a domain. When clients log on, they receive a ticket-granting ticket that can be used to obtain session tickets valid for authentication on all servers throughout the domain. These tickets contain the user's SID and the SIDs of global groups that the user belongs to, and they are used to construct access tokens on servers when sessions are established.

- There are four primary types of security groups in a domain: local groups that do not exist on domain controllers; domain local groups that are used to secure resources; global groups that are used to create groups of user accounts within a single domain; and universal groups, which are global groups that are propagated to all domains in the Active Directory tree.

C H A P T E R   3

Restricting Accounts, Users, and Groups

About This Chapter

This chapter builds on the security features introduced in Chapter 2, "User Accounts and Security Groups." It covers account policy, user rights, restricted groups, and security templates.

Account policies are restrictions that are applied to all users logging on because they must take effect before the user who is logging on is identified. For example, a restriction on the number of times that any user can mistype a password is applied to all users, because the user has not yet logged on and the account settings are not yet known. Account policies are managed by using Group Policy settings.

User rights and restricted groups are also managed on a per-machine rather than a per-user basis. *User rights* control a user's ability to perform operations that affect the system as a whole, such as shutting down the computer. User rights are required to perform these actions because they affect every program running on the computer. *Restricted groups* are security groups that have controlled memberships. Periodically (during the Group Policy refresh period described in Chapter 1, "Group Policy"), users that may have been improperly added to security groups can be removed automatically by the system.

This chapter covers the following major Windows account-based security features:

- Account policies
- User rights
- Restricted groups

This chapter also discusses using *security templates* to establish a level of security across the network. It discusses what you need to know to manage and deploy security templates and provides information about troubleshooting common problems.

Before You Begin

To complete this chapter, you must have a pair of networked test computers

- One configured with Microsoft Windows 2000 Server and with Active Directory installed
- One running Microsoft Windows 2000 Professional and joined to the server's domain
- A domain controller with Active Directory installed and a domain-wide Group Policy Object (GPO) configured
- A client workstation connected to the same domain as the Active Directory domain controller

Tip   You can use Microsoft Windows XP Professional in these exercises if you enable the Classic Start Menu option in the Taskbar Properties menu.

Lesson 1: Understanding Account Policies

Account policies are Group Policy settings stored in GPOs that affect all user accounts. They control operating system features such as the maximum number of logon attempts, automatic enforcement of high-quality passwords, and the lifetime of Kerberos tickets.

After this lesson, you will be able to

- Understand account policies
- Manage account policy settings for a domain
- Determine which account policy settings are appropriate for your network

Estimated lesson time: 20 minutes

Applying Account Policies

Account policies do not apply to individual accounts, they apply to all accounts, and their enforcement begins before a user logs on. This means that account policies apply to the Computer Configuration portion of a GPO rather than to the User Configuration portion. Account policies are located in the Computer Configuration\Windows Settings\Security Settings\Account Policies node of a GPO.

Only one account policy is valid per domain, so only account policy settings in GPOs linked to domain objects have effect on user accounts within the domain. Domain account policies automatically override account policy settings linked to organizational units (OUs). However, if a user does not log on to the domain, the OU account policy that applies to the computer the user logs on to locally remains valid. This means that

- Users who log on locally to a computer that has a security account within an OU will have the account policy restrictions located in the GPO linked to that OU.
- Users who log on to the domain will have the account policy restrictions linked to a domain GPO.

You can use this difference to change the account policy that is applied for users who log on using a local user account.

What Are the Account Policy Settings?

An account policy is comprised of several settings. The following sections explain each setting's purpose and detail its effect on your overall security posture.

Enforce Password History

Enforce Password History allows you to keep users from rotating among a small set of preferred passwords when they are forced to change them. A user who attempts to reuse a password that is stored in the password history will be forced to choose another password.

Tip   Keep a relatively long password history of at least 10 previously used passwords to prevent users from recycling a few favorite passwords.

Maximum Password Age

Maximum Password Age identifies the length of time that a user can use a specific password before being required to change it. Traditional security policy has held that forcing users to change passwords often keeps others from learning their passwords and exploiting them.

Unfortunately, the requirement that users change passwords often leads users to select shorter, simpler passwords that are easier to remember. Users also frequently select simple variations of the same password, such as a single word followed by a different set of numbers. Anyone knowing the user might still have a relatively easy time determining the user's password.

Since the advent of the Internet, the true security threat has changed from coworker shenanigans to very serious intrusions by Internet hackers. Hackers usually don't know the end users or passwords on your system. Instead, they use very large dictionary files containing all words from the major world languages, common names and surnames, slang terms, and words appearing in the religious texts of the major world religions—just about every word that most people know.

Important   It is imperative that users select long and mostly random passwords that are somewhat difficult to remember.

Because it's more difficult for users to remember highly secure passwords, use somewhat less restrictive change times. Users should not be expected to memorize long and highly random passwords routinely. For this reason, many administrators either no longer enforce password changes or set them to very long durations such as one year. Be sure to accompany relaxing password age enforcement with a dramatic increase in minimum password length and the enforcement of complexity requirements to ensure security.

Minimum Password Age

Minimum Password Age identifies the length of time that a user must use a newly assigned password before changing it. This prevents hackers from obtaining a password and then changing it to something else to secure it for their own use.

Note   The Minimum Password Age setting has the least effect of any setting on your overall security posture. The type of attack it prevents is extremely rare and very easy to detect. Most installations will not require an enforcement of minimum password age.

Minimum Password Length

Minimum Password Length identifies the shortest allowable length of a password. While simple, this setting has more impact on security posture than any other account policy setting.

Each character in a password makes the password about a hundred times harder to guess. A 1-character password can be guessed in about 80 attempts because there are about 80 characters that can appear in passwords. A 2-character password requires 80×80 (or 6400) attempts. At one guess per second, that's the difference between about one minute and about two hours.

Tip   If you create passwords for international users, remember that their keyboards can't always create the same set of punctuation and other special characters as yours. For example, the number sign (#) does not appear on keyboards in Spanish-speaking countries.

If you work in a multinational environment, restrict the punctuation you use in passwords to symbols that are internationally valid. Better yet, delegate administration to regional administrators in the target country if possible. Using localized punctuation is not particularly effective for thwarting foreign hackers, because these hackers use password lists and brute-force software that generate all possible punctuation.

Prior to the wide accessibility of the Internet, a password of 8 characters or longer was considered secure. After all, at one attempt per second, a truly random password of this length would require over a billion years to guess. Unfortunately, users don't often select truly random passwords—they select normal words and names they use every day. So, while in theory an 8-character password would be secure, a hacker could try out every word in the dictionary, or first and last names appearing in the telephone book of 8 or more characters in less than one day.

Hackers can use automated tools for password guessing that randomize their computer's name and IP address. A server can't reject multiple attempts coming from these hackers because they don't appear to be coming from the same computer. Exploiting this fact, automated tools have been created that can check up to 1200 passwords per second against a Windows 2000 server. In one hour, hackers can run well over 4 million passwords against a well-connected server attached to the Internet. When you consider that an extremely large vocabulary for a single language is just 25,000 words, hackers now have the capability to check every word that has ever been published on the Internet in any language in just one hour. What this means in practical terms is that hackers can now find words plus punctuation and two- and three-word combined passwords within a reasonable time. However, a truly random 8-character password would still require more than 40,000 years to crack even at this speed.

In practice, because users don't select truly random passwords, you should consider using no fewer than 12 characters as your minimum password length. Windows 2000 allows passwords up to 256 characters in length, but some code remains in the operating system that makes it difficult to use passwords longer than the Microsoft Windows NT limit of 14 characters. With a 12-letter minimum, users will naturally select multi-word passwords, and with complexity requirements enforced, these passwords take an extremely long time to crack.

Passwords Must Meet Complexity Requirements

With this setting enabled, all users must use complex passwords. This setting ensures that passwords will not appear in the dictionary-based password lists that hackers use. Select this option to force each user to create passwords that are not equal to any part of the user's name and must contain characters from three out of four of these classes:

- Uppercase letters
- Lowercase letters
- Numbers
- Punctuation and other special characters

Planning   This setting is mandatory for any secure network. Enabling this setting and forcing users to select new passwords will increase the security of your network more than any other single measure.

After exploiting system "bugs," exploiting low password quality is the second most likely way that hackers will get into your network. Unlike exploiting bugs, taking advantage of low password quality has always worked and will always work against some networks, so hackers routinely attempt it.

On networks with lockout policies, hackers don't try 10,000 passwords against one account; they try 10,000 accounts against one password. This ensures that no single account sees more than one logon attempt within a reasonable period, and it prevents audit measures from logging extremely high logon rates against individual accounts. The larger your network is, the more effective this sort of attack becomes.

The second most common password after "1234" is "123456," and on networks that require a minimum of 8 characters, "asdfasdf" is equally as common. On average, out of 10,000 accounts on a network that does not enforce complex password use, more than 100 accounts will have these trivial passwords. This fact almost guarantees hackers access to your network if you have a large number of accounts and you don't enforce password complexity.

Store Password Using Reversible Encryption for All Users in the Domain

Store Password Using Reversible Encryption For All Users In The Domain is a setting that weakens security to allow third-party client computers such as Apple Macintosh clients to authenticate in the domain.

Do not enable this setting unless you must for compatibility reasons. This setting makes it easier for hackers to use network analysis equipment to listen for (sniff) passwords on your network if they can gain physical access to it.

Account Lockout Duration

Account Lockout Duration identifies the amount of time that an account will remain disabled once the system has detected that the Account Lockout Threshold has been reached.

To keep high-speed automated logon attempts from working against your network, you must have this setting configured. However, to thwart high-speed logon attempts, the account lockout duration does not need to be particularly long. When hackers run dictionary attacks, they rely on logon rates faster than one per second to break into a system in a reasonable time. Any setting greater than five minutes will make an automated logon attempt take so long that it would not be worth perpetrating. Settings longer than 15 minutes are unusually burdensome for users and unnecessary to achieve the security goals of this policy setting.

Warning   The local and domain administrator account cannot be locked out, no matter how many times its password has been incorrectly entered. This is also the account that hackers want to access, so it is typically the only account they try. To remain secure, you must rename the administrator account. Don't use "root," "admin," or "supervisor" as a synonym, because these account names are routinely tried as well.

Account Lockout Threshold

Account Lockout Threshold indicates the number of times that a user can enter an incorrect password before being locked out. This setting is used to thwart high-speed logon attempts, so it is not necessary to set it to a low number. Many facilities use three, five, or seven attempts as a baseline for the number of times a user can incorrectly type a password. Fewer than four attempts is burdensome for users who must switch passwords regularly or who use different passwords frequently. More than 10 are more attempts than most valid users would make before giving up in frustration, so seven is probably a good compromise. Any reasonably low number will defeat automated logon attacks.

Reset Account Lockout Counter After

Reset Account Lockout Counter After indicates the duration before an attempt at logging on is considered separate from an earlier attempt. This value should be set to a value that is similar to your Account Lockout Duration so that users need only remember one timing value if they are having password problems.

Enforce User Logon Restrictions

Enforce User Logon Restrictions causes domain controllers to validate every request for a session ticket by examining the user rights policy on the target server to verify that the user has the right to log on through the network. This means that the Kerberos Key Distribution Center (KDC) service must go over the network to contact the target server, request its policy, and examine it.

Tip   In larger networks, enabling this restriction can cause unnecessary logon traffic if you do not deny users network access to servers.

The security effects of disabling this restriction are esoteric. If the user has a valid Kerberos session ticket, the user is logged on to the network. Unless you are in a network environment where internal network security is paramount, such as at a medical center or military installation, the effect of this setting on your security posture will be minimal.

Maximum Lifetime for Service Ticket

Maximum Lifetime For Service Ticket specifies how long session tickets are valid. This setting must be no less than 10 minutes and no more than the value specified in the Maximum Lifetime For User Ticket setting.

If normal working hours at your facility routinely exceed 10 hours (the default), change both of these values to encompass normal working hours. This will eliminate spurious logon activity when Ticket Granting Ticket (TGT) and session tickets expire. As long as these settings are less than 24 hours, you won't have to worry about ticket replay attacks.

Maximum Lifetime for User Ticket

Maximum Lifetime For User Ticket specifies the maximum lifetime for both TGT and session tickets, although the Maximum Lifetime For Service Ticket setting can further reduce the lifetime of individual session tickets.

Maximum Lifetime for User Ticket Renewal

This setting specifies the maximum time that a TGT or session ticket can be continuously renewed without requiring a physical logon. The default is seven days, which is more than long enough for most purposes.

The only real issue you might encounter that would require changing this setting is the use of user-mode software in a logged on session that runs continuously, such as IBM Lotus Notes. Software that runs in user mode should be either configured as a service using the Srvany.exe service wrapper from the *Microsoft Windows 2000 Server Resource Kit* or replaced with software that can be run as a service so that a user account doesn't need to remain logged on to run it.

Maximum Tolerance for Computer Clock Synchronization

Maximum Tolerance For Computer Clock Synchronization specifies the granularity of time-based encryption for session tickets. This setting allows you to increase the tolerance for time variances between servers. The default value for all Kerberos installations is five minutes. This means that a session ticket retrieved from a TGT must be used within this period to be valid. When the time settings on servers vary by more than this amount, session tickets will not be valid on them, and users will have no access to resources on those servers.

Normally, session tickets are used immediately so that session ticket expiration is not an issue. But it is an issue if the server being accessed doesn't have the same time set as the TGT, because the difference in time settings could easily be more than five minutes.

The disadvantage of increasing the Maximum Tolerance For Computer Clock Synchronization is that it increases the period of time during which a forged session ticket could be used. If hackers were able to decrypt a session ticket while it was still valid, they could forge the contents of the ticket and then use it to gain access to the server for which the session ticket was created. By keeping this setting short, you make this attack impossible.

Tip   Time synchronization is critical to the proper operation of Kerberos. By default, computers in a domain automatically synchronize with domain controllers. Domain controllers should be set to synchronize with an Internet time server such as *time.windows.com* or *tock.usno.navy.mil* to maintain synchrony with other domains. You can set a server's Simple Network Time Protocol (SNTP) time source by entering the following command in a command prompt and then restarting the Windows Time service:

```
net time /setsntp:time.windows.com
```

The clock synchronization tolerance setting directly affects the duration for which a session ticket can be replayed and should not be modified without good reason. Rather than changing the clock synchronization setting, set all domain controllers to synchronize daily with an atomic clock time source on the Internet, or at least with a single authoritative time server on your network.

Practice: Configuring Account Policies

To meet the threat of automated password guessing attempts, Fabrikam, Inc. has established the following account policy guidelines:

- User accounts will be locked out after seven failed attempts to log on, and will remain locked out for 15 minutes.
- Passwords must be complex, at least 12 characters in length, and consisting of no single words. While they need not be changed often, they should not be reused.

In this practice, you implement these acceptable use guidelines as domain-wide Group Policy settings.

▶ **To define account policies**

1. Click Start, point to Programs, point to Administrative Tools, and click Active Directory Users And Computers.

   The Active Directory Users And Computers management console appears.

2. Right-click domain.fabrikam.com, and click Properties.

   The domain.fabrikam.com Properties dialog box appears.

3. Click the Group Policy tab.

4. Double-click Domain Security Policy.

   The Group Policies management console appears with the Domain Security Policy GPO opened.

5. Expand Computer Configuration, Windows Settings, Security Settings, and then Account Policies.

6. Select Password Policy to view the settings, as shown in Figure 3.1.

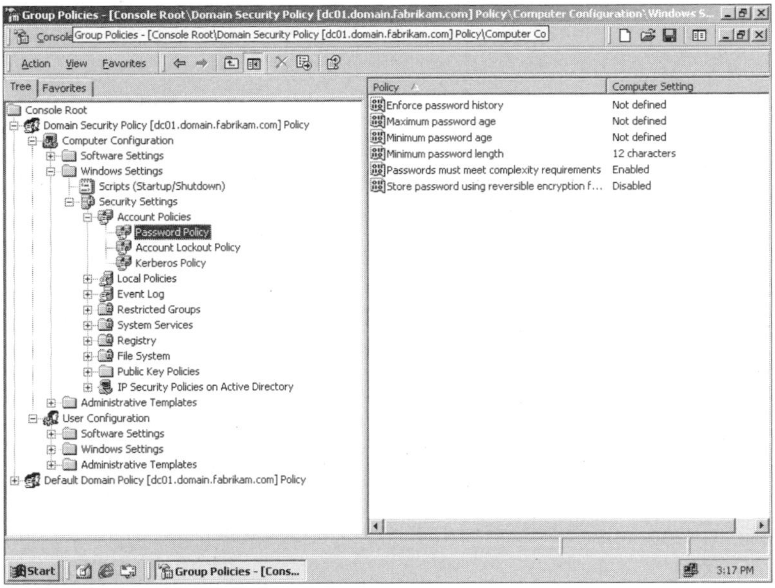

Figure 3.1   The Password Policy settings

7. Double-click Enforce Password History. The Security Policy Setting dialog box appears, as shown in Figure 3.2.

Figure 3.2   The Security Policy Setting dialog box

8. Select the Define This Policy Setting check box, and click OK to accept the default of 18 days.

9. Double-click Maximum Password Age. The Security Policy Setting dialog box appears.

10. Select the Define This Policy Setting check box, type **356**, and click OK.

11. If a dialog box appears recommending changes to other policy settings, click OK to accept the recommended changes.

12. Double-click the Minimum Password Length setting. The Security Policy Setting dialog box appears.

13. Select the Define This Policy check box, and type **12**.

14. Click OK to accept the changes, and close the dialog box.

15. Double-click Passwords Must Meet Complexity Requirements. The Security Policy Settings dialog box appears.

16. Select the Define This Policy Setting check box, and click OK.

▶ **To define account lockout policies**

1. In the Group Policies management console, click Account Lockout Policy to view the settings, as shown in Figure 3.3.

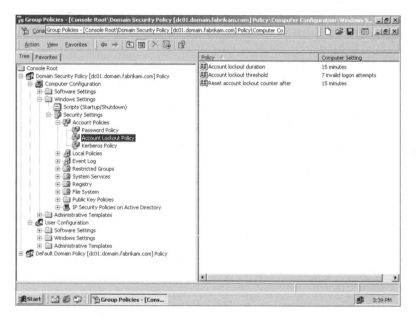

Figure 3.3   Account Lockout Policy settings

2. Double-click Account Lockout Duration. The Security Policy Setting dialog box appears.

3. Select the Define This Policy Setting check box, type **15**, and click OK.

4. If a dialog box appears recommending changes to other policy settings, click OK to accept recommended changes to other settings.

5. Double-click Account Lockout Threshold. The Security Policy Setting dialog box appears.

6. Change the setting to **7** invalid logon attempts, and click OK to close the dialog box.

7. Close the Group Policies management console.

8. Click OK to close the domain.fabrikam.com Properties dialog box.

9. Close the Active Directory Users And Computers management console.

Lesson Review

The following questions are intended to reinforce key information in this lesson. If you are unable to answer a question, review the lesson and try the question again. Answers to the questions can be found in the appendix.

1. How many logon attempts can hackers perpetrate against a Windows 2000 server in one hour?

2. What is the shortest recommended length for a password for a network connected to the Internet?

3. What is the default maximum time difference between a client and a server before Kerberos tickets can no longer be decrypted?

Lesson Summary

- The threat of automated password-guessing attacks from Internet-based hackers has risen dramatically since the rise of the Internet. To counter this threat, much stronger passwords are required than have been used traditionally.

- Windows 2000 account policy allows administrators to define domain-wide account policies to enforce password complexity and length requirements.

- Account lockout durations can be established to thwart high-speed logon guessing attacks.

- The administrator account cannot be locked out and should be renamed to prevent it from being exploited.

- Kerberos requires strict time synchronization to avoid ticket replay attacks. For this reason, all domain controllers should be time synchronized to a trusted Internet time source.

Lesson 2: Managing User Rights

User rights control security operations that can be performed on a computer by specific user accounts. User rights are not like permissions because they don't apply to specific secured objects, they apply to functions that can be performed throughout the computer's operating system, such as shutting down the computer or logging on to the local console. It is the application of user rights that makes administrative accounts different from typical user accounts.

After this lesson, you will be able to

- Understand the purpose of user rights
- Manage user rights assignment

Estimated lesson time: 20 minutes

Assigning User Rights

User rights are managed the same way as other Group Policy settings: by determining the appropriate GPO for a site, domain, or OU, and changing the user rights assignment settings in that object. User rights assignments in a GPO apply to all computers within that Active Directory container. Figure 3.4 shows the user rights that are available under Local Policies in a GPO.

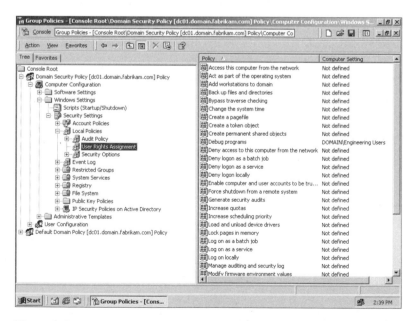

Figure 3.4   The user rights available in a Group Policy Object

User rights are assigned to user accounts and to group accounts, thereby allowing a user or group the ability to perform whatever function the user right allows on computers to which the GPO containing the user right setting applies.

Normally, user rights are applied to groups, and individual user accounts are made members of those groups to obtain the user right. However, specific user accounts frequently require the application of user rights to correctly run service software within that user account's security context. For example, a user account that is used as the security context for a backup service must have the user right to back up files and directories, and the user right to restore files and directories.

User rights take priority over permissions. Activities that might be disallowed by permissions can be overridden by the application of user rights. For example, the owner of a file applies a user right to change the access control list (ACL) of an object regardless of whether permissions in the ACL allow the owner access to the file.

The default user rights assignments are appropriate for the vast majority of organizations. Modifying user rights assignments can have wide-ranging and negative impacts on the ability of users and services to operate. You should change them only when you have specific information about a vulnerability from either Microsoft or a trusted security vendor, and you should modify them only to configurations that have been verified to work correctly in a production environment. When you need to assign user rights to users, make the users a part of an existing group that has the appropriate rights assigned.

Practice: Modifying User Rights

Engineers at Fabrikam, Inc. frequently write drivers to control the devices that Fabrikam produces. For this reason, they must be able to test, debug, and profile the performance of their software on machines inside the domain. In this practice, you expand the engineers' user rights to allow these activities, which are normally restricted due to their potential for abuse.

▶ **To expand user rights for engineers**

1. Click Start, point to Programs, point to Administrative Tools, and click Active Directory Users And Computers. The Active Directory Users And Computers management console appears.

2. Right-click domain.fabrikam.com, and choose Properties. The domain.fabrikam.com Properties dialog box appears.

3. Click the Group Policy tab.

4. Double-click Domain Security Policy. The Group Policies management console appears with the Domain Security Policy GPO opened.

5. Expand Computer Configuration, Windows Settings, Security Settings, Local Policies, and click User Rights Assignment to view the settings as shown in Figure 3.5.

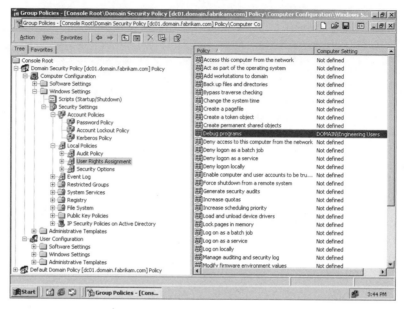

Figure 3.5   Local policies settings

6. Double-click Debug Programs. The Security Policy Setting dialog box appears, as shown in Figure 3.6.

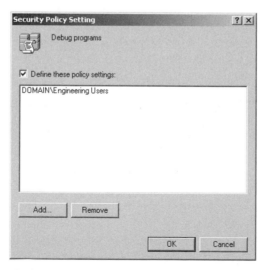

Figure 3.6   The Security Policy Setting dialog box

7. Select the Define These Policy Settings check box, and then click Add. The Add User Or Group dialog box appears.

8. Click Browse. The Select Users Or Groups dialog box appears with a list of domain users and groups.

9. Select Engineering Users from the domain.fabrikam.com list, and then click OK to close the Select Users Or Groups dialog box.

10. Click OK to close the Add User Or Group dialog box.

11. Click OK to close the Security Policy Setting dialog box.

12. Double-click Profile Single Process. The Security Policy Setting dialog box (Figure 3.6) appears.

13. Select the Define These Policy Settings check box, and then click Add. The Add User Or Group dialog box appears.

14. Click Browse. The Select Users Or Groups dialog box appears with a list of domain users and groups listed.

15. Select Engineering Users from the domain.fabrikam.com list, and then click OK to close the Select Users Or Group dialog box.

16. Click OK to close the Add User Or Group dialog box.

17. Click OK to close the Security Policy Setting dialog box.

18. Double-click Profile System Performance. The Security Policy Setting dialog box (Figure 3.6) appears.

19. Select the Define These Policy Settings check box, and then click Add. The Add User Or Group dialog box appears.

20. Click Browse. The Select Users Or Groups dialog box appears.

21. Select Engineering Users from the domain.fabrikam.com list, and then click OK to close the Select Users Or Groups dialog box.

22. Click OK to close the Add User Or Group dialog box.

23. Click OK to close the Security Policy Setting dialog box. The group policy settings you've just defined are now in effect.

24. Close the Group Policies management console.

25. Click OK to close the domain.fabrikam.com Properties dialog box.

26. Close the Active Directory Users And Computers management console.

Lesson Review

The following questions are intended to reinforce key information in this lesson. If you are unable to answer a question, review the lesson and try the question again. Answers to the questions can be found in the appendix.

1. How are user rights managed?

2. At what level in the Active Directory are user rights applied?

3. What is the typical use of user rights?

4. How often do user rights need to be modified by administrators?

Lesson Summary

- User rights are operations that can be granted to security principals to perform important operations that involve security risk on the system as a whole, rather than to specific secured objects within the system.

- User rights are managed through GPOs linked to Active Directory containers. The computers inside these containers apply the user rights settings locally.

- Rather than modifying user rights for a specific account, you make user accounts members of a group that has the right you want to assign. However, software applications and services frequently modify the rights of the user context under which they operate to perform their function.

- User rights take priority over permissions and allow users to perform activities that their permissions would otherwise not allow.

Lesson 3: Controlling Access Through Restricted Groups

In large environments where authority to create user accounts and add members to groups is broadly delegated, keeping strict control of the membership of highly sensitive groups can be difficult but essential for the security of your network. Membership in security groups provides user accounts with wide-ranging access to secure resources throughout the network. If users are accidentally (or otherwise) made members of security groups to which they shouldn't belong, they can exceed their authorization for using the system. Group Policy provides a mechanism for creating predefined restricted groups, which help ensure that users are not inappropriately added to sensitive security groups.

After this lesson, you will be able to

- Understand the restricted groups mechanism
- Use restricted groups to control security group membership

Estimated lesson time: 15 minutes

Applying Restricted Group Settings

Using restricted groups is simple: at each policy update interval, the actual membership of the security group is changed to match the membership list in the restricted group settings of the policy. Users who have been inappropriately added are removed, and valid users who have been removed are restored.

When you configure a group as a restricted group, new membership into the group can be revoked by the system at each Group Policy refresh interval, which by default is about every 90 minutes. Therefore, if a user is inappropriately added to a membership-restricted group, the membership will be revoked within 90 minutes.

To make membership changes to a restricted group, you change the membership in the GPO and let the application of Group Policy change the security member-ship. In this way, membership is changed throughout Active Directory uniformly rather than just in those areas you remember to directly change.

You can also enforce which groups the restricted group is a member of by including those groups in the policy setting on the Member Of tab in the GPO's Properties dialog box. However, the restricted groups feature adds only the restricted group to other groups—it does not remove it from groups where it appears. To remove a restricted group from another group, you must remove the other group from the Member Of list in the restricted group's GPO, and then manually remove the restricted group from the containing security group.

Practice: Creating a Restricted Group

In this practice, you limit the members of a restricted group. At Fabrikam, Inc., the only valid domain administrators are those working in the IT department. Membership in the Domain Admins group should be limited to members of the Information Technology Users group. When you are done, the members of the Information Technology Users group will be made members of the Domain Admins group at the next Group Policy refresh interval.

▶ **To create a restricted group**

1. Click Start, point to Programs, point to Administrative Tools, and click Active Directory Users And Computers. The Active Directory Users And Computers management console appears.

2. Right-click domain.fabrikam.com, and choose Properties. The domain.fabrikam.com Properties dialog box appears.

3. Click the Group Policy tab.

4. Double-click Domain Security Policy. The Group Policies management console appears with the Domain Security Policy GPO opened.

5. Expand Computer Configuration, then Windows Settings, and then click Security Settings.

6. Right-click Restricted Groups, and click Add Group. The Add Group dialog box appears, as shown in Figure 3.7.

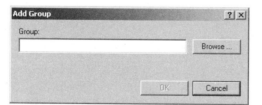

Figure 3.7   The Add Group dialog box

7. Click Browse. The Select Groups dialog box appears.

8. Select Domain Admins from the domain.fabrikam.com list, and then click OK to close the Select Groups dialog box.

9. Click OK to close the Add Group dialog box.

   Domain Admins is now added to the list of restricted groups.

10. Double-click Domain Admins in the list of restricted groups. The Configure Membership dialog box appears as shown in Figure 3.8.

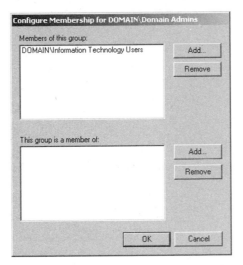

Figure 3.8   The Configure Membership dialog box for restricted groups

11. Click Add to open the Add Member dialog box.

12. Click Browse. The Select Users Or Groups dialog box appears.

13. Double-click Information Technology Users from the list, and click OK to close the Select Users Or Groups dialog box.

14. Click OK to close the Add Member dialog box.

15. Click OK to close the Configure Membership dialog box.

    The Information Technology Users security group is now a member of the Domain Admins restricted group.

16. Close the Group Policies management console.

17. Click OK to close the domain.fabrikam.com Properties dialog box.

18. Close the Active Directory Users And Computers management console.

Lesson Review

The following questions are intended to reinforce key information in this lesson. If you are unable to answer a question, review the lesson and try the question again. Answers to the questions can be found in the appendix.

1. What is the primary purpose of restricted groups?

2. What subtle difference exists between the way that restricted groups handle members and the way they handle being members of another group?

3. How should you create members of a restricted group?

Lesson Summary

- Restricted groups are implemented by Group Policy to limit the membership of security groups according to strictly defined and controlled lists and to automatically correct membership discrepancies at the Group Policy refresh interval.

- The restricted groups feature can be used to ensure that restricted groups are also members of other groups.

Lesson 4: Administering Security Templates

Security templates are text files that contain numerous policy settings pertaining to computer security, such as password policy, account policy, and other settings within the Security Settings namespace of a GPO. Because security templates are text files, they can be exported from one GPO and imported into any number of others, allowing administrators to distribute security settings among individual computers or independent domains.

Exam Tip   Security templates are the recommended way to make changes to Group Policy so that the changes can be easily documented and distributed throughout the enterprise. Be certain that you understand how to use security templates.

After completing this lesson, you will be able to

- Understand the structure and purpose of security templates
- Create security templates
- Modify predefined security templates
- Deploy security templates using a variety of tools

Estimated lesson time: 45 minutes

Understanding the Purpose of Security Templates

A *security template* is simply the settings contained in the Computer\Security Settings portion of a GPO that have been exported to a text file so that they can be imported into other GPOs. Microsoft uses security templates to establish baseline security settings for computers during installation and to distribute security standards that are more secure than the default installation. You can think of a security template as a computer GPO that has been packaged for distribution. Figure 3.9 contains an example of a security template.

Figure 3.9   A security template

Security templates are used to create a standardized security baseline that can be imported into various GPOs and local GPOs (LGPOs) throughout your organization. Security templates allow you to export the security settings from a GPO and distribute those settings as a text file (for example, through e-mail) to administrators throughout your organization.

Security templates are used primarily to modify local GPOs on workstations and servers to increase their basic security posture, whether or not they are subject to a non-local GPO. Modifying a computer's local security settings ensures that the computer remains protected from compromise whenever it is used outside a domain environment.

Security templates are also used to distribute security settings in multi-domain environments where a single GPO cannot be applied uniformly across an entire Active Directory tree or forest. By creating and managing security templates, you can manage a uniform set of security configuration standards for various classes of computers across any number of domains.

Using a security template, you can configure settings for

- Account policies (password, account lockout, and Kerberos policy)
- Local policies (audit policy, user rights assignment, and security options)
- Event log settings
- Restricted groups membership
- File system permissions
- Registry permissions
- System services startup type

Why Use Predefined Security Templates?

Windows 2000 ships with a number of predefined security templates that can be incorporated into a GPO to immediately improve security for specific situations. By default, these templates are stored in %systemroot%\Security\Templates.

The predefined security templates are as follows:

- *Default* workstation (Basicwk.inf), server (Basicsv.inf), and domain controller (Basicdc.inf) templates are the security settings applied to a standard computer after installation. You can use these templates to reverse other security settings that may have been applied to workstations, servers, or domain controllers respectively.
- The *Compatible* workstation (Compatws.inf) lowers the default security settings of the computer so that members of the Users group can successfully run applications that are not certified for Windows 2000. Normally, only Power Users can run these applications.
- *Secure* workstation or server (Securews.inf) and domain controller (Securedc.inf) templates implement Microsoft's standard security recommendations for workstations. These recommendations improve security without sacrificing backward compatibility with earlier Windows operating systems.
- *Highly secure* workstation or server (Hisecws.inf) and domain controller (Hisecdc.inf) templates establish security settings that secure network communication between computers by removing backward compatibility features. Computers with these security settings can communicate only with Windows 2000 and later computers.
- The *Dedicated* domain controller (Dedica.inf) template establishes security settings for domain controllers that remove compatibility settings allowing earlier server applications to be run locally on the domain controller.

The predefined security templates are incremental in nature and assume that basic Windows 2000 settings from a default installation of Windows are in place. For computers that have been upgraded from Windows NT 4, you will have to apply the basic security template to the computer to bring it up to the default Windows 2000 security configuration. Figure 3.10 contains an example of a predefined security template with default security settings.

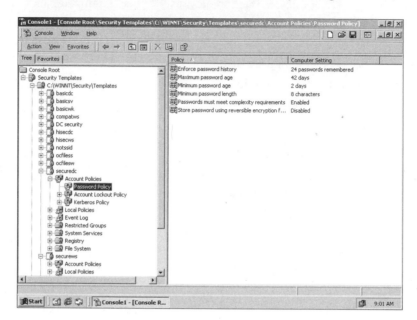

Figure 3.10   A predefined security template

Managing Security Templates

You can use five major tools to manage security templates:

- The *Group Policies management console* can be used to import and export security template files. When you import security settings into a GPO, those settings apply automatically to all computers within that GPO's scope.

- The *Local Security Settings* management console can be used to import and export security template files. When you import security settings into a local GPO, you permanently modify the computer's local security policy.

- The *Security Templates* snap-in can be used to manage entire directories of security templates quickly and easily. The Security Templates snap-in interprets the contents of a security template text file in the same familiar way that the Group Policy Editor interprets Group Policy settings, so you can browse the settings hierarchy and modify your security templates without the risk of making errors, and without having to understand the syntax of security template files.

- The *Configuration and Analysis snap-in* can be used to analyze how closely a machine's effective security posture matches a specific security template and to apply security template settings to a specific machine. The Configuration and Analysis management console can create a database of a computer's security settings and compare that database against numerous security templates
- The *SecEdit.exe* command-line utility provides powerful scripting functions to accomplish tasks that cannot be accomplished using management console snap-ins.

Tip   The simplest way to manage security templates is to create a management console containing the Security Templates snap-in and add it to your Administrative Tools folder.

Best Practices

Best practices for managing security templates include the following:

- Never edit the Setup Security.inf template. If you do, you won't be able to reapply default security settings if it becomes necessary.
- Don't apply the Setup Security.inf template through Group Policy. The Setup Security.inf template is unique for each computer, and it is very large. Apply it only to the local computer through the Security Configuration And Analysis snap-in.
- Do not apply the Compatible template to domain controllers.
- Do not modify predefined templates. Rather, copy them to a new file and edit the new file.
- Test security templates before applying them to production group policies.

Deploying Security Templates

The most effective way to deploy the settings in a security template is to import into a GPO the settings that apply to the range of computers to which you want to apply the security settings.

Tip   Importing security template settings into a GPO is the easiest and most effective way to deploy security settings throughout your company.

To deploy security template settings across multiple domains and GPOs, you must individually import the security settings into each GPO. There is no mechanism for automatically deploying security template settings across a number of domains.

Other methods of deploying security templates include manually importing settings into a computer's Local Security Settings management console or using the Security Configuration And Analysis management console to configure security settings.

Finally, you can deploy security templates using the powerful SecEdit.exe command, which is a command-line version of the Security Configuration And Analysis snap-in. Because it is a command-line tool, it can be used in startup/shutdown and logon/logoff scripts. This makes it a powerful tool for deploying changes to local security settings throughout a domain automatically, a task that cannot be accomplished any other way.

Practice: Managing Security Templates

In this practice, you use various methods to deploy the security settings contained in a security template.

Exercise 1: Creating a Security Template Management Console

The first step in managing security templates is to create a convenient security templates management console. In this exercise, you create a management console for security templates and then compare the computer's configuration to the predefined security setting in the security template.

▶ **To create a security templates management console**

1. Click Start, and click Run.
2. In the Run dialog box, type **mmc** in the Open box and press ENTER. The Microsoft Management Console appears.
3. On the Console menu, click Add/Remove Snap-In. The Add/Remove Snap-in dialog box opens.
4. Click Add to open the Add Standalone Snap-in dialog box.
5. In the list, double-click both Security Configuration And Analysis and Security Templates.
6. Click Close to close the Add Standalone snap-in dialog box.
7. Click OK to close the Add/Remove snap-ins dialog box.
8. Maximize the Console Root window within the console window, and then maximize the Console window. Resize the window, and expand the Security Templates and its child node in the console tree to show the various preconfigured security templates.
9. When you have adjusted the console to your preferences, on the Console menu, choose Save As.
10. Type **Security Templates** in the File Name box, and click Save.

You now have a security templates management tool located in the Administrative Tools folder of the Start menu.

► **To compare a computer's security settings**

1. In the Security Templates management console, right-click Security Configuration And Analysis, and click Open Database.

2. In the Open Database dialog box, type **DC01** as the name of the database, and click Open. The Import Template dialog box appears containing a list of security templates from which to choose.

3. Select the Hisecdc.inf security template as the template to compare the database to, and click Open.

   A list of instructions for analyzing security will appear in the management console. The Security Configuration And Analysis snap-in allows you to compare the effective security settings of a computer against a specific security template.

4. Right-click Security Configuration And Analysis and click Analyze Computer Now. The Perform Analysis dialog box appears asking for a file name and path for the error log.

5. Click OK to accept the error log path.

   During the analysis, a progress indicator will appear. After the analysis, the console tree structure below the Security Configuration And Analysis node will contain the configuration differences, as shown in Figure 3.11.

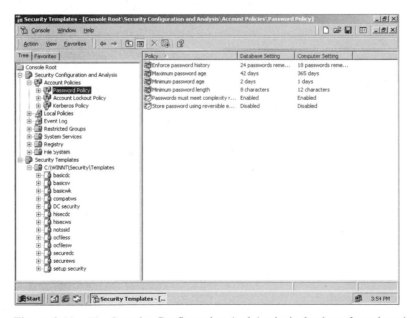

Figure 3.11   The Security Configuration And Analysis database for a domain controller

6. Expand Security Configuration And Analysis, Account Policies, and then select Password Policy.

Notice the red X icons, which indicate a difference between the computer's configuration and the security template, and the green check mark icons, which indicate that the computer's settings are the same as the security policy.

7. Double-click Enforce Password History.

The Analyzed Security Policy Setting dialog box appears, as shown in Figure 3.12. Notice that the computer is set to retain 18 passwords, while the security template specifies 24.

Figure 3.12   The Analyzed Security Policy Setting dialog box

8. Click OK.

9. Browse through the remainder of the settings that are marked with red icons to view the discrepancies between this computer's settings and the security template.

10. Close the Security Templates management console.

Exercise 2: Creating a Security Template

You can create new security templates whenever you have unique security needs that are not met by predefined security templates. The procedures in this exercise will help you create and manage a new security template.

▶   **To create a new security template file**

1. In Microsoft Windows Explorer, browse to C:\Winnt\Security\Templates and create a folder named User Defined Templates.

2. Open the Security Templates management console that you created in Exercise 1 of this practice.

3. Right-click Security Templates in the console tree, and click New Template Search Path. The Browse For Folder dialog box opens.

4. Browse to the User Defined Templates folder you created in step 1, and click OK.

   A new template folder appears in the Security Templates namespace, as shown in Figure 3.13.

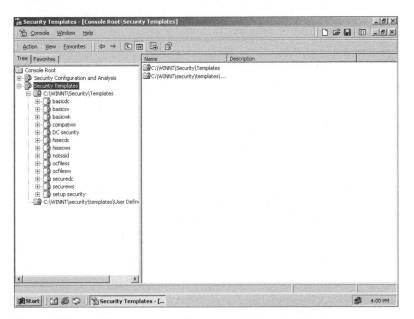

Figure 3.13   Adding a new search path to the Security Templates namespace

5. In the console tree, right-click the new User Defined Templates folder, and click New Template. The new template dialog box appears.

6. Type **Passpol** as the Template Name.

7. In the Description box, type **Company-wide password policy to be applied to all local and domain GPOs**.

8. Click OK.

   A new policy template has been created and it appears below the search path you added in step 4.

▶ **To modify settings in a newly created security template**

1. Expand the new Passpol security template, expand the Account Policies folder, and then click Password Policy, as shown in Figure 3.14.

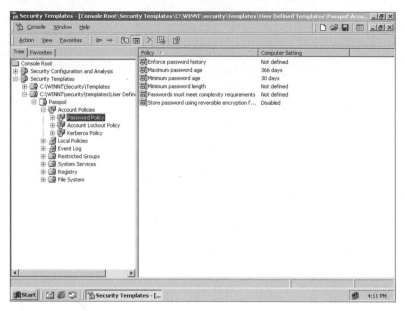

Figure 3.14   The Password Policy settings of a new security template

2. Double-click Enforce Password History.

3. In the Template Security Policy Setting dialog box, select Define This Policy Setting.

4. Type **24** in the Passwords Remembered box, and click OK to close the dialog box.

5. Double-click Maximum Password Age.

6. In the Template Security Policy Setting dialog box, select Define This Policy Setting.

7. Type **366** into the Days box, and click OK to close the dialog box.

8. In the Suggested Value Changes dialog box, click OK to dismiss the Minimum Password Age notice.

9. Double-click the Minimum Password Length policy.

10. In the Template Security Policy Setting dialog box, select Define This Policy Setting.
11. Type **12** in the Characters box, and click OK to close the dialog box.
12. Double-click the Passwords Must Meet Complexity Requirements setting.
13. In the Template Security Policy Setting dialog box, select Define This Policy Setting, and click OK to close the dialog box.
14. Double-click the Store Password Using Reversible Encryption setting
15. In the Template Security Policy Setting dialog box, select Define This Policy Setting.
16. Select Disabled, and click OK to close the dialog box.
17. Close the management console.
18. Click Yes to save the security template file.

▶ **To display security template settings**

1. In Windows Explorer, browse to C:\WINNT\Security\Templates\User Defined Templates.
2. Right-click Passpol.inf, and choose Properties. The Passpol.inf Properties dialog box appears.

   Notice that the size of the file is well under 1 KB.
3. Click OK to close the Properties dialog box.
4. Double-click Passpol.inf.

   Notepad.exe opens showing the text of Passpol.inf, as shown in Figure 3.15. The settings you just created are stored in a text file that you can read.

Figure 3.15   Viewing security templates as text in Microsoft Notepad

Exercise 4: Modifying a Predefined Security Template

In this exercise, you modify a predefined security template to customize it for your specific environment.

▶ **To customize a security template**

1. Open the Security Templates management console you created in Exercise 1 of this practice.
2. Expand the C:\WINNT\Security\Templates folder.
3. Right-click the Hisecdc security template, and click Save As. The Save As dialog box appears.
4. Browse to User Defined Templates, and save the policy as Mod Hisecdc.inf.
5. In the console tree, expand Mod Hisecdc, Account Policies, and select Password Policy.
6. Double-click Maximum Password Age.
7. In the Template Security Policy Setting dialog box, change the value in the Days box to **366** and then click OK.
8. Double-click Minimum Password Length.
9. In the Template Security Policy Setting dialog box, change the value in the Characters box to **12** and then click OK.
10. Right-click Mod Hisecdc, and choose Save.
11. Close the Security Templates management console.

Exercise 5: Local Security Settings Management Console

In this exercise, you import security settings using the Local Security Settings snap-in.

▶ **To import security settings**

1. Click Start, point to Programs, point to Administrative Tools, and click Local Security Policy. The Local Security Settings management console appears.
2. In the console tree, right-click Security Settings, and choose Import Policy. The Import Policy From dialog box opens.
3. Browse to the User Defined Templates folder, and double-click Passpol.inf.
4. Browse to Account Policies\Password Policy to verify that the local security settings now match those specified by the security template, as shown in Figure 3.16.

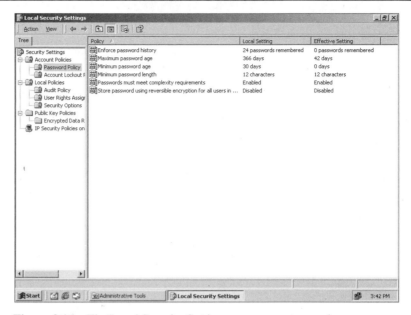

Figure 3.16   The Local Security Settings management console

5. Close the Local Security Settings management console.

Exercise 6: Using the Security Configuration and Analysis Management Console

In this exercise, you apply configuration settings to a computer.

▶ **To apply configuration settings**

1. Open the Security Templates management console you created in Exercise 1 of this practice.

2. Right-click Security And Configuration Analysis, and click Open Database. The Open Database dialog box appears.

3. Double-click the dc01.sdb security database.

4. Right-click Security And Configuration Analysis, and click Import Template. The Import Template file selection dialog box appears.

5. Browse to User Defined Templates, and double-click Passpol.inf.

6. Right-click Security And Configuration Analysis, and click Configure Computer Now.

7. In the Configure System dialog box, click OK to accept the default path.

    A progress indicator will appear briefly.

8. In the management console, expand Security Configuration And Analysis, Account Policy, Password Policy, and select Maximum Password Age.

   Notice that the effective setting does not match the policy that was just applied.

   Why have the settings on this domain controller not taken effect?

9. Close the Security Templates management console.

Exercise 7: Deploying a Security Template Using Group Policy Objects

In this exercise, you import security settings into a GPO.

▶ **To deploy security settings through a GPO**

1. Click Start, point to Programs, point to Administrative Tools, and click Active Directory Users And Computers. The Active Directory Users And Computers management console appears.

2. Right-click domain.fabrikam.com, and click Properties. The domain.fabrikam.com Properties dialog box appears.

3. Click the Group Policy tab.

4. Double-click Domain Security Policy. The Group Policies management console appears with the Domain Security Policy GPO opened.

5. Expand Domain Security Policy, Computer Configuration, Windows Settings, and then Security Settings.

6. Right-click Security Settings, and click Import Policy. The Import Policy From dialog box appears.

7. Browse to the User Defined Templates folder, and double-click Passpol.

8. Expand Security Settings, Account Policies, and then click Password Policy.

   Notice that the Enforce Password History now conforms to the settings in the template. This password policy now applies to all computers within the domain

9. Close the Group Policies management console.

10. Click OK to close the domain.fabrikam.com Properties dialog box.

11. Close the Active Directory Users And Computers dialog box.

Exercise 8: Using SecEdit.exe

In this exercise, you use the SecEdit.exe tool to change the local GPO settings for computers within a domain. Modifying the local policy settings on computers ensures that your security settings remain effective even when the computers are not attached to a domain.

To implement this functionality, you will create a share containing the security template and then use a startup script to apply that security template to each computer within the domain when it is booted.

▶ **To create a share point for user-defined security templates**

1. In Windows Explorer, browse to C:\WINNT\Security\Templates.
2. Right-click User Defined Templates, and click Sharing. The User Defined Templates Properties dialog appears showing the Sharing tab.
3. Select the Share This Folder option, and type **UserSec** as the share name.
4. Click the Permissions button. The Permissions for UserSec dialog box appears.
5. Ensure that the Everyone group has Allow Read permissions.
6. Click OK close the Permissions dialog box.
7. Click the Security tab in the User Defined Templates Properties dialog box.
8. Click Add to open the Select Users, Computers, Or Groups dialog box.
9. Double-click the Everyone group, and then click OK to close the Select Users, Computers, Or Groups dialog box.
10. Ensure that the Read & Execute, List Folder Contents, and Read permissions are selected in the Allow column.
11. Click OK to close the User Defined Templates Properties dialog box.

    Why does this exercise specify reducing security and using the Everyone group, rather than using a more secure group such as Domain Users?

▶ **To create a startup script to apply security templates**

1. Click Start, point to Programs, point to Administrative Tools, and click Active Directory Users And Computers. The Active Directory Users And Computers management console appears.
2. Right-click domain.fabrikam.com, and click Properties. The domain.fabrikam.com Properties dialog box appears.
3. Click the Group Policy tab.
4. Double-click Domain Security Policy. The Group Policies management console appears with the Domain Security Policy GPO opened.
5. Expand Domain Security Group Policy, then Computer Configuration, Windows Settings, and Scripts.

6. Double-click Startup. The Startup Properties dialog box appears, as shown in Figure 3.17.

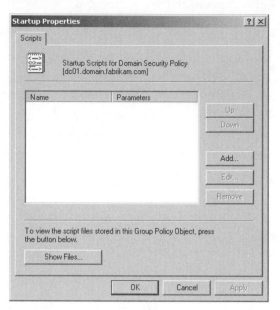

Figure 3.17   The Startup Properties dialog box

7. Click Add to open the Add A Script dialog box.

8. Click Browse. A file browser dialog box appears.

9. Right-click in the file list, select New, and then click Text Document.

10. Type **setsecurity.bat** to change the name of the file, and press ENTER. A message box appears asking you if you want to change the file type.

11. Click Yes to confirm that you want to change the file type.

12. Right-click Setsecurity.bat, and choose Edit.

    Notepad appears with Setsecurity.bat open.

13. Type the following text into the batch file:

```
secedit /analyze /DB c:\sectemp.sdb /CFG \\dc01\UserSec\pass-
pol.inf

secedit /configure /DB c:\sectemp.sdb /CFG \\dc01\UserSec\pass-
pol.inf /overwrite

del c:\sectemp.sdb
```

14. Save and close the text document.

15. Click Open in the Browse window to select the newly created Setsecurity.bat startup script.

16. Click OK to close the Add A Script dialog box.

17. Click OK to close the Startup Properties dialog box.

18. Close the Group Policies management console.

19. Click OK to close the domain.fabrikam.com Properties dialog box.

20. Close the Active Directory Users And Computers management console.

▶   **To verify the security template application**

1. Reboot a workstation that is a member of the domain.fabrikam.com domain.

2. Log on using an account local to the workstation instead of logging on to the domain.

3. Open Control Panel.

4. Double-click Administrative tools.

5. Double-click Local Policy Settings. The Local Security Settings management console appears.

6. Expand Account Policies, and then click Password Policies.

    Note that the settings from the security template have been applied to the local machine.

Lesson Review

The following questions are intended to reinforce key information in this lesson. If you are unable to answer a question, review the lesson and try the question again. Answers to the questions can be found in the appendix.

1. What is the easiest way to deploy security templates?

2. What is the primary purpose of the Security Configuration And Analysis snap-in?

3. When would it be appropriate to use the SecEdit.exe tool?

4. In what format are security templates stored?

Lesson Summary

- Security templates are text files containing security settings that apply to the Computer Configuration\Security Settings portion of a GPO.

- Security templates can be imported into and exported from GPOs to facilitate deploying a standard set of security settings throughout an enterprise.

- Security templates are managed using the Security Templates snap-in, which allows administrators to make changes to security template settings in a uniform and consistent manner.

- The Security Configuration And Analysis snap-in allows administrators to compare a computer's effective security settings to a security template, enabling them to quickly find problems with security settings deployment.

- The SecEdit.exe tool is a command-line version of the Security Configuration And Analysis snap-in that allows administrators to script various actions related to security templates, including analyzing security settings and applying security templates.

C H A P T E R   4

Account-Based Security

About This Chapter

When a user logs on, the operating system knows the user's account credentials and provides access to resources based on the user's identity. The access control mechanism in Microsoft Windows 2000 that secures various types of resources is referred to as *permissions*. Windows 2000 can apply permissions to the following types of resources:

■   Files and folders on NTFS file system volumes through the NTFS driver

■   Shared folders and shared printers through the server service

■   Registry keys through the security reference monitor

■   Active Directory objects through the Active Directory service

Security for each type of resource is managed by a separate process, and these processes vary slightly in their capabilities and effects, but the concept of permissions is uniformly applied throughout Windows 2000.

Before You Begin

To complete this chapter, you must have

- The dc01.domain.Fabrikam.com test computer configured with Microsoft Windows 2000 Server and with Active Directory installed with the Domain Security Policy defined in Chapter 1
- The example network configuration created in Chapter 2, "User Accounts and Security Groups"
- Access to a client computer running Microsoft Windows 2000 Professional or Windows XP Professional

Lesson 1: Managing File System Permissions

In this lesson, you learn about file system permissions that apply to files and folders stored on NTFS volumes. The next few lessons in this chapter cover the other types of permissions you can use to secure your system.

Exam Tip   Permissions are the foundation on which most Windows 2000 security features are based. You need to understand both how to allow access to security groups and how to deny access to security groups for purposes such as controlling access to files and controlling the application of Group Policy Objects to specific users.

After completing this lesson, you will be able to

- Understand the role of NTFS permissions in securing a computer
- Manage NTFS permissions

Estimated lesson time: 1 hour

Managing Permissions-Based Security

Windows implements authorization by attaching a security descriptor to each secured object in the system, such as a file or folder. Security descriptors contain the following information:

- The *owner SID*, which is the security identifier (SID) of the security principal that created the object, or the security principal that was assigned to be the owner by an administrator exercising the Take Ownership user right.
- The *group SID*, which is the SID of the security group that owns the object. Group ownership is used only by the Portable Operating System Interface for UNIX (POSIX). Windows does not provide an interface for establishing group ownership.
- The *discretionary access control list* (DACL), usually referred to simply as an ACL, which contains access control entries (ACEs) composed of a security principal's SID and a specific type of allowed or denied access. ACLs are described in detail in Chapter 2, "User Accounts and Security Groups."
- The *system access control list* (SACL), which contains ACEs that specify how access to the object by permitted security principals should be recorded in the audit log. Auditing is discussed in Lesson 3 of this chapter.

Technically, any resource can be controlled with security descriptors if the process that provides access to the resource is configured to manage security, and if access to the object cannot be controlled by any other process that does not respect security descriptors. In the case of file system permissions, the NTFS driver manages setting permissions, and the security reference monitor process of the Local Security Authority (LSA) checks permissions whenever files on an NTFS-formatted volume are accessed.

Why Is File System Access Control Important?

Hackers can completely circumvent any security restriction in any computer if they have the ability to modify files on disk, because this gives them the ability to change the files that store the operating system. If they can change the operating system to eliminate security checks, they need only reboot the computer to run their modified version of the operating system. Making a computer fail or "crash" is simple to accomplish, even remotely, using one of thousands of different attacks. They would subsequently have complete access to the system.

This is one of the many ways in which a seemingly small security failure can be exploited to gain full control of a computer system. File permissions and NTFS are absolutely required to secure a computer against inappropriate use.

Warning   Volumes that are formatted with FAT or FAT32 file systems do not support security descriptors, so all users have full control of these files. For this reason, you should not use FAT or FAT32 volumes on computers connected to a domain.

How Do Permissions Work?

Every file and folder on an NTFS volume has a security descriptor containing an ACL, which is comprised of any number of ACEs. An ACE is a simple combination of

- An action that can be taken on the object
- Whether the action is being permitted or denied
- The SID of the security principal to which the ACE applies

For example, an ACE might combine the Read action with the Finance security group SID, thus forming a permission. Because this ACE is contained in the ACL attached to a file called Fiscal Year Projections.xls, it is inherently joined to that file, so the relationship is established between the secured resource, the permitted activity, and the permitted user. The security principal represented by the SID in the ACE is able to perform the action on the secured resource, which is specified in the ACE. In Figure 4.1, you can see how a match between any SID in an access token and an ACE allows access.

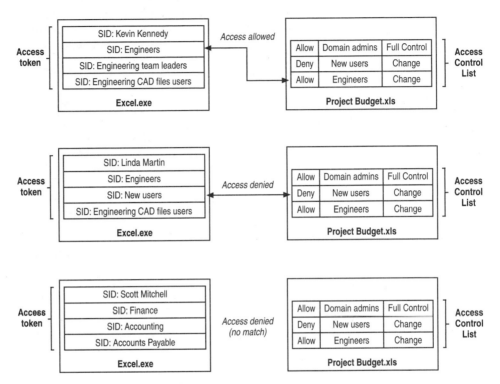

Figure 4.1   An ACE containing the SID allows access

Determining Security Requirements

When you need to create permissions, you can list your security requirements in plain language and then convert them to specific permissions. For example, here are some requirements:

"Members of the Finance Department should have the ability to read, write, and delete files in the Accounting folder."

To satisfy these requirements, you first need to create a group called Finance Department containing all the user accounts of users in that department. Next, you need to create an ACL containing an ACE that specifies that the Finance Department security group should have Read, Write, and Delete entries in the security descriptor for the Accounting folder. The Read, Write, and Delete permissions are combined into a single permission called Modify, which is appropriate in this case. (The Modify permission is described in Table 4.1.)

Using Standard File System Permissions

To secure all the resources in your network, you need to survey managers to determine exactly which users require what type of access to which documents. After you have this information, you can create meaningful security groups and use them to secure the directory structure of your networked resources.

Table 4.1 lists the standard permissions for files and folders. Standard permissions are used to define a user's or group's access to a secured resource, and they provide most of the flexibility required in most cases.

Table 4.1　Standard File System Permissions for Files and Folders

Permission	Use
Full Control	Allows full access to the resource with no restrictions
Modify	Allows users to read, write, create, and delete files, and change file attributes, but does not allow them to change permissions on files or take ownership
Read & Execute	Allows users to read files and to execute them if they are executables or scripts
Read	Allows users to read the contents of files and their attributes, but does not allow executables to be launched
Write	Allows users to write and append data to files
List Folder Contents	Allows users to display the contents of a directory (folders only)

Special Permissions

The standard file system permissions are actually combinations of more atomic permissions called *special permissions*. In some rare cases, such as serving Web pages or preventing accidental access to a database file, you might need finer control of how resources can be used than standard file system permissions allow. Table 4.2 lists the special permissions you can use to accomplish fine-tuning of permissions for files and folders.

Note　Avoid using special file system permissions unless there is no other way to accomplish a specific security goal. Because the use of special file system permissions is unusual, other administrators might not consider looking at them when they are debugging security problems.

Table 4.2 Special File System Permissions

Permission	Use
Full Control	All special permissions combined
Traverse Folder /Execute File	Allows users to change directories into the folder, but does not allow them to list the folder's content; for files, it allows execution of executables and scripts
List Folder/Read Data	Allows users to display the contents of a folder or read a file
Read Attributes	Allows users to display the file or folders attributes, such as its compression flag, archive flag, and read only flag
Read Extended Attributes	Allows users to display the file or folder's extended attributes.
Create Files/Write Data	Allows users to create files in the directory or overwrite files
Create Folders /Append Data	Allows users to create folders within the folder or append data to the file
Write Attributes	Allows users to change a file or folder's file system attributes
Write Extended Attributes	Allows users to change a file or folder's extended attributes
Delete Subfolders and Files	Allows users to delete files or folders within the folder
Delete	Allows users to delete the resource
Read Permissions	Allows users to enumerate the permissions for a resource
Change Permissions	Allows users to change the permissions on the resource
Take Ownership	Allows users to change the ownership information for the resource

Cumulative Permissions

The effective permissions allowed by an ACL for a specific user are the sum of all permissions that apply to all the SIDs in the user's access token. For example, assume that David is a member of both the Bookkeeping and Accountants groups. If Bookkeeping has Read permission to the Accounts Payable folder and Accountants has Change permission for the same folder, David has both Read and Change permissions to the folder. This occurs because the security reference monitor scans the ACL and accumulates all permissions allowed by all the SIDs in the user's access token, which contains the group SIDs as well as the user SID. When the security reference monitor has accumulated all permissions, it allows the requested type of access if it appears anywhere in the ACL for any of the SIDs in the user's access token.

Deny Access Control Entries

Users can also be denied a specific type of access using an ACE. Deny ACEs take priority over all Allow ACEs for the type of access specified. Therefore, if a Deny ACE matches any of a user's SIDs in an ACL, the specified access to the secure resource will be denied, even if it is explicitly allowed by another ACE.

Important Explicit Allow permissions applied directly to a resource will have priority over a Deny ACE inherited from a parent folder. This contradicts the purpose of Deny ACEs and is a side effect of the way that Windows 2000 manages inherited permissions.

For example, in addition to the group memberships previously described, user David is also a member of the New Employees group. New Employees has a Deny Write ACE appearing in the Accounts Payable folder. Irrespective of his accumulated permissions, the Deny ACE blocks access and prevents writing files into the folder.

Note Avoid using Deny ACEs if you can accomplish the same goal by removing a user from a security group or splitting a security group into two groups with different allowed access. Remember that a SID with no ACE allows no access, so Deny ACEs are usually not necessary. Deny ACEs are usually used to temporarily restrict access to specific users or certain groups during periods of probation.

Empty ACLs

If an ACL is empty, then no user has access to the file. However, the account having the ownership right always retains the ability to change permissions, and so can add ACEs to the ACL irrespective of the permissions.

Nonexistent ACLs

If an ACL does not exist (which is not the same as being empty), then all users have full access to the file. This occurs when the file system driver does not support ACLs, as is the case with the FAT and FAT32 file systems.

Inheritance

When a file is created, its ACL is copied from the ACL of the containing directory. For this reason, it is said to "inherit" its permissions from the containing directory.

In Windows 2000, secured resources can be set to use both their own permissions and the permissions of the containing folder. With this setting, the security reference monitor scans the containing folder's ACL and the resource's ACL to establish the entire set of permissions. When permissions on the containing folder are changed, they apply immediately to all contained folders and files without being copied into each file individually, which makes the management of permissions much simpler.

Moving and Copying Files

An ACL is created containing the permissions of the parent folder whenever a file is created on an NTFS volume. This applies to all copy operations. Because a copy is a new file, the copy inherits the permissions of the folder to which it is copied, not the permissions of the original file. Copying a file does not copy the permissions of the original file.

Moving a file or folder is a different process. If you move a file or folder *between volumes*, the move operation is accomplished by copying the file to the new volume and then by deleting the original file or folder. Because it's a copy operation, permissions are reset on the file or folder when it is moved.

However, if you move a file or folder *within the same volume*, no copy is performed. Rather, the directory entry for the file name is moved to the new directory—this is why moves within the same volume are immediate no matter how large the file is. Because the file has not been copied, its permissions remain unchanged. Moving a file within the same volume does not affect its permissions.

Tip   You can use the Xcopy command from the command prompt to copy files along with their permissions and owner information. The Xcopy /o switch specifies that permissions and ownership information should be copied along with files and is appropriate whenever permissions must be maintained during a move or copy operation.

Establishing Permissions Best Practices

Use permissions to secure all the computers in your organization against improper use. Permissions are the most important single security component of Windows 2000, and they are the foundation of all other security measures because they prevent the operating system from being changed. You cannot properly secure a Windows 2000 computer without understanding how to apply permissions properly.

Applying Base Permissions

The first and most basic practice is to apply meaningful permissions. The default permission for an NTFS-formatted volume is to allow the Everyone group Full Control permission. This allows anonymous users, guest users, and literally anyone who can connect to the computer to read and write files on it, and it is no more secure than an unsecured FAT32 volume.

Whenever you format an NTFS volume, replace the Everyone group Full Control permission with at least the Authenticated Users group Full Control permission. In this way, as new folders and files are created or copied into the volume, they will inherit these base permissions. The base permissions on file servers should be Authenticated Users: Change and Domain Administrators: Full Control.

Managing Permissions Changes Through a Single Folder

Windows creates the correct necessary permissions for the system drive of a computer, and beyond replacing the Everyone Full Control permission on the root of the C drive, you should not change permissions on folders you don't create. The best way to manage custom permissions that you've set is to create a single folder in each volume and customize permissions and shares within that folder.

Create a single folder on a volume within which all shared access to files will occur, and disable shared access to any other parts of the computer. Then set that single folder's NTFS permissions to the most restrictive allowable for the group of people who will access the computer remotely. For example, if the computer is a file server that will serve the engineering department, grant the Engineering security group and the Domain Administrators group Full Control permissions. When folders and shares are created inside this folder, you won't have to worry about base permissions because they're already set properly, and you won't have to worry about other folders on the computer's disk outside this area because there will be no remote access to them.

Note   Remember, to gain full access to a file, users with Read access to the file can copy it to another volume where they have full control (or to a FAT32 volume where permissions are not checked). However, they will not be able to copy it back, so as long as the original copy is the only copy trusted to contain the true contents, this risk implies only the theft of data. Use audit policy to determine when users read specific files of high importance, as shown in Lesson 3 of this chapter.

Mimicking Your Organizational Unit Structure in Folders and Security Groups

Map your organizational hierarchy to your shared directory folder structure. For example, create shares for each of your division- or department-level organizational units (OUs), such as accounting, marketing, engineering, and so on. After you've created the shares, create security groups that are analogous to those OUs and apply those security groups as the base permissions to the folders with the same names. Create a security group that provides Full Control for Power Users of the folder, and a security group that provides Change control for typical users. Power users, such as team leaders and department heads, can then manage permissions inside their own shared folders.

The reason for creating shares at a departmental level is that departments are highly likely to be moved as a unit as the company grows and servers are outgrown. For example, when the finance department is large enough to require its own server, you can easily move the department's files and folders along with the share structure intact to another server and re-map network drives for those users using Group Policy. If you use Microsoft distributed file system (Dfs), the shared folder locator service for Windows 2000, the change from many shared folders on a single server to many servers with a single shared folder can be completely transparent.

Tip   By mapping your OUs to analogous security groups and shared folders, you make it easy to visually determine what permissions ought to be on a shared folder.

Matching your OU structure is an excellent way to start assigning permissions. However, you don't have to be strict or rigorous about mimicking OUs with security groups. Security groups should be flexible and created on an ad hoc basis to solve immediate security issues as they arise.

Editing Existing Permissions

A wide-ranging permissions problem can be difficult to fix using Microsoft Windows Explorer. For example, if you have an existing shared folder structure where the Everyone Full Control permission is granted in many places, but where other permissions that must be retained are also present, you cannot simply go to the root of the drive and set new permissions, because those permissions will replace the unique permissions of interior folders and files.

Tip   You can use the command-prompt Cacls command to grant or remove specific ACEs without affecting or replacing other entries. Use this tool to fix permissions on volumes that contain existing data. Audit permissions on your servers on a quarterly basis to be certain that some users haven't accidentally been provided with wide access. Use the Cacls command to check for inappropriate permissions and to replace them.

Creating a Security Group with Full Control Access to All Resources

To correctly troubleshoot security problems and to perform some administrative functions, you will need unfettered access to files and resources without expending the time and effort required to take ownership. Set up one security group that has Full Control access to every resource on your network. This group should be a universal security group in Active Directory. Membership in this group should be severely restricted—most of the time it might contain no members at all. You can add an individual administrator when access is required. Use the restricted groups feature to prevent users from being made members of this group.

Troubleshooting Permissions Problems

The security provided by permissions is a double-edged sword—while necessary for security purposes, permissions can cause problems that can be extremely difficult to troubleshoot in production systems. For example, applications can fail to start correctly or can be unable to store documents. Some applications might not report Access Denied error messages correctly and might fail when they attempt to use resources to which the user has no access.

Determining Whether a Permissions Problem Exists

The first step in troubleshooting permissions is to determine whether the problem has to do with permissions. First, make the user who is experiencing the problem a temporary member of a security group with universal access to all resources (such as Domain Admins), and then have the user log on with this new temporary membership. One of three things will happen that can guide your troubleshooting efforts:

- If the problem disappears when the user logs on with full access, you have a permissions problem.
- If the problem changes in nature or the error messages change, you have at least two different issues and one of them is permissions.
- If the error indications do not change, there is no permissions problem.

Now that you know if you're dealing with a permissions problem, remove the user from membership in your universal access group.

Finding the Problem Resources

Remember that, although the problem might be a permissions problem, it might not be a file or folder access problem. Registry keys can also be secured, so keep in mind that your permissions problem can be a registry permissions problem. Applications that rely on Active Directory services can also behave unexpectedly if you have increased the security of Active Directory objects. These troubleshooting principles remain the same no matter what type of secured resource you're having problems with.

Once you know that you have a permissions problem, the next step is to determine which resources are too restricted. When a user is attempting to load a document into a Microsoft Office program, this is simple: it's the file. However, when applications fail to run correctly without providing useful error messages, you can have difficulty determining exactly what is going wrong.

To determine which files or other restricted resources are causing the access problem, you need to narrow the scope of likely suspects, and then enable access failure auditing on those files. Then have the user attempt to use the resource, and check the audit log to see which files the user has attempted to access. Establishing auditing is covered in Lesson 3 of this chapter.

Tip   You can shorten this process by downloading the File Monitor tool from *www.sysinternals.com*. (At publication time, this was a free download.) The File Monitor tool shows all file access on the system and makes it simple to see which files a program is attempting to open. To find permissions problems, run this utility, and then run the application you are having problems with. The related Registry Monitor tool does the same thing for registry access.

Determining the Problem

Once you know which files are causing the error, you need to determine what the user's effective permissions to the file are. Start with the file or folder in question and determine the contents of its ACL by logging on as the administrator and viewing the file's security properties. Record all the group SIDs in the ACL, paying special attention to any Deny ACE. Once you know all the group SIDs, determine the membership of those groups until you've tracked down all the users with access.

You will find one of two results: either the user does not have membership in a group that has appropriate access or the user is a member of a group that has a specific Deny ACE on the resource. After you know exactly why the user does not have appropriate access, you can solve the permissions problem.

Don't add users to existing security groups to solve security-related problems. Existing groups are likely to have wide access to resources beyond those required to solve the immediate problem. Determine the full scope of the problem and create a new resource security group with the access required to solve the specific permissions problem. Then you can add account groups to the resource group to eliminate the permissions problem for several groups of users without inappropriately increasing access to other resources. This is a prime example of why separating account and resource groups makes security administration more flexible.

Practice: Securing Files and Folders

In practice, managing permissions is quite easy—the interface is intuitive and simple. In this practice, you will use the recommended method of separating users and resources into two types of security groups and make the account groups members of the resource groups. While slightly more convoluted than simply securing resources using account groups, this method scales very well to larger networks and actually simplifies security administration after the initial configuration.

Tip   You will notice that resource groups parallel the folder structure and that account groups parallel the Active Directory structure. Keeping this parallelism intact throughout your network will keep security administration simple in any size of network.

Exercise 1: Setting Permissions on Files and Folders

In this exercise, you create a set of secured folders for each of the OUs in the Fabrikam corporation. You use global security groups to contain user accounts, and you secure the folders using resource security groups. To provide access to users, you then make the global security groups containing the user accounts members of the resource groups that are used to secure the folders. To accomplish this, you need to create a number of security groups and folders. You will use these groups and folders in other lessons.

▶ **To create a security group**

1. Start the Active Directory Users And Computers management console.

2. Expand domain.fabrikam.com and Departments.

3. Click Design, and then click New Group on the toolbar.

4. Type **Design Users** in the Group Name and Group Name (Pre-Windows 2000) boxes as shown in Figure 4.2, and click OK.

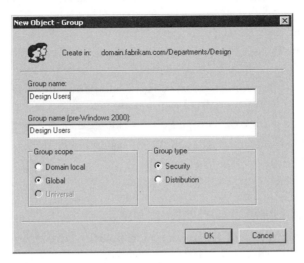

Figure 4.2   Naming a security group

5. Double-click the Design Users group.

6. Click the Members tab, and click Add.

7. Double-click the following users: Syed Abbas, Kim Abercrombie, Humberto Acevedo, and Pilar Ackerman.

8. Click OK to finish adding members, and then click OK to confirm.

▶ **To create numerous security groups**

1. Create a global security group called Engineering Users in the Engineering Department OU with the following members: Amy E. Alberts, Francois Ajenstat, Jay Adams, Kim Akers, and Terry Adams.

2. Create a global security group called Finance Users in the Finance Department OU with the following members: Gary E. Altman, Gregory F. Alderson, Michael Allen, Michelle Alexander, and Sean P. Alexander.

3. Create a global security group called Human Resources Users in the Human Resources OU with the following member: Nancy Anderson.

4. Create a global security group called Information Technology Users in the Information Technology OU with the following members: Chris Ashton, John Arthur, Karen Archer, Pamela Ansman-Wolfe, and Zainal Arifin.

5. Create a global security group called Marketing Users in the Marketing OU with the following member: Chris Ashton.

▶ **To create a resource group**

1. In the Active Directory Users And Computers management console, expand domain.fabrikam.com and Departments.

2. Click Design, and click New Group on the toolbar.

3. Type **Design Folder** in the Group Name and Group Name (Pre-Windows 2000) boxes (see Figure 4.2).

4. Select the Domain Local scope as an optimization because this group will contain only users from this domain, and click OK.

5. Double-click the Design Folder resource group, and click the Members tab.

6. Click Add, and double-click the Design Users global security group to add its members to the resource group.

7. Click OK, and then click OK again.

▶ **To create numerous resource groups**

1. Create a domain local security group called Engineering Folder in the Engineering OU. Add the Engineering Users global security group as a member of this group.

2. Create a domain local security group called Finance Folder in the Finance OU. Add the Finance Users global security group as a member of this group.

3. Create a domain local security group called Human Resources Folder in the Human Resources OU. Add the Human Resources Users global security group as a member of this group.

4. Create a domain local security group called Information Technology Folder in the Information Technology OU. Add the Information Technology Users global security group as a member of this group.

5. Create a domain local security group called Marketing Folder in the Marketing OU. Add the Marketing Users global security group as a member of this group.

▶ **To create a secure folder**

1. In Windows Explorer, double-click My Computer, and double-click the C drive.
2. Right-click in the C drive window, and choose New Folder.
3. Type **Departments** to name the folder.
4. Right-click the Departments folder, and choose Properties.
5. Click the Security tab. Figure 4.3 shows the Security tab for the Departments Properties dialog box.

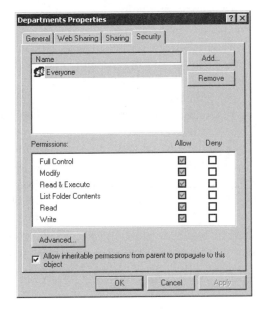

Figure 4.3   The Security tab

6. Clear the Allow Inheritable Permissions check box, and click Remove in the message box that appears. Notice that the ACL list now contains no ACEs.
7. Click Add. The Select Users, Computers, Or Groups dialog box appears.
8. Double-click Domain Admins and Domain Users, and then click OK to close the Select Users, Computers, Or Groups dialog box.
9. Click Domain Admins, and select the Full Control check box in the Allow column.
10. Click Domain Users, and select the Modify check box in the Allow column.
11. Click OK to finish setting permissions.

▶   **To create numerous secure folders**

1. In Windows Explorer, double-click the Departments folder.

2. In the Departments folder, create a folder called Design. In the folder's Properties, clear the Inherit Permissions check box, and click Copy to copy the inherited permissions. Remove the Domain Users ACE, and add an ACE to allow the Design Folder group Full Control.

3. In the Departments folder, create another folder called Engineering. In this folder's properties, clear the Inherit Permissions check box, and click Copy to copy the inherited permissions. Remove the Domain Users ACE, and add an ACE to allow the Engineering Folder group Full Control.

4. In the Departments folder, create a folder called Finance. In this folder's properties, clear the Inherit Permissions check box, and click Copy to copy the inherited permissions. Remove the Domain Users ACE, and add an ACE to allow the Finance Folder group Full Control.

5. In the Departments folder, create a folder called Human Resources. In this folder's properties, clear the Inherit Permissions check box, and click Copy to copy the inherited permissions. Remove the Domain Users ACE, and add an ACE to allow the Human Resources Folder group Full Control.

6. In the Departments folder, create a folder called Information Technology. In this folder's properties, clear the Inherit Permissions checkbox, and click Copy to copy the inherited permissions. Remove the Domain Users ACE, and add an ACE to allow the Information Technology Folder group Full Control.

7. In the Departments folder, create a folder called Marketing. In this folder's properties, clear the Inherit Permissions check box, and click Copy to copy the inherited permissions. Remove the Domain Users ACE, and add an ACE to allow the Marketing Folder group Full Control.

Exercise 2: Troubleshooting Permissions Problems

After you implement the scenario in the previous exercise, the user named Chris Ashton reports that he has access to the Information Technology folder, which is inappropriate. This exercise shows how to troubleshoot permissions problems.

▶ **To determine effective permissions**

1. In Windows Explorer, browse to C:\Departments\Information Technology.

2. Right-click the Information Technology folder, and choose Properties. Click the Security tab to view the folder's ACL, as shown in Figure 4.4.

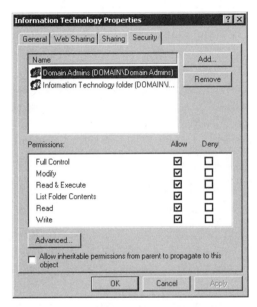

Figure 4.4   The Information Technology folder's ACL

The information contained in the ACL is correct—Chris Ashton does not have a specific SID giving him access. Therefore, his SID must be contained in the Information Technology Folder resource group.

3. Close Windows Explorer.

4. Open the Active Directory Users And Computers management console.

5. Browse to the Information Technology OU.

6. Double-click the Information Technology Folder security group, and click the Members tab, shown in Figure 4.5.

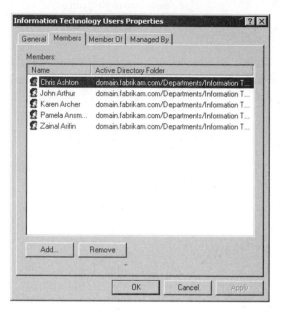

Figure 4.5   The security group's Members tab

The information contained in this folder is correct; there are no inappropriate SIDs listed. Therefore, the security problem must be located in a group that is a member of this group.

7. Click Cancel.

8. Double-click the Information Technology Users security group, and select the Members tab.

   Chris Ashton is incorrectly listed as a member of this group.

9. Select Chris Ashton, and click Remove. Click Yes to confirm the removal, and then click OK to close the Properties dialog box.

When user Chris Ashton logs off and logs on again, his new access token will not contain the SIDs necessary to access the Information Technology folder.

Lesson Review

1. What does Windows attach to a secured resource to manage permissions?

2. What is an access control list?

3. If a user has Read and Write permission because of a membership in one group, has Full Control because of membership in a second group, and has a Deny Write ACE because of membership in a third group, what are the user's effective permissions?

4. If a resource has no ACL, what are the effective permissions?

Lesson Summary

- Windows secures resources by attaching a security descriptor that contains an ACL to each resource. ACLs contain ACEs that specify exactly which security principals are allowed to perform specific actions upon the secured resource.
- Permissions are managed by the NTFS driver. FAT volumes do not support permissions, so all users have full control of resources stored on a FAT volume. For this reason, you should use FAT volumes only for backward compatibility.
- The standard file system permissions are Full Control, Modify, Read & Execute, Read, Write, and List Folder Contents.
- Permissions are cumulative—a user can access a file in any way that is specified by the ACL for any of the SIDs in the user's access token. For example, if membership in one group provides Write access, while membership in another provides Read access, the user's effective permissions are Read and Write access.
- Deny ACEs have priority over Allow ACEs. If a Deny ACE exists for any type of access, access will be denied regardless of the number or type of existing ACEs that allow the specific type of access.

- If an ACL is empty, all users will have no access. The owner can still use the ownership right to set permissions, however. If there is no ACL because the file is stored on a file system that does not support ACLs, then all users have full control.

- When files or folders are created inside a folder, they inherit the permissions settings of the parent folder. When you copy a file, this rule is respected, and the copy receives a copy of the permissions of the recipient folder. When you move a file within the same volume, this rule is not respected, and the original permissions are retained. This occurs because file move operations do not re-create the file—they simply change the directory entries.

Lesson 2: Implementing Share Service Security

Shares are folders that an administrator has published on the local network in which users can store files. *Share security* is the term for restrictions placed on shares. This lesson will teach you to manage share security as an integral part of managing a secure network.

After completing this lesson, you will be able to

- Understand the role of share security in network security
- Create and manage shares
- Manage share security

Estimated lesson time: 30 minutes

Understanding Share Security

Share security consists of account-based access restrictions that are placed on shared folders and implemented by the file-sharing service (Server.exe). User authentication and authorization are managed and enforced by the server service, and file system permissions are managed separately by the file system on the volume that stores the folder. The server service actually manages both file and print sharing, and the ACLs for both types of service are similar.

Note   Share security was the first form of user access control provided by Windows operating system networks, before NTFS permissions were available. You should rely on share permissions only when you need to share a volume that cannot be upgraded to NTFS.

When a user connects to the file-sharing service by mapping a network drive or accessing a file remotely, the service authenticates the user when the session is established in one of the following ways:

- Receiving a valid session ticket during a Windows 2000 domain log on
- Performing Windows NT LAN Manager Authentication during a Microsoft Windows NT domain log on
- Requesting credentials through NetBIOS during Workgroup log on

In all three cases, the server service on the server that is hosting the shared files creates an access token representing the user from the SIDs that are either provided to it (domain log on) or that are determined from the user's local account (workgroup log on). The access token is associated with the user's session and is used for all subsequent access until the user logs off the machine or the session is timed out and destroyed.

Warning   Only Windows NT–based servers create an access token that allows user permissions to be checked by the file system. Earlier versions of Windows and third-party file-sharing services are not capable of checking file system permissions and can use only share security to protect shared files.

Whenever the user's session requests a file, Server.exe compares the user's access token to the share's ACL and determines whether to allow or deny the request. If the request is allowed, the service performs the operation on the file using the user's access token. Because the user's access token contains the SIDs for the user, the security reference monitor can still check NTFS permissions to determine whether the user has permission to operate on the file requested.

This method essentially means that permissions are checked in two places for shared files: once by the sharing service for the share as a whole, and then by the security reference monitor for NTFS files. Because these two mechanisms act independently of one another, any access not allowed by either service will prevent access. Share and NTFS permissions together are not cumulative; users must have permissions from both services to perform an action on a file.

Keep these points in mind when you create share security:

- Share permissions can be applied to FAT and FAT32 volumes because they are enforced by the server service, not the file system.
- Share security applies only to the share point, not to files within the share. Once a user has access to a share, only file system permissions can be used to restrict access to interior files and folders.
- NTFS security is more flexible, more detailed, and more configurable than share security.

Rely on NTFS for file security because it is more robust than share security and cannot be circumvented by connecting to the disk through another file-sharing mechanism such as FTP or by logging on locally. You can use share security as a supplemental security service, but because it can be relied upon only to secure access to the share as a whole and only through the Windows file-sharing service, it is not robust enough to provide for all possible security requirements.

Important   Never share files from a FAT or FAT32 volume on a server because security cannot be controlled for individual files and folders from these volumes.

Managing Shares and Share Security

Creating shares is simple: right-click a folder you want to share and choose Sharing. You can set the share name and permissions directly, and the share will be immediately created and available for use.

You can manage and view all the shares on a server through the Shared Folders snap-in in the Computer Management console of MMC. Using this console, you can easily delete existing shares without browsing through the file system. You can also view open files and sessions using this snap-in. Figure 4.6 shows the Shared Folders snap-in.

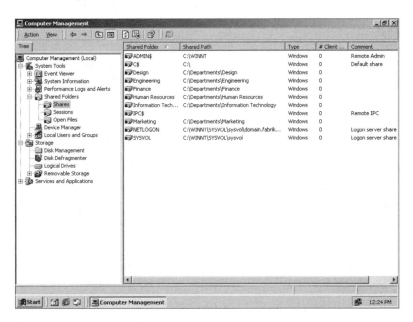

Figure 4.6   The Shared Folders snap-in

Share Security Best Practices

Deciding when to use share security is simple: rely on NTFS permissions for security, and use share security as a supplemental security measure. You cannot rely on share security alone to prevent access to files because it is possible to circumvent share security by connecting to the shared resource through another service such as FTP or Terminal Services. Although share security isn't perfect, there's no reason not to supplement NTFS security with share security. Because NTFS and share security complement each other, inappropriate access can still be prevented if one or the other is improperly configured.

Create separate shares for major groups of users instead of creating monolithic shares that contain numerous folders to which users do not have access. Users will be less likely to attempt to circumvent security if they can't see the folders that they don't have access to. Use the distributed file system (Dfs) to make share management more convenient and scalable.

More Info   For more information about Dfs, see *Microsoft Windows 2000 Server Distributed Systems Guide* (Microsoft Press, 2002).

Practice: Applying Shares and Share Permissions

In this practice, you will use the secure folder structure created in Lesson 1, and apply different shares and share permissions. Rather than creating a single share at the root level of the Departments folder, you will be sharing each department's secured folder separately. In this way, only users who are members of a department can use its folder. If you shared the Departments folder, all domain users could create and attach their own folders at that level, because the permissions on that folder are not restrictive enough to prevent them from doing so.

Exercise 1: Managing Security for Shared Folders

In this exercise, you create a share for each of the major OUs in domain.fabrikam.com. These shared folders will be secured with both share permissions and NTFS permissions.

▶   **To create a shared folder**

1. Browse to C:\Departments\Design in Windows Explorer.
2. Right-click the Design folder, and choose Sharing.

3. Select Share This Folder. The Share Name will default to the folder's name, as shown in Figure 4.7.

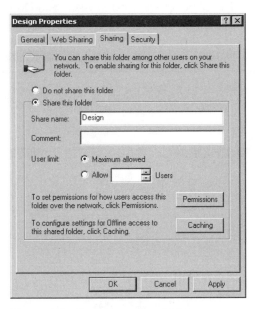

Figure 4.7   Creating a shared folder

4. Click Permissions to view the Permissions settings as shown in Figure 4.8.

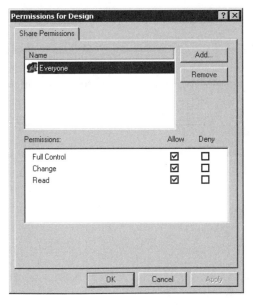

Figure 4.8   Setting permissions for a shared folder

5. Select the Everyone permission, and click Remove.

6. Click Add to open the Select Users, Computers, Or Groups dialog box shown in Figure 4.9. Double-click the Design Users and Domain Admins security groups, and click OK.

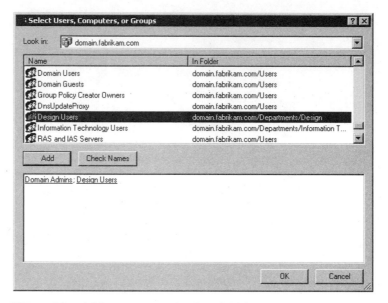

Figure 4.9   Adding groups to the shared folder

7. Select Domain Admins, and, in the Allow column, select the Full Control check box.

8. Select Design Users, and, in the Allow column, select the Change check box.

9. Click OK to close the Permissions dialog box, and then click OK to close the Sharing dialog box. Notice that the folder's icon now indicates that it is being shared.

▶ **To create multiple shares**

1. Share the Engineering folder. Remove the Everyone permission, and add Full Control permission for Domain Admins and Change permission for Engineering Users.

2. Share the Finance folder. Remove the Everyone permission, and add Full Control permission for Domain Admins and Change permission for Finance Users.

3. Share the Human Resources folder. Remove the Everyone permission, and add Full Control permission for Domain Admins and Change permission for Human Resources Users.

4. Share the Information Technology folder. Remove the Everyone permission, and add Full Control permission for Domain Admins and Change permission for Information Technology Users.

5. Share the Marketing folder. Remove the Everyone permission, and add Full Control permission for Domain Admins and Change permission for Marketing Users.

Exercise 2: Managing Share Security

In this exercise, you modify permissions to the Information Technology share. This share is intended to be used as a repository for IT resources such as installable application packages, IT users who are not administrators do not require Read access. You will create the share using Windows Explorer and then modify permissions using the Shared Folders snap-in in the Computer Management console. All share management operations can be managed using either method.

▶   **To modify share permissions**

1. In Windows Explorer, right-click My Computer, and choose Manage.

2. Expand Shared Folders, click Shares, and double-click Information Technology.

3. Click the Share Permissions tab, shown in Figure 4.10.

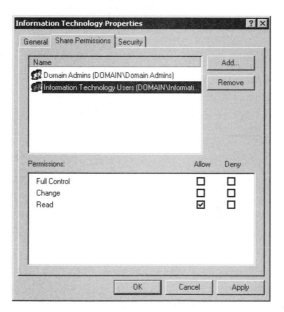

Figure 4.10   The Share Permissions tab

4. Select Information Technology users.

5. In the Allow column, clear the Change permission check box.

   What is the effective difference between clearing the Allow check box and selecting the Deny check box?

6. Click the Security tab, and click the Information Technology Folder group.

7. Clear all the permissions except Allow Read, and click OK to close the Properties dialog box.

Lesson Review

1. If you set NTFS permissions on a shared folder that allow Full Control to the Domain Admins group and no other permissions, but the share security settings allow Full Control to the Everyone group, what are the effective permissions for the folder?

2. Why is it important to rely on NTFS permissions for share security?

3. Why should you set share permissions when NTFS permissions can perform the same security function on an NTFS volume?

Lesson Summary

- Shares have ACLs that can be used to prevent users from connecting to the share through the file server service.

- Share permissions cannot be used to prevent access to specific files or folders within a share. Share permissions are effective on all supported file system types.

- The more restrictive of either the share or the NTFS permission is a user's effective permission. Either security service can be used to prevent access to shared folders, but NTFS security cannot be circumvented by other methods that provide access to the file.

- You should rely on NTFS security to secure shares, and use share security as a supplemental security mechanism.

Lesson 3: Using Audit Policies

In this lesson, you will learn how to use audit policies to track authorized access to secure resources and the exercise of user rights. Auditing allows you to determine when valid users are misusing their authority or when hackers have maliciously made use of a valid user account.

After completing this lesson, you will be able to

- Understand the role of auditing in securing a computer
- Manage the auditing of user rights
- Manage the auditing of file and Active Directory access

Estimated lesson time: 30 minutes

Which Security Mechanisms Are Used in Auditing?

There are two entirely different theories of security in the world:

- Authorization systems seek to prevent unauthorized users from accessing restricted resources, but these systems do not track the activities of valid users. Authorization systems are similar to lock and key systems that prevent theft in the real world. Authorization is implemented through permissions in Windows 2000.

- Accountability systems allow open access to all resources, but they hold users responsible for the way they use resources. Accountability systems are similar to legal restrictions that do not restrict access or behavior but punish perpetrators after the fact. Accountability is implemented through auditing in Windows 2000.

Neither theory works perfectly well by itself. Pure authorization systems cannot ensure that valid users won't cause harm, and pure accountability systems cannot prevent damage to critical resources, they can only allow events to be reconstructed so that the perpetrator can be held accountable. Both systems are used in the real world, and both systems are used in security for the Windows operating system.

How Auditing Works

The Windows operating system has extremely strong support for accountability through its support for auditing. Windows makes it possible for administrators to potentially record every action that a user makes in a system, from logging on or exercising user rights to reading and writing files.

The resulting list of activities is called an *audit trail*, and it creates a body of evidence that can be used to reconstruct a user's activities should it become necessary. The audit trail can also be used to search for anomalous activities, such as user account logon attempts during off hours or an extraordinary number of logon attempts across multiple accounts in a short period.

Auditing is managed and enforced similarly to permissions and rights in Windows. With the combination of permitted activities and user rights, it is possible to record virtually every activity that every user takes on the system.

For securable objects like files or registry keys, a special type of ACL called a *system access control list* (SACL) is contained in the object's security descriptor. Rather than specifying permissions for security principals, the ACEs in an SACL specify the activities that should be audited (recorded in the system log). You can audit every type of access that can be permitted. The security reference monitor makes audit log entries after it checks for proper permissions.

Just as normal permissions can permit or deny activities, auditing can record the success or failure of a potential operation. For example, you can choose to audit only successful logon attempts, only failed logon attempts, or both.

In addition to auditing file access, Windows 2000 can audit the exercise of user rights, such as the right to log on locally or interactively, or the right to take ownership of files. If you choose, every exercise of user rights can be recorded.

Identifying Audit Categories

The types of events you can audit are broken down into a number of categories, based on the services that audit events. For example, the security reference monitor is responsible for monitoring object access, while the WinLogon process is responsible for monitoring logon events. The following list describes the various audit categories:

- *Account logon events* allow you to audit network-based access to the computer, such as attempts to connect to shares.
- *Account management* allows you to audit the creation, deletion, and management of user accounts.
- *Directory services access* allows you to audit access to Active Directory. For example, you could audit attempts to manage certain critical user accounts, domains, or security groups. Monitoring numerous Active Directory service access events creates numerous audit log entries and can put domain controllers under some load.

- *Logon events* allow you to audit the success or failure of local user logon attempts.
- *Object access* enables the auditing of files, folders, and printers.

Planning   You must enable this policy setting to audit these types of objects. Monitoring object access can put the system under extreme load and create numerous audit log entries. You should enable object access monitoring only for specific folders and files that contain sensitive information.

- *Policy change* allows you to audit changes made to Group Policy Objects (GPOs).
- *Privilege use* allows you to audit the use of user rights, such as taking ownership of files. Monitoring privilege use can put the system under load and will create numerous audit log entries.
- *Process tracking* allows you to audit the execution of processes in the system, as well as their attempts to access memory and objects. Monitoring process tracking will create numerous audit log entries.
- *System events* allow you to audit events that affect the security of the system as a whole, such as starting up or shutting down the system, or clearing the event log.

Managing Auditing

To establish auditing for all of the various categories, you must enable audit policy in a GPO linked to either the local GPO or a domain or OU GPO. For most types of auditing, this is all that is necessary to begin recording audited activities in the security log. Audit policy is contained in the computer portion of the GPO, and it applies to all machines within the Active Directory container to which the audit policy GPO is linked.

For file system or printer access, you must enable auditing of object access and then create a SACL in the audited object's security descriptor. This process is very similar to setting permissions on the object and is handled through the Advanced section of the object's Security tab. To audit Active Directory object access, you must enable directory service access and then enable auditing on the specific objects you want to monitor.

All audit events are recorded in the computer's security log. To view audit information, use Event Viewer to read events in the security log. Figure 4.11 shows a server's security log with various audit log entries.

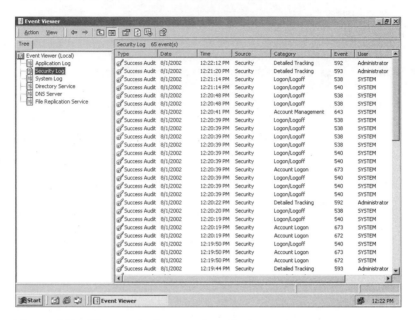

Figure 4.11   The security log records audited events

Avoiding Auditing Problems

There are downsides to the powerful recording capabilities of auditing:

- Auditing can put a significant load on the system, because recording to a log file requires Disk Write access and CPU time. If you enabled auditing for all files on a system, the amount of load caused by auditing would make the machine so slow that it would not be able to operate effectively as a server for multiple users.

- Excessive auditing also fills the security log with events that you don't care about, making it harder to find critical events. Enabling auditing on events like process tracking and privilege use can create a tremendous number of audit log entries, making crucial hacking indicators such as numerous failed logon attempts more difficult to see.

Important   Keep your security log clean by auditing only those types of events that actually indicate hacking activity or abuse by employees.

Administering Auditing Activities

You must administer auditing judiciously by enabling the auditing of rare events that are potentially dangerous and which have a high likelihood of indicating abuse, while allowing routine activities and activities with low potential for abuse to go untracked.

Typically, administrators monitor:

■ Account management operations, such as adding or deleting user accounts and security groups

■ Group Policy changes

■ System events, such as starting up or shutting down the system

■ Network and local logon failure

■ Read and Write access to specifically identified, extremely sensitive documents.

When you enable auditing for relatively rare events, the audit mechanism will not create a noticeable load on your server.

Practice: Enabling Auditing

In this practice, you enable the auditing of easily abused user rights as well as accesses to the Information Technology folder in the domain.fabrikam.com domain.

Exercise 1: Auditing Log On and Log Off Attempts

In this exercise, you establish audit policy to monitor many user and administrative activities. These specific audit policies will not create a significant load on a server because they are relatively rare activities.

▶ **To establish audit policies for users and computers**

1. Open the Active Directory Users And Computers management console.

2. Right-click domain.fabrikam.com, and choose Properties. Click the Group Policy tab shown in Figure 4.12, and double-click Domain Security Policy.

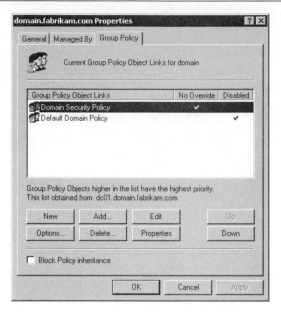

Figure 4.12   The Group Policy tab

3. In the Group Policies console, expand Domain Security Policy, Computer Configuration, Windows Settings, Security Settings, Local Policies, and click Audit Policy to view the various policies. See Figure 4.13.

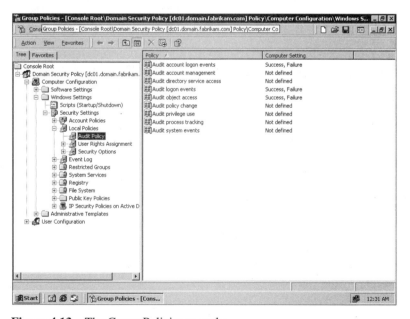

Figure 4.13   The Group Policies console

4. Double-click Audit Account Logon Events, select Define These Policy Settings, select Failure, and click OK. The audit log will report account logon events that fail.

5. Double-click Audit Logon Events, select Define These Policy Settings, select Failure, and click OK. The audit log will report logon events that fail.

6. Double-click Audit Account Management, select Define These Policy Settings, select Success and Failure, and click OK. The audit log will report the creation of or change to any user account or group.

7. Double-click Audit Policy Change, select Define These Policy Settings, select Success and Failure, and click OK. The audit log will report any attempts to change the GPO.

8. Close the GPO, and click OK to close the Properties dialog box.

Exercise 2: Auditing File and Folder Permissions

In this exercise, you establish file and folder auditing for documents contained within a specific folder that stores highly sensitive information. All file activity in this folder will be monitored.

▶   **To enable file system object auditing**

1. Open the domain.fabrikam.com Domain Security Policy.

2. Expand Domain Security Policy, Computer Configuration, Windows Settings, Security Settings, Local Policies, and click Audit Policy.

3. Double-click Audit Object Access to open the Security Policy Setting dialog box as shown in Figure 4.14.

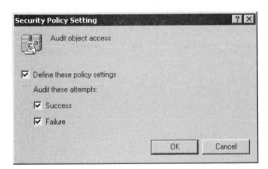

Figure 4.14   Defining the policy for object access

4. Select Define These Policy Settings, select Success and Failure, and click OK. The audit log will report any attempts to access the object.

5. Close the GPO and any other open windows.

▶ **To set audit policy on a specific folder**

1. In Windows Explorer, browse to C:\Departments.
2. Right-click Finance, and choose Properties.
3. Click the Security tab, and click Advanced.
4. Click the Auditing tab, and click Add.
5. In the Select User, Computer, Or Group dialog box, double-click Everyone to open the Auditing Entry dialog box, as shown in Figure 4.15.

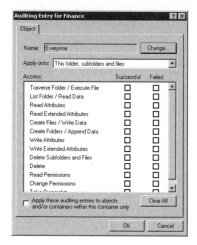

Figure 4.15   Auditing Entry dialog box

6. Select the Successful and Failed check boxes for
   - Create Files /Write Data
   - Create Folders /Append Data
   - Delete Subfolders And Files
   - Delete
   - Change Permissions
   - Take Ownership
7. Click OK to finish setting Audit ACEs, click OK to close the Access Control Settings dialog box, and click OK to close the folder Properties dialog box.

Exercise 3: Monitoring the Audit Log

In this exercise, you create an audit trail by creating and deleting a file in the Finance folder. Once the audit trail is created, you can view the audit log.

▶ **To create an audit trail**

1. In Windows Explorer, browse to C:\Departments\Finance.
2. Right-click in the folder, point to New, and choose Text Document.
3. Type **Finance Data.txt** as the name of the document.
4. Double-click Finance Data.txt to open the document.
5. Type **This is sample Data**.
6. Save and close the text document.
7. Right-click Finance Data.txt, and choose Delete.
8. Click Yes to confirm that you want to delete the text document.
9. Close all open folder windows.

▶ **To view the audit log**

1. Click Start, point to Programs, point to Administrative Tools, and click Event Viewer.
2. Click Security Log.
3. Browse through the security log from the bottom up as shown in Figure 4.16. Find the event marking the creation of the file New Text Document.txt.

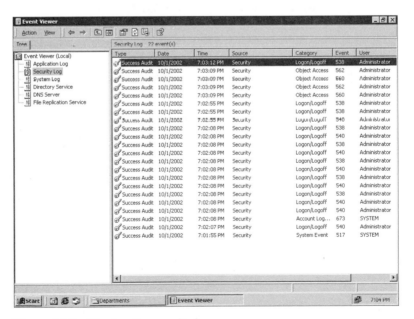

Figure 4.16   Viewing the security log

4. Browse through subsequent object access events.

You will notice a delete event for the New Text Document.txt, which actually indicates that the file has been renamed. Subsequent audit log entries for this file will refer to it as Finance Data.txt.

5. Browse up through subsequent object access events for the Finance Data.txt file.

You will notice a write data event and a delete event for this file.

6. Close the Event Viewer.

Lesson Review

1. Why should you be judicious in your use of auditing rather than audit all possible events?

2. How would you use auditing to determine if hackers are attempting to run a password list against the administrative account of a computer attached to the Internet?

3. How would you use auditing to determine if an employee has been changing the reported hours worked in a Microsoft Excel spreadsheet after the accounting department has left at 5:00 P.M.?

4. How does auditing prevent users from damaging files to which they have access?

Lesson Summary

- Windows supplements its authentication-based security by providing support for event auditing, which allows authorized users to be held accountable for their activities in the system.

- Windows can audit numerous categories of events, including access to specific files, folders, printers, and Active Directory objects, as well as the use of user rights such as logging on to a system.

- Certain types of auditing can create excessive load on the system. To avoid excessive load, you should audit object access only for files and folders that contain sensitive information.

- Most computers should be audited, at a minimum, for user account creation and management, failed local and network logon attempts, and changes to group policy. These events should be relatively rare, and they can alert you to hacking activity.

Lesson 4: Including Registry Security

In this lesson, you will learn about registry security and the RegEdt32 security registry editor.

After completing this lesson, you will be able to
- Understand the role of registry security in securing computers
- Modify permissions on registry keys

Estimated lesson time: 15 minutes

Why Use Registry Security?

The *registry* is the central configuration database for Windows and most software installed on a Windows-based computer. Internally, the registry is viewed as a hierarchical structure of keys, which can contain either keys or values. Values are named identifiers containing simple data types such as integers (whole numbers) or strings (text) that store configuration information required for the operating system and installed applications that make use of the registry.

Because the information stored in the registry controls the configuration of the operating system, indiscriminate changes to it can dramatically affect the security of the system as a whole. For example, hackers could insert keys that would cause kernel-level drivers to be loaded, which would have open access to the system inside the kernel's security boundary. It would be possible to replace nearly any component of the operating system with a non-secure mimic, which would subsequently fail to prevent inappropriate access. Therefore, controlling access to the registry is critical to keeping a computer secure.

The registry itself is read from files on disk. This fact might lead you to believe that file system security could be used to secure the registry. However file system security can be used only to secure files as a whole—it cannot be used to secure internal portions of a file independently. Because each registry file contains numerous keys, and because the keys require different security settings depending upon their function, file system security is not granular enough to provide security for the registry.

More Info   To learn more about the registry, its purpose, and structure, refer to the *Microsoft Windows 2000 Server Resource Kit* (Microsoft Press, 2002).

To properly implement security, registry keys have ACLs that determine exactly how security principals are able to access and modify the keys. ACLs in the registry work in exactly the same way as ACLs do for the rest of the system—they contain ACEs, which bind a specific security principal to a certain type of access that can be allowed or denied.

Editing the Registry

There are two primary registry editing tools:

- *Regedit*, which was first included with Microsoft Windows 95, presents the registry as a single hierarchical tree. Because Windows 95 did not implement ACL security on registry keys, Regedit cannot manage registry permissions.
- *RegEdt32*, which was first included with Windows NT 3.5, presents the registry in five different windows corresponding to the different files (also called hives) from which the keys are loaded. RegEdt32 is the only registry editing tool that allows administrators to directly modify registry key ACLs.

Warning   Indiscriminately editing the registry is extremely likely to cause unintended malfunction. You should never edit the values or the ACL of a registry key unless you fully understand the impact on the operation of the system.

The operating system establishes registry security settings for crucial keys during its installation. Likewise, applications set permissions for their own registry keys when they are installed. Editing the registry is usually not required for routing administration, and modifying registry security is very rare.

However, various security tools such as the Internet Information Services (IIS) Lockdown tool and the Microsoft Baseline Security Analyzer will increase, or recommend manually increasing, the security of many registry keys. The settings in these tools have been established and tested by Microsoft and are appropriate for the level of security implemented by the specific tool.

Tip   Stay up to date on Microsoft security tools, practices, and checklists at *http://www.microsoft.com/technet/security/tools/tools.asp*

For the most part, registry key permissions are established so that users cannot modify registry keys outside the HKEY Current Users hive. Administrators are permitted wide access to registry keys and are prevented only from seeing and modifying the portions of the registry where the Security Accounts Manager security database is stored. These settings are appropriate for the vast majority of users.

For facilities with a hierarchy of network administrators, it may be appropriate to create customized security settings. However, custom registry security settings must be rigorously tested in the context of every affected security group to ensure that computers operate properly. Strange and obscure errors are likely to result from the inability of applications and the operating system to read and change registry keys.

The registry in Windows 2000 is secure against all known registry attacks, and it is not normally necessary for administrators to modify registry security to keep users from causing problems. When registry permissions problems are discovered that allow hackers to exploit systems, Microsoft releases hotfixes to change security, so registry permissions are kept up to date through the normal patching mechanism.

Practice: Exploring the Registry

In this practice, you lower registry security to allow the administrator to explore the registry structure of the Security Accounts Manager for training purposes on a test machine. You will modify the permissions on a registry key to enable administrators to view the contents of the Security Accounts Manager.

Warning   This practice will reduce the security of the system that you perform it on, and it should only be performed on a test machine.

▶   **To view the contents of the Security Accounts Manager**

1. Click Start, and click Run.
2. Type **regedt32** in the Run dialog box, and press ENTER.
3. Click the HKEY_LOCAL_MACHINE window.
4. Double-click SAM. Click the dimmed SAM key that appears below the top-level SAM key, as shown in Figure 4.17.

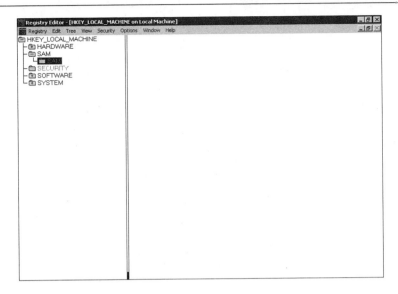

Figure 4.17   The Registry Editor

5. From the Security menu, choose Permissions.

6. Select Administrators, and then select Allow Read. Click OK. Notice that the SAM key is now available.

7. Double-click the SAM key to show its subkeys.

8. Explore the SAM key to view details about how local accounts are stored on the server, as shown in Figure 4.18.

Figure 4.18   Viewing key details in the Registry Editor

9. Click the SAM subkey under the SAM key in HKEY_LOCAL_MACHINE.
10. From the Security menu, choose Permissions.
11. Click Administrators, and clear the Allow Read check box. Click OK.
12. Close the registry editor.

Lesson Review

1. What security mechanism is used to provide security for registry keys?

2. How are registry permissions problems in Windows 2000 normally dealt with?

3. What tool is used to modify registry permissions in Windows?

Lesson Summary

- The Windows 2000 registry stores configuration settings for the operating system and installed applications. Because these configuration settings affect security, controlling access to the registry is critical. Windows 2000 uses permissions to control access to registry keys.

- Registry security is strong by default in Windows 2000, and it is not normally managed by administrators. Administrators can use RegEdt32 to immediately strengthen registry security when vulnerabilities are discovered.

C H A P T E R 5

Certificate Authorities

About This Chapter

This chapter covers certificate authorities and Microsoft Certificate Services. A *certificate authority* (CA) is a service that accepts and completes or revokes certificate requests. *Certificate Services* is the Microsoft Windows 2000 tool that allows users to request and obtain encryption certificates for use by numerous security services of Windows 2000, such as smart card logon and e-mail encryption.

Chapter 6, "Managing a Public Key Infrastructure," covers the various ways that certificates can be used specifically, including detailed information about how to request certificates within a domain and outside a domain.

Exam Tip   Be sure you understand the differences between a root CA and a subordinate CA, as well as the difference between an enterprise CA and a stand-alone CA. You should also know how to protect a root CA from hacking attempts.

Before You Begin

To complete this chapter, you must have

- The dc01.domain.fabrikam.com Windows 2000 Server configured with Active Directory
- Windows 2000 Server joined to the domain as a member server—Active Directory need not be installed on this server
- Your original Windows 2000 Server installation CD-ROM

Lesson 1: Understanding Certificates

Before you can begin to use certificates and certificate authorities, you need to understand what certificates are and how they work. This lesson covers the core concepts of certificates, along with encryption, public key encryption, and digital signatures.

After completing this lesson, you will be able to

- Understand encryption
- Understand public key encryption
- Explain the difference between secret keys, public keys, and private keys
- Understand digital signatures
- Understand certificates

Estimated lesson time: 20 minutes

How Encryption Works

Encryption is the technological basis behind certificates. While certificates use public key encryption, you must understand basic secret key encryption to understand public key encryption.

Secret Key Encryption

With *secret key encryption*, also called symmetric key encryption, you use a single key for both encrypting and decrypting data. In traditional secret key encryption systems, a document (called a plain text) is encoded by performing a mathematical operation (called an algorithm) on each character in the text using another number (called the key). For example, you might encrypt a locker combination of 21-17-42 using the algorithm "add" and a key of 21:

$$21 + 21 = 42$$
$$17 + 21 = 38$$
$$42 + 21 = 63$$

The resulting encrypted combination is 42-38-63. Only users who know the algorithm ("add") and the key (21) can decrypt the combination, so you can publicize the encrypted value without fear that anyone will know the true combination.

To decrypt the encrypted text, the reverse function must be used. In this example, "add" was used to encrypt the text, so "subtract" must be used to decrypt the encrypted value. However, the same key is used to perform the decryption. Because the same key value is used for encryption and decryption, secret key algorithms are referred to as *symmetrical algorithms*.

Note While this example is simple, all secret key cryptosystems work this way. Only the complexity of the algorithm and the length of the key changes.

There's a problem with secret key algorithms, though: while you can transmit the encrypted text to any party without fear of it being decrypted, you cannot transmit the key to the party that should decrypt it because, if the key is intercepted during transmission, it can be used to decrypt the text. The inability to transmit a secret key to remote parties makes pure secret key systems inappropriate for transmitting information over public venues like the Internet.

Public Key Encryption

The solution to the key transfer problem was discovered in 1975 by cryptographic researchers. They arrived at a class of mathematical functions that have two different keys: one key to encrypt data, and a different key to decrypt the data. Because they use different keys for encryption and decryption, these algorithms are referred to as *asymmetrical algorithms*.

You still can't transmit the decryption key across a public medium because it could be intercepted and used to decrypt the encrypted data. But you can transfer the encryption key across a public medium without compromise because it cannot be used to decrypt the message.

To transmit a message securely, the sender asks the receiver for its encryption key. Because the encryption key can't be used to decrypt the message, this transfer is safe no matter how it's sent. The sender then uses the encryption key to encrypt the message, and sends the encrypted text to the receiver. The encrypted text is indecipherable without the decryption key, so this transfer is also safe. Finally, the receiver uses the decryption key to decode the message. The decryption key has never left the receiver's possession, so it has remained secure throughout the process, as shown in Figure 5.1.

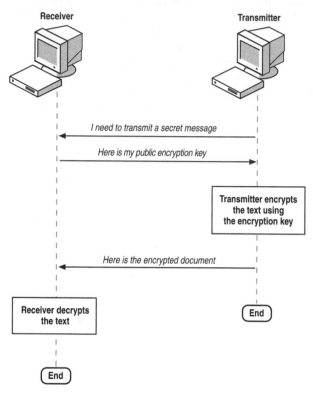

Figure 5.1   The public key exchange process

Because the encoding key is sent over a public medium, it is referred to as the *public key*. The decryption key cannot be revealed, so it is referred to as the *private key*.

Note   Anyone can encrypt a message to a receiver using an intercepted public key. Public key encryption cannot be used to verify identity because the ability to transmit messages to the receiver is open to anyone. However, once encrypted, the messages cannot be decrypted by anyone but the intended receiver.

Verifying Identities with Digital Signatures

Digital signatures are used to verify identities by encrypting identity information, such as contact information, in such a way that anyone can decrypt the information to verify it, but only the originator can encrypt the information. This is similar to the concept of a traditional signature: anyone can read and verify it, but only the person who developed the signature can sign a valid copy of it.

Digital signatures work by using the concept of public key encryption in reverse. Using the same type of algorithms as public encryption (in many cases, the same algorithms), digital signatures reverse the role of the encryption and decryption keys.

- In a public key cryptosystem, the encrypting key is the public key and the decrypting key is the private key.
- In a digital signature system, the encrypting key is the private key and the decrypting key is the public key.

By holding the encryption key privately and publicizing the decryption key, digital signatures allow transmitters to prove that they are undoubtedly the same security principal that encrypted the message using the original encryption key that they hold private.

By appending a digital signature to any plain text document, the receiver of the document can prove the document's validity by decrypting the digital signature using the decryption key. Of course, that proves only that the digital signature is valid—the remainder of the plain text is unprotected.

To extend this protection to the entire document, the plain text portion of the document is processed through a checksum algorithm, one that can be as simple as adding all the data in the document into a single, large number, and including the resultant number inside the encrypted digital signature. The receiver can verify the entire contents of the document by running the same checksum algorithm on the document and ensuring that its calculated checksum equals the stored checksum inside the encrypted portion of the digital signature.

To summarize, digital signatures can guarantee that the entity that created a certain digital signature key is the same entity that later used it to transmit various documents. But no algorithm can tie the identity of an individual or organization to a specific pair of keys.

Combining Encryption and Certificates

Certificates combine numerous features of public key encryption and digital signatures to create a complete encryption and proof-of-identity solution.

Certificates are data structures that can contain numerous public keys, private keys, secret keys, and digital signatures. Primarily, certificates are used to perform trusted third-party authentication. Trusted third-party authentication allows trust to exist between parties who have no trust relationship, but who both trust a third-party service, called a *certificate authority* (CA), to process certificate requests. Both parties trust that the certificate authority has verified the identity of the other party.

To create a certificate:

1. The user generates a pair of encryption keys for use in public key encryption, and optionally another pair for use in digitally signing documents. These keys, along with identity information like the user's name, taxpayer ID, and e-mail address, are then encoded into a certificate request.
2. The certificate request is sent to a CA for certification.
3. The CA applies its own standards for verifying the identity of the requester and either rejects the request, if it's determined to be invalid, or signs the request.

At this point, the certificate contains the digital signature decryption key of the user, which has been validated by the digital signature of the CA. That signature contains a checksum that validates the user's digital signature decryption key. This signature key can be used to validate any remaining information in the certificate, such as a separately generated public key that can be used to encrypt documents going to the user who generated the certificate.

Because the transmitter's digital signature decryption key was decryptable using the CA's decryption key, the CA has vouched for the identity of the transmitter. The receiver can add the user's digital signature decryption key to its cache of trusted entities and can use it to validate documents from the user in the future. By this mechanism, trust in the CA has been conferred upon the user whose signature was signed by the CA. When a CA vouches for an entity by signing its digital signature, it is certified.

Note   *Signing* with a digital signature means that the CA first uses some physical means to verify the user's identity, such as an administrator identifying the person by sight, then performs a checksum operation on the user's digital signature, and finally includes that checksum in an additional digital signature that is appended to the certificate.

Certificate Hierarchies

A hierarchy of CA certification can go on indefinitely—any CA can be certified by any other CA, ad infinitum. For example, engineers at Fabrikam can have their certificates signed by the engineering CA at Fabrikam. This means that any two engineers at Fabrikam can trust each other because their identities have been verified by the engineering CA. The engineering CA can in turn be certified by the Fabrikam enterprise CA, which certifies all the subordinate CAs in the enterprise. With this certification, an engineer can present his certificate to any other user at the company, and that receiver can extend trust because they can decrypt the Fabrikam enterprise CA digital signature, which allows them to trust the engineering CA digital signature, which allows them to trust the engineer's digital signature.

When certificates are used pervasively throughout an enterprise and the CAs that have issued these certificates have the same root CA, the collection of CAs and certificate-based services is referred to as a *public key infrastructure* (PKI).

If users at Fabrikam need to trust engineers at Microsoft, both companies can have their enterprise root certificates signed by a third party that they both trust, such as VeriSign, Inc. When both companies have their enterprise root certificates signed by the same trusted third party, trust can be extended across corporate boundaries, with the parties secure in the knowledge that all are who they say they are. Figure 5.2 shows a list of some of the CAs that are, by default, trusted by Microsoft Internet Explorer.

Figure 5.2   Certificate authorities in Internet Explorer

Root Certification Authorities

Ultimately, users and companies have to trust some authority to act as a root certifying authority. In an ideal world, there would be one single root certifying authority that everyone trusts, but because trust cannot be legislated, this single authority might never exist.

Currently, users and companies choose a certifying authority that they reasonably believe will authenticate the identities of everyone that they certify. There are numerous companies that perform this function for a fee. When two independent organizations need to establish a trust relationship, they must agree on a third party to certify each of them. The other option is to sign each other's root certificates and agree to trust one another without a third party.

In the United States, the National Institute of Standards and Technology (NIST) is establishing a government-run root certifying authority for purposes of authenticating communications among government agencies. However, the government lags far behind commercial certifying authorities, which are currently available world wide to perform validation services and to provide certificates rooted in their trust hierarchies.

Planning   Anyone can create a root CA by setting up a CA that does not have its certificate signed by another CA. To establish a trust hierarchy, this root CA can sign the certificates of other CAs. It is not necessary to have a CA's certificates signed by anyone if all parties involved in the certified transaction trust the CA. For most businesses, this means that certificates used entirely within the company, such as to perform logon authentication or encrypt internal e-mail, can be self-certified by the company without relying on external trust providers. In fact, it's safer, because trust won't be conferred on anyone who has managed to forge a certificate from a popular certifier.

Certificate Expiration

Certificates have a built-in expiration date included in their identity information that tells recipients when the certificate should no longer be trusted. Expiration is important in digital certificates to prevent factoring, or brute force, attacks against the certificate.

In a *brute force* or *factoring attack*, a hacker attempts to determine the private key by signing a document using all possible values until the digital signatures match. With a single computer, this would take an extraordinarily long time, but with the Internet's ability to pool the resources of millions of computers in a single attack, it would become possible to factor all possible values of an extremely important digital signature—for example, a digital signature used by Microsoft to prove the validity of an update or a root certificate used by a popular CA like VeriSign or Thawte. If the private keys for these digital signatures could be factored, the hackers could forge certificates using their identities and convince any party that trusted the exploited party to trust them. Once these single certificates have been factored, trust in the CA would evaporate. Therefore, root certificates for public certifiers are a likely target for massive factoring efforts by large groups of hackers.

Certificate expiration thwarts this attack by telling certificate receivers to distrust the certificate after a reasonably short period of time, such as two years. Because no factoring attack could take less time using means available before the expiration date, factoring attacks will not succeed in time for them to be useful. If computing methods become available that make decryption easier, future certificates can use shorter expiration times or change the algorithm to a stronger mechanism.

Figure 5.3 shows the Certificate dialog box for a selected certificate. This information includes the certificate's expiration date.

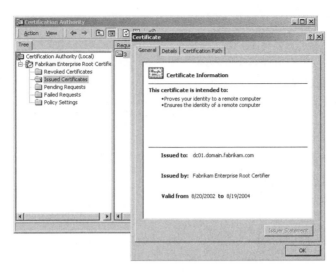

Figure 5.3   The Certificate dialog box

Before a certificate expires, most CA implementations negotiate with the trusted CA to which the certificate applies to receive an updated certificate with new keys (and potentially, specifying a new and stronger encryption algorithm). If the expiration date goes by without a new certificate exchange, both parties must manually establish trust using the same method that was used to establish trust originally.

Certificate Revocation Lists

Brute force attacks are only one possible reason why certificates should be periodically invalidated. The most important reason to invalidate a certificate is that the association between the CA and the certified entity has changed. For example, an employee might change positions within a company or leave the company. This means that the company should no longer certify that employee's certificates.

It's also possible that a hacker might have obtained access to a user's computer and extracted the private keys for that user's certificate. This would enable the hacker to impersonate the user by signing documents.

In these and many other cases, it's important for a CA to be able to revoke certificates before their expiration date. The mechanism for revoking specific certificates is simple: the CA publishes a list of certificates that are no longer valid. This list is called a *certificate revocation list* (CRL). When a certificate is received, the receiver can check the CA's published CRL to ensure that the certificate has not been revoked. Figure 5.4 shows an example of a CRL.

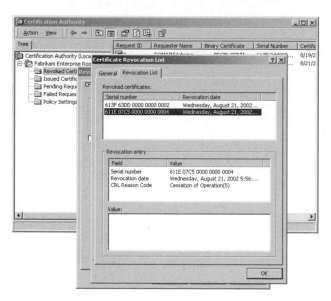

Figure 5.4   A CA's certificate revocation list

The actual mechanism of publishing a CRL is not standardized. Some PKI systems publish their CRL using HTTP; others publish text files on FTP sites. Microsoft uses two methods: publishing a text file using Internet Information Services (IIS), and publishing the CRL in Active Directory. All Microsoft services use the Active Directory-integrated CRL, while third-party services that are not Active Directory-integrated can use the text file published by IIS to determine whether certificates have been revoked.

Uses for Certificates

Because certificates validate identity and can contain other useful information, they are used primarily in situations where verifying identity is critical, such as logon authentication and computer authentication. For example, Windows 2000 can be configured to use certificates stored on smart cards for log on rather than storing them in the registry and asking users for a user name and password.

More Info   Chapter 6, "Managing a Public Key Infrastructure," details the issuance and use of encrypted certificates.

Because certificates can contain information in addition to the digital signature keys, they are often used to transport public keys for encryption. The certificate simultaneously validates the identity of the person publishing the public key and delivers the key, so that the receiver can send encrypted texts to the publisher.

Important   By including public keys for encryption inside certificates, both parties to a secure exchange can be certain of each other's identity. In this way, certificates are used to assure identity in a way that public key encryption alone cannot.

Public key encryption is primarily used to send encrypted e-mail and to establish Secure Sockets Layer (SSL) encrypted Web sessions between a Web browser and a Web server.

Finally, the PKI system uses certificates to validate the identities of CAs to create a hierarchy of trust.

Lesson Review

The following questions are intended to reinforce key information in this lesson. If you are unable to answer a question, review the lesson and try the question again. Answers to the questions can be found in the appendix.

1. What is the difference between a symmetrical algorithm and an asymmetrical algorithm?

2. How does a digital signature system differ from a public key cryptosystem?

3. How does a certificate authority sign a document?

4. How does a CA certify another CA?

Lesson Summary

- Secret key encryption allows two parties to exchange documents securely over a public medium by encrypting the documents using an algorithm and a secret key known to both parties. There is no way to transmit the secret key without risking interception, however.

- Public key encryption solves the key transmission problem by using asymmetrical algorithms that use a public key to encrypt data and a separate private key to decrypt data. The public key can be sent over a public medium because it cannot be used to decrypt the encrypted text.

- Digital signatures reverse the purpose of the keys used in public key encryption to allow any recipient to decrypt a text that can be encrypted only by the holder of the secret key. As long as the original digital signature public key is trusted, any document sent by the signer can be trusted.

- Certificates are digital signatures that have themselves been signed by one or more CAs.

- CAs vouch for the identity of the entities whose certificates they've signed. CAs themselves are verified by superior CAs up to a root CA that is self-certified. As long as all participants trust the root CA, the identities of all participants in the trust hierarchy can be trusted.

Lesson 2: Installing Windows 2000 Certificate Services

Windows 2000 creates a public key infrastructure (PKI) through the use of Microsoft Certificate Services, which establishes a CA on a server. In this lesson, you will learn how to install and configure a CA for use in Windows 2000 and for use with third-party PKI products.

After completing this lesson, you will be able to

- Install Certificate Services for use in a Windows 2000 domain
- Install Certificate Services for use in third-party PKI systems
- Install Certificate Services as a root CA
- Install Certificate Services as a subordinate CA

Estimated lesson time: 20 minutes

Installing Certificate Authorities

To use certificates in your organization, you must either have your own CA or request certificates from an organization that does. Because there is usually a charge associated with each certificate request from a commercial certifier, it is almost always advantageous to generate certificates locally. Furthermore, to use the advanced authentication features like smart card authentication allowed by Windows 2000 enterprise CAs, you must create your own CA.

Creating a CA in Windows 2000 is simple: install Certificate Services and answer a few questions about the type of CA you want to install. Windows 2000 supports two types of CAs:

- *Enterprise CAs* are part of an enterprise-wide security infrastructure and require Active Directory.
- *Stand-alone CAs* are separate from Active Directory and can issue certificates for extranet or intranet use.

When you install Certificate Services, you must determine which type of CA you intend to install. In addition, you need to determine whether you are installing a *root CA*, which is the topmost CA in the certification hierarchy, or a *subordinate CA*, which requires a CA certificate from the root CA. Your final installation decision is about which *cryptographic service providers* (CSPs) you will use to perform the cryptographic operations for the programming interfaces provided with Certificate Services.

Enterprise CAs

Enterprise CAs are stored in a CA object in Active Directory. Certificates are published in Active Directory, and the CA can be used to generate certificates for specific Windows 2000 purposes such as logging on using smart cards, as well as all purposes for which a stand-alone CA can be used.

Installing an enterprise CA requires the following:

- The installing user must be a member of the Enterprise Admins group.
- A fully-functioning, Active Directory–integrated DNS infrastructure must be available.

Note   Although enterprise CA objects are stored in the Active Directory database, the CA need not be installed on a domain controller.

Users requesting a certificate from an enterprise CA must have an Active Directory account. Certificate requests can be made through Active Directory services by applications that require them.

More Info   Requesting certificates is discussed in Chapter 6, "Managing a Public Key Infrastructure."

Stand-Alone CAs

Installing a stand-alone CA requires administrative privilege on the server. Active Directory is not required, but a stand-alone CA can make use of Active Directory if it is available. Stand-alone CAs are primarily used in situations where Active Directory services are not available, such as for public Web or e-mail services.

Stand-alone CAs can generate certificates for such purposes as exchanging public keys for SSL secure Internet connections and Secure/Multipurpose Internet Mail Extensions (S/MIME) encrypted e-mail. Certificates for stand-alone CAs can be issued and managed through a Web site that is installed during the Certificate Services installation process. This Web site is located at *http://localhost/certsrv* (Figure 5.5) on all machines with both Certificate Services and IIS installed. IIS must be installed for this functionality to work.

Note   Replace *localhost* with the DNS name or IP address of the CA if you are not requesting the certificate from a Web browser on the local machine.

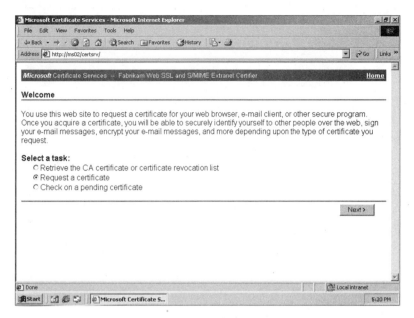

Figure 5.5   The stand-alone CA certificate management Web site

Stand-alone CAs cannot issue certificates that can be used to log on to a Windows 2000 domain.

Root and Subordinate Certificate Authorities

In addition to choosing between the two primary types of CAs, you must also determine whether your CA will be a self-certified root CA or a subordinate CA. Most organizations initially install a root CA and then use that CA to certify all other CAs in the organization. However, you might have multiple root CAs in an organization if you have multiple purposes for which transitive trust is not necessary. For example, you might have an enterprise CA used to create certificates for smart card log on, and a separate root CA for generating S/MIME e-mail encryption certificates for business partners that should not receive the same level of trust as employees.

If you choose to create a subordinate CA, you have to configure the new CA to contact an existing CA to receive its certification. Alternatively, you can finish the installation without certification and later activate the CA by installing a certificate from a parent CA. In Figure 5.6, a certificate is being requested for a subordinate CA during Certificate Services installation.

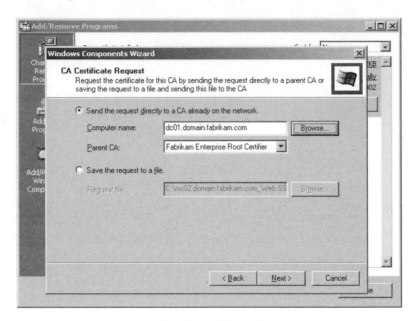

Figure 5.6   Requesting a subordinate CA certificate

Cryptographic Service Providers

The final decision you must make when installing a CA is to determine which CSP you want to use. CSPs determine which algorithms are used to generate keys, encrypt data, and digitally sign documents. The primary difference between them is the strength of their encryption algorithms.

The following list identifies the primary encryption algorithms provided by default CSPs in Windows:

- RC2 is a secret key algorithm used for block encryption of files stored on disk.
- RC4 is a secret key algorithm used for stream encryption of Internet connections such as SSL.

- DES (Data Encryption Standard) is a secret key algorithm used for TCP/IP packet encryption and numerous other uses.
- SHA-1 is used for public key encryption.
- MD5 is used for message signing, password encryption, and digital signatures.

The length of the encryption key directly affects how long it will take to factor all possible values. Each bit of additional key length doubles the length of time (or the number of computers) required to factor the key. Currently, 64 bits is the minimum required length to remain secure for the two-year default period of a certificate if the key is being factored by a single powerful machine (defined as an Intel Pentium 4 running at 2 GHz). Currently, 1 million PC-grade computers connected by the Internet could factor an 80-bit key within two years. A 112-bit double-key DES could be factored by 4 billion PCs in the space of 130,000 years. As you can see, increasing the key length by trivial amounts dramatically improves the security of an encrypted key.

Microsoft provides three primary CSPs:

- Base CSP provides 40-bit RC2, RC4, and 56-bit DES, with 512-bit public keys for signatures and exchanges. Base CSP was originally developed to provide a CSP that could be exported.
- Strong CSP provides 128-bit RC2, RC4, 112-bit double key DES or 168-bit Triple DES.
- Enhanced CSP is the same as Strong CSP with improved encryption of keys.

Warning The Base CSP is weak and should not be used unless backward compatibility is more important than security. On standard computers, 40-bit keys can be factored in just a few days. Base CSP is also the default CSP if you do not select Advanced Options when you install Certificate Services.

Note Strong and Enhanced cannot generate 40-bit keys, but they are backward compatible with the Base CSP and can import 40-bit keys.

Windows 2000 is also distributed with third-party CSPs developed by other software developers for use with their security products. When you install Certificate Services, select Advanced Options in the Certification Authority Type page to see the Public And Private Key Pair page (Figure 5.7), in which you can select the CSPs.

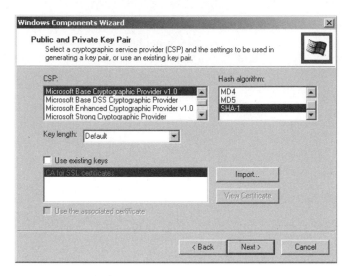

Figure 5.7   Assigning a CSP

Best Practices

Determining how to create your CA hierarchy is not difficult. The first question is whether to install as a root CA or as a subordinate to a third-party trust provider. The simple answer to this question is that, because you can always configure your root CA to trust a third party CA later, there's no reason not to install as a root CA.

The next question is whether your root CA should be a Windows 2000 Active Directory–integrated enterprise CA or a stand-alone CA. Because it is easier to create a certificate hierarchy using enterprise CAs that are Active Directory integrated, your root CA should be an enterprise CA. You can always create stand-alone CAs that are subordinate to your enterprise CA, and you can always root your enterprise CA to an external stand-alone CA later if you need to.

Larger enterprises that plan to issue certificates to other business organizations may want to initially begin with a stand-alone root CA and have that CA certify an enterprise root CA. This will allow the organization to create certificates for external parties that are not trusted for enterprise use. By starting with a stand-alone CA, you can easily shut down the CA after it has certified the enterprise CA to ensure that no hacker can forge a request to the root CA to gain wide trust.

Tip   For maximum security, create a stand-alone root CA that certifies a subordinate enterprise CA that will actually be used for certificate issuance, and then turn off and store the root CA until it is needed to refresh the certificate issuer's certification or affirm certificate requests from new CAs. This methodology prevents hackers or malicious users from exploiting an administrator's account to certify their own CAs.

Finally, you need to determine how many CAs you need to install. In organizations with more than one CA, your first CA should be used only to certify other CAs. In general, your CA architecture should be somewhat analogous to your Active Directory structure, so it's common practice to install the enterprise root CA on the same machine as was used to create the Active Directory forest. Because this CA certifies only other CAs, Certificate Services does not generate much load.

Once you have an enterprise root CA, you can create CAs as necessary to keep up with the demand for certificates. By creating a first tier of CAs in the first domain level below the top of your Active Directory tree, you can determine whether the CA infrastructure is large enough to keep up easily with demand. If it cannot, you can deploy another tier of CAs at the domain level below, and continue expanding your hierarchy until you have enough CAs to keep up with the demand placed upon them.

Tip   You should always use the Microsoft Enhanced CSP unless you have a specific reason for using another CSP, such as instructions from a third-party cryptographic provider. The Enhanced CSP provides the strongest security of the Microsoft standard CSPs and is backward compatible with both the Base CSP and the Strong CSP.

Practice: Establishing a CA Hierarchy

In this practice, you create a CA hierarchy by first creating the enterprise root CA. You then install IIS so that you can create a stand-alone subordinate CA. For larger enterprises or those with strong security requirements, you would first create a stand-alone CA, use that CA to certify the enterprise CA, and then shut down the stand-alone root CA and continue as shown in this practice.

Exercise 1: Installing Certificate Services for an Enterprise Root CA

In this exercise, you establish an enterprise root CA. To complete this exercise, you must log on to the dc01.domain.Fabrikam.com server as a member of the Enterprise Admins group. The default Administrator account for the domain is a member of this group and can be used to complete this exercise.

▶ **To install Certificate Services**

1. Click Start, point to Settings, and click Control Panel.
2. In Control Panel, double-click Add/Remove Programs.
3. In the Add/Remove Programs dialog box, click Add/Remove Windows Components. This launches the Windows Components Wizard.
4. In the Windows Components Wizard, select the check box for Certificate Services. A Microsoft Certificate Services message box appears.
5. Click Yes to acknowledge the warning that the computer cannot be renamed or have its domain affiliation changed once Certificate Services is installed.
6. Click Next.

Note   If you have Terminal Services installed, the Terminal Services Setup page will appear in the wizard. Click Next to accept the default Terminal Services remote administration mode and continue.

---

7. The Certificate Authority Type page (Figure 5.8) appears. Select Enterprise Root CA, select Advanced Options, and click Next.

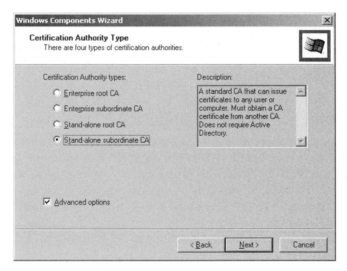

Figure 5.8   Selecting the CA type

Note   You can use this procedure to create a stand-alone root CA by selecting Stand-alone Root CA in this page. All other options are the same.

---

8. The Public And Private Key Pair page (Figure 5.7) appears. Select Microsoft Enhanced Cryptographic Provider as the CSP, and click Next.

9. In the CA Identifying Information page (Figure 5.9), Type **Fabrikam Enterprise Root Certifier** in the CA Name box.

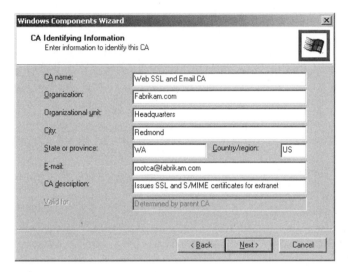

Figure 5.9   The CA Identifying Information page

10. Type **Fabrikam, Inc.** in the Organization box.

11. Type **Redmond** in the City box.

12. Type **WA** in the State box.

13. Type **US** in the Country/Region box.

14. Type **rootca@fabrikam.com** in the E-mail box.

15. Type **Fabrikam Root Certifier** in the CA Description box.

16. Leave the 2 year default duration, and click Next. The Data Storage Location page appears.

17. Ensure that you have placed the Windows 2000 Server installation CD in your CD-ROM drive. To identify where the CA's files will be stored, leave the default setting for the Certificate Database and Certificate Database Log, and click Next.

18. If IIS is running, a message box appears stating that the service must be stopped before proceeding. Click OK to stop IIS and continue.

The service will now generate cryptographic certificates and copy the files necessary for the certificate service from your CD-ROM drive.

Important   Make sure you use a storage location that is backed up on a regular basis.

---

19. Click Finish. Certificate Services is now installed on your server.
20. Click Close to close the Add/Remove Programs window.
21. Close Control Panel.

Exercise 2: Installing Certificate Services for a Stand-alone Subordinate CA

In this exercise, you install a stand-alone CA that is subordinate to the previously installed enterprise CA. For this functionality to work, you must install IIS. You must then install the CA on a member server in the domain.Fabrikam.com domain. The procedure for installing a stand-alone CA is very similar to installing an enterprise CA. If IIS is already installed, you can skip this procedure.

▶ **To install a stand-alone subordinate CA**

1. Click Start, point to Settings, and then click Control Panel.
2. Double-click Add/Remove Programs.
3. In the Add/Remove Programs window, click Add/Remove Windows Components. This launches the Windows Components Wizard.
4. In the Windows Components Wizard, select Certificate Services. A Microsoft Certificate Services message box appears.
5. Click Yes to acknowledge the warning that the computer cannot be renamed or have its domain affiliation changed once Certificate Services is installed.
6. Click Next.

Note   If you have Terminal Services installed, the Terminal Services Setup page will appear. Click Next to accept the default Terminal Services remote administration mode and continue.

---

7. In the Certificate Authority Type page (Figure 5.8), select Stand-alone Subordinate CA, select Advanced Options, and click Next.

8. In the Public And Private Key Pair page (Figure 5.7), select Microsoft Enhanced Cryptographic Provider as the CSP, and click Next.

9. In the CA Identifying Information page (Figure 5.10), type **Fabrikam Web SSL and S/MIME Extranet Certifier** in the CA Name box.

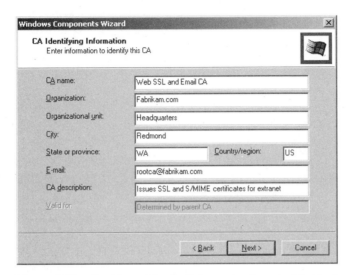

Figure 5.10   Certificate Identity Information is embedded in the certificate

10. Type **Fabrikam, Inc.** in the Organization box.

11. Type **Redmond** in the City box.

12. Type **WA** in the State box.

13. Type **US** in the Country/Region box.

14. Type **rootca@fabrikam.com** in the E-mail box.

15. Type **Issues SSL and S/MIME certificates for extranet** in the CA Description box, and click Next.

16. Leave the default certificate database and log settings as they are. The Data Storage Location page appears.

17. Select Store Configuration Information In A Shared Folder to identify where the CA's files will be stored.

18. Type C:\CAConfig as the name of the shared folder, and click Next.

19. The Root CA selection dialog box appears. Click Browse, select Fabrikam Enterprise Root Certifier, and click OK. The Root CA selection dialog box now appears as shown in Figure 5.11.

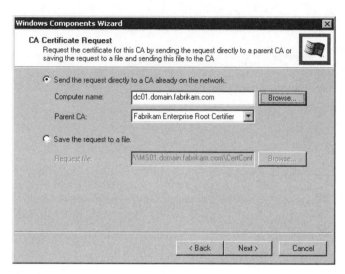

Figure 5.11   The Root CA selection dialog box

20. In the Root CA selection dialog box, click Next. A message box appears asking whether you want to stop IIS. Ensure that you have placed the Windows 2000 Server installation CD in your CD-ROM drive. Click OK to stop IIS.

    The service generates cryptographic certificates and copies the files necessary for the Certificate Service from your CD-ROM drive.

21. Click Finish. Certificate Services is now installed on your server.

22. Click Close to close the Add/Remove Programs dialog box.

23. Close Control Panel.

Lesson Review

The following questions are intended to reinforce key information in this lesson. If you are unable to answer a question, review the lesson and try the question again. Answers to the questions can be found in the appendix.

1. What is the strongest standard CSP provided by Microsoft?

2. How are certificates normally requested from a stand-alone CA?

3. What is the primary difference between an enterprise CA and a stand-alone CA?

4. How many certificate authorities can a single server host?

Lesson Summary

- Stand-alone CAs can be used to generate SSL, S/MIME, and other types of Internet standard certificates. Certificates from stand-alone CAs are requested through the certificate services Web site on the server that hosts the CA.

- Enterprise CAs have all the functionality of stand-alone CAs and can also generate certificates for use within a Windows 2000 domain for purposes such as logging on using a smart card. Active Directory account holders can request certificates through enterprise CAs.

- CAs can be either self-certifying, stand-alone CAs, or subordinate to another CA. The top CA in any organization's CA hierarchy can be configured as a subordinate to a third-party trust provider. To configure a CA as a subordinate CA, you can select the parent CA from the Active Directory list if the server is a member of the domain, or request and install the CA certificate manually.

- CAs can use different CSPs to change the algorithms and key lengths used for the various certificate encryption functions. The Microsoft Enhanced CSP provides the best quality of encryption for most purposes and is backward compatible with the Base CSP and the Strong CSP.

Lesson 3: Maintaining Certificate Authorities

CAs don't require much in the way of specific maintenance. The most important administrative tasks in addition to regular backup are the revocation of certificates that should no longer be used and the maintenance of the CRL.

After this lesson, you will be able to

- Revoke certificates
- View and publish the CRL
- Back up the CRL
- Restore the CRL

Estimated lesson time: 20 minutes

Revoking Certificates

Certificate authorities are designed to issue certificates, but they can also take them back. Certificates are designed to be autonomous—once issued, they contain all the information necessary to validate themselves, so contacting the issuing server is not necessary.

But that doesn't cover the case in which a certificate must be rescinded. There are numerous reasons why a certificate might be obsolete before it expires:

- The business activity using the certificate has been discontinued.
- The association between the organization and the employee represented by the certificate has changed.
- The administrator suspects that the keys have been compromised.

The certificate protocol does not allow for any intrinsic mechanism to rescind a certificate other then expiration. For this reason, the X.509 protocol includes a procedure for listing certificates by serial number that the administrator wants to rescind. This list is called the *certificate revocation list* (CRL).

In Windows 2000, the CRL is stored in Active Directory for enterprise CAs and as a text file in a shared directory for stand-alone CAs. Because of the potential size of the CRL, it is not published to the Active Directory database or the CRL text file each time that a certificate is revoked. Rather, the CRL expires and is republished on a periodic basis that can be set by the administrator. The default period is one week, which is sufficient for most purposes.

Note   It is up to the service receiving the certificate to check the issuing CA when the certificate is presented to determine if the CA has been revoked.

When a particularly important revocation occurs or a large number of certificates have been revoked by administrative action, an administrator can choose to immediately publish the CRL before the normal expiration period.

Issuing Certificates

When a user requests a certificate through Active Directory in an enterprise CA, the certificate is issued by the CA by default. This is automatic because the user's identity is already certified; the user holds a user account in the Active Directory database.

For stand-alone certificates, an administrator must choose to issue each pending certificate request. The administrator must validate the identity of the user and verify that the user issued the request. For example, the administrator might telephone the requestor for verification.

Once the administrator has determined that the request is valid, the administrator can select the certificate in the Pending Requests folder within the CA management console and select Issue. The CA digitally signs the certificate and places it in the Issued Certificates folder so that the user can download it.

Note   The Exchange 2000 Key Management Service (KMS) uses the Windows 2000 Certificate Authority service to automatically generate certificates for Exchange and Outlook users. KMS provides an easy method for recovering lost private keys for users: By right-clicking on the Key Manager and selecting All Tasks, and then clicking Recover Keys, you can select the users who require key recovery. Those users will receive an e-mail from the KMS detailing the steps they need to follow to re-install their private key. More information about KMS is provided with Exchange Server 2000 and the *Microsoft Exchange Server 2000 Resource Kit.*

Backing Up and Restoring CAs

As with all crucial enterprise data, certificates must be backed up to avoid losing them in the event of a hardware failure. If the CA database is lost, a new CA will have to be established. Existing issued certificates would not be revocable, and certificates previously on the CRL could no longer be revoked.

Routine CA Database Backups

Although the CA management console contains a facility for backing up and restoring the certificate database, your primary mechanism for backing up the CA should be the Windows 2000 Backup tool or your enterprise backup management software. The Certificate Database will be picked up as a part of any normal server backup process and can be retained along with your traditional full system backup.

As long as you perform regular full system backups, there is no need to use the backup and restore mechanism provided by the CA management console for the purpose of restoring a CA. The backup and restore mechanism provide by the CA management console is primarily used to transfer a CA from one server to another.

Backing Up the Certificate Database Using the CA Management Console

The Certificate Authority management console provides a mechanism for backing up the CA's certificate as well as the database of issued, pending, and revoked certificates. You can use the CA Backup Wizard to manually back up the CA database, but there is no mechanism for performing automatic periodic backups.

Tip   Treat the CA backup facility as a secondary, manual backup mechanism for such purposes as transferring an existing CA from one server to another or retaining a permanent record of CA certificates.

The CA Backup Wizard is capable of creating full backups or incremental backups. Making incremental backups of the certificate authority, while supported, is not recommended. The problem with incremental backups is that the entire body of backup files from the last full backup through the most recent incremental backup is required to restore the database. The sum total size of all of these backups is no larger than the size of a current full backup. Figure 5.12 provides an example of the contents of a CA Backup folder after a CA backup operation.

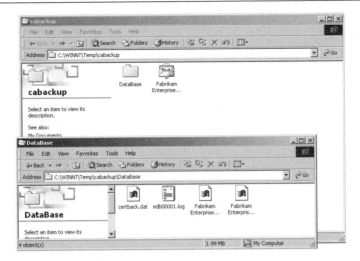

Figure 5.12   A CA Backup folder

Incremental backups are used in traditional backups so that many older sets of data can be retained in case a file is lost. But keeping old copies of a CA has no value. Previous backups of a CA do not contain the most recent CRL, so if you had to restore one, you would not know which certificates were no longer revoked. CA databases are not particularly large. Even very large CAs can be backed up to a file that would be less than a few gigabytes in size. Given the problems that incremental backups can cause and the lack of any real benefit to performing them for a CA, you should always run full backups.

Tip   Consider backing up your CA to flash memory, and keeping a single CA backup on your flash memory device. USB flash memory devices are easy to mount in servers and come in sizes up to 1 GB, which is large enough to back up most CAs. Flash memory is the most reliable form of digital storage available.

Practice: Managing CAs

In this practice, you manage CAs by revoking a certificate, verifying the information in a CRL, updating a CRL, and then changing the CRL publication date. You'll finish by backing up and then restoring a CA.

Exercise 1: Revoking a Certificate

In this exercise, you revoke a certificate that is being discontinued.

▶ **To revoke a certificate**

1. Click Start, point to Programs, Administrative Tools, and choose Certificate Authority. The Certificate Authority console opens.
2. In the console, expand Certification Authority, Fabrikam Enterprise Root Certifier, and select Issued Certificates.
3. In the right pane of the console, right-click the certificate with the Issued Common Name of Fabrikam Web SSL And S/MIME Extranet Certifier, select All Tasks, and then choose Revoke Certificate (Figure 5.13).

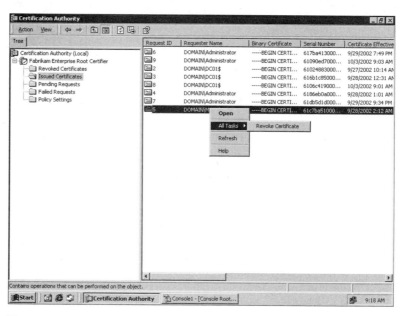

Figure 5.13   Revoking a certificate in the Certification Authority console

4. The Certificate Revocation dialog box appears, as shown in Figure 5.14. In the Reason Code box, select Cease Of Operation, and click Yes. The certificate will disappear from the Issued Certificates list.

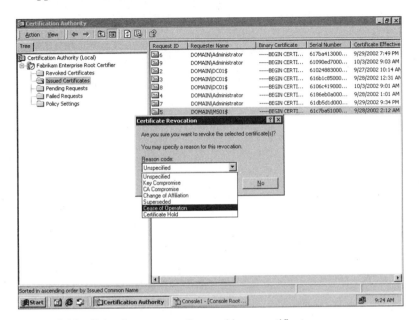

Figure 5.14   Selecting a reason for revoking a certificate

5. Click the Revoked Certificates folder. Note that the certificate now appears in this folder.

Exercise 2: Managing the CRL

This exercise walks you through the procedures for viewing and updating the CRL, and for updating the publication interval.

▶ **To view the CRL**

1. Click Start, point to Programs, Administrative Tools, and then click Certificate Authority. The Certificate Authority console opens.

2. Expand Certification Authority and Fabrikam Enterprise Root Certifier.

3. Right-click Revoked Certificates and choose Properties. The Revoked Certificates Properties dialog box appears.

4. Click View Current CRL.

5. When the Certificate Revocation List dialog box appears, click the Revocation List tab. Verify that the CRL is empty.

   Why does the CRL appear to be empty when certificates have been revoked?

6. Click OK to close the Certificate Revocation List dialog box.
7. Click OK to close the Revoked Certificates Properties dialog box.

▶ **To immediately update the CRL**

1. Right-click Revoked Certificates, point to All Tasks, and choose Publish.
2. A message box appears informing you that the current CRL is still valid. Click Yes to publish a new CRL.
3. Repeat the procedure for viewing the CRL to verify that the revoked certificates now appear in it.

▶ **To change the CRL publication interval**

1. Click Start, point to Programs, Administrative Tools, and click Certificate Authority.
2. Expand Certification Authority and Fabrikam Enterprise Root Certifier.
3. Right-click Revoked Certificates, and select Properties. The Revoked Certificates Properties dialog box appears, as shown in Figure 5.15.

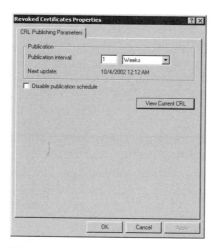

Figure 5.15   The CRL Publication Parameters

4. For the Publication Interval, type **2** in the box, and select Days from the drop-down list box.

5. Click OK. The CRL will now be published every two days.

Exercise 3: Backing Up a CA

In this exercise, you back up a CA to avoid losing the ability to issue, revoke or renew certificates for the CA.

▶ **To back up a CA**

1. Start the Certificate Authority management console.

2. Right-click Fabrikam Enterprise Root Certifier, point to All Tasks, and choose Backup CA. The Certification Authority Backup Wizard appears.

3. Click Next. The Items To Back Up page appears, as shown in Figure 5.16.

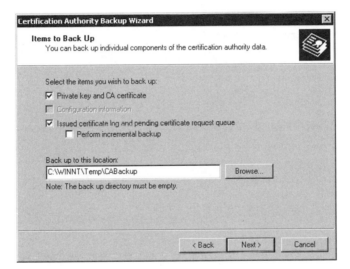

Figure 5.16   Backing up items using the Certification Authority Backup Wizard

4. In the Items To Backup page, select Private Key And CA Certificate, and select Issued Certificate Log And Pending Certificate Request Queue.

5. Type C:\WINNT\Temp\CABackup in the Back Up To This Location box, and click Next.

6. A dialog box appears asking if you want to create the directory. Click OK.

7. Type the same random secure password in both the Password and Confirm Password boxes. Click Next.

8. Click Finish. A progress bar will appear indicating backup progress. When it disappears, the backup is complete.

9. In Windows Explorer, browse to C:\WINNT\Temp\CABackup. Notice that a file called Fabrikam Enterprise Root Certifier.p12 exists, along with a folder called Database, as shown in Figure 5.17. The .p12 file is an export of the CA's certificate. The files inside the Database folder are Active Directory backup files containing all the certificates for the CA.

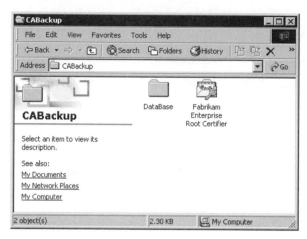

Figure 5.17   A CA Backup certificate and database

Exercise 4: Restoring a CA

In this exercise, you use the Certification Authority Restore Wizard, which is very similar to the Certification Authority Backup Wizard. Using this wizard, you stop the Certificate Services and restore from the files you previously backed up.

▶ **To restore a CA**

1. Start the Certificate Authority management console.

2. Right-click Fabrikam Enterprise Root Server, point to All Tasks, and click Restore CA.

3. A message box appears asking if you want to stop Certificate Services. Click OK.

4. When the Certification Authority Restore Wizard appears, click Next.

5. In the Items To Restore page, select Private Key And CA Certificate, and select Issued Certificate Log And Pending Certificate Request Queue.

6. Click Browse and browse to C:\WINNT\Temp\CABackup, select CABackup, and click OK. Click Next.

7. The Provide Password page appears. Type the password you entered in the previous exercise, and click Next.

8. Click Finish to restore the database.

9. You might see a message box asking for additional incremental files. Click No to indicate that there are no additional files.

10. You might see a message box asking if you would like to start Certificate Services. If so, click Yes. Otherwise, right-click Fabrikam Enterprise Root Certifier, select All Tasks, and click Start Service.

Lesson Review

The following questions are intended to reinforce key information in this lesson. If you are unable to answer a question, review the lesson and try the question again. Answers to the questions can be found in the appendix.

1. What are the two mechanisms through which a certificate can be rendered invalid?

2. What are the two methods by which the CRL is published in Windows 2000?

3. What is the best way to back up a CA?

Lesson Summary

- CAs require very little administration. Outside of normal server backup, administrators can choose to independently back up the CA's certificate and the certificate database using the Certificate Authority management console.

- Certificates can be revoked by the CA that issued them at any time. Reasons for revoking a certificate include no longer offering the service for which the certificate is required, suspected compromise of the certificate's private keys, or a change in relationship between the issuing organization and the certified entity.

- Certificates that have been revoked are listed in the server's CRL, the list of certificate serial numbers that have been revoked. The CRL can be published by any network mechanism. In Windows 2000, the CRL is published in the Active Directory database or in a text file within a shared directory.

- All certificate management functions are performed through the Certificate Authority management console.

C H A P T E R   6

Managing a Public Key Infrastructure

About This Chapter

Your infrastructure of Certificate Authorities (CAs) and certificate-enabled services is called a public key infrastructure (PKI). In Chapter 5, "Certificate Authorities," you learned how to deploy and manage CAs. In this chapter, you learn about the types of certificates that CAs can create and how they are used within Microsoft Windows 2000.

Exam Tip   You need to understand the differences between computer certificates and user certificates, and what each type of certificate is used for.

Before You Begin

To complete the lessons in this chapter, you must have

- An enterprise root CA as configured in Chapter 5
- A stand-alone subordinate CA as configured in Chapter 5
- A Windows 2000 computer configured as a domain member
- A smart card reader attached to the Windows 2000 domain member
- One unused smart card

Tip   You can purchase Windows 2000-compatible smart cards and readers directly from Schlumberger at their Web site: *www.smartcards.net*.

Lesson 1: Working with Computer Certificates

Windows 2000 uses computer certificates to bind the identity of a computer to a public/private key pair. This key pair can subsequently be used for a myriad of security purposes, such as creating an Internet Protocol Security connection to another computer or proving the computer's identity.

After this lesson, you will be able to

- Understand the purpose and function of computer certificates
- Deploy computer certificates

Estimated lesson time: 30 minutes

Understanding the Purpose of Computer Certificates

Computer certificates are used for five primary purposes in Windows 2000:

- Internet Protocol Security (IPSec) encrypts data flowing between two computers in the same domain.

  More Info   Computer certificates are required to establish IPSec communication between Windows 2000 computers. Read more about IPSec in Chapter 8, "IP Security."

- Layer 2 Tunneling Protocol (L2TP) encrypts data flowing between computers based on user authentication and allows users to log on securely from remote locations. L2TP is the subject of Chapter 9, "Remote Access and VPN."
- Secure Sockets Layer (SSL) encrypts data flowing between computers that have not otherwise agreed to trust one another. SSL does not provide identity of the user or machine, but does encrypt the connection between them. SSL is covered in Chapter 12, "Web Service Security."
- Smart card log on validates the identity of users, and stores the secret keys used to encrypt their data.
- Secure/Multipurpose Internet Mail Extensions (S/MIME) encrypts e-mail messages when they are created, and provides a mechanism to exchange encryption keys between e-mail users.

Identifying How a Certificate Is Used

Windows 2000 CAs create X.509v3 certificates. *X.509v3* is a format that specifies how information in a certificate is organized, and it provides enough detail so that software from different vendors can create, manage, and use certificates from any source if they contain the correct type of information for the application.

Multiple types of certificates exist because each type of application requires specific information within a certificate. When a certificate contains information that pertains to more than one application, the certificate can be used for each of those applications. The following are some examples of applications and their specific requirements for certificates:

- Some applications, such as a code signature verifier, might require only that a certificate contain identity information and be digitally signed by a CA that the applications are configured to trust.

Note   A *code signature* is a digital signature appended to a program that guarantees that the program has not been modified when in transit between the vendor and the end user.

- Other applications, such as a *smart card* logon suite, might require access to a public or private key embedded within the certificate. Smart cards are the subject of Lesson 3 in this chapter.
- Some applications might require specific information in the identity portion of the certificate that other applications do not need. For example, an e-mail client might require that the user's e-mail address appear in the certificate, while a file encryption package would have no use for that information.

Using Certificate Templates

Windows 2000 CAs create certificates specifically for applications, depending on the requirements of the application. These applications select a standard certificate template to ensure that the information they require will be embedded within the certificate. A *certificate template* is a file that specifies exactly what information is required by the application that is requesting the certificate. Figure 6.1 shows the general information for a specific certificate.

Figure 6.1   A certificate's information

For example, the Encrypting File System (EFS), which encrypts files in Windows 2000, requests certificates by specifying the file encryption certificate template. This guarantees that the proper information has been provided by the client (or the request will be rejected) in order for the CA to create a certificate that will be compatible with the EFS encryption service.

Most often, you will request certificates using the certificate templates listed in Table 6.1, which are built into Windows 2000. Other templates exist that are used automatically by various services; you will not need to administer those templates.

Table 6.1   Windows 2000 Certificate Templates

Template name	Purpose
Computer	IPSec, L2TP, SSL
User	Authentication, e-mail security, file encryption
EFS	File encryption
S/MIME	E-mail security
Smart card logon	Log on through smart cards
Smart card user	Authentication, e-mail security, and file encryption through smart card
Enrollment agent	Authorization of administrators to sign smart card certificates
Subordinate CA	Authorization of a CA to issue certificates within a trust hierarchy

Deploying Computer Certificates

There are two ways to deploy computer certificates:

- Manually on an individual computer
- Automatically on a domain or organizational unit (OU)

Manual Deployment

Deploy computer certificates manually when you need to deploy only a few certificates for a specific purpose, such as establishing an IPSec link between two computers, and you don't want to incur the planning or network overhead of automatic deployment.

To perform a manual deployment, you create a Certificates management console (Figure 6.2) on the computer for which you want to create the certificate, and specify that the console be used to manage computer certificates. The exercises in this lesson show you exactly how to do this. You then request the computer certificate. The CA issues the certificate, and your Certificates management console installs it.

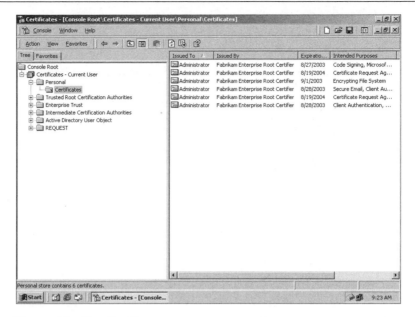

Figure 6.2   The Certificates management console

Automated Deployment

Deploy computer certificates automatically when you want to deploy certificates to large groups of computers. Automatic computer certificate deployment works very well—so well, in fact, that you need to plan for the additional network and computer load that will occur when computers throughout your domain or OU simultaneously request certificates.

To deploy certificates automatically, establish a Group Policy setting in a Group Policy Object (GPO) that is linked to the container holding the computers to which you want to deploy certificates. At the Group Policy refresh interval, the automatic certificate request policy is applied to the computers, and the computers will request certificates from the enterprise CA configured in the policy.

In general, you should have a CA for every 100 to 1000 computers that will be requesting certificates, depending on how much noticeable load you are willing to let your users see. If you postpone your deployment to a non-work time such as a weekend, you might be able to deploy 10,000 to 100,000 certificates from a single CA. Apply the policy changes at the end of the workday on Friday, and let the CA issue certificates throughout the weekend.

While deployment is usually performed at a domain level, you can load-schedule the deployment by creating an OU designed solely for certificate deployment. Create the OU as a subordinate to the domain, and then move computers into the OU in batches. Once they've gone through a Group Policy refresh interval, they will request and install the certificates automatically. You can then move the computer objects back to their original OUs and move a new batch in.

Tip   Be certain that you aren't obviating any important GPO settings by moving computers—you should always make your certificate deployment OU a subordinate to the OU that contains computers to ensure that you aren't accidentally removing settings.

Practice: Using Two Methods to Deploy Computer Certificates

In this practice, you use two different methods to deploy computer certificates: manually on a per-computer basis, and automatically through Group Policy to all computers within the Active Directory container.

Exercise 1: Deploying Computer Certificates Manually

In this exercise, you create a Certificates management console and manually request a computer certificate for a specific computer. Perform this exercise on a Windows 2000 Professional workstation joined to the domain.

▶   **To create a Certificates management console**

1. Log on as a domain administrator.
2. Click Start, and then click Run. The Run dialog box appears.
3. Type **mmc**, and click OK. An empty management console window will appear.
4. From the Console menu, choose Add/Remove Snap-In. The Add/Remove Snap-in dialog box appears.
5. Click Add. The Add Standalone Snap-in dialog box appears with a list of snap-ins.
6. Double-click certificates. The Certificates Snap-in Wizard appears with a list of the types of certificates that the snap-in can manage.
7. Select Computer Account, and click Next. The Select Computer Wizard page now asks which computer you would like to manage.
8. Select Local Computer, and click Finish.
9. Click Close to close the Add Standalone Snap-in dialog box. The Certificates snap-in is now in the Add/Remove Snap-ins list box.
10. Click OK to close the Add/Remove Snap-in dialog box.
11. From the Console menu, choose Save. The Save As dialog box appears.
12. Type **Certificates** in the File Name box, and click Save.

    A Certificates management console now appears in the Administrative Tools folder of the Start menu.

▶ **To request a certificate**

1. From the Certificates management console that you created in the first procedure, expand the Certificates Snap-in.

2. Right-click the Personal folder, click All Tasks, and select Request New Certificate. The Certificate Request Wizard appears.

3. Click Next. The Certificate Template dialog box appears. Computer is the only option.

4. Click Next to view the dialog box for the certificate-friendly name and description, as shown in Figure 6.3.

Figure 6.3   The Certificate Request Wizard

5. Type **Workstation Certificate** as the Friendly Name for the certificate.

6. Type **IPSec enabling certificate** as the Description for the certificate.

7. Click Next, and then click Finish. A message box appears indicating that the certificate request was successful.

8. Click OK to acknowledge that the certificate request was successful.

9. Click the Certificates folder under the Personal folder. The certificates contained within this folder appear in the leftmost panel of the screen.

10. Double-click the CLIENT01.domain.Fabrikam.com certificate to view the certificate information. The window that appears will be similar to the window shown in Figure 6.1.

Exercise 2: Deploying Computer Certificates Through Group Policy

In this exercise, you configure Group Policy to automatically deploy computer certificates to computers when they are booted or at the next Group Policy update interval.

▶ **To configure domain security policy for automatic computer certificate deployment**

1. Click Start, point to Programs, point to Administrative Tools, and click Active Directory Users And Computers. The Active Directory Users And Computers management console appears.

2. Right-click domain.fabrikam.com in the domain tree, and click Properties. The domain.fabrikam.com Properties dialog box appears.

3. Click Group Policy.

4. Double-click Domain Security Policy. The Group Policy editor appears with the Domain Security Policy open.

5. Expand Domain Security Policy, Computer Configuration, Windows Settings, Security Settings, and Public Key Policies.

6. Right-click Automatic Certificates Request Settings, point to New, and click Automatic Certificate Request, as shown in Figure 6.4. The Automatic Certificate Request Setup Wizard appears.

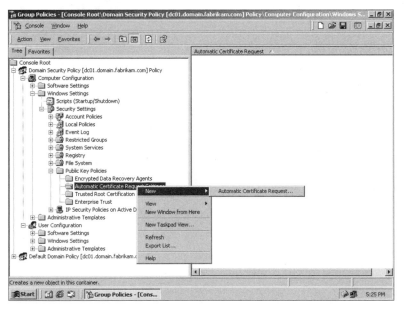

Figure 6.4   The Group Policy editor showing the Public Key Policies container

7. Click Next. The Certificate Template page appears, as shown in Figure 6.5.

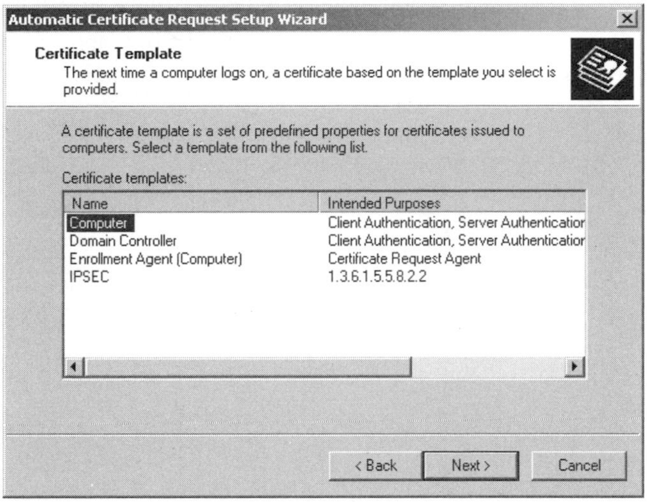

Figure 6.5   The Automatic Certificate Request Setup Wizard

8. Select the Computer template, and click Next. The Certification Authority page appears, with Fabrikam Enterprise Root Certifier selected.

9. Click Next, and then click Finish.

10. Close the Group Policy editor window.

11. Click OK to close the domain.fabrikam.com Properties dialog box.

12. Close the Active Directory Users And Computers management console.

▶ **To verify certificate deployment**

Perform this procedure on a Windows 2000 Professional workstation joined to the domain.

1. Restart the client computer.

2. Log on and open the Certificates management console.

3. Verify that the new certificate is listed under the Personal Certificates folder.

► **To verify certificate deployment at the CA**

1. On the domain controller, open the Certification Authority management console.

2. Expand Fabrikam Enterprise Root Certifier, and select Issued Certificates. A list of all certificates issued by the CA appears in the management console, as shown in Figure 6.6.

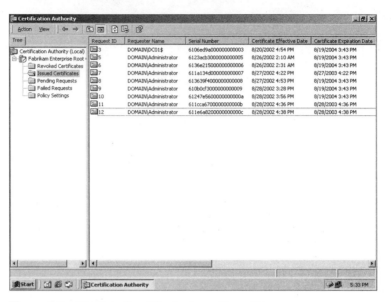

Figure 6.6   The list of certificates issued by a CA

3. Double-click the most recently issued certificate to view the certificate information, as shown in Figure 6.7. This is the certificate automatically issued to the client computer.

Figure 6.7   Verifying the deployment of a certificate

Lesson Review

The following questions are intended to reinforce key information in this lesson. If you are unable to answer a question, review the lesson and try the question again. Answers to the questions can be found in the appendix.

1. What is the primary purpose for computer certificates in Windows 2000?

2. When would you choose to use manual computer certificate deployment?

3. When would you choose to use automatic computer certificate deployment?

4. What tool do you use to perform manual deployment?

5. What tool do you use to perform automatic deployment?

Lesson Summary

- Computer certificates are used to perform network link encryption between computers. Depending on the circumstance, computer certificates can be used to perform IPSec, L2TP, and SSL encryption.
- Computer certificates can be manually deployed by using the Certificates management console on the computer that requires the certificate.
- Computer certificates can be automatically deployed using Group Policy to computers within a Group Policy container such as a domain or an OU.

  You must take special precautions to avoid overloading the certificate authority when you deploy computer certificates automatically, because all computers in the container will request certificates more or less simultaneously. Either perform the deployment when the CA has plenty of time to respond to requests or use subordinate OUs to isolate computers into smaller groups so that certificates can be deployed in batches.

Lesson 2: Deploying User Certificates

Certificates can be used to bind a user's identity to a public/private key pair for purposes such as logging on to Web sites, securing e-mail, and encrypting files. Windows 2000 supports these functions through the user certificates template, which generates certificates appropriate for each of these purposes for individual users within the domain.

The user certificates deployment methodology is designed for users to request and install their own certificates, primarily because user certificates are stored within the profile of each user logged on.

After this lesson, you will be able to
- Deploy user certificates using the Certificates management console
- Deploy user certificates using the Microsoft Certificate Services Web site

Estimated lesson time: 30 minutes

Deploying Certificates to Users

User certificates allow you to combine numerous functions, such as securing e-mail, encrypting files, and authenticating with extranets, in a single certificate that can be thought of as a user's digital identity. This certificate can perform all functions in Windows 2000 that are specific to a user.

Note   For the purpose of securing e-mail, user certificates are compatible only with Microsoft Outlook. Other e-mail packages require more identity information than a user certificate provides. Certificates can be created for these packages using the S/MIME certificate template on a stand-alone CA.

Allowing Users to Request and Install Certificates

User certificates are digitally signed by the CA when they are requested. The certificates are immediately returned to the requesting user unless you configure the CA to require administrative intervention by modifying its exit policy in the CA Administrative console. This means that users can request and immediately install their own certificates from the enterprise CA by using the Microsoft

Certificate Services Web site (CertSrv), shown in Figure 6.8. This Web site is installed by default when a CA is created on a machine where Internet Information Services (IIS) is installed.

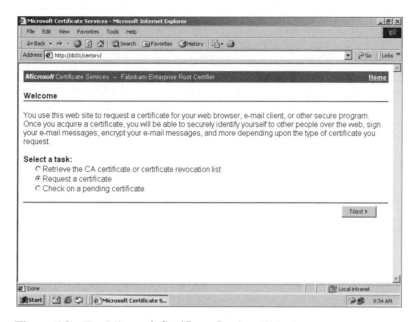

Figure 6.8   The Microsoft Certificate Services Web site

Tip   If you installed IIS after Certificate Services, you will not have the CertSrv virtual directories or files installed. Run **certutil –vroot** from the command prompt to install them.

Certificates are issued automatically only to users who have proven their identity by logging on using an Active Directory account. If you would still like to confirm each certificate before it is issued, you can change the CA's exit policy for the specific template by opening the template's Properties dialog box, selecting Exit Policy, and clearing the option to automatically issue certificates to authenticated users.

To ensure that certificates are issued correctly to a domain user, you must ensure that the domain user has authenticated with the CA through the IIS CertSrv Web site. Because the connection is made through IIS, the CertSrv virtual directory on the Certificate server must be configured to authenticate using domain authentication. Allow integrated Windows authentication only to prevent any other type of authentication from taking place. This will automatically log on users so that the correct credentials are requested. If other types of authentication are allowed, the user's correct credentials might not be passed, and certificate generation might fail or a useless certificate might be generated.

Users can also request certificates using the Certificates snap-in if they have access to the Microsoft Management Console (MMC). However, this method requires more administrative talent and is less familiar to end users than navigating a Web site, and access to the MMC is usually restricted by Group Policy.

Tip   An easy way to roll out certificates throughout an enterprise is to send a mass e-mail message to users with an embedded link to their proper CA. Include step-by-step instructions with screen shots showing how to request and install their certificates. You can use the Certification Authority management console to determine which users have successfully completed the steps and which require further assistance.

Automated Deployment of User Certificates

EFS encryption certificates are requested, created, and deployed by the system whenever they are needed to encrypt files in a domain. User or administrator intervention is not required for this specific type of certificate.

User certificates must be deployed to users from within their own user profiles, which means that for the most part, users must request their own certificates. While it is technically possible for administrators to log on as each user and per-form the request in an environment that uses roaming profiles, the network and administrative overhead to do this would be prohibitive.

Microsoft does not support any automated means for administrators to bulk deploy user certificates or even to create user certificates on behalf of users.

Caution   It is possible to use the Certreq.exe command-prompt utility to create a logon script that can automate the request and retrieval of certificates. Performing this sort of certificate rollout involves considerable capacity planning and programming expertise and is therefore beyond the scope of this book.

Manually Creating Certificates

User certificates are designed for deployment by end users rather than by administrators. While it is possible to configure the CertSrv Web site on a CA to request credentials each time a user connects so that an administrator can create certificates for individuals manually, you must take special precautions, such as closing Microsoft Internet Explorer between certificate requests, to ensure that the administrator is working within the correct user's account logon context in the Web session. User certificates created within the wrong user context will be useless.

Caution   Internet Explorer will remain logged on using the same user's credentials for as long as it is open. If administrators will be generating certificates for multiple users in a single logon session, you must ensure that you close and reopen Internet Explorer between sessions. You should also configure the CertSrv virtual directory for Basic Authentication so that administrators can log on as each of the various users independently. If integrated authentication is used, every certificate requested will be generated for the user who is logged on to the machine, rather than the user specified in the certificate, so the certificate will be useless.

Once created, the certificates have to be exported and then manually imported into each user's profile before they can be used.

Moving Certificates

When users change computers, their certificates must move with them. There are three ways to move certificates between workstations:

- Back up and restore the operating system on the workstation.
- Enable roaming profiles.
- Export certificates on one machine and import them on another.

Backing Up and Restoring the Operating System

Performing a complete backup and restoration of a workstation operating system, while somewhat extreme, successfully moves all aspects of a user's working environment as long as the target machine is sufficiently similar to the source machine for the restore to work. In most cases, full machine backup and restore will work without fail.

Of course, backing up and restoring a full machine is time intensive, administratively complicated, usually unnecessary, and destructive to the configuration of the target machine. It has the advantage of moving encrypted files intact without problems, however, and it may be your first choice if your environment makes use of EFS to encrypt local files.

Using Roaming Profiles

User certificates are stored in a user's profile in a special location referred to as the *certificate store*. Users in environments that support roaming profiles do not need to be concerned with moving certificates manually because the certificates follow the user wherever they log on.

Enabling roaming profiles is the easiest method of moving certificates and is frequently the only convenient way to move certificates. It also preserves the user's desktop settings and files. Even if the change is temporary and used only to transport a user's certificates and settings, you should convert a user's profile to a roaming profile using the system Control Panel and have the user download the profile to the destination machine by logging on, if possible. You can then convert the roaming profile back to a local profile on the destination machine.

Exporting and Importing Certificates

Certificates can be imported and exported in a variety of formats. The format you use will depend on the application that needs to import it.

PKCS #12 Personal Information Exchange format is required to export Windows 2000 certificates that contain a private key. This certificate format is designed for the transport of private keys that are specific to a certain user. Windows 2000 allows you to export a certificate only if you specified the exportable option under advanced settings when you generated it using the CertSrv Web site or if it is an EFS encryption certificate. PKCS #12 is the only format that can export a private key.

Warning   You must specify that a certificate is exportable using advanced settings on the Certificate Services Web site before the certificate is created. Certificates that have not been marked for export cannot be exported. To move certificates that have not been marked for export, you must enable roaming profiles instead.

To export a certificate, open the Certificates management console, right-click the certificate, point to All Tasks, and choose Export. Follow the prompts to create an exported PKCS #12 certificate file that can be imported on another workstation. Figure 6.9 shows the wizard window that appears at the end of the process of exporting a certificate.

Caution   Don't weaken your security posture or the privacy of user certificates by marking them as exportable when they are created. Use the roaming profiles feature of the operating system, even if only temporarily, to move personal certificate stores when necessary. If you are moving a certificate store between physically separate facilities, consider using the backup/restore method rather than the import/export method.

Figure 6.9   Exporting a certificate to a file

Practice: Deploying and Moving Certificates

In this practice, you deploy a user certificate for a single user, and then export the certificate for use on another machine. Because user certificates are designed to be deployed by end users rather than by administrators, this process shows you the steps each user needs to perform when requesting certificates.

Exercise 1: Deploying User Certificates Through the Certificates Services Web Site

In this exercise, you establish that Integrated Windows authentication is the only authentication method that is allowed. After defining the authentication method, you request and install a user certificate.

▶ **To set Certificate Services Web site authentication**

1. Log on to the domain controller.
2. Click Start, point to Programs, point to Administrative Tools, and click Internet Services Manager. The Internet Information Services management console appears.
3. Expand Internet Information Services, then dc01, and then Default Web Site.
4. Right-click the CertSrv virtual directory, and click Properties. The CertSrv Properties dialog box appears.

5. Click the Directory Security tab, and click Edit in the Anonymous Access And Authentication Control group. The Authentication Methods dialog box appears, as shown in Figure 6.10.

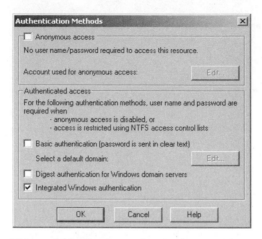

Figure 6.10   Setting authentication methods for a Web site

6. Select Integrated Windows Authentication, and clear all other check boxes.

7. Click OK to close the Authentication Methods dialog box.

8. Click OK to close the CertSrv Properties dialog box.

9. Close the Internet Information Services management console.

► **To request a certificate**

1. From the client computer, log on as user **packerman** in domain.Fabrikam.com.

2. Browse to *http://dc01/certsrv/*. The Microsoft Certificate Services Web site appears.

3. Select Request A Certificate, and click Next. The Choose Request Type page appears.

4. Leave the User Certificate Request option selected, as shown in Figure 6.11, and click Next.

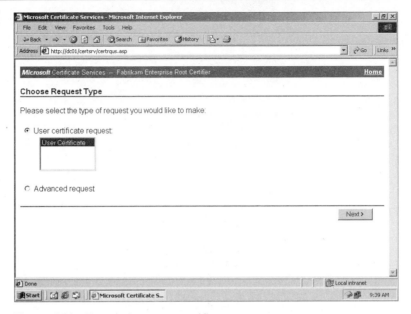

Figure 6.11   Requesting a user certificate

5. Click Submit. The Protected Item dialog box appears.

6. Click OK. The dialog box will appear again. Click OK again.

7. When the Certificate Issued dialog box appears, click Install This Certificate.

8. From the Tools menu, choose Internet Options.

9. When the Internet Options dialog box appears, click the Content tab.

10. Click Certificates. The Certificates dialog box displays a list of installed certificates, as shown in Figure 6.12.

Figure 6.12   Certificates installed in the current user's profile

11. Double-click the Pilar Ackerman certificate. When the Certificate Information window appears (Figure 6.13), verify the certificate's uses.

Figure 6.13   Properties of a certificate

12. Close the dialog boxes and the Web browser.

Exercise 2: Moving a Certificate Between Workstations

In this exercise, the EFS certificate for the domain administrator account is exported from a file server and imported to a workstation. In this domain, users do not have access to the MMC, and their certificates have not been marked as exportable, so it would not be possible to export and import user certificates for non-administrative users.

▶ **To automatically generate an EFS certificate**

Perform this procedure on the Windows 2000 Server.

1. Log on as Administrator.
2. Right-click a blank area of the desktop, point to New, and click Text Document. A new text document icon appears on the desktop.
3. Change the document's name to Encrypted.txt.
4. Right-click Encrypted.txt, and click Properties. The Properties dialog box for Encrypted.txt appears.

5. Click Advanced to view the Advanced Attributes for Encrypted.txt, as shown in Figure 6.14.

Figure 6.14   Setting the advanced attributes for a document

6. Select Encrypt Contents To Secure Data, and click OK.

Note   Setting encryption for a file results in the automatic generation of an EFS certificate.

---

7. Click OK to close the Encrypted.txt Properties dialog box. An encryption warning message appears.

8. Select Encrypt The File Only, and click OK.

The server will request an EFS encryption certificate from the CA; the certificate will be automatically issued and used to encrypt the text file.

▶ **To create a certificates console for the administrator**

Perform this procedure on the Windows 2000 Server while logged on as Administrator.

1. Click Start, and then click Run to open the Run dialog box.

2. Type **mmc** in the Open field, and click OK. A blank management console appears.

3. On the Console menu, click Add/Remove Snap-in. The Add/Remove Snap-in dialog box appears.

4. Click Add. The Add Standalone Snap-in dialog box appears.

5. Double-click Certificates. The Certificates snap-in dialog box appears with options for the type of certificates to manage.

6. Select My User Account, and click Finish.

7. Click Close to close the Add Standalone Snap-in dialog box.

8. Click OK to close the Add/Remove Snap-in dialog box.

9. From the Console menu, choose Save.

10. Type **Administrator Certificates** in the File Name box, and then click Save.

▶ **To export the EFS certificate**

1. In the Administrator Certificates console, expand Certificates – Current User, expand Personal, and then select the Certificates folder.

   Certificates issued to the administrator are listed in the window, as shown in Figure 6.15.

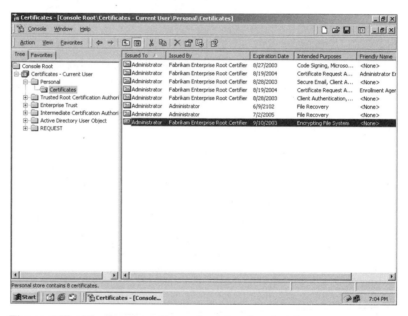

Figure 6.15   The list of certificates issued to the administrator

2. In the Intended Purposes column, find the certificate issued to the administrator Encrypting File System.

3. Right-click the certificate, point to All Tasks, and then click Export. The Certificate Export Wizard appears.

4. Click Next. The Export Private Key page appears asking if you want to export the private key along with the certificate.

5. Select Yes, Export The Private Key, and click Next. The Export File Format page appears, providing options for exporting the certificate.

6. Leave the default Enable Strong Protection check box selected, and click Next. The Password window appears.

7. Type and confirm a password for the certificate, and then click Next.

> **Important**   Use a more complex password than the account's logon password to secure private certificates.

8. On the File To Export page, click Browse. When the Save As dialog box appears, insert a blank formatted floppy disk into the computer's floppy disk drive, and browse to the floppy disk drive.

9. Type **AdminEFS.pfx** as the File Name of the certificate, and then click Save. A:\AdminEFS.pfx should appear in the File Name box.

10. Click Next, and then click Finish.

11. In the message box that appears, click OK to acknowledge that the export was successful.

▶ **To import an EFS certificate file**

Perform this exercise on a workstation joined to the domain.

1. Insert the floppy disk containing the Administrator's EFS certificate.

2. Open the floppy disk drive in Windows Explorer.

3. Double-click AdminEFS.pfx. The Certificate Import Wizard appears.

4. Click Next. The File To Import page appears, requesting the name of the file to import. The correct file name already appears in the File Name box.

5. Click Next. The Password page appears requesting the password that was used to encrypt the certificate.

6. Enter the password you used to secure the certificate, and click Next. The Certificate Store page appears, asking which store you want to add the certificate to.

7. Leave Automatically Select Certificate Store selected, and click Next.

8. Click Finish.

9. In the message box that appears, click OK to acknowledge that the import was successful.

Lesson Review

The following questions are intended to reinforce key information in this lesson. If you are unable to answer a question, review the lesson and try the question again. Answers to the questions can be found in the appendix.

1. Can administrators create user certificates on behalf of users without knowing their account user name and password?

2. For which purposes can user certificates be used?

3. Where is a user's certificate store permanently stored?

4. What is the recommended method for moving certificate stores when a user changes workstations?

5. Which certificate format is used to export and import user certificates?

6. Which type of certificates can be exported without being explicitly marked as exportable?

Lesson Summary

- User certificates are designed to accomplish most of the purposes for which end users require public keys: file encryption, e-mail security, and authentication with third parties.
- User certificates are automatically issued by the CA when they are requested unless the administrator changes the CA's exit policy. This means that users can request and immediately install certificates through the CA's CertSrv Web site.
- User certificates can be used to secure e-mail in Outlook, but they do not contain the required identity information for most other e-mail packages.
- Personal certificates are stored in a user's profile, so they will automatically move in a roaming profiles environment. You can manually export and import user certificates that have been marked as exportable by using the Certificates management console.

Lesson 3: Using Smart Card Certificates

Smart cards provide a mechanism for securely storing private keys in a manner that cannot be compromised (without tremendous effort and very expensive equipment) and for associating those private keys with specific individuals. Windows 2000 can store certificates on smart cards to support logging on, digitally signing and encrypting e-mail, and encrypting files on disk.

After this lesson, you will be able to

- Understand the operation and function of smart cards
- Deploy smart cards using a smart card enrollment station
- Log on using smart cards

Estimated lesson time: 30 minutes

Using Smart Cards

Smart cards are security devices the size of a credit card (in fact, they are used as credit cards) that contain a microprocessor and an amount of permanent flash memory. When a card is inserted into a smart card reader, the card's processor and memory are powered by the reader and used to securely store information such as private keys and digital certificates, and other private information.

Note   Smart cards come in many types, and all of them contain permanent memory, but only a few types contain the type of microprocessor needed to perform the PKI functions required by Windows 2000. Be certain that the smart cards you purchase specifically state that they are compatible with Windows 2000 logon requirements. Most smart card readers that can be attached to a PC will function correctly.

In Windows 2000, smart cards are used for three purposes:

- To log on to a Windows computer
- To encrypt e-mail
- To encrypt disk files using EFS

To perform these functions, a smart card reader must be attached to the computer. Typically, you attach a smart card reader to a serial port, USB port, or PCMCIA port. All PCs have either a serial port or a USB port, and all laptop computers have a PCMCIA port, so smart card readers are available for all computers. Even PDAs have serial ports that can be used to support smart cards.

How Public and Private Keys Are Stored

When a public/private key pair is created for a smart card, the key pair is generated by the microprocessor in the card, not by the host computer. The private key is stored in a secure area of the smart card's memory that cannot be accessed from the host computer. The public key is stored in a publicly available area of memory that can be read by the host computer.

Note   The private key is never accessible to the host computer (or any other computer) and cannot be compromised. However, if the smart card is ever lost or re-initialized, the private key and any data that has been encrypted by it is irretrievably lost.

Once a private key has been generated and stored by a smart card, it cannot be removed. The host computer sends the encrypted data to the card, and the microprocessor on board the smart card decrypts the encrypted data using the private key and then transmits the decrypted data back to the computer. Typically, the encrypted data consists of only a secret key that is used to bulk encrypt an e-mail message or a disk file. Because only the secret key is encrypted by the card, the amount of data and processing required is minimal.

Using a Personal Identification Number

Smart cards are issued to individuals who assign to the card a *personal identification number* (PIN), or numeric password, known only to them. The PIN is created at the time they receive the card.

The smart card's processor requires the PIN to unlock any use of the private memory on the smart card. PINs do not have to be particularly strong, because the smart card will erase itself after three or five incorrect attempts (depending on the manufacturer) to use the PIN. Most PINs are 4 to 8 characters in length, which is sufficient to protect the card from unauthorized use, because brute force attacks cannot be used to guess the PIN.

Guaranteeing Security

Smart cards use two measures to guarantee security:

- Possession of a controlled device (the card) to authorize access
- Knowledge of an secret (the PIN) to authenticate identity

A user can lose a password and user name but cannot lose control of a smart card by losing the PIN, because both the PIN and the device are required to gain access to the system. If the device is lost, then the user can report it, and its certification in the system can be invalidated to prevent it from being used.

Types of Smart Card Certificates

There are two types of smart card certificates that a Windows 2000 enterprise CA can issue:

- Smart card logon certificates
- Smart card user certificates

Note   Stand-alone CAs cannot issue smart card certificates.

The difference between the two types of certificates is that the smart card logon certificate can only be used for logging on, whereas the smart card user certificate can be used for logging on as well as for EFS encryption and S/MIME e-mail encryption. Unless there is a reason to restrict users from using S/MIME and EFS, you will want to deploy smart card user certificates to allow their increased functionality.

Tip   The CA policy required to issue smart card certificates must be explicitly enabled. The exercises in this lesson show how to do this.

For purposes of logging on, both types of smart card certificates are identical. A computer running Windows that has a smart card reader installed will present the smart card icon in the logon prompt dialog box. When you insert a smart card, a dialog box appears, prompting you for the smart card PIN. After you enter the PIN, the logon process proceeds as usual.

Issuing Smart Cards

In contrast to most types of certificates, users cannot request smart cards and create them on their own. Smart cards must be signed by a specific type of administrative certificate to certify that they are allowed to be used in the domain. The administrator's *enrollment agent certificate* digitally signs the certificates stored on the smart card to prove that they were issued by a legitimate administrator on the network. The administrator who creates the smart card certificates and writes them to the smart card must have an enrollment agent certificate installed on the smart card enrollment station to deploy smart cards.

To issue certificates, an administrator can work from any smart card–equipped workstation in the domain. After installing an enrollment agent certificate on the machine using the Certificates management console, the administrator can browse to the Smart Card Enrollment Station page on the CertSrv Web site on an enterprise CA (as shown in Figure 6.16) that has the policy settings required to issue smart cards and begin enrolling smart cards in bulk.

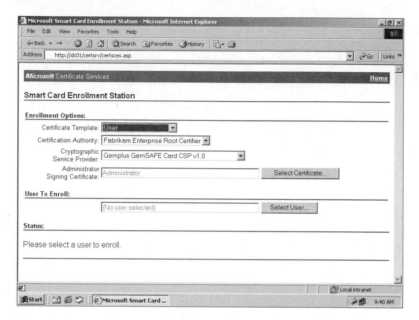

Figure 6.16   The Smart Card Enrollment Station page of the CertSrv Web site

During the enrollment process, which takes approximately one minute per card, you must physically label the smart cards with the user account for which they have been enrolled. This is most easily accomplished by either writing on the smart card with a permanent marker or affixing a label from a preprinted label sheet as you work.

You must also decide on a PIN assignment strategy. You can

- Leave the manufacturer's default PIN in place if the card comes from the factory pre-initialized. This option is not secure and should never be used outside a test environment.
- Randomly assign PINs as you initialize cards. While this is the fastest secure method, it requires you to securely transmit the PIN to the users and assume that they won't forget it, because if they do (and if you don't retain it), you will have to reinitialize the card. Unfortunately, this option is likely to cause you to

reinitialize a large percentage of the cards you deploy. If you want to use this method to deploy smart cards, write the randomly assigned PINs on the inside flap of envelopes and then seal the smart cards in the envelopes to securely deploy them to users in large batches.

■ Create a PIN changing station at the smart card distribution location and guide users through the process of setting their PIN. This is the most reliable solution because it allows users to assign their own PINs, which they are more likely to remember. You can use this as an opportunity to explain the function of the smart card and show them the smart card removal behavior, which is covered in the next section. This option is the most secure way to deploy smart cards.

■ Leave or assign a default PIN to all cards, and have users log on with it when they receive their card. Once they've logged on with the default PIN, you can run the PIN changing application provided by the card manufacturer to assist them in changing their PIN. You must ensure that all users actually change their PIN for this method to be secure.

Caution   Caution users not to use their street addresses, telephone numbers, or social security numbers as (or as portions of) their PINs. Hackers try this publicly available information first when they try to hack smart cards.

Including PIN changing and user training, you should probably assume that it will take five minutes per user to deploy a smart card infrastructure. For a network of 100 users, it would constitute one work day for a single administrator. For a network of 10,000 users, it would take 10 administrators two weeks to deploy a smart card infrastructure to end users.

Modifying the Smart Card Removal Behavior Policy

To maintain perfect accountability in a smart card environment, users must retain control of their smart cards whenever they are logged on to the network. Otherwise, the logged on workstation card could fall into the hands of another party, and the smart card could no longer prove identity. To maintain the security concept that the smart card represents the user at all times, smart card systems usually require that the smart card be present in the smart card reader while the computer is in use.

The default behavior for removing a smart card is to force a log off. You can change this behavior by modifying the security policy setting for smart card removal in the domain GPO to which the workstation belongs. Figure 6.17 shows the Security Policy Setting dialog box.

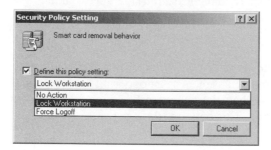

Figure 6.17 Changing the smart card removal behavior in a GPO

Important Carefully consider the security ramifications of these options before you choose one. Each of these actions has a dramatic effect on the behavior of the people who use smart cards and can increase or decrease the odds of losing control of a smart card or a logged on computer.

The Security Policy Setting dialog box lets you choose one of three smart card removal behavior options:

- The *No Action* option creates the strong possibility that users will insert and remove their smart cards when logging on. While this reduces the odds of leaving a smart card in a reader unattended, it dramatically increases the odds that a logged on workstation will be left logged on and unattended when a user steps away from the computer. This means that other users could perform actions on the system within the security context of the smart card user. Because smart card environments require more security than typical logon environments, this is usually not acceptable.

- The *Force Logoff* option is the opposite extreme from a security standpoint, but it also has unintended consequences. This option forces users to leave their smart cards inserted into the smart card readers to perform their work. The idea is that whenever the user leaves a workstation, the user will remove the smart card. The problem is that a forced log off causes the user to lose any unsaved work that is open on the desktop. In many situations, this will encourage users to leave their smart cards sitting unattended in the readers so they won't lose data when they must unexpectedly leave their workstations.

- The *Lock Workstation* option is the best option in most environments. Locking a workstation prevents unauthorized users from exploiting it, but does not lose a user's work. Because users can remove their cards quickly without losing their work, locking workstations allows you to preserve the security concept that the user is present if the smart card is present, and eliminates all of the subtle reasons users might use to justify circumventing smart card security.

Tip   Select the Lock Workstation policy setting as your domain default unless you have a good reason for doing otherwise.

Troubleshooting Smart Card Enrollment

Smart cards are a mature technology, but they have only recently been introduced to PCs for use as logon and security devices. Windows 2000 provides a sophisticated environment in which to use smart cards, and as with any sophisticated environment, complex problems can occur that may be difficult to troubleshoot.

Troubleshooting Errors Attempting to Initialize Smart Cards

If you cannot select an administrator's enrollment certificate during the enrollment process, you do not have an enrollment agent certificate installed on the enrollment workstation. Using the certificate's management console, request an enrollment agent certificate and reattempt the enrollment process.

If you get an error stating that you must select a certificate type with a CA, you have not enabled the CA to issue the specific type of certificate that you are requesting. On the CA, open the Certificate Authority management console, right-click the Policies folder, and add the specific type of certificate you wish to deploy.

Troubleshooting Errors During Smart Card Initialization

When you enroll users using the Enrollment Station Web site, you might encounter an error when you insert the smart card to be written to. There are two common reasons for this error message to appear:

- The card has not been correctly initialized and does not have a PIN assigned. Use the manufacturer's initialization software and instructions to initialize the card. Some brands of cards come pre-initialized with default PINs. If you don't know the PIN number for the smart card, it is probably not initialized.
- The card is not compatible with Windows 2000 Logon. There are hundreds of different types of smart cards, but only a few types work correctly with Windows 2000 Logon. Obtain cards of the correct type that conform to the Windows 2000 Logon requirements for smart cards. If your smart card does not specifically state that it is compatible with Windows 2000 Logon, it probably isn't.

Practice: Deploying a Smart Card

In this practice, you deploy a smart card to a user in the enterprise. The process remains the same no matter how many users you enroll. To complete this practice, you will need a smart card reader and at least one uninitialized smart card.

Exercise 1: Deploying Certificates for Smart Cards

In this exercise, you set the CA policy to allow for certificate deployment, create a deployment workstation, and create an enrollment agent certificate. This exercise needs to be performed only once per enrollment station to enroll any number of users.

▶ **To configure the CA to issue smart card certificates**

Perform this procedure on the enterprise Root CA server.

1. Open the Certification Authority management console.
2. Expand Fabrikam Root Certifier.
3. Right-click Policy Settings, point to New, and then click Certificate To Issue. The Select Certificate Template dialog box appears.
4. Double-click Enrollment Agent. Make sure you do not click Enrollment Agent (Computer).
5. Right-click Policy Settings, point to New, and then click Certificates To Issue. The Select Certificate Template dialog box appears.
6. Double-click Smart Card User.
7. Close the Certification Authority management console. The CA is now configured to issue enrollment agent certificates to administrators and smart card user certificates to end users.

▶ **To create a Certificates management console**

Perform this procedure on the workstation that you will be using as a smart card enrollment station. You can use the CA server as the enrollment workstation if you want.

Tip   If a Certificates management console for the current user account already exists because you've already added one to this computer, you do not need to perform this procedure.

---

1. Click Start, click Run, type **mmc**, and then click OK. A blank management console appears.
2. On the Console menu, choose Add/Remove Snap-in. The Add/Remove Snap-in dialog box appears.

3. Click Add. The Add Standalone Snap-in dialog box appears, displaying a list of snap-ins.

4. Double-click Certificates. The Certificates Snap-in Wizard appears with a list of the types of certificates that the snap-in can manage.

5. Select My User Account, and then click Finish.

6. Click Close to close the Add Standalone Snap-in dialog box.

7. Click OK to close the Add/Remove Snap-in dialog box.

8. From the Console menu, choose Save As.

9. In the Save As dialog box, type **Certificates** in the File Name box and click Save.

▶ **To obtain a smart card enrollment certificate**

Perform this procedure on the workstation that you will be using as a smart card enrollment station.

1. Open the Certificates management console.

2. Expand Certificates – Current User, right-click Personal, point to All Tasks, and then click Request New Certificate. The Certificate Request Wizard appears.

3. Click Next. The Certificate Template page appears, showing the types of certificates you can request.

4. Select Enrollment Agent, and then click Next.

5. If the Certification Authority page appears, select Fabrikam Enterprise Root Certifier, and click Next. The Certificate Friendly Name And Description page appears.

6. In the Friendly Name box, type **Smart card enrollment**.

7. In the Description box, type **Allows administrators to digitally sign smart card certificates**.

8. Click Next.

9. Click Finish to request the certificate. The Certificate Request Wizard displays a message box prompting you to install, view the certificate, or cancel.

10. Click Install Certificate.

11. In the message box that appears, click OK to acknowledge that the certificate request was successful.

Exercise 2: Enrolling Smart Cards

In this exercise, you enroll a smart card on behalf of a user and log on as the user. You then modify the default security policy settings for the smart card. The steps in this exercise must be repeated for every user that you enroll.

▶ **To deploy smart cards on behalf of users**

Perform this procedure on the workstation that you will be using as a smart card enrollment station.

1. Open Internet Explorer, type **http://dc01/certsrv** in the address bar, and then press ENTER. The Microsoft Certificate Services Web site appears (Figure 6.8).

2. Select Request A Certificate, and click Next. The Choose Request Type page appears (Figure 6.11).

3. Select Advanced Request, and click Next.

4. Select Request A Certificate For A Smart Card On Behalf Of Another User Using The Smart Card Enrollment Station, and click Next. The Smart Card Enrollment Station page appears, as shown in Figure 6.18.

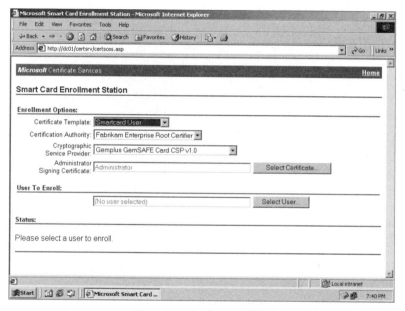

Figure 6.18   The Smart Card Enrollment Station Web site

5. If the Active X security dialog box appears prompting for permission to install Microsoft Smart Card Enrollment Station control, click Yes.

Note   If you have problems getting past this step, lower the security settings of your Web browser in the Internet Options security properties dialog box to allow you to download ActiveX controls.

---

6. In the Certificate Template list on the Smart Card Enrollment Station page, select Smartcard User.

7. In the Cryptographic Service Provider list, select the CSP appropriate for your card reader. For example, if your smart card has oval contacts, select the Gem-plus CSP. If your smart card has square contacts, select the Schlumberger CSP.

8. Verify that the Administrator Signing Certificate box contains Administrator. If it does not, click Select Certificate, and select the Smart Card Enrollment Certificate.

9. Click Select User. The Select User dialog box appears.

10. Double-click Syed Abbas to identify the user you are enrolling.

11. Insert a blank smart card into the smart card reader, and click Enroll. Figure 6.19 shows the Smart Card Enrollment Station window with the message indicating that the user is being enrolled.

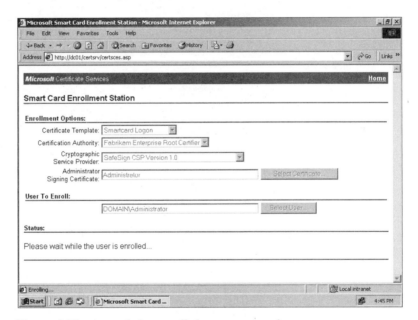

Figure 6.19 A user being enrolled on a smart card

Note If you receive an error message indicating that an unknown error has occurred, it probably means that you're using an uninitialized smart card or a smart card that is not compatible with Windows 2000.

12. When the PIN prompt appears, type the PIN for the smart card.

Tip Check your smart card provider's documentation for the default PIN number for their smart cards or the method used to assign a PIN to a smart card.

The Smart Card Enrollment Station page reappears, as shown in Figure 6.20. The status area indicates that the smart card is ready and the user is enrolled.

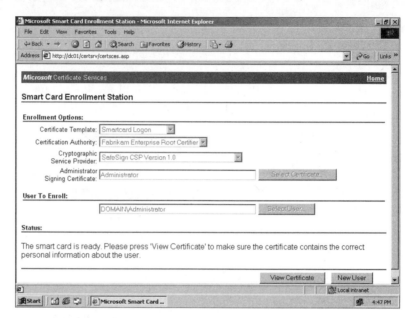

Figure 6.20 The CertSrv Web site indicates that the smart card is ready

13. When the enrollment process is completed, click View Certificates to view the certificates that have been installed on the smart card.
14. Close Internet Explorer.

▶ **To perform a smart card log on**

Perform this procedure on the enrollment station or another workstation with a smart card reader attached. If you are currently logged on, log off before performing this procedure.

1. Ensure that the smart card icon appears in the Windows logon prompt, as shown in Figure 6.21. Insert your smart card into the attached smart card reader.

Figure 6.21   The smart card–enabled logon prompt

2. When the Log On To Windows dialog box appears, as shown in Figure 6.22, type the PIN you assigned to this smart card, and click OK. Windows completes the logon process.

Figure 6.22   Entering a PIN to prove identity during a smart card log on

3. Remove the smart card from the smart card reader. Windows logs off the computer. The default smart card removal behavior is to log off when the smart card is removed from the reader.

▶ **To modify the domain security policy**

1. Log on to the domain controller as Administrator.

2. Click Start, point to Programs, point to Administrative Tools, and then click Active Directory Users And Computers. The Active Directory Users And Computers management console appears.

3. Right-click domain.fabrikam.com in the domain tree, and click Properties. The domain.fabrikam.com Properties dialog box appears.

4. Click Group Policy.

5. Double-click Domain Security Policy. The Group Policy editor appears with the Domain Security Policy open.

6. Expand Domain Security Policy, Computer Configuration, Windows Settings, Security Settings, Local Policies, and then select Security Options. Figure 6.23 shows the Group Policy editor opened to this policy setting.

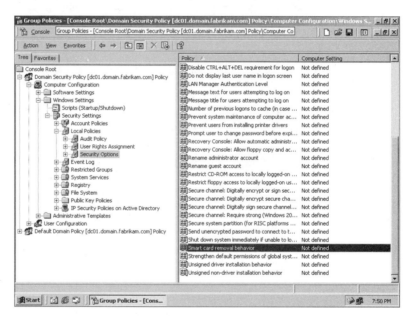

Figure 6.23   The Smart Card Removal Behavior policy setting

7. Double-click Smart Card Removal Behavior. The Security Policy Setting dialog box appears.

8. Select Define This Policy Setting.

9. Select Lock Workstation from the list, as shown in Figure 6.24.

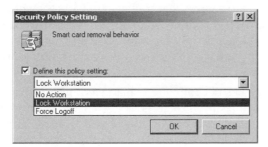

Figure 6.24 The Smart Card Removal Behavior policy options

10. Click OK.

11. Close the Group Policy editor.

Lesson Review

The following questions are intended to reinforce key information in this lesson. If you are unable to answer a question, review the lesson and try the question again. Answers to the questions can be found in the appendix.

1. What is a smart card?

2. Are there any types of computers that cannot support smart card readers?

3. For what purposes are smart cards used in Windows 2000?

4. What does an administrator do to authorize a smart card to function in the domain?

5. What program is used to deploy smart cards?

Lesson Summary

- Smart cards are devices that contain a microprocessor and permanent memory that can be used to securely store private keys for domain log on, e-mail signing and encryption, and file encryption. Because the keys are stored on the card, they are transported with the user wherever the user moves within the enterprise. To use a smart card, the workstation must have a smart card reader attached.

- The major steps in deploying a smart card infrastructure: add the appropriate smart card policy to the enterprise CA, install an enrollment agent certificate on the enrollment workstation, and use the Smart Card Enrollment Station page on the CertSrv Web site to create Windows 2000 smart cards.

- Smart cards are deployed in bulk by administrators and issued to users after they have been enrolled. Administrators can set the PIN required to use the card or allow users to set the PIN when the smart cards are deployed.

- Users are logged off by default when their smart cards are removed from the smart card reader. You can change this default behavior by modifying the domain group policy to either lock the workstation or to take no action.

Lesson 4: Deploying S/MIME Certificates

Digitally signing and encrypting e-mail is one of the primary reasons for deploying a PKI, and it is the only way to truly secure e-mail from forgery and sniffing attacks. Creating and deploying S/MIME certificates that are compatible with a wide range of e-mail clients is a key feature of Windows 2000 Certificate Services.

After this lesson, you will be able to

- Request and issue S/MIME certificates
- Send digitally signed e-mail from Microsoft Outlook Express

Estimated lesson time: 20 minutes

How S/MIME Certificates Are Used

While standard Windows 2000 user certificates allow users to digitally sign and encrypt e-mail from Outlook, many third-party e-mail clients as well as Outlook Express require specially formatted S/MIME certificates that contain the user's e-mail address in the identity field. This requirement exists as a way to foil attempts to forge certificates that claim to be from a certain user but specify return e-mail addresses other than the user's legitimate e-mail address.

Because users' identities in a domain have been certified by their logging on, an embedded e-mail address is not required in a user certificate to certify that they are who they say they are. This requirement makes standard user certificates from an enterprise CA inappropriate for use in e-mail applications that don't trust domain log on.

Enterprise CAs cannot issue S/MIME certificates because enterprise user certificates are optimized to acquire all their information directly from the system and to be issued automatically without user or administrative intervention. Because e-mail addresses are not stored by default in Active Directory, enterprise CA certificates do not necessarily contain all the information in the certificate that some e-mail clients require. Outlook is optimized to work with enterprise CA–issued user certificates, but most other e-mail clients, including Outlook Express, are not.

Stand-alone CAs are capable of producing S/MIME certificates that will work in all X.509 compliant e-mail clients by using the S/MIME certificate template and providing an interface through the CertSrv Web site that allows users to enter their e-mail addresses. To request these types of certificates, you must have a stand-alone CA configured to issue certificates using the S/MIME certificate template.

Troubleshooting S/MIME Deployment

If your e-mail client will not successfully import a certificate, the certificate does not conform to the e-mail client's requirements for S/MIME certificates. The most likely cause for this is that the e-mail client requires the Identity field of the certificate to contain the user's e-mail address, and the user certificate either does not contain it or the e-mail address doesn't match the configured address in the client.

Remember that you can create "e-mail only" S/MIME certificates that conform to embedded e-mail address requirements only from a stand-alone CA. However, enterprise CAs can create user certificates that can be used by some e-mail clients, including Outlook, to sign and encrypt e-mail messages.

Practice: Sending Digitally Signed E-mail

In this practice, you will configure Outlook Express for a user, request an S/MIME certificate appropriate for use in Outlook Express, install that certificate, and use it to digitally sign an e-mail message. This practice requires access to the stand-alone subordinate CA created in Chapter 5, "Certificate Authorities" and will not work correctly if you attempt to use an enterprise CA. It also requires access to the Windows 2000 Professional workstation from which the user will actually send and request e-mail messages.

Note   Because the Outlook Express configuration depicted in this practice refers to a fictitious e-mail server, Outlook Express will warn that it cannot find the e-mail server at each attempted connection. For the purposes of this exercise, actually transmitting e-mail is not necessary, so these warnings can be ignored. You may elect to configure Outlook Express using your actual e-mail credentials if you'd like to see the process complete without errors.

▶   **To configure Outlook Express**

1. Log on to the client workstation as user Pilar Ackerman, user name packerman.
2. Click Start, point to Programs, and then click Outlook Express. If the Internet Connection Wizard appears continue with step 5.
3. If the Internet Connection Wizard does not appear, choose Accounts from the Tools menu. The Internet Accounts dialog box appears.
4. In the Internet Accounts dialog box, click Add, and choose Mail. The Internet Connection Wizard appears.
5. Type **Pilar Ackerman** as the Display Name, and press ENTER.
6. Type **packerman@fabrikam.com** in the E-mail Address box, and press ENTER.
7. Type **mail.Fabrikam.com** in the Incoming Mail Server box.
8. Type **mail.Fabrikam.com** in the Outgoing Mail Server box.
9. Type **packerman** in the Account Name box.

10. Click Next, and then click Finish.

11. If you opened the Internet Accounts dialog box in step 3, click Close to close the dialog box. Outlook Express is now configured and ready to use.

▶ **To verify that no S/MIME certificate is installed**

Perform this procedure on the workstation logged on as user **packerman**.

1. In Outlook Express, click New Mail. The New Message window opens.

2. Type **sabbas@fabrikam.com** in the To box.

3. Type **Test Message** in the Subject box.

4. Type **Test** as the body of the message.

5. Click the Sign button in the toolbar, as shown in Figure 6.25.

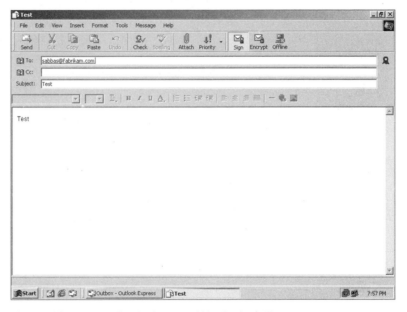

Figure 6.25   Digitally signing e-mail in Outlook Express

6. Click Send. A dialog box appears stating that you cannot send digitally signed messages because you do not have a digital ID for this account.

7. Click Cancel, and close the e-mail message. Click No when asked to save changes.

8. Close Outlook Express.

▶ **To request an S/MIME certificate**

Perform this procedure on the workstation logged on as user **packerman**.

1. Open Internet Explorer.
2. Browse to *http://ms02/certsrv/*.

   The Microsoft Certificate Services Web site appears.

Note   You must browse to the CA configured as a stand-alone subordinate server. You cannot request S/MIME certificates appropriate for use in Outlook Express from an enterprise CA. However, the user certificate from an enterprise CA is appropriate for use in standard Outlook.

---

3. Select Request A Certificate, and click Next. The Request Type page appears.
4. Select E-Mail Protection Certificate, and then click Next. The E-Mail Protection Certificate – Identifying Information window appears, as shown in Figure 6.26.

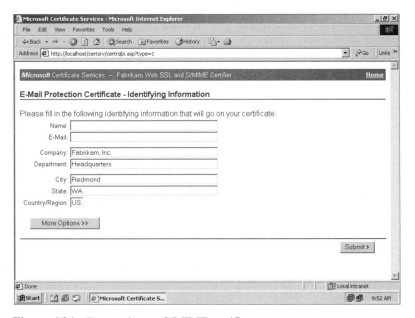

Figure 6.26   Requesting an S/MIME certificate

5. Type **Pilar Ackerman** in the Name box.
6. Type **packerman@fabrikam.com** in the E-Mail box.
7. Click Submit. The Certificate Pending page appears.
8. Close Internet Explorer.

▶ **To issue the certificate**

Perform this procedure on the stand-alone subordinate CA server.

1. Open the Certification Authority management console.
2. Expand Fabrikam Web SSL and S/MIME Certifier, and select Pending Requests. A list of pending certificate requests appears in the management console.
3. Right-click the certificate with the Request Common Name of Pilar Ackerman, point to All Tasks, and then click Issue.
4. Close the management console.

▶ **To install the issued certificate**

Perform this procedure on the workstation logged on as user **packerman**.

1. Open Internet Explorer and browse to *http://ms02/certsrv*. The Microsoft Certificate Services Web site appears.
2. Select Check On A Pending Certificate, and click Next.
3. Select the E-Mail Protection Certificate, and click Next. The Certificate Issued dialog box appears.
4. Click Install This Certificate.
5. From the Tools menu, choose Internet Options. The Internet Options dialog box appears.
6. Click the Content tab, and then click the Certificates button.
7. Double-click the Pilar Ackerman certificate. The Certificate dialog box appears, containing information about the issued certificate.
8. Verify the certificate's uses.
9. Close all of the dialog boxes and the Web browser.

▶ **To send digitally signed e-mail messages**

1. Open Outlook Express. If an error message appears stating that mail.Fabrikam.com cannot be reached, click Hide.
2. Click New Mail. An empty e-mail message window appears.
3. Type **sabbas@fabrikam.com** in the To box.
4. Type **Test Message** in the Subject box.
5. Type **Test** as the body of the message.
6. Click the Sign button.
7. Click Send.
8. Click Outbox. Notice that the e-mail is transferred to the outbox with a digital signature.

Note   You cannot encrypt e-mail to a recipient until you receive a digitally signed e-mail message from that person containing a public key. The key is added to your e-mail client's key store and can encrypt future e-mail messages to that person.

Lesson Review

The following questions are intended to reinforce key information in this lesson. If you are unable to answer a question, review the lesson and try the question again. Answers to the questions can be found in the appendix.

1. Why can't you use user certificates in many e-mail clients to sign and encrypt e-mail?

2. Why is an e-mail address usually required in the Identity field of an S/MIME certificate?

3. Why don't user certificates contain e-mail addresses?

4. Why does Outlook accept user certificates if they don't contain an e-mail address?

Lesson Summary

S/MIME certificates are required to sign and encrypt e-mail messages for S/MIME-compliant e-mail clients such as Outlook, Outlook Express, and most other independent software vendor e-mail programs. Most of these packages require the Identity field to be set to the e-mail address configured in the user settings.

The user certificate template can be used as an S/MIME certificate for e-mail programs that don't require the e-mail address to be configured in the certificate's Identity field, such as Outlook. For all other e-mail applications, you must use S/MIME certificates generated from the S/MIME template. The S/MIME template runs only on a stand-alone CA and asks users for their e-mail addresses to embed in the certificate's Identity field.

You must use a stand-alone CA to generate S/MIME certificates for most e-mail clients. If you use Outlook, you can use an enterprise CA to generate user certificates that will work as S/MIME certificates.

C H A P T E R   7

Increasing Authentication Security

About This Chapter

This chapter discusses how to keep your network as secure as possible while allowing access to network resources for clients that run earlier versions of Microsoft Windows and third-party operating systems such as Apple Macintosh. It also discusses how to keep authentication secure when transiting between domains within the same organization.

Exam Tip   You need to understand how to require NTLM version 2 authentication on servers and how to install support for NTLM version 2 on Windows 98, Windows NT, and Apple Macintosh computers.

Before You Begin

Chapter 2, "User Accounts and Security Groups," dealt with authentication on local computers and the Kerberos mechanism for logging on to a domain network after the client initially authenticates with the authentication service on a domain controller. You should be familiar with Chapter 2 before reading this chapter.

To complete the lessons in this chapter, you must have

- A Microsoft Windows 2000 domain controller attached to the network
- A Windows 2000 domain controller for another forest attached to the network
- A Microsoft Windows 98 client computer attached to the network
- A Macintosh client computer attached to the network

Lesson 1: Supporting Earlier Versions of Windows Clients

In environments that have not completed the migration to Windows 2000, you might need to support earlier versions of clients (also called down-level clients) such as Microsoft Windows 95, Windows 98, and Windows NT. This lesson will teach you how to improve security by replacing earlier authentication protocols with Microsoft NTLM version 2 on servers and clients.

To complete this lesson, you will need

■   A Windows 98 client attached to the domain

Estimated lesson time: 30 minutes

Authentication Basics

Network authentication is the process by which users prove their identity to a remote computer to gain access to its resources after having logged on to a local computer. Single Sign On (SSO) systems, such as Kerberos, automate this process but do not eliminate the requirement of logging on to each server that the user accesses. The illusion of "logging on to the network" is maintained because the user is not interrupted for credentials—they are automatically provided by the client through a traditional exchange of credentials or by possession of a secret key.

When you attempt to access resources on a remote computer or server, either you must have an account on the remote server or the remote server must trust a domain controller on which you have an account. In Windows, this trust can be automatically conferred by participation in the same domain or by participation within a trusted domain.

In a Kerberos network, clients contact a domain controller to retrieve a session ticket, which they can then use to prove their ability to log on. But, because Kerberos authentication is not available to clients prior to Windows 2000, either the LAN Manager or the NTLM authentication protocol must be used.

Both the LAN Manager and the NTLM authentication protocols are *challenge/ response* authentication protocols. Challenge/response authentication is a method of proving that two computers each know a password without revealing what that password is. When the client requests a log on by sending the account name, the server looks up the account name and finds the encrypted password associated with it. The server then sends a random number called a *nonce* to the client. Both the client and server encrypt the nonce using the password, and the client returns the result. If the result computed on the client matches the result computed on the server, both computers used the same password to reach that result, but they passed only a random number and an encrypted random number over the network.

When a client contacts a domain member server and requests a logon session using LAN Manager or NTLM authentication, the member server performs a pass-through challenge/response authentication with the client. In *pass-through* authentication, the member server, which does not store the user's account information, passes the credentials, nonce, and results to and from the domain controller, and accepts the domain controller's word that the authentication succeeded. If the credentials are valid on the domain controller, the domain controller replies with the security identifiers (SIDs) that are valid for the client account, and the member server constructs an access token and creates a session for the user.

Windows 2000 Network Authentication

To authenticate a user name and password, Windows 2000 uses the Kerberos V5 or NTLM authentication protocol to encrypt the user name and password. Kerberos V5 is the default in a Windows 2000 (and Windows XP) environment. However, NTLM authentication is used when the client is an earlier version of the Windows operating system, such as Windows 98 or Windows NT. Windows 2000 provides authentication with these clients by supporting

- *LAN Manager*, an early Microsoft technology for client/server environments. The least secure authentication method, LAN Manager is used only when connecting to shared folders on computers running Microsoft Windows for Workgroups, Windows 95, Windows 98, and Windows Me.

Tip   If you do not need to support clients earlier than Windows 2000, improve network security by disabling support for LAN Manager protocols in Group Policy.

- *NTLM version 1*, used to connect to Windows NT servers if the environment includes a domain controller running Windows NT 4 Service Pack 3 or earlier.
- *NTLM version 2*, used to connect to workstation computers running Windows 2000 (or Windows XP) or to Windows NT servers in a domain where all controllers are running Windows NT Service Pack 4 or higher.
- *Kerberos V5*, used when Windows 2000 or Windows XP clients connect to domain member servers or when Windows 2000 servers connect to other Windows 2000 servers.

LAN Manager Authentication

LAN Manager authentication was developed to connect computers running MS-DOS, IBM OS/2, and UNIX operating systems. Modern computers can decrypt any LAN Manager–encrypted password in a trivial amount of time, so avoid its use. On Windows 95 and Windows 98 computers, you can install the Directory Services client to upgrade their authentication to NTLM version 2. For Windows NT 4, you can install any service pack after Service Pack 4 to provide compatibility with NTLM version 2. Earlier clients should be upgraded to more modern and secure operating systems because they do not support secure authentication protocols.

Warning   Support for LAN Manager authentication is enabled by default in Windows 2000. If your network does not include non-Microsoft legacy clients, such as computers running OS/2, disable support for LAN Manager authentication using the procedure shown in Exercise 1.

NTLM Authentication

NTLM authentication is more secure than LAN Manager authentication. It uses 14-character passwords and 56-bit encryption to increase the difficulty of acquiring the password in a brute-force attack. However, NTLM authentication is still not secure enough to withstand a concerted decryption attack. All NTLM passwords can be decrypted in a matter of three to six hours with dedicated hardware, and weak or short passwords can be decrypted in a few hours on any modern computer.

Warning   NTLM authentication has been superseded by NTLM version 2. Upgrade all clients to support NTLM version 2 rather than support NTLM authentication in your network.

NTLM Version 2 Authentication

NTLM version 2 increases the security of NTLM encryption by using 128-bit encryption, which provides enough security to make brute-force attacks impractical with current technology. Dictionary attacks can still be successful, so passwords must be strong to avoid compromise.

NTLM version 2 is enabled for Windows NT 4 Service Pack 4 and later. For Windows 95 and Windows 98, you can enable support for NTLM version 2 by installing the Windows 2000 Directory Services client and ensuring that support for 128-bit encryption has been added by installing the latest version of Microsoft Internet Explorer.

Caution   Consider moving all earlier Windows platforms to Windows 2000 so that you have a homogeneous Windows 2000 network and can disable all forms of NTLM authentication. While NTLM version 2 is significantly stronger than earlier versions, it's still not nearly as secure as Kerberos authentication.

Creating a Secure Environment

Enabling support for NTLM version 2 requires 128-bit security. To see if your Windows 95 or Windows 98 computer already supports 128-bit security, open Internet Explorer, click Help, and then choose About Internet Explorer. Internet Explorer displays an About Internet Explorer dialog box, as shown in Figure 7.1.

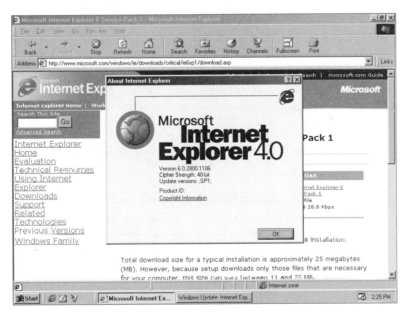

Figure 7.1   Windows 95 and Windows 98 shipped with 40-bit security

If the cipher strength is anything less than 128-bit, you must upgrade to the current version of Internet Explorer.

Practice: Enabling a Secure Mixed-Client Environment

In this practice, you update earlier versions of Windows clients to take advantage of NTLM version 2 and disable support for the earlier, less secure LAN Manager authentication protocols. You also install the Directory Services client on a Windows 95 or Windows 98 computer, and modify registry settings to support NTLM version 2 authentication.

Exercise 1: Removing Support for Earlier Authentication Protocols in the Domain

In this exercise, you increase the logon protocol security for a Windows 95 or Windows 98 client network to better safeguard passwords on the network against brute-force decryption attacks. You upgrade the client to NTLM version 2 authentication and ensure that Internet Explorer is providing 128-bit encryption.

► **To force NTLM version 2 authentication in the domain**

1. Log on as the Administrator and open the Domain Security Policy management console. The Group Policy editor appears.

2. Expand Domain Security policy, Windows Settings, Security Settings, Local Policies, and then select Security Options. The Group Policy namespace appears as shown in Figure 7.2.

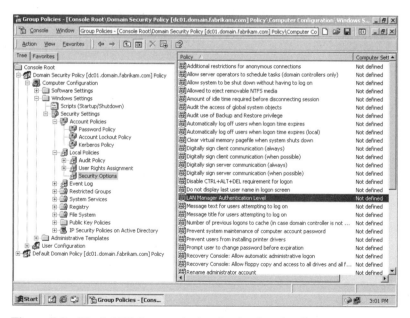

Figure 7.2   The LAN Manager Authentication Level policy

3. Double-click LAN Manager Authentication Level. The Security Policy Setting dialog box appears as shown in Figure 7.3.

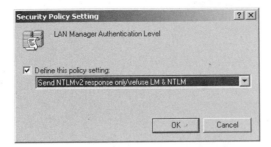

Figure 7.3   Security Policy Setting dialog box

4. Select the Define This Policy Setting check box, and then select Send NTLMv2 Responses Only\Refuse LM & NTLM from the list.

5. Click OK to establish a security policy that accepts NTLM version 2 authentication responses only. Responses from earlier authentication protocols will be rejected.

6. Close the Group Policy editor.

▶ **To upgrade to 128-bit security**

1. Open Internet Explorer and go to the following address: *http://www.microsoft.com/windows/ie/downloads*.

   Depending on the version of Internet Explorer you are using, you may receive error messages when Internet Explorer tries to access the Microsoft download Web site. Click Yes to any of these messages to continue loading the Web site. If you cannot reach the download Web site from your version of Internet Explorer, install a newer version of Internet Explorer from CD. See *http://www.microsoft.com/ie* for information about obtaining an Internet Explorer CD.

2. Follow the links to download the latest version of Internet Explorer.

3. When the File Download dialog box appears, select Run This Program From Its Current Location, and click OK.

4. A Security Warning message box appears. Click Yes to install the current version of Internet Explorer. The Windows Update: Internet Explorer And Internet Tools Wizard appears.

5. Select I Accept The Agreement, and click Next. The Installation page appears.

6. Select Install Minimal to keep the download time to a minimum, and click Next.

7. On the Component Options page, leave the defaults as they are, and click Next.

   Windows Update proceeds to download components. This could take a few seconds or a few hours, depending on the speed of your Internet connection. The Restart Computer message box appears at the end of the file download.

8. Click Finish to restart your computer.

9. If a logon dialog box appears, you can either log on or click Cancel.

A Windows 98 Setup progress bar appears while Internet Explorer updates system settings during the boot process. System startup will be unusually long because numerous system updates are applied. At the end of the boot process, Windows has been updated to use 128-bit security. You can verify this in the About Internet Explorer dialog box, as shown in Figure 7.4.

Figure 7.4   Verifying that 128-bit security is installed

▶ **To install the Directory Services client**

1. Insert the Windows 2000 Server CD into the client computer's CD-ROM drive.

2. In Windows Explorer, double-click the CD-ROM drive icon. Then double-click the Clients folder, the WIN9X folder, and the Dsclient.cab file.

   A progress bar appears briefly while the files in the cabinet file are decompressed, and the Directory Service Client Setup Wizard appears next.

3. Click Next, and click Next again to begin copying files.

4. Click Finish after the files are copied.

5. Click Yes to restart your computer.

Exercise 2: Enabling NTLM Version 2 on Earlier Versions of Windows Clients

In this exercise, you modify the registry on an earlier Windows client, such as Windows 95, Window 98, and Windows NT, so that it authenticates using NTLM version 2.

Note   Windows NT 4 clients must have Service Pack 4 or later installed for this procedure to be effective.

▶ **To modify the registry to support NTLM version 2**

1. Click Start, and click Run.

2. In the Run dialog box, type **regedit,** and press ENTER. The Registry Editor appears.

3. Expand HKEY_LOCAL_MACHINE, System, CurrentControlSet, Control, and then Lsa.

Note   The Lsa registry key might not exist if you have not installed Internet Explorer. If it does not exist, create it by right-clicking Control, pointing to New, clicking Key, and changing the name to Lsa.

---

4. Right-click the Lsa key, point to New, and then click DWORD Value.

5. Type **LMCompatibility** as the name of the value.

6. Double-click the LMCompatibility value.

7. In the Edit DWORD Value dialog box, type **3** in the Value Data box, and click OK. The value 3 is the registry value required to force NTLM version 2 authentication and reject LAN Manager and NTLM version 1 authentication.

   In the Registry Editor, LMCompatibility appears with the value of 3, as shown in Figure 7.5.

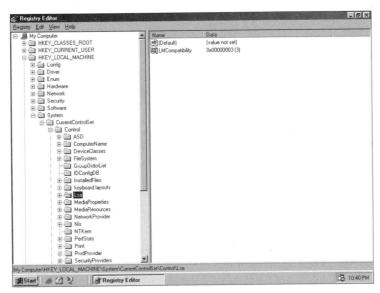

Figure 7.5   Configuring a Windows 98 client to use NTLM version 2 authentication

8. Close the Registry Editor.

9. Restart the computer.

   Upon rebooting, the client computer will be able to log on to the domain using NTLM version 2 authentication.

Lesson Review

The following questions are intended to reinforce key information in this lesson. If you are unable to answer a question, review the lesson and try the question again. Answers to the questions can be found in the appendix.

1. What are the four types of authentication supported by Windows 2000 to support current and earlier versions of Windows clients?

2. Which two authentication protocols are considered the most secure?

3. What components must be installed in Windows 98 to use NTLM version 2?

4. What encryption strength is used to secure NTLM version 2 passwords?

Lesson Summary

- Windows 2000 supports LAN Manager, NTLM, NTLM version 2, and Kerberos authentication for authenticating Windows clients.
- LAN Manager authentication was originally used in IBM OS/2, MS-DOS, and Windows for Workgroups. It is especially weak and should not be used in secure networks.
- NTLM was developed to improve LAN Manager security for Windows NT and was superseded by NTLM version 2 in Windows NT Service Pack 4. NTLM authentication is not as strong and should therefore be replaced by NTLM version 2 authentication.
- NTLM version 2 improves NTLM authentication by increasing the encryption strength from 56 bits to 128 bits.
- Kerberos is considerably stronger than earlier authentication methods. If security is of paramount importance, earlier clients should be replaced with Windows 2000 or later, and Kerberos should be used exclusively for authentication.

Lesson 2: Supporting Macintosh Clients

Windows 2000 includes strong support for Macintosh clients by supporting the Apple File Protocol (AFP) as a native networking protocol. AFP is the file sharing protocol used by Apple products. Installing Services for Macintosh on Windows 2000 servers allows them to share files seamlessly with Macintosh clients.

Note   Apple authentication is weak by default, but can be strengthened to NTLM version 2 by installing the Microsoft User Authentication Module (UAM).

To complete this lesson, you will need

■   A Macintosh client

Estimated lesson time: 20 minutes

Supporting Macintosh Computers Securely

Because Macintosh computers present their passwords without encryption by default, a malicious user can easily sniff them on the network. In addition, to check plaintext passwords, you must enable password storage using reversible encryption on domain controllers, which puts passwords at risk for decryption if the server is physically compromised.

Tip   In Windows 2000, AFP can be used with TCP/IP as well as AppleTalk, so AppleTalk is not necessary if all Macintosh clients are TCP/IP capable.

Both of these problems can be solved by installing the Microsoft User Authentication Module (UAM) on Macintosh clients that need to attach to the domain. The UAM implements NTLM version 2 with 128-bit encryption, and eliminates the requirement for storing passwords using reversible encryption. To provide secure Macintosh service, install the latest UAM on every Macintosh client and configure servers to require NTLM version 2 authentication.

When you install Services for Macintosh, the installer creates a Macintosh-compatible share called the Microsoft UAM Volume. An earlier version of the UAM is installed in this share, which allows Mac OS 8 and 9 computers to connect to the server and download the UAM easily. The current UAM, which is compatible with NTLM version 2, is not installed by default.

Servers that are already secured to require NTLM version 2 authentication will not allow Macintosh clients to connect to this share to obtain the UAM. Rather than reducing server security to deploy the UAM, solve this problem by downloading the UAM client directly from Microsoft through the client's Web browser. Automate the deployment by e-mailing Macintosh users a link to the file and letting them install it themselves.

The current version of the UAM provides NTLM version 2 128-bit encryption for Macintosh clients. There are two versions of the UAM:

- UAM for Mac OS 8.5 through 9.2
- UAM for Mac OS X 10.1 and later

Note   The Mac OS X is entirely different from earlier versions of the Mac OS and requires a different version of the UAM to be compatible with NTLM version 2.

The NTLM version 2 compatible UAM does not require passwords to be stored using reversible encryption, and you should not enable reversible encryption to support Macintosh clients that use this UAM.

Note   Macintosh OS X 10.1 clients can connect natively to Server Message Block (SMB) shares on workstation computers, but they cannot authenticate with domains.

Practice: Enabling Macintosh Clients to Access Windows 2000 Servers

In this practice, you configure the domain controller to serve Macintosh clients, and you configure a Macintosh client to connect to the server using NTLM version 2 authentication.

Exercise 1: Preparing a Windows 2000 Server to Support Macintosh Clients

In this exercise, you prepare a Windows 2000 server to serve Macintosh clients. Perform these procedures on a domain controller.

▶   **To install Services for Macintosh**

1. Log on as Administrator.
2. Click Start, point to Settings, and then click Control Panel.

3. In Control Panel, double-click Add/Remove Programs. The Add/Remove Programs window appears.

4. Click Add/Remove Windows Components. The Windows Components Wizard appears.

5. In the wizard, double-click (do not select) Other Network File And Print Services. The Other Network File And Print Services dialog box appears.

6. Select File Services For Macintosh and Print Services For Macintosh, as shown in Figure 7.6.

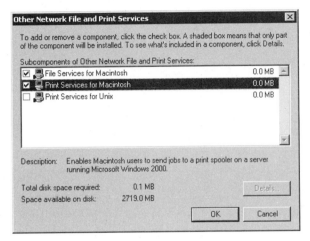

Figure 7.6   Installing File Services and Print Services for Macintosh

7. Click OK, and click Next. The Configuring Components window appears with a progress indicator.

8. When the configuration completes, click Finish.

9. Click Close to close the Add/Remove Programs window.

10. Close the Control Panel window.

▶ **To create a Macintosh-compatible file share**

1. Log on as the Administrator.

2. On the desktop, right-click My Computer, and click Manage. The Computer Management console appears.

3. Expand Shared Folders, and then click Shares. Your screen should look like Figure 7.7.

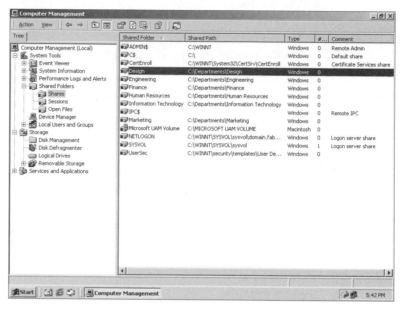

Figure 7.7   Shared folders in the Computer Management console

4. Right-click in a blank area of the rightmost pane, and click New File Share. The Create Shared Folder Wizard (Figure 7.8) appears.

Figure 7.8   Creating a Macintosh-compatible shared folder

5. Type **C:\Departments** (or use the browse button to browse to that location).

6. Type **Departments** as the Share Name.

7. Type **Macintosh Accessible Share** in the Share Description box.

8. Select the Apple Macintosh check box in the Accessible From The Following Clients group, and verify that Microsoft Windows is selected.

9. Click Next to open the share permissions page.

10. Leave the All Users Have Full Control option set, and click Finish. A message box will appear asking if you want to create another shared folder.

11. Click No, and close the Computer Management console.

Exercise 2: Connecting to Windows 2000 from a Macintosh

In this exercise, you connect a Macintosh OS X 10.1 client computer to a Windows 2000 server using the AFP. The process for Macintosh OS 8.5-9.2 clients is very similar.

In this exercise, the UAM is downloaded directly from the Microsoft Web site because the version created automatically in the Microsoft UAM share on the Windows 2000 server is not compatible with Mac OS X. Perform this exercise from a Macintosh client running Mac OS X 10.1 or higher.

Important   Adopt a habit of acquiring the latest revision of any security-related software that you use on your network. Vulnerabilities are routinely patched in security-related software, so installing the latest version ensures that your system is as secure as possible.

▶   **To install the Microsoft UAM**

1. Open Internet Explorer and browse to the following address:
   www.microsoft.com/mac/products/win2ksfm/.

   The Mactopia Services For Macintosh Web page appears.

2. Click the download link for the Microsoft User Authentication Module (UAM) appropriate for your version of Mac OS.

   The download manager appears, then a MSUAM installation package icon appears on the desktop, and finally a MSUAM folder appears on the desktop.

3. Double-click the UAM folder on the desktop.

4. Double-click the Install MSUAM icon within the folder.

   The Macintosh installer appears. In Mac OS X, an authorization dialog box appears requesting the Administrator password.

5. Click the lock icon. An Authenticate dialog box appears.

6. Type the administrator's password, and click OK. The Authenticate dialog box closes, returning the installer to the front.

7. Click Continue. The MS UAM Read Me document appears, as shown in Figure 7.9.

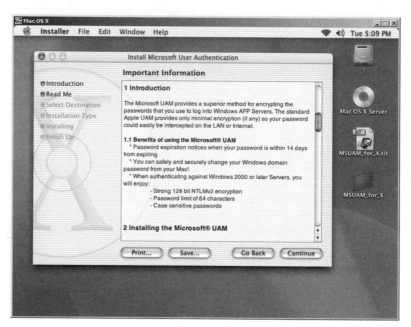

Figure 7.9   Installing the Microsoft User Authentication Module on a Macintosh

8. Click Continue to open the Select A Destination dialog box.

9. Click the icon representing your internal hard disk, and then click Continue.

10. Click Install. The Macintosh installer will inform you that the installation was successful.

11. Click Close.

12. Close the open window on your desktop, and delete the installation package file and folder left by the installation process.

▶   **To connect securely to a Windows share from a Macintosh client**

1. In the Mac Finder (the desktop), click the Go menu, and then click Connect To Server.

   Use the Connect To Server dialog box, shown in Figure 7.10, to create the shared drive mappings.

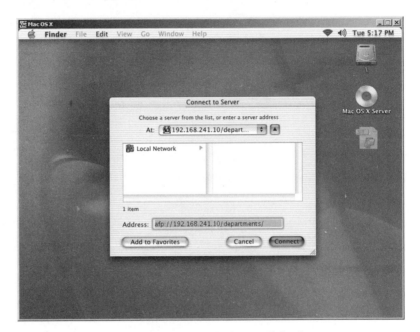

Figure 7.10   The Macintosh Connect To Server dialog box

2. Type **afp://192.168.241.10/departments/** in the Address box, and click Connect.

Note   Use the IP address for your server, or its domain name if your Macintosh client has been configured to receive DNS service from the domain controller.

A UAM authentication dialog box appears, as shown in Figure 7.11, that you can use to ensure the authentication process is secure.

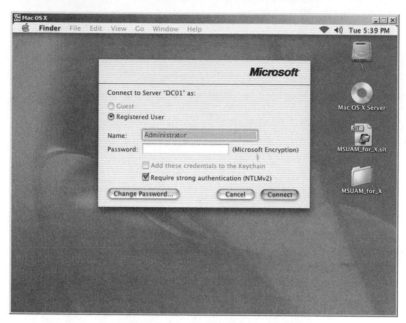

Figure 7.11   The Macintosh UAM authentication dialog box

3. Verify that Registered User is selected, type **Administrator** in the Name box, and then type the administrator's password in the Password box.

4. Ensure that the Require Strong Authentication check box is selected, and click Connect. A Departments icon appears on the desktop representing the network share.

5. Double-click the Departments icon to view the contents of the Departments share, as shown in Figure 7.12.

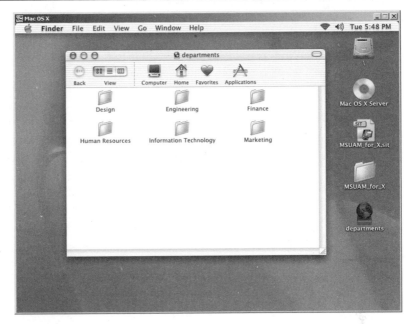

Figure 7.12   A Windows 2000 share as viewed from a Macintosh client

Lesson Review

The following questions are intended to reinforce key information in this lesson. If you are unable to answer a question, review the lesson and try the question again. Answers to the questions can be found in the appendix.

1. What server component is used to provide the Apple File Service?

2. Is AppleTalk required to provide service to Macintosh clients?

3. What client component provides NTLM version 2 authentication for Macintosh computers?

4. Does the NTLM version 2 compatible Microsoft UAM require reversible encryption to support Macintosh clients?

Lesson Summary

- Windows 2000 Server provides strong support for Macintosh computers in the Services for Macintosh and AppleTalk protocols. Installing these services and enabling password storage with reversible encryption will allow access by Macintosh computers using non-secure plaintext authentication.

- You can secure Macintosh client access by requiring NTML version 2 on servers and installing the Microsoft User Authentication Module (UAM). The UAM enables Macintosh clients to authenticate securely using NTML version 2, and eliminates the requirement for reversible password encryption on servers.

- The UAM client for earlier versions of Mac OS is installed by default in the Microsoft UAM volume that is created when Services for Macintosh is installed. You must download the UAM for Mac OS X clients from Microsoft.

Lesson 3: Trust Relationships

Trust relationships allow members of one domain to access resources in another domain without possessing an account in the target domain. This relationship simplifies administration by allowing you to determine on a large scale which groups of users should have access to pools of resources across domains. Windows 2000 creates trust relationships automatically.

To complete this lesson, you will need

- A domain controller named dc01.domain.fabrikam.com
- A domain controller named gdi-dc-01.extranet.graphicdesigninstitute.com that is in a separate forest but on the same physical network
- A workstation in the domain.fabrikam.com domain

Estimated lesson time: 30 minutes

Understanding Trust Relationships

When one domain trusts another domain's account holders, a *one-way trust relationship* exists. When both domains trust each other's account holders, a *two-way trust relationship* exists. When trust in a central domain allows the edge domains to trust each other, a *transitive trust relationship* exists.

Adding a domain to a forest creates a two-way transitive trust relationship with the parent domain that, due to the transitive nature of trust in Windows 2000, translates to an automatic trust relationship with all other domains in the forest. These trust relationships do not need to be managed.

There are three reasons to explicitly manage trust relationships in a Windows 2000 forest:

- To establish trust relationships with Windows NT 4 domains
- To establish trust to a domain in a foreign forest
- To create a shortcut trust relationship between two domains in a very large forest

Important   Rather than explicitly manage Windows NT 4 trust relationships, upgrade Windows NT 4 domains to Windows 2000 as quickly as possible.

When authentication is performed between two widely separated domains in Windows 2000, a trust path must be computed between them, which can take a considerable amount of time if the path is heavily used. Explicitly creating a two-way trust relationship between these domains shortens the trust-path computation and optimizes authentication processing. However, shortcut trust relationships have no effect on security, so they are not specifically covered in this book.

Managing External Trust Relationships

Creating a trust relationship to a foreign domain allows users to log on to the foreign domain directly. External trust relationships are one-way and non-transitive, so you can create a two-way trust relationship by creating two reciprocal trust relationships between the domains. Because external trust relationships are non-transitive, you must create an explicit trust relationship for every trusted domain.

Create trust relationships between forests through the Active Directory Domains And Trusts management console by opening the Properties dialog box for the domain. To establish a trust relationship, create an entry in the trusted domain list on the domain controller in the domain containing the target resource, and then create an entry in the trusting domain list on the domain controller containing the user accounts that will access the target resource. Security is established by entering the same secret key as a password on both systems.

After the second entry has been made, the domain controllers verify the trust relationship and pass information about security principals to the target domain so their SIDs can be entered into the access control lists (ACLs) of resources in the target domain.

Practice: Creating an External Trust Relationship

In this practice, you create an external trust relationship to a resource domain belonging to a business partner of the Fabrikam Corporation, the Graphic Design Institute. The purpose of this trust relationship is to allow Fabrikam designers to create and manage Fabrikam graphic files that will be produced by the Graphic Design Institute directly on their own servers.

After you've created a trust relationship, you will add users from the Fabrikam domain to the ACL of a resource in the Graphic Design Institute domain—users from a trusted domain. Finally, you will access those resources from the trusted domain.

To perform this practice, you need to set up a domain controller for a domain called extranet.GraphicDesignInstitute.com.

Note   To reduce the complexity of this exercise, NetBIOS names are used to refer to both domains and servers rather than fully qualified domain names. Normally, the two domains are not within the same physical network, so using the NetBIOS name to resolve the foreign domain or server would not work. To create trust relationships between domains using the fully qualified domain name, you must configure DNS name resolution with entries for the foreign domain.

Exercise: Establishing a Trust Relationship

In this exercise, you establish a trust relationship from the extranet.graphicdesigninstitute.com domain to the domain.fabrikam.com domain so that Fabrikam users can log on to the Graphic Design Institute server.

Note   Perform this exercise on the Graphic Design Institute domain controller.

▶   **To create an external trust relationship**

1. Log on as the domain administrator.
2. Click Start, point to Programs, point to Administrative Tools, and click Active Directory Domains And Trusts. The Active Directory Domains And Trusts management console appears.
3. Right-click extranet.graphicdesigninstitute.com, and click Properties. The extranet.graphicdesigninstitute.com Properties dialog box appears.
4. Click the Trusts tab, shown in Figure 7.13.

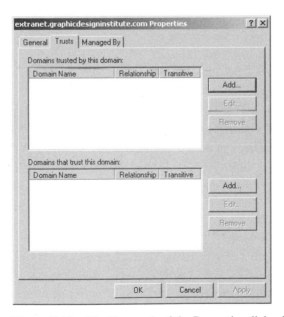

Figure 7.13   The Trusts tab of the Properties dialog box

5. Click the Add button for the Domains Trusted By This Domain control group. The Add Trusted Domain dialog box appears, as shown in Figure 7.14.

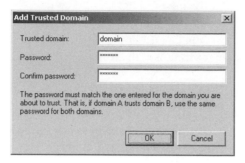

Figure 7.14   Adding an explicit trust relationship

6. Type **domain** in the Trusted Domain box, and type the password for the domain in both the Password and Confirm Password boxes. Click OK to continue.

7. Click OK when a warning appears that the trust cannot be verified.

8. Click OK to close the extranet.graphicdesigninstitute.com Properties dialog box.

9. Close the Active Directory Domains And Trusts management console.

▶ **To create the reciprocal trust entry**

1. Log on as the domain administrator on the domain.fabrikam.com domain controller.

2. Click Start, point to Programs, point to Administrative Tools, and click Active Directory Domains And Trusts. The Active Directory Domains And Trusts management console appears.

3. Right-click domain.fabrikam.com, and click Properties. The domain.fabrikam.com Properties dialog box appears.

4. Click the Trusts tab.

5. Click the Add button for the Domains That Trust This Domain control group. The Add Trusting Domain dialog box appears.

6. Type **Extranet** in the Trusting Domain box, and type the password you used in the previous procedure in both of the Password boxes.

7. Click OK. A dialog box appears asking if you want to verify the trust relationship.

8. Click Yes. A dialog box appears asking for an administrator's credentials in the foreign domain.

9. Type **Administrator** in the User Name box, and type the administrator's password for the extranet.graphicdesigninstitute.com domain in the Password box.

10. Click OK. A message appears indicating that the trusting domain has been added and the trust verified.

11. Click OK. The domain.fabrikam.com dialog box appears, as shown in Figure 7.15, with extranet.graphicdesigninstitute.com listed as a domain that trusts this domain.

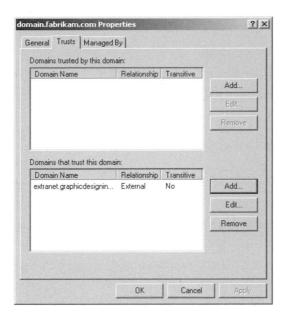

Figure 7.15   The other side of a trust relationship

12. Click OK, and close the Active Directory Domains And Trusts management console.

► **To secure a resource for users in a foreign domain**

1. Log on as the domain administrator on the extranet.graphicdesigninstitute.com domain controller.

2. Create a folder in the C drive named **Fabrikam**. This folder will be used to store files from Fabrikam.

3. Right-click the Fabrikam folder, and click Properties to open the Properties dialog box.

4. Select the Security tab, and click Add. The Select Users, Computers, Or Groups dialog box appears.

5. In the Look In list, select domain.fabrikam.com.

6. Double-click Design Users. You have now added users from a trusted domain to the resource's ACL.

7. In the Look In list, select extranet.graphicdesigninstitute.com.

8. Double-click Administrators, and click OK to close the Select Users, Computers, Or Groups dialog box. The resource is now accessible by users in both domains.

9. With Design Users selected in the Properties dialog box, select the Full Control Allow check box.

10. Clear the Allow Inheritable Permissions check box.

11. The Security dialog box appears asking if you want to copy or remove inherited permissions. Click Remove.

    The Everyone group is removed from the list of allowed security principals.

12. Click OK to close the Fabrikam Properties dialog box.

13. Right-click the Fabrikam folder, and click Sharing. The Properties dialog box opens.

14. Select Share This Folder, and click OK.

    The folder is now shared.

▶ **To access an external resource**

1. Log on as user **sabbas** from a workstation in the domain.fabrikam.com domain.

2. On the desktop, double-click My Network Places.

3. Double-click Add Network Place. The Add Network Place Wizard appears.

4. Type **\\GDI-DC1-01\Fabrikam** as the name of the network place, and click Next.

   What would you type as the name of this server if the two servers were not on the same network?

5. Click Finish. The Fabrikam window opens.

6. Right-click in the window, point to New, and click Text Document.

   A new text document appears in the window, proving that the user has Write access to the share.

Lesson Review

The following questions are intended to reinforce key information in this lesson. If you are unable to answer a question, review the lesson and try the question again. Answers to the questions can be found in the appendix.

1. What are the three reasons why you would explicitly modify trust relationships?

2. What is the difference between transitive and non-transitive trust?

3. What is the difference between one-way and two-way trust relationships?

4. What type of trust relationship results when you manually create a trust relationship?

5. What type of trust relationship is automatically created when a domain is added to a forest?

Lesson Summary

- Trust relationships allow servers in a domain to trust accounts in a foreign domain so that users in the foreign domain can access resources in the local domain. A two-way trust relationship exists when both domains trust each other's accounts. A transitive trust relationship exists when trust in a domain is automatically conferred to domains that it trusts.

- Windows 2000 automatically creates two-way transitive trust relationships between domains whenever a domain is created within a forest. For this reason, it is normally not necessary to explicitly manage trust relationships. Domains within a forest all trust each other's accounts.

- You explicitly manage trust relationships to create a trust path shortcut, establish trust with a Windows NT 4 server, or establish trust with a server outside the forest. Explicitly managed trust relationships are one-way non-transitive trust relationships.

- Trust relationships are managed using the Active Directory Domains And Trusts management console. Creating a trust relationship requires making an entry containing the same secret key on a domain controller in the trusted domain as the one in the trusting domain.

C H A P T E R   8

IP Security

About This Chapter

Internet Protocol security (IPSec) is an Internet Engineering Task Force (IETF) body of standards that defines a protocol for authenticating and encrypting IP traffic between hosts on an IP network. IPSec allows the hosts to negotiate encryption and authentication methods that are compatible with both the Internet and private IP networks, and appropriate for the type of traffic flowing over the connection.

IPSec operates at the network layer as a component of IP. It can be passed by any intermediate gateways that can route IP packets and can encapsulate IP to create private tunnels for secure point-to-point communications on the Internet. Because it operates at the network layer, it is transparent to higher-level programs and can be added to supplement security for any network application.

Because it is so flexible, configuring IPSec is complex and multifaceted. You use a number of tools to perform configuration and troubleshooting, and there is usually more than one way to accomplish the same goal.

Exam Tip   Ensure that you understand the role of IPSec in a network, why you would deploy AH and ESP, and the different methods used to distribute IPSec keys.

Before You Begin

To complete this chapter, you will need

- A domain controller for the domain.fabrikam.com domain named dc01
- A domain controller for the extranet.graphicdesigninstitute.com named gdi-dc-01 with an IP address of 192.168.241.60
- A member server in domain.Fabrikam.com named ms01 with an IP address of 192.168.241.63
- A client workstation in the domain.Fabrikam.com domain named CLIENT01

All three of these servers should be on the same local network. You can modify the IP addresses if desired, but remember to use the revised addresses consistently throughout the exercises in this chapter.

Lesson 1: Configuring IPSec Within a Domain

IPSec provides the ability to encrypt TCP/IP communications between computers. While it was originally developed to provide encryption between public Internet hosts, there are many private environments in which encrypted communications between servers and clients would improve security, including loosely controlled environments such as universities, high-security environments such as military operations, and industries such as finance that have a need to protect sensitive information or trade secrets.

Within a domain, enabling IPSec between servers and clients is easy, and IPSec can be deployed throughout a domain of any size with minimal administrative effort.

To complete this lesson, you will need

- The dc01 domain controller
- The ms01 member server
- The CLIENT01 client computer

After this lesson, you will be able to

- Understand the purpose of IPSec
- Enable secure encrypted communications on servers and clients within a domain

Estimated lesson time: 30 minutes

Understanding the IPSec Basics

IPSec is the standard method of authenticating and encrypting traffic between IP hosts. IPSec provides the IP packet structure and protocols necessary to automatically exchange keys between hosts and negotiate encryption and authentication protocols. IPSec performs these two primary functions using two complementary features:

- *Authenticated Headers* (AH) digitally encrypts the IP header (the portion of a packet containing the source and destination address) and the payload (the portion of a packet containing the user's data) to ensure that they have not been modified at any time during their transit between hosts. AH does not encrypt traffic.

- *Encapsulating Security Payload* (ESP) encrypts packets and applies a new non-encrypted header to facilitate routing. Beyond providing encryption, ESP does not guarantee the authenticity of header data.

These two methods can be used together to provide both authenticated headers and encrypted data payload.

Note   Windows 2000 and Windows NT 4 both contain support for SMB message signing, which provides the ability to authenticate each SMB (Windows file and print sharing) packet between a server and its clients. This functionality has been superceded by IPSec AH, which works for SMB as well as all other protocols. Configure SMB message signing only when you can't use IPSec, such as when you must support backward compatibility with Windows NT 4 machines.

ESP Modes

ESP functions in two modes, as determined by the functionality that is required and the capability of the IPSec aware hosts or routers:

- *Transport mode*, in which data payload is encrypted but header data is unchanged. Transport mode is intended to encrypt data between two hosts that are IPSec aware and capable of decrypting the payload data directly, as is the case with Microsoft Windows 2000 systems.

- *Tunnel mode*, in which the entire original packet is encrypted and becomes the payload of a new packet, which is then transmitted between IPSec aware routers. Tunnel mode enables IPSec aware routers to encapsulate and encrypt network traffic from non-IPSec aware hosts, transmit it over a non-secure network, and then decrypt it for use on the destination network by other hosts that are not IPSec aware. Tunnel mode in Windows 2000 is provided primarily for interoperability with third-party IPSec solutions when Windows 2000 is being used as a router.

IPSec Applications

IPSec is employed in three widely used scenarios:

- *Host-to-host* (H2H) signifies secure connections between individual computers that are both IPSec capable. H2H connections are used frequently to secure communications in internal networks, extranets, and on the Internet. H2H applications use AH and ESP in transport mode.

- *Host-to-gateway* (H2G) specifies secure connections between hosts and a network gateway to a private network. H2G applications are used to provide secure telecommuting for remote clients. Windows uses Layer 2 Tunneling Protocol (L2TP) to support H2G applications. L2TP is essentially Point-to-Point Protocol (PPP) that has been encrypted using IPSec transport mode, and it is covered in Chapter 9, "Remote Access and VPN."

- *Gateway-to-gateway* (G2G) specifies secure connections between border gateways to create a secure wide area network (WAN) connection over the Internet. IPSec tunnel mode is supported to create a single encrypted link between two networks when the link must be compatible with earlier IPSec-compliant routers that do not support L2TP. Using IPSec tunnel mode is not recommended for use in other scenarios, because it is less secure and more difficult to configure than L2TP.

More Info   IPSec tunnel mode is not specifically covered in this chapter, but by using the exercises in this chapter, you will learn enough to create this type of IPSec security association if necessary. L2TP is covered in Chapter 9. This chapter covers only host-to-host scenarios, which comprise the majority of IPSec configuration problems.

Establishing IP Security Using Internet Key Exchange

IPSec itself does not provide encryption or authentication algorithms. Instead, it provides a framework for existing algorithms to work within. Determining which encryption and authentication algorithms to use for an IPSec session is performed by a protocol within IPSec, the Internet Key Exchange (IKE) protocol. IKE establishes secure communications by proving trust between hosts, negotiating a compatible set of encryption and authentication algorithms, and performing other minor functions so that IPSec security associations (SAs) do not have to be manually specified and keyed. To prove trust between hosts, IKE requires that both hosts have knowledge of the same shared secret key. Once trust has been established between the hosts, bulk encryption keys are exchanged using public key cryptography and are automatically refreshed according to intervals defined in the IPSec policy. A reasonably short key refresh time reduces the lifetime of a key, and therefore the length of time that attackers have to use brute-force methods to crack it.

IPSec in Windows 2000

Windows 2000 makes the security of IPSec easily accessible by integrating it with the standard Windows 2000 configuration management system, Active Directory. By defining IPSec configuration using Group Policy and distributing secret keys using standard Windows mechanisms, administrators can completely automate the deployment of IPSec within an Active Directory forest.

Manual methods of keying, distributing secret keys, and configuring IPSec are also provided for situations in which centralized configuration management is not possible or is not a concern, such as when creating a security association between untrusted hosts or when establishing a single security association for a specific one-time purpose.

Distributing IKE Secret Keys

In Windows 2000, you can use three methods to distribute the shared secret key required by IKE to automatically negotiate security associations:

- Use Kerberos to distribute the secret key within a domain or between trusted domains, and whenever a domain or trust relationship exists between the hosts involved.
- Install certificates with private keys that are both rooted in the same trusted certificate authority (CA). Use certificates when you can't use Kerberos.
- Type it directly in the IPSec filter (manual keying). Use manual keying when you can't use Kerberos or certificates, and use it for IPSec testing.

IPSec Within a Private Network

IPSec is most commonly used to secure traffic between hosts on the Internet, but it is designed to operate in any context where network layer security is important. Many modern private networks are very large IP networks, spanning vast distances. IPSec can be used within a private network in the following scenarios:

- Within an Active Directory forest, IPSec can be used to authenticate or encrypt traffic between servers and clients as necessary. Authentication can be based on the Kerberos protocol to ensure security for specific applications.
- Between clients or servers within a domain, creating encrypted or authenticated sessions is a simple matter of creating a Group Policy that organizes the clients and servers according to their roles and then applying a GPO with the proper IPSec configuration. Once the GPO is created and applied to the OUs, the policy will deploy automatically to the affected servers and clients, and IP communications will be secured as described in the policies.
- Within a domain or between domains, where a trust relationship exists, configuring IPSec is particularly easy, because Kerberos can be used to provide the secret keys necessary for IKE to establish the requisite IPSec security associations without administrator intervention.

Determining IP Security Method by Server Role

Windows 2000 makes it easy to enable security within a domain, but you cannot simply require IPSec on all computers within a domain and consider the problem solved. Here are two potential issues:

- IPSec can create a "chicken before the egg" problem. If IPSec is required by domain controllers, new computers that do not have IPSec configured cannot contact domain controllers to join the domain. Because IPSec keys are distributed only to domain members, they can't be used to configure a new computer. The inability to join a domain without an existing IPSec configuration and the inability to configure IPSec without an existing domain association creates a mutually exclusive problem that can prevent new computers from being added to a domain. To avoid this problem, domain controllers must be configured to allow both IPSec and non-secure communications.

- Overly restrictive IPSec policy can cause widespread problems for administrators because of the increased complexity required to administer IPSec, the addition of a new possibility for failure, and the fact that encrypted communications can make many key troubleshooting tools, such as sniffers, impossible to use.

Rather than applying blanket IPSec policy within your domain, consider moving sensitive applications and data to a few servers (as few as possible, considering the amount of data and the various security compartmentalization issues you have) and then requiring IPSec security on those servers only.

Certain services within your domain should be available whether or not clients can negotiate IP security with them. These services include domain log on and authentication, DNS services, DHCP, and other infrastructure services. If these services are not available to all clients, you might wind up with mutually exclusive requirements that cannot be resolved, such as computers that cannot receive an IP address from a DHCP server without already having an IPSec connection (which requires a valid IP address).

You can apply IPSec to computers in Windows 2000 by choosing one of three different policy modes:

- Require security (the default Secure Server role)
- Request security without requiring it (the default Server role)
- Respond to security requests without making them (the default Client role)

Tip   It is good practice to accumulate infrastructure services such as DNS and DHCP on domain controllers and to allow those servers to speak to any clients by setting their IPSec policy mode to request security without requiring it.

Clients within a domain should be configured to accept IP security if a server requests it, except for any clients that you explicitly want to prevent from accessing secure servers. For example, you might want to prevent access for computers used as guest kiosks, Internet browsing stations, or for untrusted users, such as students in a university environment.

Practice: Enabling IPSec Between Domain Members

Trade secrets at Fabrikam, Inc. have to be transmitted using authentication and encryption even within the enterprise. To facilitate this requirement, all trade secret information is stored on member server ms01.domain.Fabrikam.com, which you will configure to require IPSec security. To allow access to the information, you will configure clients to respond to IP Security requests.

In this practice, you create a set of GPOs to require security for member servers and enable IPSec on clients if the servers request IPSec. This configuration will prevent servers within the Secure Servers OU from communicating with any client that is not specifically configured as an IPSec client, which by extension eliminates any computers that are not within the same or a trusted domain.

Exercise 1: Configuring IPSec Logging and Monitoring

The first step in any IPSec configuration session is to allow troubleshooting by enabling IPSec logging. Follow the procedures in this exercise to enable IPSec logging.

Note   Perform this exercise while logged on to the domain controller as the Administrator.

▶   **To enable IPSec security logging**

1. Click Start, point to Programs, point to Administrative Tools, and click Active Directory Users And Computers. The Active Directory Users And Computers management console appears.

2. Right-click domain.fabrikam.com, and click Properties.

3. In the domain.fabrikam.com Properties dialog box, click the Group Policy tab.

4. Double-click the Domain Security Policy GPO. The Group Policy management console appears.

5. Expand Computer Configuration, Windows Settings, Security Settings, and Local Policies.

6. Click Audit Policy. Your screen should now appear similar to Figure 8.1.

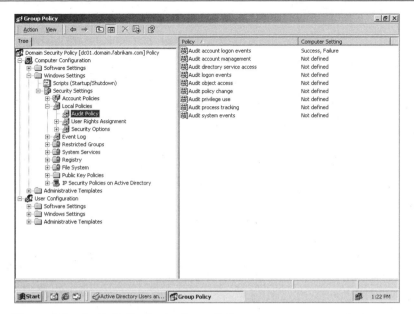

Figure 8.1   Audit Policy in the Group Policy management console

7. Double-click Audit Logon Events. The Security Policy Setting dialog box, shown in Figure 8.2, appears.

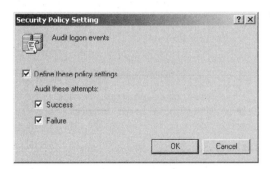

Figure 8.2   Enabling IPSec auditing

8. Select Define These Policy Settings, select Success, select Failure, and click OK.

9. Double-click Audit Object Access. The Security Policy Setting dialog box appears.

10. Select Define These Policy Settings, select Success, select Failure, and then click OK.

11. Close the Group Policy management console.

12. Click OK to close the domain.fabrikam.com Properties dialog box.

13. Leave the Active Directory Users And Computers management console open for the next procedure.

Exercise 2: Enabling IPSec on Servers

In this exercise, you create an OU for secure servers and apply an IPSec policy that forces them to require security to communicate.

Note   Perform this exercise while logged on to the domain controller as the Administrator with the Active Directory Users And Computers management console open.

▶ **To create organizational units for secure servers**

1. Right-click the domain.fabrikam.com domain, point to New, and then click Organizational Unit. The New Object – Organizational Unit dialog box appears.

2. Type **Secure Servers** in the Name box, and click OK.

3. Click the Computers container, as shown in Figure 8.3, in the domain.fabrikam.com domain.

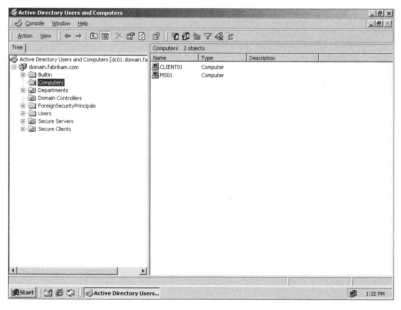

Figure 8.3   Member servers and computers are located in the Computers folder by default

4. Right-click MS01, and click Move to open the Move dialog box.

5. Click Secure Servers, and then click OK.

   MS01 is removed from the list in the Computers container and appears in the list of Secure Servers.

▶ **To create a GPO for Secure Servers**

1. Right-click the Secure Servers OU, and click Properties.

2. In the Secure Servers Properties dialog box, click the Group Policy tab.

3. Click the New button. A new GPO appears in the Group Policy Object Links list.

4. Type **Secure Servers IPSec Policy** as the name of the GPO and press ENTER.

5. Double-click Secure Servers IPSec Policy. The Group Policy management console appears.

6. Expand Computer Configuration, Windows Settings, and Security Settings.

7. Click IP Security Policies On Active Directory. A list of available IPSec policies appears in the right panel.

8. Right-click the Secure Server policy, and click Assign.

9. Close the Group Policy management console.

10. Close the Secure Servers Properties dialog box.

11. Leave the Active Directory Users And Computers management console open for the next exercise.

Exercise 3: Enabling IPSec on Clients

In this exercise, you create an OU for clients that will be able to establish IPSec communications.

▶ **To create an OU for secure clients**

Perform this procedure while logged on to the domain controller as the Administrator, with the Active Directory Users and Computers management console open.

1. Right-click the domain.fabrikam.com domain, point to New, and then click Organizational Unit. The New Object – Organizational Unit dialog box appears.

2. Type **Secure Clients** in the Name box, and click OK.

3. Click the Computers container.

4. Right-click CLIENT01, and click Move to open the Move dialog box.

5. Click Secure Clients, and click OK.

   CLIENT01 is removed from the list in the Computers container and appears in the list of Secure Clients.

► **To create a GPO for secure clients**

Perform this procedure while logged on to the domain controller as Administrator with the Active Directory Users And Computers management console open.

1. Right-click the Secure Clients OU, and click Properties.
2. In the Secure Clients Properties dialog box, click the Group Policy tab.
3. Click the New button. A new GPO appears in the Group Policy Object Links list.
4. Type **Secure Clients IPSec Policy** as the name of the GPO and press ENTER.
5. Double-click the Secure Clients IPSec Policy. The Group Policy management console appears.
6. Expand Computer Configuration, Windows Settings, and Security Settings.
7. Click IP Security Policies On Active Directory. A list of available IPSec policies appears in the right panel.
8. Right-click the Client policy, and click Assign.
9. Close the Group Policy management console.
10. Close the Secure Clients Properties dialog box.

► **To test IPSec connectivity between computers**

Perform this exercise on the workstation CLIENT01.

1. Click Start, and click Run. The Run dialog box appears.
2. Type **ipsecmon** and click OK. The IP Security Monitor appears as shown in Figure 8.4.

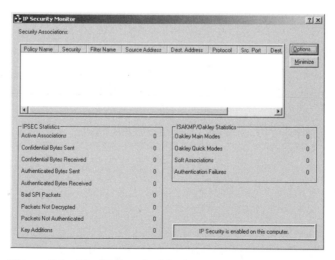

Figure 8.4   The IP Security Monitor

3. Click Start, point to Programs, Accessories, and then click Command Prompt. The command prompt appears.

4. Type **net view \\ms01** and press ENTER.

 The command prompt displays a list of shares on the server. The list might be empty.

5. Type **exit** and press ENTER.

 The IP Security Monitor now shows a security association existing between the client and the server, as shown in Figure 8.5.

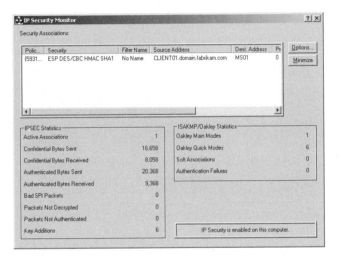

Figure 8.5   The list of active security associations in the IP Security Monitor

6. Close the IP Security Monitor.

Exercise 4: Enabling IPSec on Domain Controllers

In this exercise, you configure domain controllers to respond to secure requests if an IPSec security association can be converged. IPSec is said to have *converged* if IKE can successfully negotiate a compatible set of encryption and authentication protocols at both ends and successfully transmit data between hosts. By allowing domain controllers to accept secure communications, you enable secure servers that require security to communicate with them.

In this scenario, because you're using default IPSec templates, Internet Control Message Protocol (ICMP) communications will pass even when an IPSec has not been negotiated, but higher-level communications will fail.

▶ **To test connectivity to the domain controller**

Perform this exercise on the member server ms01.

1. Click Start, and click Run. The Run dialog box appears.
2. Type **cmd** and click OK. The command prompt appears.
3. Type **ping dc01**.

   Notice that dc01 can be pinged.

4. Type **net view \\dc01**.

   Notice that the operation fails, as shown in Figure 8.6.

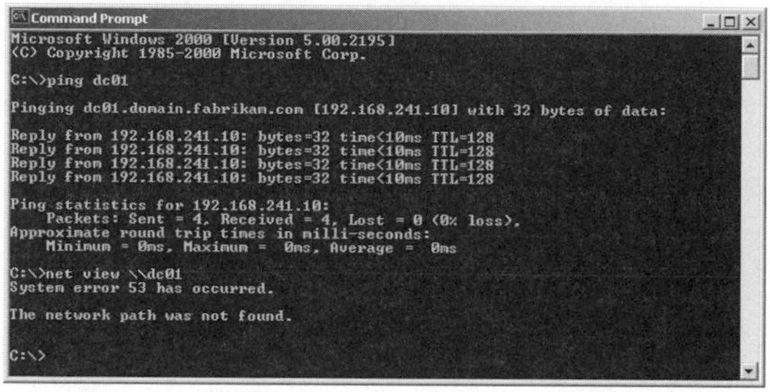

Figure 8.6   Testing high-level network connectivity without an IPSec security association

5. Close the command prompt window.

▶ **To enable discretionary IPSec on domain controllers**

Perform this procedure while logged on to the domain controller as the Administrator.

1. Click Start, point to Programs, point to Administrative Tools, and click Active Directory Users And Computers. The Active Directory Users And Computers management console appears.
2. Expand domain.fabrikam.com.
3. Right-click Domain Controllers, and click Properties.
4. In the Domain Controllers Properties dialog box, click the Group Policy tab.
5. Click New. A new GPO appears in the Group Policy list.
6. Type **IPSec Policy for Domain Controllers** and click Edit.
7. Expand Computer Configuration, Windows Settings, and Security Settings and click IP Security Policies.

8. Right-click the Server policy, and click Assign.

9. Close the Group Policy management console.

10. Click OK to close the Domain Controllers Properties dialog box.

11. Close the Active Directory Uses And Computers management console.

▶ **To test connectivity to the domain controller**

Perform this exercise on the member server.

1. Click Start, and click Run to open the Run dialog box.

2. Type **cmd** and click OK. The command prompt appears.

3. Type **ping dc01**.

    Notice that dc01 can be pinged.

4. Type **net view \\dc01**. The operation succeeds, as shown in Figure 8.7.

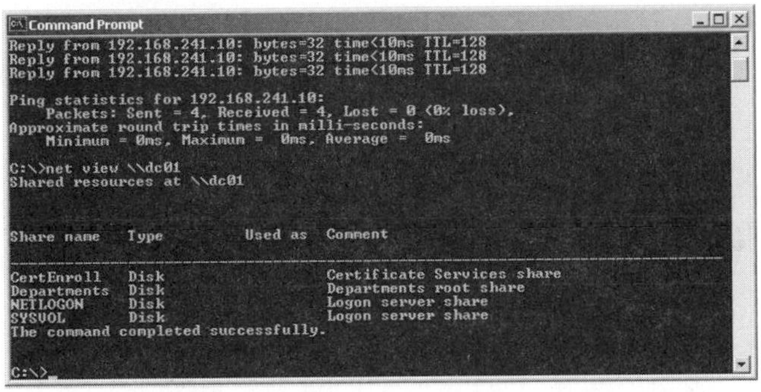

Figure 8.7   Testing high-level connectivity with an IPSec security association in place

5. Close the command prompt window.

Lesson Review

The following questions are intended to reinforce key information in this lesson. If you are unable to answer a question, review the lesson and try the question again. Answers to the questions can be found in the appendix.

1. What are the two primary methods IPSec uses to authenticate and encrypt IP packets?

2. What are the two encrypted payload modes that IPSec supports?

3. Explain the difference between transport mode and tunnel mode.

4. How does IKE determine whether to trust the participants when it establishes a security association?

5. How is IPSec managed in Windows 2000?

6. What mechanism would you use to distribute secret keys automatically in a domain?

Lesson Summary

- IPSec provides mechanisms to authenticate and encrypt IP traffic between hosts in any IP network. IPSec operates at the network layer and is transparent to higher-level applications, which need not be aware of IPSec to benefit from it.

- Authenticated Headers (AH) provides the functionality to authenticate packets and guarantee that they have not been modified. *Encapsulating Security Payload* (ESP) provides the functionality to encrypt packet payloads. ESP transport mode encrypts data, while tunnel mode encrypts and encapsulates entire packets.

- Internet Key Exchange (IKE) is used to prove trust between hosts using shared secrets, and it creates security associations by negotiating keys and compatible encryption and authentication algorithms. IKE also periodically refreshes keys in existing security associations.

- IPSec in Windows 2000 is managed using Group Policy and can use Kerberos secret keys as IKE secret keys. With these two capabilities, IPSec security can be deployed throughout an Active Directory forest at large scale using only Group Policy configuration.

- A computer's role on the network determines which of three IPSec negotiation methods should be used. Secure servers should require security, standard servers should request security, and clients should respond to security requests.

Lesson 2: Configuring IPSec Between Untrusted Networks

Using IPSec between networks requires some method of exchanging secret keys for IKE negotiation other than Kerberos because Kerberos-based key exchange is available only to machines within the same domain or with an existing trust relationship. For testing purposes, it is desirable to use the simplest method: manual keying. Manual keying enables administrators to type matching secret keys (pass phrases) at both end systems to establish that IPSec policies are functioning correctly.

To complete this lesson, you will need

- Member server ms01
- Domain controller dc01
- Domain controller gdi-dc-01

After this lesson, you will be able to

- Configure IPSec using manual keys
- Understand IPSec filters

Estimated lesson time: 30 minutes

Providing a Secret Key

Windows 2000 allows administrators to manually type in a secret key to be used in IKE negotiation. This method is the simplest way to provide secret keys for IKE. However, manual keys have a number of problems:

- Manual keys cannot be distributed automatically—each participant must be individually administered.
- Manual keys are generated by humans, and are usually far less random than most machine-generated keys.
- It is difficult to securely distribute manual keys over any significant distance.

In a high-security application, you cannot simply phone another administrator over a non-secure telephone and speak the key, because the telephone conversation might be overheard. E-mailing the information is also not secure. Your key is only as secure as the method used to transmit it. Arguably, the only secure method would be to have the same administrator key both sides from memory by traveling to the two locations.

Certificates solve these problems by using public key security to distribute the secret key necessary for IKE negotiation. Even though using certificates is the preferred solution, it's more complex because it adds all the possible failure modes of certificate distribution to the already complex configuration of IPSec.

In a ground-up deployment, you can use manual keying with non-secure keys to prove that the IPSec configuration works as long as the servers in question do not yet have secure data on them. When you've established that your IPSec policies are working, it's a simple matter to upgrade from manually keyed IKE to certificate-based IKE. Once that has been done, you can begin using the servers in production, secure in the knowledge that no intermediate party will be able to decrypt your communications.

Creating IPSec Policy in Windows 2000

IPSec policy is applied to packets when they are transmitted or received depending on how their headers match the IPSec filters that are applied to the computer. On an individual basis, if a packet's header matches an IPSec filter, then

- The packet is blocked.
- The packet is permitted.
- An IPSec filter action is applied to the packet.

The first two options are obvious. All IPSec actions are based on the third option.

Creating IPSec Filters

To enable IPSec, administrators first define a filter list that applies to the computer. Once the filter list is defined, any number of individual IP filters can be created.

IPSec filters describe the packets that the filter will apply to. Any number of combinations can be used, and packets can be described by a specific IP address, a network range, or a domain name, as well as by protocol and port number.

Once you've created a filter, you can apply any number of filter actions to the filter. *Filter actions* allow you to specify whether security is required, which protocols are allowed, and what IPSec mechanisms to use, such as AH, ESP, and tunnel mode.

IPSec requires two-way communications between hosts. Filters are actually unidirectional—they create only an inbound or an outbound rule. Because the vast majority of scenarios require bi-directional functionality, Windows 2000 can automatically mirror the filter to create the reciprocal filter by transposing the source and destination addresses.

Tip   Always mirror your filters when you create them unless you have a specific reason to do otherwise.

What Are the IPSec Exceptions?

A few types of packets are always exempted from IPSec filters because they must be passed in order for IPSec to function, or they represent a type of service that cannot be secured. They are

- Broadcast addresses.
- Multicast-addresses (224.0.0.0 - 239.255.255.255).
- Quality of Service requests. RSVP (IP protocol 46) allows Quality of Service (QOS) requests to pass. If QOS requests were encrypted, intermediate systems could not use them to prioritize traffic, and QOS would not function.
- Kerberos (UDP port 88), used for IPSec's IKE negotiation service, which is used for authentication of other computers in a domain. IKE is secure by itself.
- IKE (UDP port 500), required to allow IKE to negotiate parameters for IPSec security. All IPSec implementations must pass IKE messages.

These exemptions do not apply to tunnel mode filters—tunnel mode passes all IP traffic without inspecting the contents of the interior packets because it is designed to function as an intermediate system. Tunnels cannot filter based on protocol type for the same reason.

Practice: Creating a Simple Encrypted Tunnel Between Domains

Fabrikam has a business partner, Graphic Design Institute, which produces the collateral print materials for Fabrikam products. Design documents and requirements must be securely transmitted to GDI, and finished print materials must remain secure when they are returned to Fabrikam.

In this practice, you create a manually keyed IPSec security association between two hosts on foreign networks (networks between which no trust relationship exists) using manual keying. This procedure is a prelude to creating a security association that is keyed using certificates.

Exercise 1: Configuring a Foreign Server for IP Security

In this exercise, you establish connectivity between the local and remote server, secure the remote server, and then ensure that communication has been disrupted by the security requirement.

▶ **To establish a test environment**

Perform this procedure on member server ms01.domain.Fabrikam.com while logged on as Administrator.

1. Click Start, point to Programs, point to Accessories, and click Command Prompt. The command prompt appears.

2. Type **Ping 192.168.241.60 -t**, replacing the IP address with the address of gdi-dc-01.graphicdesigninstitute.com on your network.

A ping reply will appear once per second until the screen is full. Leave this procedure running on the console throughout the remainder of this lesson.

▶ **To create an IPSec Policy management console on the remote host**

Perform this procedure on the gdi-dc-01.extranet.graphicdesigninstitute.com.

1. Click Start, and click Run to open the Run dialog box.
2. Type **MMC** and then click OK. An empty management console appears.
3. From the Console menu, choose Add/Remove Snap-in.
4. In the Add/Remove Snap-in dialog box, click Add.
5. In the Add Standalone Snap-in dialog box, double-click IP Security Policy Management.
6. In the Select Computer Wizard, leave Local Computer selected, and click Finish.
7. Click Close to close the Add Standalone Snap-in dialog box.
8. Click OK to close the Add/Remove Snap-in dialog box.

The IP Security Policies Snap-in appears in the management console as shown in Figure 8.8.

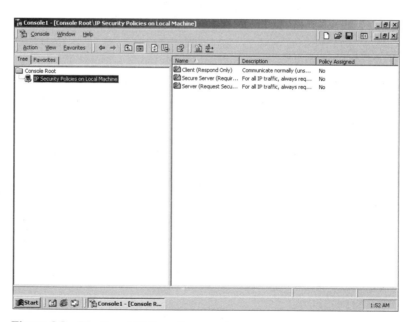

Figure 8.8   The Local IP Security console

9. From the Console menu, choose Save. The Save As dialog box appears.

10. Type **IP Security (local)** in the File Name box and click Save.

    The IP Security (local) management console will appear on the Administrative Tools menu.

▶ **To create an IPSec policy on the remote host**

Perform this procedure on gdi-dc-01.graphicdesigninstitute.com.

1. In the IP Security (Local) management console, right-click IPSecurity Policies On Local Machine, and click Create IP Security Policy.

2. When the IP Security Policy Wizard appears, click Next.

3. Type **Encrypted Link to Fabrikam** in the Name box, as shown in Figure 8.9, and then click Next.

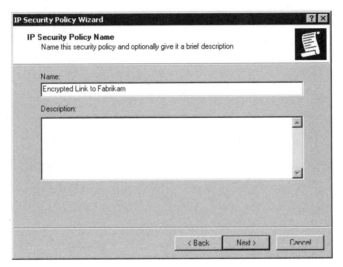

Figure 8.9   The IP Security Policy Wizard

4. Clear the Activate The Default Response Rule check box, and click Next.

5. Ensure that the Edit Properties check box is selected, and click Finish.

   The Encrypted Link To Fabrikam Properties dialog box appears, as shown in Figure 8.10.

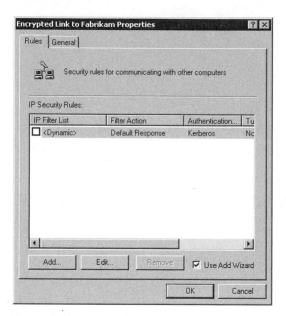

Figure 8.10 The IP filter list

6. Ensure that the Use Add Wizard check box is selected, and click Add.

7. When the Security Rule Wizard appears, click Next.

8. On the Tunnel Endpoint page, leave This Rule Does Not Specify A Tunnel selected, and click Next.

9. On the Network Type page, leave All Network Connections selected, and click Next.

10. On the Authentication Method page, select Use This String To Protect The Key Exchange.

11. Type **test_preshared_key** in the box, as shown in Figure 8.11.

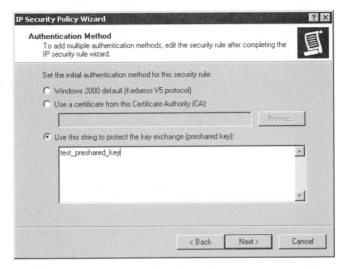

Figure 8.11   Using a pre-shared secret key to encrypt traffic between machines

12. Click Next.

13. On the IP Filter list page, click Add. The IP Filter List dialog box appears, as shown in Figure 8.12.

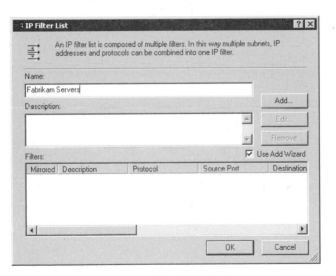

Figure 8.12   The IP Filter List dialog box

14. Type **Fabrikam Servers** in the Name box.

15. Clear the Use Add Wizard check box.

16. Click Add. The Filter Properties dialog box appears.

17. In the Destination Address list, select A Specific IP Address. An IP Address box and a Subnet Mask box appear.

18. Type **192.168.241.63** in the Address box, replacing the IP address with the IP address of member server ms01.domain.Fabrikam.com on your test network.

    The Filter Properties dialog box should now be similar to Figure 8.13.

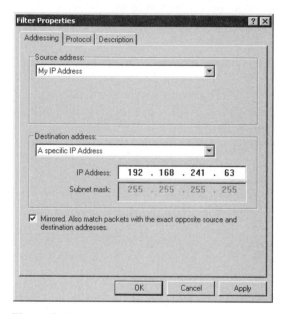

Figure 8.13   The Filter Properties dialog box

19. Ensure that the Mirrored check box is selected, and click OK.

20. Click Close to close the IP Filter List dialog box.

Fabrikam Servers now appears in the list of IP Filter Lists shown in the Security Rule Wizard, as shown in Figure 8.14.

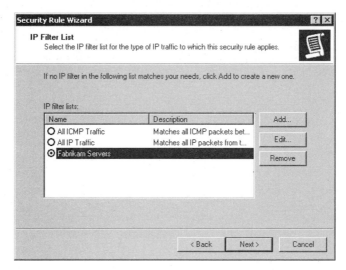

Figure 8.14   Selecting the Fabrikam Server IP filter

21. Select Fabrikam Servers, and click Next. The Filter Action page appears.

22. Ensure that the Use Add Wizard check box is selected, and click Add.

23. When the IP Security Filter Action Wizard appears, click Next.

24. Type **Encrypt Fabrikam Traffic** in the Name box, and click Next.

25. On the Filter Action General Options page, leave Negotiate Security selected, and click Next.

26. On the Communicating With Computers That Do Not Support IPSec page, leave Do Not Communicate With Computers That Do Not Support IPSec selected, and click Next.

27. On the IP Traffic Security page, leave High (Encapsulated Secure Payload, Data Will Be Encrypted, Authenticated, and Unmodified) selected, and click Next.

28. Click Finish. Encrypt Fabrikam Traffic now appears in the Filter Action dialog box as shown in Figure 8.15.

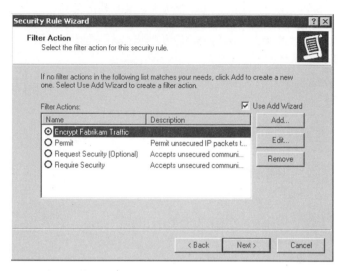

Figure 8.15 Creating a IP Security Filter Action

29. On the Filter Action page, select Encrypt Fabrikam Traffic, and click Next.

30. Click Finish to close the Security Rule Wizard, and return to the Encrypted Link To Fabrikam Properties dialog box.

31. Click Close to return to the IP Security (Local) management console.

32. Right-click the Encrypted Link to Fabrikam policy, and click Assign.

    Notice that the constant ping on ms01.domain.Fabrikam.com now fails with a Request Timed Out message, as shown in Figure 8.16. This indicates that gdi-dc-01 is no longer accepting traffic from ms01.domain.Fabrikam.com because of the IPSec policy now in place.

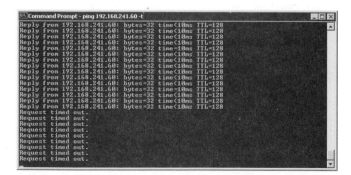

Figure 8.16 ICMP traffic between hosts fails if matching authentication for IKE cannot be resolved

33. Close the IP Security (Local) management console.

Exercise 2: Configuring Servers in a Domain for IPSec with a Foreign Server

In this exercise, you extend the existing security policy for servers to allow communications with a foreign server.

▶ **To create an IPSec policy for secure servers in the domain**

Perform this procedure on the dc01.domain.Fabrikam.com domain controller.

1. Click Start, point to Programs, point to Administrative Tools, and click Active Directory Users And Computers. The Active Directory Users And Computers management console appears.
2. Right-click Secure Servers, and click Properties.
3. In the Secure Servers Properties dialog box, click the Group Policy tab.
4. Double-click Secure Servers IPSec Policy. The Group Policy management console appears.
5. Expand Computer Configuration, Windows Settings, and Security Settings.
6. Right-click IP Security Policies On Active Directory, and click Create IP Security Policy.

▶ **To work with the IP Security Policy Wizard**

1. When the IP Security Policy Wizard appears, click Next.
2. On the IP Security Policy Name page, type **Encrypted Link to Graphic Design Institute** in the Name box, and then click Next.
3. On the Requests For Secure Communication page, clear the Activate The Default Response Rule check box, and click Next.
4. Ensure that the Edit Properties check box is selected, and click Finish. The Encrypted Link To Fabrikam Properties dialog box appears.
5. Ensure that the Use Add Wizard check box is selected, and click Add.
6. When the Security Rule Wizard appears, click Next.
7. On the Tunnel Endpoint page, leave This Rule Does Not Specify A Tunnel selected, and click Next.
8. On the Network Type page, leave All Network Connections selected, and click Next.
9. On the Authentication Method page, select Use This String To Protect The Key Exchange.
10. Type **test_preshared_key** in the box, as previously shown in Figure 8.11, and click Next.
11. On the IP Filter List page, click Add to open the IP Filter List dialog box.

12. Type **GDI Servers** in the Name box, clear the Use Add Wizard check box, and click Add. The Filter Properties dialog box appears.

13. In the Destination Address list, select A Specific IP Address. An IP Address box and a Subnet Mask box appear.

14. Type **192.168.241.60** in the IP Address box, replacing the IP address with the IP address of member server gdi-dc-01.graphicdesigninstitute.com on your test network.

The Filter Properties dialog box should now be similar to Figure 8.17.

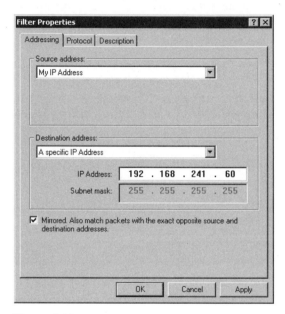

Figure 8.17   The Filter Properties dialog box showing a specific IP address as the destination

15. Ensure that the Mirrored check box is selected, and click OK.

16. Click Close to close the IP Filter List dialog box.

Fabrikam Servers now appears in the list of IP Filter Lists shown in the Security Rule Wizard.

17. Select GDI Servers, and click Next. The Filter Action page appears.

18. Ensure that the Use Add Wizard check box is selected, and click Add.

19. When the IP Security Filter Action Wizard appears, click Next.

20. On the Filter Action Name page, type **Encrypt GDI Traffic** in the Name box, and click Next.

21. On the Filter Action General Options page, leave Negotiate Security selected, and click Next.

22. On the Communicating With Computers That Do Not Support IPSec page, leave Do Not Communicate With Computers That Do Not Support IPSec selected, and click Next.

23. On the IP Traffic Security page, leave High (Encapsulated Secure Payload, Data Will Be Encrypted, Authenticated, and Unmodified) selected, and click Next.

24. Click Finish. Encrypt GDI Traffic will now appear in the Filter Action dialog box, as shown in Figure 8.18.

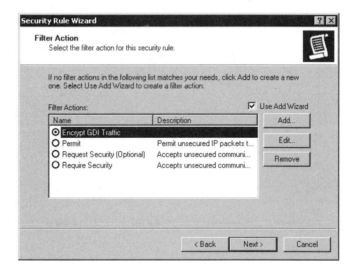

Figure 8.18   Selecting a Filter Action to encrypt traffic between servers

25. Select Encrypt GDI Traffic, and click Next.

26. Ensure that the Edit Properties check box is cleared, and click Finish to close the Security Rule Wizard and return to the Encrypted Link To Graphic Design Institute Properties dialog box.

    GDI Servers should appear selected in the IP Security Rules list, as shown in Figure 8.19.

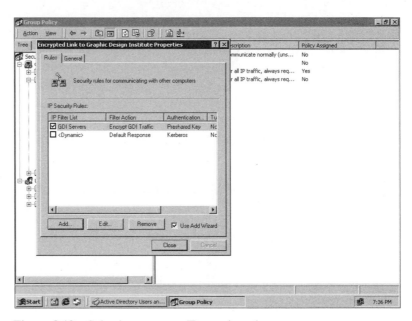

Figure 8.19   Selecting a custom IP security rule

27. Click Close to return to the Group Policy management console. Encrypted Link To Graphic Design Institute now appears in the list of IP Security Policies.

28. Right-click the Encrypted Link To Graphic Design Institute policy, and click Assign.

29. Close the Group Policy management console.

30. Click OK to close the Secure Servers Properties window.

31. Close the Active Directory Users And Computers management console.

▶ **To test the policy application**

Perform this procedure on member server ms01.domain.Fabrikam.com.

1. Verify that the command prompt you set to continuously ping
    gdi-dc-01.graphicdesigninstitute.com is still showing Request Timed Out.
    Leave this window open for this procedure.

2. Click Start, point to Programs, point to Accessories, and click Command
    Prompt. A second command prompt appears.

3. Type **secedit /refreshpolicy MACHINE_POLICY** and press ENTER.

The Secedit program will report that a policy refresh has been initiated. In a few
seconds, the Request Timed Out message will be replaced by a Negotiating IP
Security Message, which will shortly be replaced by Reply From messages indicating
that encrypted communications are now operating between the servers, as shown
in Figure 8.20.

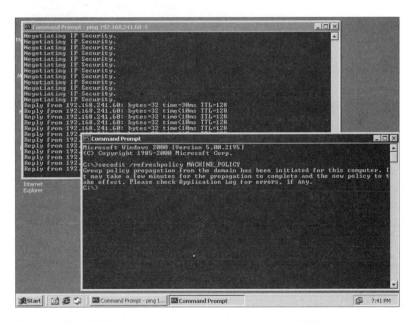

Figure 8.20   ICMP messages begin passing as soon as IKE negotiation converges

4. Type **Exit**.

5. Click Start, and click Run to open the Run dialog box.

6. Type **ipsecmon**, and click OK. The IP Security Monitor appears as shown in Figure 8.21.

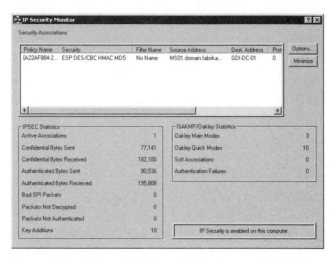

Figure 8.21   Using the IP Security Monitor to verify IPSec connectivity

7. Verify the IP Security connection between ms01.domain.Fabrikam.com and gdi-dc-01.

8. Close the IP Security Monitor.

9. Select the Command Prompt running ping and press CTRL+C. The ping will stop.

10. Type **Exit** at the command prompt to close the window.

Lesson Review

The following questions are intended to reinforce key information in this lesson. If you are unable to answer a question, review the lesson and try the question again. Answers to the questions can be found in the appendix.

1. Which methods are available to distribute IKE secret keys in Windows 2000?

2. When would you use manual keying rather than Kerberos or certificates?

3. How is IPSec policy defined in Windows 2000?

4. Name the types of traffic that are never secured by IPSec.

Lesson Summary

- There are three methods that can be used to distribute secret keys for IKE negotiation: Kerberos, manual keying, and certificates rooted in the same trusted certificate authority.

- Manual keying is appropriate for use in situations where neither Kerberos nor certificates can be used, for testing IPSec without the complexity of certificates, and when establishing individual IPSec associations on an infrequent basis, where security is not paramount.

- IPSec policy in Windows 2000 is defined by using filter lists comprised of filters that specify the hosts, networks, and ports that should trigger IPSec actions. Valid IPSec actions include blocking traffic, permitting traffic, and securing traffic using IPSec.

- There are some types of packets that are never secured using IPSec: broadcast, multicast, RSVP-QOS, Kerberos, and IKE traffic. These types of traffic must remain unsecured in order for IPSec to work correctly. Exceptions don't apply to tunnel mode traffic, which encrypts everything.

Lesson 3: Configuring IPSec on Internet Servers

Certificates are the perfect mechanism for distributing the secret keys required to establish IPSec security associations. IPSec security associations can be established by using certificates that have secret keys attached to them and that are rooted in a CA trusted by all parties.

To complete this lesson, you will need

- Domain controller dc01
- Member server ms01
- Domain controller gdi-dc-01

After this lesson, you will be able to
- Distribute IPSec keys using certificates
- Configure an enterprise CA to deploy IPSec certificates
- Deploy IPSec certificates automatically by using Group Policy
- Deploy IPSec certificates manually by using the Certificate Services Web site

Estimated lesson time: 20 minutes

Using Certificates to Distribute IPSec Secret Keys

IPSec was originally designed to provide secure, authenticated communications between hosts on the Internet, where security is often required but relationships are not necessarily strict. On the Internet, any communication might be allowed as long as identity is verified, or where, for example, a public service provider provides services to a vast array of clients and cannot create manual keys for each of them.

Internal networks, which have a single administrative authority, present an entirely different set of administrative challenges. So do associations between business partners where protocols and keys can be mutually agreed on.

In private networks, Kerberos provides a mechanism for distributing secret keys, which are required by IKE to prove that two computers should trust one another. In simple configurations, administrators can manually enter these secret keys. But in situations where a large number of parties are involved, where security is paramount, or where the participants are not necessarily known in advance, certificates provide the ideal solution.

Certificates provide an IKE trust mechanism when they contain private keys and are rooted in the same CA. IKE negotiates trust using the public/private key pair contained in the certificates. Once trust is established, an IPSec security association can be negotiated automatically in the same way as any trust relationship would be.

Tip   You can use certificates designed for any purpose so long as they contain a private key. It is not necessary to use certificates specifically created for IPSec, although they are more likely to work without requiring troubleshooting.

You can use the Certificates snap-in to determine whether certificates stored on the local machine contain the necessary private key.

Practice: Using Certificates to Exchange IKE Secret Keys

Fabrikam has extended its security requirements to encompass all partner companies. To avoid creating excessive administrative burden, partners will be given access to the Fabrikam Enterprise Root Certifier to request and install a certificate that will enable Fabrikam hosts to securely access their extranet servers.

In this scenario, you will modify the IPSec security association created in the previous lesson to use certificates rather than manual keys to provide secret keys. This method is far more scalable and secure than manually keying secrets.

Exercise 1: Configuring the Enterprise CA to Deploy IPSec Certificates

In this exercise, you configure the Fabrikam Enterprise Root Certifier to issue IPSec certificates and then configure the domain GPO to automatically deploy them to domain participants.

▶ **To enable the CA to issue IPSec certificates**

Perform this exercise on the Fabrikam Enterprise Root Certifer.

1. Click Start, point to Programs, point to Administrative Tools, and click Certification Authority. The Certification Authority management console appears, as shown in Figure 8.22.

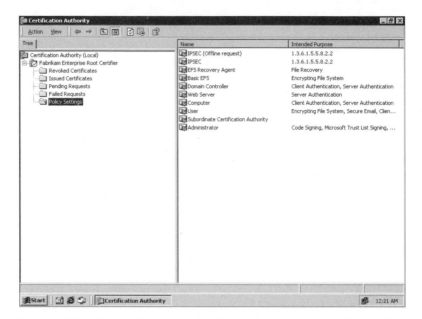

Figure 8.22   The Certification Authority configured to issue IPSec certificates

2. Expand Fabrikam Enterprise Root Certifier.

3. Right-click Policy Settings, point to New, and click Certificate To Issue. The Select Certificate Template dialog box appears.

4. In the Select Certificate Template dialog box, select IPSEC, and click OK.

5. Right-click Policy Settings, point to New, and then click Certificate To Issue. The Select Certificate Template dialog box appears.

6. Select IPSEC (Offline Request), and then click OK.

7. Close the Certification Authority management console.

▶ **To configure Group Policy to automatically deploy IPSec certificates**

1. Click Start, point to Programs, point to Administrative Tools, and click Active Directory Users And Computers. The Active Directory Users And Computers management console appears.

2. Right-click domain.fabrikam.com, and click Properties. The domain.fabrikam.com Properties dialog box appears.

3. Click the Group Policy tab, and double-click Domain Security Policy. The Group Policy management console appears.

4. Expand Computer Configuration, Windows Settings, Security Settings, and Public Key Policies.

5. Right-click Automatic Certificate Request Settings, point to New, and click Automatic Certificate Request. The Automatic Certificate Request Setup Wizard appears.

6. Click Next to open the wizard. Your wizard page will be similar to the one shown in Figure 8.23.

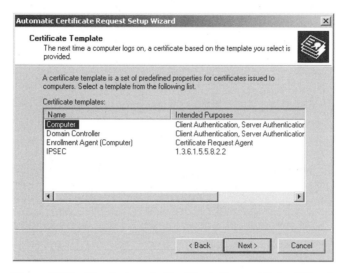

Figure 8.23   The Automatic Certificate Request Setup Wizard

7. In the Certificate Template drop-down list, click IPSEC and then hold down SHIFT and click IPSEC (Offline Request). Both policies should be selected.

8. Click Next.

9. On the Certification Authority page, accept the default Fabrikam Enterprise Root Certifier as the certificate authority, and click Next.

10. Click Finish. IPSEC will appear in the list of Automatic Certificate Requests.

11. Close the Group Policy management console.

12. Click OK to close the domain.fabrikam.com Properties dialog box.

13. Close the Active Directory Users And Computers management console.

Exercise 2: Deploying Certificates for IPSec Encryption

In this exercise, you request a certificate from the Fabrikam Enterprise Root Certifier of the foreign domain. By requesting the certificate directly from the root CA for the target enterprise, you guarantee that both parties have certificates rooted in the same CA.

▶   **To request a certificate from a foreign certification authority**

Perform this procedure on the gdi-dc-01.extranet.graphicdesigninstitute.com server.

1. Open Internet Explorer and browse to *http://dc01/certsrv/*. The Microsoft Certificate Services Web site appears.
2. On the Welcome page, select Request A Certificate, and click Next.
3. On the Choose Request Type page, select Advanced Request, and click Next.
4. On the Advanced Certificate Requests page, select Submit A Certificate Request To This CA Using A Form, and click Next.
5. On the Advanced Certificate Request page, select IPSEC (Offline Request) in the Certificate Template drop-down list.
6. Type **Fabrikam IPSEC Administrator** in the Name box.
7. Type **rootca@fabrikam.com** in the E-Mail address box.
8. Select Microsoft Enhanced Cryptographic Provider in the CSP drop-down list.

   Select Exchange in the Key Usage group. The Web page should appear as shown in Figure 8.24.

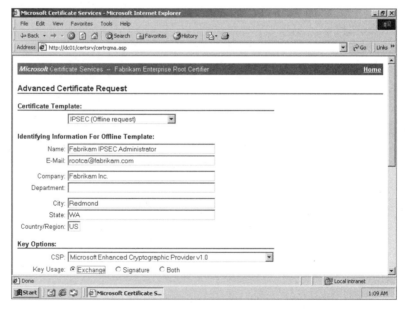

Figure 8.24   Requesting a certificate using the Microsoft Certificate Services Web site

9. Type **1024** in the Key Size box.

10. Select Use Local Machine Store, and click Submit.

   After waiting for the certificate to be issued, the Certificate Issued Web page appears, as shown in Figure 8.25.

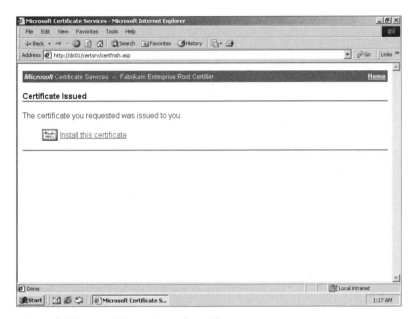

Figure 8.25   Installing an issued certificate

11. Click the Install This Certificate link.

12. Close Internet Explorer.

▶ **To convert an existing IPSec filter to use certificate-based IKE authentication**

Perform this procedure on server gdi-dc-01.graphicdesigninstitute.com while logged on as Administrator.

1. Click Start, point to Programs, point to Administrative Tools, and click IP Security (Local). The IP Security (Local) management console appears.

2. Double-click Encrypted Link To Fabrikam. The Encrypted Link To Fabrikam Properties dialog box appears, as shown in Figure 8.26.

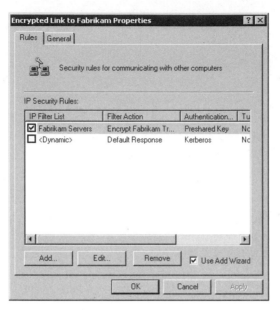

Figure 8.26   Encrypted link properties

3. Double-click Fabrikam Servers in the IP Security Rules list. The Edit Rule Properties dialog box appears, as shown in Figure 8.27.

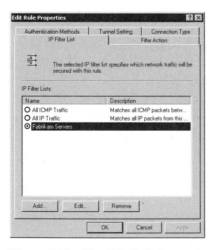

Figure 8.27   The Edit Rule Properties dialog box

4. Click the Authentication Methods tab.

5. With the Preshared Key method selected, click Edit. The Edit Authentication Method Properties dialog box appears.

6. Select Use A Certificate From This Certificate Authority, and click Browse. The Select Certificate dialog box appears.

7. Click Issued By to sort the certificates in alphabetical sequence by issuer.

8. Double-click the certificate issued by Fabrikam Enterprise Root Certifier.

9. Click OK to close the Select Certificate dialog box.

10. Click OK to close the Edit Authentication Method Properties dialog box.

11. Click OK to close the Edit Rule Properties dialog box.

12. Click Close to close the Encrypted Link To Fabrikam Properties dialog box.

13. Close the IP Security (local) management console.

▶ **To modify Group Policy-based IPSec configuration to use certificates**

Perform this procedure on the dc01.domain.Fabrikam.com domain controller.

1. Click Start, point to Programs, point to Administrative Tools, and click Active Directory Users And Computers. The Active Directory Users And Computers management console appears.

2. Right-click the Secure Servers OU, and click Properties. The Secure Servers Properties dialog box appears.

3. Click the Group Policy tab, and click the New button. A new GPO appears in the Group Policy Object Links list.

4. Type **Secure Servers IPSec Policy** as the name of the GPO, and press ENTER.

5. Double-click Secure Servers IPSec Policy. The Group Policy management console appears.

6. Expand Computer Configuration, Windows Settings, and Security Settings, and click IP Security Policies On Active Directory.

7. Double-click Encrypted Link To Graphic Design Institute. The Encrypted Link To Graphic Design Institute Properties dialog box appears.

8. Double-click GDI Servers. The Edit Rule Properties dialog box appears.

9. Click the Authentication Methods tab.

10. Ensure that Preshared Key is selected, and click Edit. The Edit Authentication Method Properties dialog box appears.

11. Select Use A Certificate From This Certificate Authority, and click Browse.

12. When a warning message appears stating that Active Directory does not contain a shared certificate store, click Yes.

13. Select any certificate issued by Fabrikam Enterprise Root Certifier, and click OK.

14. Click OK to close the Edit Authentication Method Properties dialog box.

15. Click OK to close the Edit Rule dialog box.

16. Click Close to close the Encrypted Link To Graphic Design Institute Properties dialog box.

17. Close the Group Policy management console.

18. Click OK to close the Secure Servers Properties dialog box.

19. Close the Active Directory Users And Computers management console.

▶ **To test connectivity with certificate-based IKE negotiation**

Perform this procedure on the member server ms01.domain.Fabrikam.com.

1. Restart the server.

Note Restarting the server is not necessary. However, domain policy refresh needs to occur, a certificate must be downloaded from the Certification Authority, and you may have to restart the policy agent service for the modification of the IPSec filter policy to take effect. The easiest way to accomplish these tasks is simply to restart the server.

---

2. Log on as Administrator, and open a command prompt.

3. Type **ping 192.168.241.60**, replacing the IP address with the address of gdi-dc-01.graphicdesigninstitute.com.

   Initially, the ping tool will report that IP Security is being negotiated. In a few seconds, reply messages will appear, indicating that encrypted communications have been successfully established between servers.

Lesson Review

The following questions are intended to reinforce key information in this lesson. If you are unable to answer a question, review the lesson and try the question again. Answers to the questions can be found in the appendix.

1. When would it be appropriate to use certificates to distribute IKE secrets?

2. What are the two requirements for certificates to work correctly for IKE negotiation?

3. What two portions of a GPO apply to certificate deployment?

Lesson Summary

- Certificates are the most secure way to distribute IKE secrets for servers that do not have a domain trust relationship.

- You can configure trust between any two servers that have certificates rooted in the same certificate authority. You specify the specific trusted certificate authority when you create the IPSec filter policy.

- Certificates must contain a private key in order to work with IKE. IKE uses the private key to negotiate trust between the two intermediate systems. Certificates don't need to be created for IPSec specifically.

- Certificate-based authentication is configured based on Group Policy either locally or through Active Directory–based Group Policy. The machine component of the GPO's IP Security namespace defines IPSec policies and allows administrators to apply them to the GPO.

- You can configure Group Policy to automatically deploy machine certificates suitable for IPSec to members of an OU or domain. Use the Automatic Certificate Request feature to create and deploy certificates to all machines in the domain or OU the next time the policy is applied to the machine in question.

Lesson 4: Troubleshooting IPSec Configuration

IPSec is an extremely complex protocol, and when using certificates to perform IKE Authentication, you will find IPSec configuration probably more difficult and error prone than any other configuration task in Windows 2000. There are literally hundreds of things that can go wrong, but if you consider your scenarios carefully, understand the IPSec mechanisms, start with simpler manual keying to ensure IPSec works before you deploy certificates, and use troubleshooting tools to narrow the scope of the problem, you will be able to fix IPSec problems quickly.

To complete this lesson, you will need

- Domain controller dc01
- Member server ms01
- Domain controller gdi-dc-01

After this lesson, you will be able to

- Determine why IPSec might fail
- Fix problems with IKE keying
- Fix IPSec problems due to certificates that are not valid

Estimated lesson time: 15 minutes

Why IPSec Might Fail

In Windows 2000, IPSec can fail in two ways:

- Communication does not occur.
- Communication is not encrypted.

Of these two, the first is problematic, but the second is disastrous. It's easy for an administrator to think that IPSec is configured and working, while communication is flowing without being secured at all. This provides a false sense of security. When communication is not flowing, you know that you at least have security. Be careful to test that encryption is actually occurring by examining communications using a sniffer between the two end systems.

Caution   If the IPSec Policy Agent service is not running, all IP communications will automatically be accepted. You won't have any warning that IPSec is not in place when this service isn't running.

Despite the complexity of IPSec communications, there are only a few reasons why IPSec fails:

- Communication between the end systems doesn't function correctly.
- Filters are not set up correctly.
- IKE does not have a matched set of secret keys.
- IPSec cannot negotiate a compatible set of encryption or authentication algorithms.
- An intermediate system is modifying packets between the end systems.

Don't be fooled by this short list, however, because a myriad of problems might cause any one of these failures. The following sections detail troubleshooting techniques and will help you determine in which of the problem domains you should be troubleshooting.

Communication Between the End Systems Doesn't Function Correctly

All the IPSec troubleshooting in the world won't fix a routing problem or a down circuit. You absolutely must ensure that you have proper connectivity between systems before you attempt to secure communications using IPSec. Test all protocols that you will be using over IPSec when your configurations are complete, including ICMP (ping) and DNS.

Filters Are Not Configured Correctly

IPSec configuration is performed by setting up IP filters. If the filters are not created correctly and do not exist reciprocally on both systems, IPSec communications will not occur.

Common problems include mistaking IP addresses; mismatching AH, ESP, and tunnel mode on each end; and selecting different filter actions on each end. Ensure that your IPSec filters are exactly the same on both ends, and don't include mutually exclusive filters, such as one filter that specifies all protocols or addresses, and another that specifies a certain action for only certain protocols or addresses.

IKE Does Not Have a Matched Set of Secret Keys

This problem can be difficult to differentiate from all the other types of problems. If you suspect you're having problems with secret key exchange, you can enable IKE logging to get detailed information about IPSec negotiations and determine exactly what's going wrong.

It is possible to "over specify" IKE methods. Only one authentication method is valid between a pair of hosts, and the hosts will both choose the first method found that appears to be compatible. If more than one IKE method is specified by policy between the two hosts, a mismatch can occur. Be certain that you haven't specified more than one method that could be misapplied on the hosts involved.

Better yet, as a test, simplify IKE negotiations by manually keying. After both end systems are manually keyed using IKE, and communication is working correctly between systems, IKE will succeed.

Tip   Manual keying can be used to determine whether your problem really is IKE.

Once you know you have a problem with IKE, it's time to look at the keying method. If you're using Kerberos, the only requirement is that the servers are in the same domain or that a bi-directional trust relationship exists between the domains.

If you are using certificates for IKE, you must ensure that the certificates are rooted in the same trusted CA and contain private keys. IKE uses a certificate's private key as its secret key to authenticate clients. The certificate need not be specifically created for IPSec. Any valid certificate in the machine local store containing a private key should work. You can verify whether a specific certificate has a private key by using the Certificates management console.

You might find it necessary to restart the IPSec policy agent if you've changed the authentication method and you can't determine why IKE has not converged.

Warning   If you stop the IPSec policy agent, communications will flow unsecured between the hosts without warning. It is safest to restart the computers involved if you need to restart the IPSec policy agent to ensure that traffic does not flow in an unencrypted state when security is critical.

Remember to be patient when applying changes through Group Policy, because it takes time for Group Policy to propagate and to be refreshed on servers. Consider using Local IPSec policy for testing purposes, because it takes effect immediately.

IPSec Cannot Negotiate a Compatible Set of Encryption or Authentication Algorithms

This problem occurs when servers don't have a compatible set of authentication or encryption protocols. This problem typically does not occur between Windows 2000 hosts, because the same set of protocols is available to them all, but it can occur if you've removed lower-quality Data Encryption Standard (DES) encryption from your policy but have not enabled high encryption on hosts. This is not a problem with Windows 2000 Service Pack 2 and later, which includes high encryption by default.

You might find that security protocols cannot be authenticated correctly because multiple policies exist that apply to both servers. Be certain that only a single policy applies between any two hosts in an IPSec security association.

An Intermediate System Is Modifying Packets Between the End Systems

Tampering with AH packets will cause them to fail and could potentially be used as a denial of service attack in a rare and sophisticated type of "man-in-the-middle" attack. A far more common scenario is that Network Address Translation (NAT) is being used somewhere between the end systems, and the NAT gateway is modifying header addresses, which causes AH to fail due to checksum errors.

AH is not compatible with NAT, and depending on the version of NAT, ESP transport mode might not be compatible either. ESP tunnel mode tends to be the most compatible form of IPSec for transport through NAT, because it uses typical IP headers.

The only good way to get IPSec working when NAT is being used is to disable NAT, which might not be an option for the interior of most networks. If you need to get IPSec traffic through a NAT device, you may have no option except to use an IPSec tunnel that ends on the NAT router. Typically, border routers perform NAT for the interior network and can be used as end points for IPSec tunnels. This is how the majority of existing IPSec connections between private networks work today.

Practice: Troubleshooting IPSec Communications

In this practice, you explore various troubleshooting methods that can be used to determine what might be wrong with an IPSec link that you are trying to establish.

Exercise 1: Refreshing Domain IPSec Security Policy

In this exercise, you refresh domain IPSec policy. Use this procedure whenever you make a change to a domain GPO and you want to test its effect on a specific computer that the GPO applies to.

▶ **To refresh domain IPSec policy**

1. Click Start, and then click Run to open the Run dialog box.
2. Type **cmd**, and press ENTER. A command prompt appears.
3. Type **secedit /refreshpolicy MACHINE_POLICY**, and press ENTER.
4. Type **exit**, and press ENTER.

Exercise 2: Determining Whether a Certificate Has a Private Key

In this exercise, you determine whether a machine certificate contains a private key, which is required for IKE to negotiate a security association.

▶ **To create a Certificates console**

1. Click Start, and then click Run to open the Run dialog box.
2. Type **mmc,** and click OK.
3. From the Console menu, choose Add/Remove Snap-in.

4. In the Add/Remove Snap-in dialog box, click Add.

5. In the Add Standalone Snap-in dialog box, double-click Certificates. The Certificates Snap-in Wizard appears.

6. Select Computer Account, and click Next.

7. Select Local Computer.

8. Click Finish.

9. Click Close to close the Add Standalone Snap-in dialog box.

10. Click OK to close the Add/Remove Snap-in dialog box.

11. From the Console menu, choose Save.

12. Type **Certificates (local machine)** as the name of the management console, and then click Save.

▶ **To determine whether a certificate includes a private key**

1. Open the Certificates (Local Machine) management console.

2. Expand Certificates and Personal, and then select Certificates.

3. Double-click the certificates shown in the certificates list. The Certificate Information dialog box will appear, as shown in Figure 8.28.

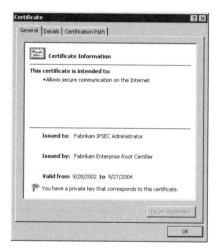

Figure 8.28   A certificate's information shows whether it contains a private key

If the certificate contains a private key, it will be noted at the bottom of the certificate.

4. Click OK and close the Certificates (Local Machine) management console.

Exercise 3: Restarting the IPSec Policy Agent

In this exercise, you restart the IPSec policy agent to solve any problems that might have occurred when an authentication method was changed.

Warning   Communications are not secured when the IPSec policy agent is not running.

▶ **To restart the IPSec policy agent**

1. Open a command prompt.
2. Type **Net stop policyagent**, and press ENTER.
3. Type **Net start policyagent**, and press ENTER.

Exercise 4: Enabling IKE Logging

In this exercise, you enable IKE logging on a computer to determine exactly why an IKE negotiation has failed. Use this procedure whenever you suspect that you have a problem with IKE and you cannot determine what is failing.

▶ **To enable IKE logging**

1. Click Start, and then click Run to open the Run dialog box.
2. Type **regedt32**, and then click OK. The Registry Editor appears.
3. Select the HKEY_LOCAL_MACHINE window.
4. Expand System, CurrentControlSet, Services, and PolicyAgent.
5. If the Oakley key doesn't exist, from the Edit menu, choose Add Key. The Add Key dialog box appears.
6. Type **Oakley** as the name of the key, and click OK.
7. Right-click Oakley, and click Add Value.
8. Type **EnableLogging** as the name of the value.
9. Select Data Type: REG_DWORD, and click OK.
10. Enter value **1** and click Hex as the Radix.
11. Click OK, and close the Registry Editor.
12. Restart the policy agent. The log file will be written to windir\debug\oakley.log.

Lesson Review

The following questions are intended to reinforce key information in this lesson. If you are unable to answer a question, review the lesson and try the question again. Answers to the questions can be found in the appendix.

1. What IPSec problem could have the most serious consequences?

2. What utility is used to refresh Group Policy on a computer that receives its IPSec configuration from a domain GPO?

3. What utility is used to enable IKE logging?

4. What's the easiest way to eliminate IKE as a potential problem source?

5. What problems might cause certificate-based IKE negotiations to fail?

Lesson Summary

- IP Security fails for the following common reasons: communication doesn't work correctly between the end systems, filters are not set up correctly, IKE secrets don't match, IKE could not negotiate a matched set of protocols, or an intermediate system is modifying packets between the end systems.

- The first step in troubleshooting IPSec is to troubleshoot everything else— ensure that the network is functioning correctly and that higher-layer protocols like DNS, Kerberos, and ICMP are all functioning correctly before attempting to get IPSec functioning.

- Creating custom filters can be an error-prone process. Be sure that you understand clearly what you're trying to accomplish, and design your policies in advance before attempting to implement them.

- IKE problems are the problem that most commonly affects IPSec communications in Windows 2000. Typical problems include mismatched or incompatible certificates, incorrectly specified manual keys, and multiple IKE policies that could be applied. Only one IKE policy is selected, so ensure that you know which one it is by having only one available.

- Test IKE problems with certificates by using manual keying. Once you have IPSec working correctly with manual keying, attempt to use certificates and troubleshoot any problems as certificate problems.

- There must be compatible IPSec algorithms on both end systems. Normally, this isn't an issue, but if you've removed some encryption methods to force high encryption or you are attempting to get IPSec working with a third party system, you might need to compare both systems closely to make sure that they have a set of encryption protocols in common.

- IPSec is incompatible with Network Address Translation (NAT). NAT is widely deployed at the boundary between private networks and the public Internet, so it's likely that you won't be able to create IPSec connections that go from the private to a public network. Clever planning and security design will be required to solve problems like these.

C H A P T E R   9

Remote Access and VPN

About This Chapter

Routing and Remote Access Service (RRAS) is the Microsoft Windows 2000 component that manages both routing between networks and remote access to networks. RRAS runs on a Microsoft Windows 2000 Server or Advanced Server computer and provides the following functions:

- Secure dial-up access to the network through the public telephone network (using analog or ISDN modems)

- Secure, encrypted communications between private networks (a Virtual Private Network)—or between a client and a private network—across a public network, usually the Internet

- TCP/IP packet routing, with support for static routes and routing protocols such as Routing Information Protocol (RIP) and Open Shortest Path First (OSPF), which automate the process of discovering nearby routers and determining which routes packets should take

- Network Address Translation (NAT), which allows you to share, or multiplex, a single public IP address among a number of computers on a private network, each with its own private address

This chapter concentrates on the security aspects of RRAS: securing RRAS servers and clients, authentication by the Internet Authentication Service (IAS), and creating a VPN using Layer 2 Tunneling Protocol (L2TP).

Exam Tip   Make sure that you know how L2TP tunneling works and that it is the recommended method to link remote clients with RRAS gateways.

Before You Begin

To complete the lessons in this chapter, you will need

- A computer running Windows 2000 Server
- The RRAS Server component installed on the server
- A modem or other remote access device
- A computer with a modem to dial in to the network
- Internet connections on the server and on a client for testing VPN features

Lesson 1: Securing RRAS Servers

Because RRAS allows access to a network from remote locations, configuring it for maximum security is essential. In this lesson you learn to properly secure a Windows 2000 server providing RRAS services and manage the VPN and authentication functions of RRAS.

After this lesson, you will be able to

- Understand security concerns that are specific to RRAS
- Perform initial configuration of an RRAS server
- Manage RRAS security options

Estimated lesson time: 20 minutes

Understanding RRAS Security

RRAS not only provides access to a network from remote locations, it also serves as the end point for VPN connections, which use encryption to securely connect private networks over a public network, such as the Internet. Because any remote access point is a potential network vulnerability, you must be especially vigilant to set up RRAS as securely as possible.

Windows 2000 includes several tools to help you configure a secure RRAS system. On the server side:

- *Remote access policies* enable you to grant or deny remote access to all users on a server according to any specific set of conditions.
- *Internet Authentication Service (IAS)* provides a central management facility for remote access security. The remote access policies in IAS can provide authentication and security for any number of RRAS servers.

On the client side:

- *Remote access properties of user accounts* provides a way to grant or deny remote access to individual users. This permission applies to all types of remote access, including dial-up, VPN, and 802.1x port authentication (discussed in Chapter 10, "Wireless Security").
- *Connection Manager Administration Kit (CMAK)* allows you to create customized client access software for dial-up or VPN access to a network.

All of these components are described in detail in this chapter, but this lesson focuses on configuring RRAS for remote access and giving users permission to connect remotely.

Remote Access Security Issues

Remote access is one of the four major ways that hackers get into your network (through the Internet, through wireless networks, and through direct log on to a LAN-connected workstation are the others).

Although the Internet has replaced dial-up as the most important hacking vector, most hacking resulted from remote access through dial-up modems until as recently as 1998. Hackers continue to attack networks using dial-up connections, so expect dial-up access to be exploited by anyone who is specifically targeting your network or who has an insider's knowledge of how your network is set up. You cannot simply deploy remote access and assume that hackers won't bother with it.

Dial-back policy was the earliest form of remote access security. When a *dial-back policy* is enforced, remote access occurs only after the user connects to the server and provides a telephone number. The remote access server then checks a list of valid connecting points and calls back if the telephone number is on the list. Dial-back policy is reasonably secure because it authenticates users by their telephone numbers and prevents connections from unauthorized locations. Typically, user authentication is then required to prove the identity of the user.

Planning   Dial-back security is an excellent way to secure dial-in access if users will be dialing in only from a fixed set of locations.

More and more frequently, users do not dial in from fixed locations. Traveling business professionals, sales representatives, and executives often require access from many locations, and cannot predict what their telephone numbers will be. To service this group, you can configure dial-back security to allow access to all telephone numbers, but the server records the numbers that it dials. Administrators can then audit these records to determine if unexpected telephone numbers have appeared. This approach uses the *accountability security model* rather than the *restriction model* to secure the system, and it's effective unless hackers can dial in, gain administrative access, and then erase the remote access logs.

Recently, it has become popular to require the use of VPN software in addition to dialing in to the network and to place remote access servers outside the interior firewall. In this approach, users dial in (or request a dial back) to a remote access server that gives them access to the Internet and initiates a VPN connection with the firewall to gain access to the interior of the network.

Planning   Using a VPN connection provides the best level of real security and allows you to centrally administer security on your firewall by handling dial-up users the same way you handle any other VPN user.

When you use a VPN connection, your RRAS servers are out in the perimeter network, and they cannot be joined to the domain. Under these circumstances, Windows-integrated authentication is not a good option for dial-up users. You can configure your RRAS servers to connect to an IAS RADIUS server inside your firewall (allowing access only for the RADIUS protocol from the remote access server) to support integrated account names and passwords, but you should strongly consider having a separate set of user accounts on the remote access machines. Credentials for dial-up networking are frequently stored on network laptops where they can be retrieved and decrypted by laptop thieves, which would subsequently allow access to your entire network if those credentials worked with your VPN solution.

Security Consequences of Single Sign-On

Remember that convenience is the opposite of security in most cases. In Single Sign-On (SSO) systems, you can use the same user name and password everywhere. While this is convenient, the password only has to be discovered in one service to be valid everywhere, so SSO systems like Active Directory improve convenience, not security.

Important   Publicly accessible networks should always use separate security domains with different sets of user accounts from private networks.

You should also strongly urge users not to use the same user name and password that they use on your network, or use their work e-mail address when they sign up for third-party services such as subscription Web sites. Web sites are routinely exploited by hackers who download and analyze the lists of user names and passwords they gain access to.

Finally, you should always enforce separate e-mail addresses and user names. Although Microsoft Exchange integrates closely with Active Directory and automatically generates e-mail boxes with the same names as user accounts, you should create a name mapping policy in Exchange to modify the e-mail addresses of users so that they're different from those in their user accounts.

Caution   Consider the consequences of using Active Directory connected services in their default configurations on both your public and private networks. Microsoft Exchange would automatically generate e-mail addresses that were the same as user names. RRAS users would be assigned dial-in permissions using their standard account names and passwords. VPN access via PPTP and L2TP would allow users to connect from the Internet. If hackers found an account named "kkennedy@Fabrikam.com" with a password of "theiwproyf13#" on the list of subscribers to a Web site, they would have all the information they'd need to reach the interior of your network using a valid user account—including which network the credentials are valid on.

Configuring a New RRAS Server

RRAS is installed by default on Windows 2000 Server, but its features are not enabled by default. Windows 2000 Server provides a wizard, the Routing and Remote Access Server Setup Wizard, which you can use to enable a basic set of features on the RRAS server, depending on how you intend to use the server.

Default RRAS Configurations

RRAS provides a number of possible configurations from which you can choose:

- **Internet Connection Server.**   Acts as an Internet gateway.
- **Remote Access Server.**   Provides dial-in access to the network.
- **Virtual Private (VPN) Server.**   Allows remote computers that have Internet access to connect to the network using a VPN.
- **Network Router.**   Configures the server to act as a router between networks.
- **Manually Configured Server.**   Uses default settings rather than a specific configuration.

Tip   These configurations are only preset combinations of properties. You can change any configuration using RRAS server properties and remote access policies.

RRAS Configuration Options

In addition to its default configurations, the Routing And Remote Access Server Setup Wizard displays a list of its currently supported network protocols, and provides the option for you to configure support for additional protocols, You can use these additional protocols for Novell Netware servers or other legacy systems. You can also choose whether to enable the Guest account for users who don't have user names or passwords. When you enable the Guest account, you allow clients to attach to the RRAS server without authenticating. This is necessary for some legacy systems, but represents an extreme security risk because you can't determine who is connecting to the system.

Caution   Using the Guest account significantly reduces RRAS security so enable it only to serve a specific need, such as supporting Apple Macintosh clients, that cannot be satisfied any other way.

When you set up RRAS, you are also prompted to choose an IP addressing method. RRAS supports two methods of assigning IP addresses:

- **Automatically.**   Uses a Dynamic Host Configuration Protocol (DHCP) server to assign addresses.
- **From A Specified Range Of Addresses.**   Specifies a range of addresses to be used as a static address pool. Using this option does not require you to configure a DHCP server.

In addition to these options, you can choose whether to enable Remote Authentication Dial-In User Service (RADIUS) authentication support for the server. RADIUS is a mechanism for centralizing authentication for numerous RRAS servers and protocols. The primary purpose of RADIUS is to allow third-party access equipment to authenticate with the operating system's accounts. Because OS integrated authentication is already supported by RRAS, you can enable RADIUS, as described in Lesson 2, only when you must integrate third-party access equipment in addition to RRAS servers.

Managing RRAS Security Options

The primary method for managing the security of a RRAS server is to set its properties in the Routing And Remote Access management console. This console becomes available on the Administrative Tools menu after you've enabled RRAS on a Windows 2000 computer.

Configuring RRAS Server Properties

For each server you select in the Routing And Remote Access management console, you can modify its settings using options on the following tabs in the server Properties dialog box:

- **General.**   Includes options to control whether the server acts as a router, remote access server, or both.
- **Security.**   Allows you to configure security and authentication options. These options are described later in this chapter.
- **IP.**   Includes IP routing and remote access options, and the option to configure a DHCP server or static address pool for assigning IP addresses.
- **AppleTalk.**   Includes options for AppleTalk routing.
- **PPP.**   Includes global options for the dial-up Point-to-Point Protocol (PPP).
- **Event Logging.**   Allows you to specify whether warning and error messages are logged. You can view log messages in the Event Viewer console.

Configuring User Properties

In addition to modifying the RRAS server's security features, you can also set the dial-in properties for user accounts. This allows you to control the ability of individual users to dial in. Using remote access policies, you can set the user dial-in properties to allow access, deny access, or control access. Remote access policies are described in detail later in this chapter.

Note   RRAS remote access policies are not available in mixed-mode Active Directory domains. To enable RRAS remote access policies, you must migrate all backup domain controllers to Windows 2000 and switch the domain mode to native mode. More information about how to accomplish this is provided in the *Microsoft Windows 2000 Server Resource Kit* (Microsoft Press, 2000).

Practice: Securing RRAS Servers

In this practice, you configure and enable RRAS on a Windows 2000 Server computer and explore the server and user properties that you can use to manage RRAS security settings.

Exercise 1: Configuring a Server for RRAS

In this exercise, you configure a new RRAS server on a Windows 2000 Server computer as a Remote Access Server. You might need the Windows 2000 Server CD or a network installation share to complete this procedure.

Important   This procedure is necessary only on a new Windows 2000 Server installation where RRAS has not yet been configured.

▶ **To configure RRAS in Windows 2000 Server**

Perform this procedure on a Windows 2000 Server computer, logged on as the Administrator.

1. Click Start, point to Programs, point to Administrative Tools, and click Routing And Remote Access Service. The Routing And Remote Access management console is displayed.

2. Select the server (dc01) in the list in the left column. The console message area indicates that the server needs to be configured for RRAS, as shown in Figure 9.1.

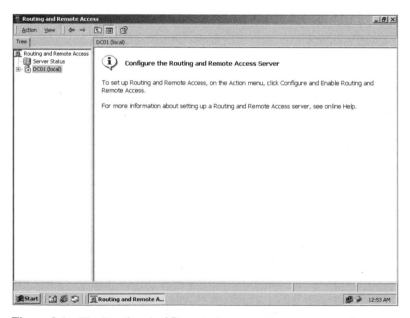

Figure 9.1   The Routing And Remote Access management console

3. From the Action menu, choose Configure And Enable Routing And Remote Access.

4. On the introductory page of the Routing And Remote Access Server Setup Wizard, click Next to continue. A list of common RRAS server configurations is displayed, as shown in Figure 9.2.

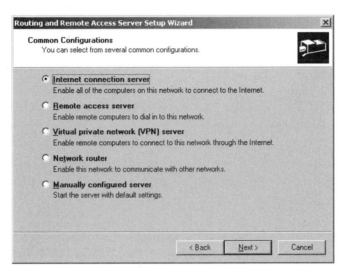

Figure 9.2   The Routing And Remote Access Server Setup Wizard

5. On the Common Configurations page of the wizard, select the Remote Access Server option, and click Next. A list of currently installed protocols is displayed, as shown in Figure 9.3.

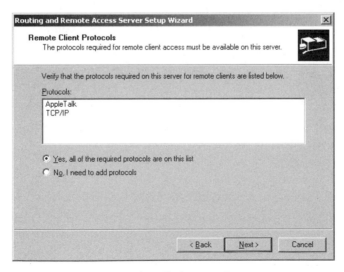

Figure 9.3   The default installed protocols

6. On the Remote Client Protocols page, select the Yes, All Of The Required Protocols Are On This List option, and click Next. A message indicates that you can optionally enable the Guest account for Apple Macintosh users.

7. Click Next. The IP Address Assignment options are displayed, as shown in Figure 9.4.

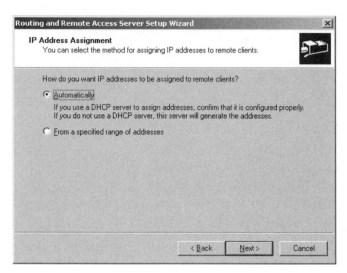

Figure 9.4   Selecting a method of IP address assignment

8. On the IP Address Assignment page, select Automatically, and click Next. The RADIUS options are displayed, asking whether RADIUS will be the authentication method.

9. Select No, and click Next.

10. Click Finish to complete the RRAS server configuration. RRAS is now started.

Exercise 2: Managing an RRAS Server

In this exercise, you add a remote RRAS server to the console so it can be managed, and you configure properties for an RRAS server.

▶ **To manage RRAS server properties**

Perform this procedure from the Routing And Remote Access management console on the RRAS server.

1. Select the server (dc01) from the list in the left column.

2. From the Action menu, Choose Properties. The server Properties dialog box is displayed.

3. Click the IP tab. The IP Properties are displayed.

4. Select the Static Address Pool option, and click Add. You are prompted for an IP address range.

5. Type **192.168.241.160** for the Start IP Address and **192.168.241.175** for the End IP Address. The IP range you've added is now shown in the list, as shown in Figure 9.5.

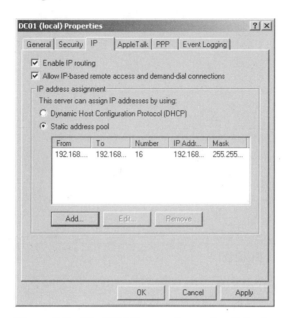

Figure 9.5   The RRAS server Properties dialog box

6. Click OK to add the address range to the address pool.

7. Click OK to close the Properties dialog box and save the new settings.

▶ **To manage user dial-in properties**

1. Log on to the domain controller as an Administrator

2. From the Administrative Tools menu, choose Active Directory Users And Computers. The Active Directory Users And Computers management console is displayed.

3. Select a user to manage, and from the Action menu, choose Properties. The Properties dialog box for the user is displayed.

4. Click the Dial-in tab. The Dial-in Properties are displayed, as shown in Figure 9.6.

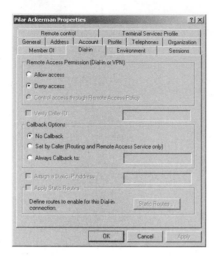

Figure 9.6 User account dial-in properties

5. Select the Allow Access option, and click OK.

Lesson Review

The following questions are intended to reinforce key information in this lesson. If you are unable to answer a question, review the lesson and try the question again. Answers to the questions can be found in the appendix.

1. Which utility do you use to manage most of Windows 2000's RRAS settings?

2. If you select automatic IP address assignment for an RRAS server, where do IP addresses come from?

3. What is the easiest way to set up an RRAS server on a Windows 2000 Server computer?

4. How can you change the settings of a server, such as its IP addressing, after configuring RRAS?

5. How can you allow a user to connect to RRAS without using remote access policies?

Lesson Summary

- Routing and Remote Access Service (RRAS) is included with Windows 2000 Server. It allows the server to act as a dial-in remote access server, Internet gateway, VPN server, or network router.

- RRAS is installed by default with Windows 2000 Server, but it is not configured. You can configure it using the Routing And Remote Access Server Setup Wizard in the Routing And Remote Access console. This console also provides access to properties and security settings for RRAS.

- User accounts include dial-in properties. Using the Active Directory Users And Computers console, you can grant or deny dial-up access for a user, or specify that the user's access will be controlled by remote access policies.

Lesson 2: Managing RRAS Authentication

To provide truly secure remote access, you need more than a simple scheme of user names and passwords. RRAS provides a wide variety of authentication methods, from simple, unencrypted passwords for low-security applications to highly secure authentication schemes for applications in which security is paramount. Windows 2000 also supports Remote Authentication Dial-In User Service (RADIUS), a dedicated service for authenticating remote users with high security and detailed accounting that works with a broad range of third-party remote access devices and services.

After this lesson, you will be able to

- Configure Windows RRAS authentication
- Install IAS
- Configure RADIUS authentication

Estimated lesson time: 30 minutes

Configuring Windows RRAS Authentication

Windows 2000 provides a number of standard authentication methods for remote users. This section describes how to choose authentication methods for users.

PAP and CHAP

Most of the authentication methods available in RRAS are based on Password Authentication Protocol (PAP), which supports simple password authentication, and Challenge Handshake Authentication Protocol (CHAP), a more sophisticated protocol that uses two-way handshakes to authenticate users. These protocols are all descendents of PAP and are increasingly secure and resilient. As with all protocols, always select the newest and most secure protocol that your range of clients support. You can enable any of the following variations of these protocols:

- *Unencrypted password (PAP)* is the basic PAP protocol. It sends passwords as clear text so it is vulnerable to network snooping. You should not use PAP unless you must support a legacy application that requires it.
- *Shiva Password Authentication Protocol (SPAP)* is an extension to the PAP protocol used to support Shiva LAN Rover devices. It supports basic encryption of passwords, but is not challenge and response, so it is vulnerable to replay attacks in which hackers capture encrypted passwords and re-use them in encrypted form.
- *Encrypted authentication (CHAP)* provides authentication with encrypted passwords. In this protocol, the server sends a challenge to the client, and the client uses the data from the challenge to calculate a one-way encrypted value,

or hash, from the user name and password that can be used to authenticate the user without sending the password across the network.

- *Microsoft encrypted authentication (MS-CHAP)* is a Microsoft extension of CHAP that improves security by storing passwords in encrypted form. This is the authentication used by Microsoft Windows 95 and Windows 98 clients.

- *Microsoft encrypted authentication version 2 (MS-CHAP v2)* is the Windows 2000 implementation of MS-CHAP. It does not support earlier Windows client versions. MS-CHAP v2 improves security by eliminating support for LAN Manager encryptions and performs mutual authentication (the client validates the server) to ensure that no man-in-the-middle attack can occur. You should use MS-CHAP v2 whenever possible.

EAP

Extensible Authentication Protocol (EAP) is an authentication protocol that can be extended with additional authentication methods that you can install separately. This protocol is commonly used for smart card authentication or certificate-based authentication. Click the EAP Methods button to open a dialog box that lists the EAP methods that are installed on the current RRAS server.

Unauthenticated Access

If you enable the Allow Remote Systems To Connect Without Authentication option, remote systems that do not support authentication can connect without supplying a user name and password. You can use this method when another system is providing security, such as Dialed Number Identification Service (DNIS). When this option is enabled, clients can also connect using the Guest user account.

Warning   The Allow Remote Systems To Connect Without Authentication option is a security risk and should not be enabled unless you must accommodate non-Windows clients. If you use unauthenticated access, ensure that some other authentication service prevents hackers from reaching private resources, such as a firewall that you've placed between the RRAS server and the interior of the network.

Using RADIUS and IAS

RADIUS is a standard service for user authentication, which provides centralized authentication, multiple authentication servers, and detailed activity logging for remote access users. RADIUS provides a way to decouple user authentication from the server or device that receives the connection or provides access to the port. It allows Administrators to centralize the authentication function on a small group of servers dedicated to authentication while distributing remote access servers or devices throughout the enterprise. Furthermore, by decoupling authentication from remote access, it allows the authentication service to be used by other services that require authentication, such as the 802.1x port authentication protocol provided to secure wireless access, as described in Chapter 10, "Wireless Security."

Understanding IAS

Microsoft's implementation of RADIUS, provided in Windows 2000 Server, is called IAS (Internet Authentication Service). The IAS server uses the Active Directory database to store authentication information so all IAS servers can be managed from a single console.

When you use IAS to provide remote access authentication, the remote clients do not directly communicate with the IAS server. Instead, clients connect to a normal RRAS server, known in RADIUS terminology as the network access server (NAS). Dial-up clients connect to network access servers, which then contact the nearest IAS server to authenticate each user. A network access server can be any RADIUS aware device or service that allows users to connect to a port, such as an RRAS server, an 802.11b wireless access point, or an 802.1x compliant Ethernet switch. Figure 9.7 shows how this process works in detail.

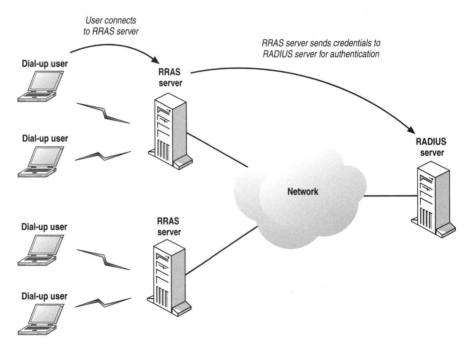

Figure 9.7   Dial-up clients connect to an RRAS server, which trusts the IAS RADIUS server for authentication

---

Tip   The same Windows 2000 Server computer can be used as both the RRAS server and the IAS server. Alternatively, you can use any number of IAS servers and RRAS servers your network architecture requires to provide authentication across a WAN. In most situations, a single IAS server is capable of handling authentication for many thousands of users.

Configuring RADIUS Authentication

If an IAS server is available on the network, you can configure RRAS servers to use RADIUS authentication. After you select RADIUS authentication, you must restart the RRAS server before the changes will take effect.

Note   Before an RRAS server can authenticate with an IAS server, you must add the RRAS server as a client of the IAS server.

Configuring RADIUS authentication is simple. After selecting the RADIUS server in the RRAS Server Properties dialog box, you can specify the following options for each server:

- **Server Name.**   The name of the RADIUS server.
- **Secret.**   A shared secret (password) used to control access to the RADIUS server. You must specify the same password later when you add the server as a client for the IAS server. The NAS (RRAS server) and RADIUS server use this shared secret to authenticate and encrypt communications among themselves.
- **Time-out.**   The number of seconds the RAS server will wait for a response from a RADIUS server before trying a different server. The default is five seconds.
- **Initial Score.**   A simple measure of availability for RADIUS servers. The server with the highest score will be queried first.
- **Port.**   The UDP port used on the RADIUS server for incoming authentication requests. The default value, 1813, is correct for most current RADIUS servers, including Microsoft IAS. UDP port 1645 is also used for some devices.

Note   Dial-up computers are not RADIUS clients. Each RADIUS client is an RRAS server or other hardware or software that provides remote access. Dial-up clients connect to this server, which in turn authenticates using the RADIUS server.

Practice: Configuring RRAS Authentication and an IAS Server

In this practice, you configure authentication on an RRAS server, including Windows authentication and RADIUS, and install and configure an IAS server. To complete this practice, you will need a Windows 2000 Server computer with the RRAS component installed.

Exercise 1: Selecting Windows Authentication Methods

In this exercise, you configure an RRAS server to use Windows authentication and select the authentication methods that will be permitted for remote clients. Some of the options described might already be selected on your server.

▶ **To use Windows authentication**

Perform this procedure on the RRAS server computer.

1. Log on as Administrator.
2. Click Start, point to Programs, point to Administrative Tools, and click Routing And Remote Access Service.
3. Select the RRAS server (dc01) in the console tree. The right-hand pane displays a list of components of the RRAS server.
4. From the Action menu, choose Properties. The Properties dialog box opens.
5. Select the Security tab. The Security properties are displayed, as shown in Figure 9.8.

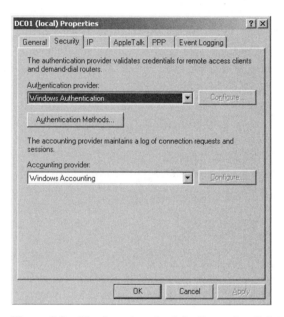

Figure 9.8 The Security tab of the Properties dialog box

6. In the Authentication Provider list, click Windows Authentication.
7. Click OK to complete the change.

Important If you were previously using a different authentication method, you will need to restart the RRAS server before this change takes effect.

▶ **To select authentication methods**

1. Select the server (dc01) in the console tree, and, from the Action menu, choose Properties. The Properties dialog box is displayed.

2. Select the Security tab.

3. Click Authentication Methods. The Authentication Methods dialog box is displayed, as shown in Figure 9.9.

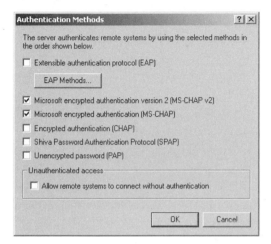

Figure 9.9   The Authentication Methods dialog box

4. Select the MS-CHAP v2 check box, and clear the other check boxes.

   Why would you limit authentication options rather than simply select them all?

5. Click OK to close the Authentication Methods dialog box, and click OK to close the Properties dialog box and complete the process.

Exercise 2: Working with RADIUS and IAS

In this exercise, you configure an RRAS server to use RADIUS authentication and configure it to access a RADIUS server. You also install the IAS Server component and configure the IAS server to support the RRAS server as a client.

▶ **To select RADIUS authentication**

1. Select the RRAS server (dc01) in the console tree of the Routing And Remote Access management console. The right-hand pane displays a list of components of the RRAS server, as shown in Figure 9.10.

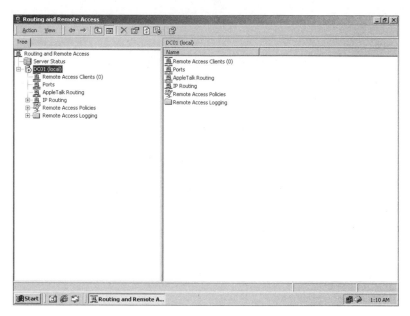

Figure 9.10   The components of the RRAS server

2. From the Action menu, choose Properties, and select the Security tab.
3. In the Authentication Provider list, click RADIUS Authentication.
4. Click OK to complete the change.

Important   If you were previously using a different authentication method, you will need to restart the RRAS server before this change takes effect.

▶ **To install the IAS server**

Perform this procedure on the RRAS server computer, logged on as the Administrator. As an alternative, you can use a different Windows 2000 Server computer for the IAS server.

1. In Control Panel, double-click Add/Remove Programs.
2. Click Add/Remove Windows Components. A list of current Windows 2000 components is displayed.
3. Click Networking Services in the list, and click Details. A list of networking components is displayed, as shown in Figure 9.11.

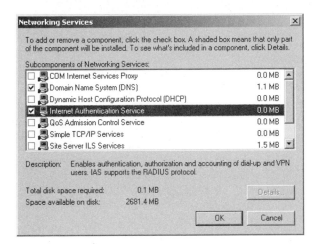

Figure 9.11   The Networking Services dialog box

4. Select the Internet Authentication Service check box, and click OK.
5. In the Windows Components Wizard, click Next to install the component.

   The new components you selected are now installed. The IAS server will be started automatically.

▶ **To configure a RADIUS server**

Perform this procedure on the RRAS server computer, logged on as the Administrator. The Routing And Remote Access console should be started.

1. Select the RRAS server (dc01) in the console tree. The right-hand pane displays a list of components of the RRAS server.
2. From the Action menu, choose Properties, and select the Security tab.

3. Click the Configure button next to the RADIUS Authentication provider.

    The RADIUS Authentication dialog box is displayed, as shown in Figure 9.12. The local IAS server (dc01) appears in the list if you have previously installed the IAS server.

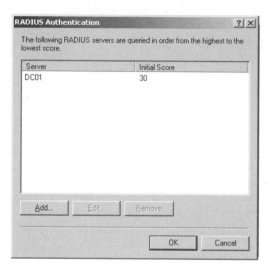

Figure 9.12 The RADIUS Authentication dialog box

4. Select the local server in the list, and click Edit. The Edit RADIUS Server dialog box is displayed, as shown in Figure 9.13.

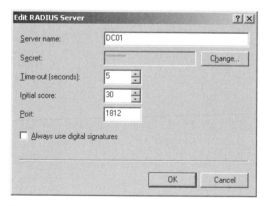

Figure 9.13 The Edit RADIUS Server dialog box

5. Change the Time-out setting to 10 seconds.

Tip   To use a shared secret, specify it in this page. You will also need to specify the same shared secret when you configure the client from the IAS console in the next procedure.

---

6. Click OK to complete the edit, and click OK to close the RADIUS Authentication dialog box. A message appears reminding you to restart the RRAS server.

7. Click OK to save the changes.

Important   You must restart the RRAS server before the changes you made here will take effect.

▶ **To add a client for the IAS server**

Perform this procedure from the computer on which you installed IAS Server. You should be logged on as the Administrator.

1. From the Administrative Tools menu, choose Internet Authentication Service. The Internet Authentication Service management console is displayed, as shown in Figure 9.14.

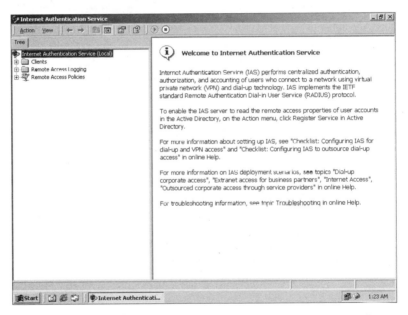

Figure 9.14   The Internet Authentication Service management console

2. Select Clients in the console tree. Any existing clients are listed in the right-hand pane.

3. From the Action menu, choose New Client. The Add Client Wizard is displayed, as shown in Figure 9.15.

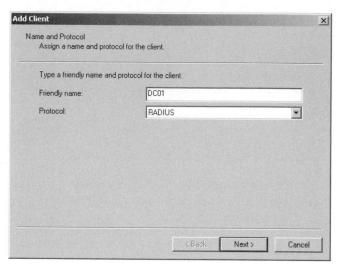

Figure 9.15   The Add Client Wizard

4. In the Friendly Name box, type **DC01**. Click Next to continue. The Client Information page is displayed, as shown in Figure 9.16.

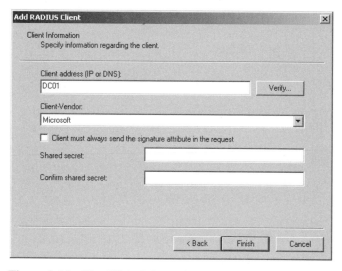

Figure 9.16   The Client Information page

5. Type **DC01** in the Client Address box.
6. Click Microsoft in the Client-Vendor list.
7. Click Finish to add the client.

Tip   To use a shared secret, type it in the two boxes provided on the Client Information page. You must specify the same shared secret in the RADIUS Authentication dialog box of the RRAS console.

Lesson Review

The following questions are intended to reinforce key information in this lesson. If you are unable to answer a question, review the lesson and try the question again. Answers to the questions can be found in the appendix.

1. Which RRAS authentication type can be used with an RRAS server to provide centralized authentication?

2. Which Windows authentication method uses completely unencrypted passwords?

3. What Windows authentication method would you use to support smart card authentication?

4. How do you manage authentication and security policy settings for an RRAS server when RADIUS authentication is in use?

5. In a network using an IAS server to provide centralized management of dial-in authentication for several RRAS servers, to which machine do dial-up clients send authentication requests?

Lesson Summary

- Windows 2000 Routing and Remote Access Service (RRAS) supports two basic authentication systems, Windows authentication and RADIUS. Windows authentication uses separate security settings for each RRAS server, while RADIUS supports centralized control of authentication and security settings.

- Windows authentication methods include unencrypted PAP and SPAP, which extends this protocol using encrypted passwords. CHAP uses a handshake system with a one-way encryption to avoid sending passwords over the network. MS-CHAP is an enhanced version of CHAP. MS-CHAP version 2 improves the security of MS-CHAP authentication by eliminating weak LAN Manager encryptions and by mutually authenticating the client and server to eliminate man-in-the-middle attacks.

- Remote Authentication Dial-In User Service (RADIUS) is a standard for centralized authentication, management, and accounting for remote access. You can configure Windows 2000 RRAS to use RADIUS authentication instead of Windows authentication.

- Windows 2000 Server includes Internet Authentication Service (IAS), a RADIUS server implementation. A computer running IAS can provide centralized security management and authentication for any number of RRAS servers, and it stores its settings in the Active Directory. An Internet Authentication Service management console allows you to configure authentication and security settings.

Lesson 3: Securing Remote Clients

In addition to fixing settings in the RRAS console, you can manage RRAS security on a per-user basis by using RRAS remote access policies. RRAS remote access policies allow you to control the duration of sessions, the authentication methods that remote clients can use, and other options that can increase the security of connections.

To make it easy for users to select the necessary RRAS policy options on their client computers, you can create a custom version of the RRAS client software called Connection Manager, with preset options for your particular remote access needs.

After this lesson, you will be able to

- Manage security using a remote access policy
- Use Connection Manager Administration Kit
- Use Connection Manager from remote clients

Estimated lesson time: 30 minutes

Managing Remote Access Policy

Windows 2000 RRAS provides comprehensive support for remote access policies, which provide you with complete control over client access to the RRAS server. You can specify one or more policies, each with conditions that a client must match to connect. The possible conditions include time of day and day of the week, client name and IP address, client and server telephone numbers, and other options.

You can also determine whether a user account's remote access permission enables the user to connect through RRAS. If you choose Allow Access, the client can connect only if it matches one of the remote access policies. If the user permission is set to Deny Access, all connections for that user are refused. If the user permission is set to Control Access through remote access policy, the policy's Allow or Deny option determines whether the connection is allowed.

Accessing Remote Access Policy

Where you manage the remote access policies depends on whether Windows authentication or IAS is in use. For Windows authentication, remote access policy is located under the RRAS server in the Routing And Remote Access management console. For IAS, remote access policy is located in the Internet Authentication Service management console. This lesson discusses IAS policy management.

Important Because IAS provides centralized management of remote access, it allows you to create remote access policies that apply to all servers. If IAS is not in use, each RRAS server has its own set of remote access policies. Always use IAS when you have more than one RRAS server in your enterprise, to ensure that a consistent remote access policy is in use throughout your network. Consider using IAS even if you only have one RRAS server so that policy management won't change as your network grows.

Creating and Editing Remote Access Policies

The Remote Access Policies window displays all of the currently active policies. You can change the sequence of policies to control which policy will be applied when two or more policies match the connection. When a connection attempt is made, RRAS uses this sequence to check the policies and uses the first policy whose conditions match the connection.

Note By default, a single policy is included: allow access if dial-in permission is enabled. This policy includes a condition that matches all connections, and it is set to deny access unless it is explicitly granted to the user.

When you add a policy to the list, you name the policy and then apply a list of conditions that must be matched by a connection for the policy to be used. The conditions you can use are listed in Table 9.1.

Table 9.1   Remote Access Policy Conditions

Condition	Description
Called-Station-Id	The telephone number dialed by the client
Calling-Station-Id	The originating telephone number
Day-and-Time-Restrictions	Connections during specified hours or days of week
Framed-Protocol	The connection protocol in use
Service-Type	The type of service requested
Tunnel-Type	The VPN tunneling protocol in use
Windows-Groups	Group memberships of the connecting user

Several additional conditions are available when you use RADIUS authentication. Most of these conditions examine the characteristics of the NAS (network access server), which is the client that makes a request to the RADIUS server (remember that RRAS acts as a NAS client). This allows you to change the authentication method based on which type of NAS the client has attached to. For example, checking the NAS port type allows you to prevent a policy you created for dial-up access from being applied to a wireless LAN user. Table 9.2 lists these additional conditions.

Table 9.2 IAS/RADIUS Remote Access Policy Conditions

Condition	Description
Client-Friendly-Name	The friendly name set in the IAS client list
Client-IP-Address	The IP address of the RADIUS client
Client-Vendor	The vendor of the NAS
NAS-Identifier	The identifier of the NAS
NAS-IP-Address	The IP address of the NAS
NAS-Port-Type	The physical port used by the NAS

Depending on the condition you select, you will be prompted for additional information. For example, the Day-and-Time-Restrictions condition prompts you for the hours and days of the week that access will be allowed or denied, and the Windows-Groups condition prompts for a list of groups.

The final step when creating a policy is to specify whether the policy will grant or deny remote access permission to users who match the conditions. If access is denied by a remote access policy, it can still be allowed on a per-user basis by the user's remote access properties.

Tip When you attach third-party NAS clients to an IAS server, the NAS vendor will typically provide an example of a correct IAS policy to allow the device to function correctly and securely on your network.

Managing the Profile for a Policy

If a connection attempt matches the policy you have created and the policy's Grant Remote Access permission option is selected, the user will be allowed access. The user will also be allowed access if explicitly granted access in the user account's remote access permission. Once a connection is made using a policy, you can further restrict the activities of the connection using policy profile settings. The profile includes six sets of properties:

- **Dial-in Constraints.** Contains various constraints that can be placed on dial-in users matching the current policy conditions. The following options are available:
  - Disconnect if idle for the specified number of minutes
  - Restrict maximum session to a specified number of minutes
  - Restrict access to specified dates and times
  - Restrict dial-in access to a particular telephone number
  - Restrict the media (modem, ISDN, DSL, Ethernet, and so on) on which connections will be allowed

- **IP.** Includes settings relating to client IP addresses. You can specify that the server must supply an IP address to the client, that the client can request an address, or that policy will be based on the server's settings.

  These IP settings also include options for packet filtering. You can create both incoming packet filters, and outgoing packet filters to restrict the ports and services that a user will be allowed to access when connected to the RRAS server. For example, you could use IP filters to allow access only to the company intranet Web site, preventing dial-up users from connecting directly to file servers. Packet filters are used only in RRAS policies, not IAS policies.

- **Multilink.** Controls whether clients using the current security policy can connect using Multilink, which allows a client to connect to two or more modems or other ports and use the combined bandwidth available from these devices. You can choose to disable Multilink entirely, allow Multilink with a specified maximum number of ports, or default to the RRAS server's settings.

  Using the bandwidth allocation protocol (BAP) options, you can specify a minimum percentage capacity for the dial-in lines and a time limit. If the capacity falls below this level for the specified time, the RRAS server will remove lines from Multilink connections to increase the available capacity.

- **Authentication.** Controls the authentication methods that will be allowed for connections that match the current policy. The options available are the same as those described earlier in this chapter, including PAP, SPAP, CHAP, MS-CHAP, MS-CHAP version 2, and EAP.

  You can also specify which types of EAP connections are allowed and their specific settings. For example, you can allow EAP connections using a smart card or certificate and specify the certificate that the server will use to authenticate itself.

- **Encryption.** Controls the level of encryption that will be allowed for connections matching the current policy. The options include No Encryption, Basic, Strong, and Strongest. These options apply only to communication between Windows 2000 clients and Windows 2000 RRAS servers.

- **Advanced.** Allows you to specify additional security attributes. Click Add to add an attribute. The list of available attributes includes standard options for RADIUS servers, as well as a variety of vendor-specific options.

Using the Connection Manager Administration Kit

The Connection Manager Administration Kit (CMAK), included with Windows 2000 Server, enables you to customize many features of the Connection Manager software used for clients of the RRAS server. Connection Manager is the Windows component that clients see when they dial a modem connection. By creating a custom Connection Manager profile with the CMAK, you are pre-setting the connection options that clients will need to meet your RRAS or IAS policies and successfully establish a dial-in connection. This is useful for ISPs that provide dial-up access as well as enterprises with dial-up or VPN access to networks.

The CMAK is a wizard that prompts you for various information and then creates a service profile for the Connection Manager utility. The following sections describe how to use this wizard.

Working with Service Profiles

When you start the Connection Manager Administration Kit Wizard, you are prompted to either create a new service profile or open and modify an existing service profile. Service profiles are stored with the .cms extension.

Tip   Another page of the wizard allows you to merge one or more existing service profiles into the current profile.

Specifying Service Names and Support Information

The initial pages of the Connection Manager Administration Kit Wizard prompt you for various text items that will be used to customize the Connection Manager interface:

- **Service Name.**   A friendly name for the service, up to 40 characters long.
- **File Name For Service Profiles.**   A file name used to prefix the files created by CMAK. This file name is limited to 8 alphanumeric characters.
- **Support Information.**   An optional message, up to 50 characters long, displayed in the Connection Manager dialog box.
- **Realm Name.**   An optional prefix (such as a domain or organizational unit name) or suffix (such as an Internet domain name) to be added to all user names.

Network and Dial-Up Connections

You can specify that Connection Manager will create one or more entries for your service in the Network And Dial-Up Connections window. For each of these, you can specify DNS and WINS addresses, if the server does not assign them automatically, and an optional script file.

You can also include a telephone book file in the service profile, specifying one or more dial-up telephone numbers. Connection Manager can also use the URL of a server running Connection Point Services to automatically download updated lists of telephone numbers.

VPN Support

If you enable VPN support in the Connection Manager Administration Kit Wizard, the resulting connection profile can be used to connect to the RRAS server through a public network, such as the Internet, rather than directly through a dial-up connection. The Internet connection used for a VPN can be any existing dial-up connection or always-on broadband connection, such as DSL or LAN.

Using Actions and Applications

The Connection Manager Administration Kit Wizard allows you to specify a number of actions, or programs, that will run at various points within the connection process. The following actions are available:

- *Pre-connect actions* run before connecting.
- *Pre-tunnel actions* run before connecting using a VPN.
- *Post-tunnel actions* run after a successful VPN connection.
- *Disconnect actions* run after the user disconnects from the service.

In addition to these actions, you can specify one or more auto-applications. These are applications that run when connected to the network. The network connection will be disconnected automatically after the user exits the last auto-application.

Modifying Graphics and Icons

Using CMAK options, you can change many of the graphics and icons used in Connection Manager dialog boxes from the default choices. Table 9.3 lists the elements you can customize.

Table 9.3 Customizable Connection Manager Elements

Element	Pixel size	Description
Logon graphic	330 x 141	Displayed at top of logon dialog box
Phonebook graphic	114 x 304	Displayed at left of Phone Book dialog box
Large program icon	32 x 32	The desktop icon
Title bar icon	16 x 16	Appears in title bar and taskbar
Status area icon	16 x 16	Appears in status area while connected

Software and Documentation

The Connection Manager Administration Kit Wizard prompts you to indicate whether to include the Connection Manager software with the service profile. You can also specify a custom Windows help file if you have created your own documentation, or use the default Connection Manager help file. Options are also provided for a custom license agreement and additional help or documentation files.

Using Connection Manager

After you complete all of the CMAK settings, the CMAK saves a number of files to complete the profile. These include a .cms file, which stores the information the wizard prompted for, and a self-extracting .exe file that installs the Connection Manager software and the service profile on a client computer. These files use the 8-character file name you specified. They can be copied to a floppy disk, CD-R, or network share to deploy the service profile to clients.

Practice: Securing Remote Clients

In this practice, you create remote access policies and modify the settings of existing policies. You also install and use the CMAK and test a customized version of Connection Manager from a client machine.

Note   To complete this practice, you will need a Windows 2000 Server computer with the RRAS component enabled and a client computer for testing.

Exercise 1: Managing Remote Access Policy

In this exercise, you create remote access policies, edit an existing policy, and edit settings in the policy profile. You will need to use either the Routing And Remote Access console or the Internet Authentication Service console to access the policy, depending on whether your RRAS server is configured to use RADIUS authentication.

▶   **To create a remote access policy with day and time restrictions**

Perform this procedure on the RRAS server.

1. From the Administrative Tools menu, choose Routing And Remote Access to open the Routing And Remote Access management console.
2. Select Remote Access Policies in the console tree. The list of current policies is displayed.
3. From the Action menu, choose New Remote Access Policy. The Add Remote Access Policy Wizard is displayed, as shown in Figure 9.17.

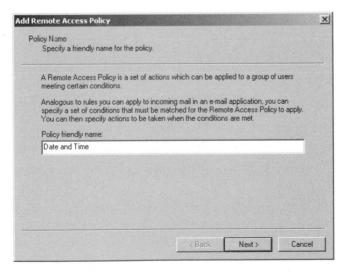

Figure 9.17   The Add Remote Access Policy Wizard

4. On the Policy Name page, type **Date and Time** in the Policy Friendly Name box, and click Next.

5. On the Conditions page, click Add to add a condition to the policy.

   As shown in Figure 9.18, the Select Attribute dialog box lists the available conditions you can add to the policy.

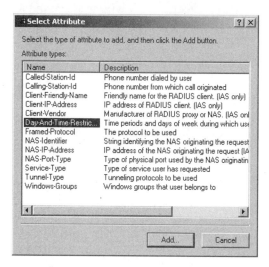

Figure 9.18   The Select Attribute dialog box

6. In the dialog box, select Day-and-Time-Restrictions from the list, and click Add. The Time Of Day Constraints dialog box is displayed, as shown in Figure 9.19.

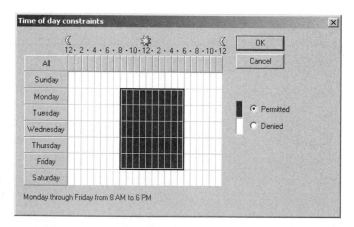

Figure 9.19   The Time Of Day Constraints dialog box

7. Click and drag to draw a box from Monday 8:00 A.M. to Friday 6:00 P.M., and then select Permitted. This enables access from 8:00 A.M. to 6:00 P.M., Monday through Friday.

8. Click OK, and click Next. The Permissions options are displayed, as shown in Figure 9.20.

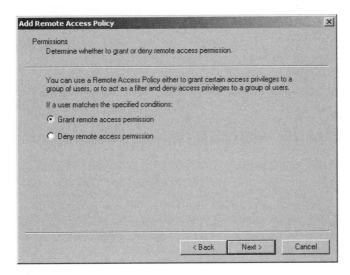

Figure 9.20   The Permissions options page

9. On the Permissions page, select Grant Remote Access Permission, and click Next.

10. On the User Profile page, click Finish to complete the new policy.

    This policy allows all users access if they connect in the specified time period.

▶ **To create a remote access policy with Windows group restrictions**

1. In the console tree of the Routing And Remote Access console, select Remote Access Policies, and choose New Remote Access Policy from the Action menu. The Add Remote Access Policy Wizard appears.

2. On the Policy Name page, type **Design Group Access** in the Policy Friendly Name box, and click Next.

3. On the Conditions page, click Add. The Select Attribute dialog box lists the available condition attributes.

4. Select Windows-Groups in the list, and click Add. The Groups dialog box appears.

5. In the Groups dialog box, click Add. The Select Groups dialog box is displayed, as shown in Figure 9.21.

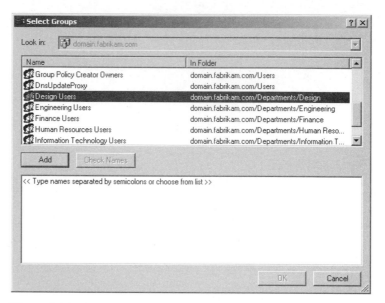

Figure 9.21   Selecting Windows groups for a policy

6. Select Design Users in the list of groups, and click Add. The Design Users group is added to the group list.

7. Click OK to close the Select Groups dialog box, and then click OK in the Groups dialog box. The condition you added is now included in the list.

8. Click Next to continue. The Permissions options are displayed.

9. On the Permissions page, select the Grant Remote Access Permission option, and click Next.

10. On the User Profile page, click Finish to complete the policy.

This policy allows access to users in the Design Users group regardless of the day or time.

▶ **To edit an existing policy**

1. In the console tree of the Routing And Remote Access console, select Remote Access Policy.

2. Select Date And Time from the list, and from the Action menu, choose Properties. The Date And Time Properties dialog box is displayed, as shown in Figure 9.22.

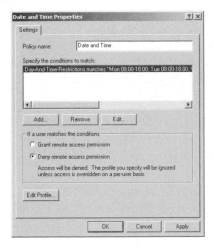

Figure 9.22   Date And Time Permissions dialog box

3. Select Deny Remote Access Permission, and click OK.

The policy now denies access during the selected times. Users can still connect if they match a different policy or if the user properties explicitly grant the remote access permission.

▶ **To change policy profile settings**

1. In the console tree of the Routing And Remote Access console, select Remote Access Policy.

2. Select Design Group Access from the list, and from the Action menu, choose Properties. The Design Group Access Properties dialog box is displayed, as shown in Figure 9.23.

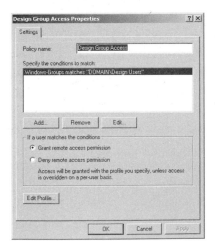

Figure 9.23   The Design Group Access Properties dialog box

3. Click Edit Profile. The Dial-in Constraints tab is displayed in the Edit Dial-in Profile dialog box shown in Figure 9.24.

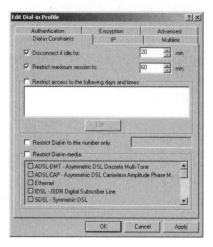

Figure 9.24   The Edit Dial-in Profile dialog box

4. Select the Disconnect If Idle For check box, and change the idle time to 20 minutes.

5. Select the Restrict Maximum Session To check box, and change the corresponding time to 60 minutes.

6. Click OK, and click OK in the Design Group Access Properties dialog box.

   Users who connect using this profile are now restricted to 60-minute sessions, and they are disconnected after 20 minutes of idle time.

Exercise 2: Connection Manager

In this exercise, you set up the CMAK on a Windows 2000 Server computer. You then use the CMAK to create a service profile, and install the customized version of Connection Manager on a client machine.

▶   **To install the Connection Manager Administration Kit**

Perform this procedure from the RRAS Server.

1. In Control Panel, double-click Add/Remove Programs.

2. Click Add/Remove Windows Components. A list of installed Windows components is displayed.

3. Select Management And Monitoring Tools in the list, and click Details. A list of monitoring components is displayed, as shown in Figure 9.25.

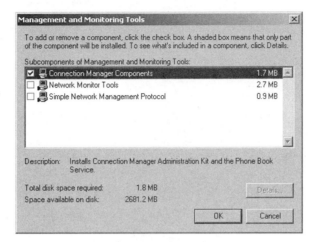

Figure 9.25   The Management And Monitoring Tools components list

4. Select the Connection Manager Components check box, and click OK.

5. In the Windows Components Wizard, click Next to install the new components. (This might take several minutes.) The Connection Manager components are now installed.

Note   You might be prompted to insert the Windows 2000 Server or Service Pack CD during the installation process.

6. Click Finish to return to Control Panel.

▶   **To create a service profile using the CMAK**

1. Click Start, point to Programs, point to Administrative Tools, and click Connection Manager Administration Kit. The Connection Manager Administration Kit Wizard displays an introductory page.

2. Click Next to continue. The Service Profile Source page, shown in Figure 9.26, appears. You can indicate whether to create a new profile or edit an existing one.

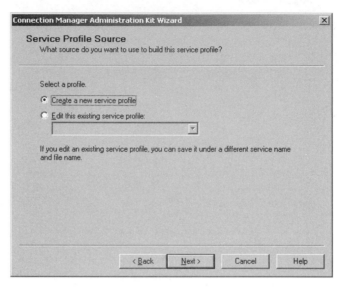

Figure 9.26   Creating a new service profile

3. Select Create A New Service Profile, and click Next.

4. On the Service And File Names page, type **Fabrikam** in the Service Name and File Name boxes, and click Next. The next page allows you to merge existing service profiles.

5. On the Merged Service Profiles page, click Next to continue. The Support Information page allows you to add a line of support information that will be displayed in the logon dialog box.

6. On the Support Information page, click Next to continue.

7. On the Realm Name page, select Do Not Add A Realm Name, and click Next to continue.

8. Click Next on both the Dial-Up Networking Entries page and the VPN Support page.

9. On the Connect Actions page, clear all check boxes, and click Next.

10. On the Auto Applications page, click Next.

11. Click Next on the Logon Bitmap, Phone Book Bitmap, Phone Book, and Icons pages.

12. On the Status-Area-Icon Menu page, click Next.

13. On the Help File page, select Use The Default Help File, and click Next.

14. On the Connection Manager Software page, select Include The Connection Manager 1.2 Software, and click Next.

15. Click Next on both the License Agreement and the Additional Files pages.

16. On the Ready To Build Service Profile page, click Next to begin building the service profile. A command prompt window opens and builds the profile.

    The path of the .exe file name is displayed when the wizard completes; typically, the file name is \Program Files\Cmak\Profiles\Fabrikam\Fabrikam.exe.

17. Click Finish to exit the wizard.

18. Copy the files in the \Program Files\Cmak\Profiles\Fabrikam folder to a floppy disk to use in the next procedure.

▶ **To connect with a customized Connection Manager**

1. On the client machine, insert the floppy disk containing the service profile, and open the floppy disk from My Computer.

2. Double-click the Fabrikam.exe file you created in the previous procedure. A dialog box asks whether you want to install the connection.

3. Click Yes to install the new connection. A dialog box opens allowing you to choose whether to make the connection available to all users or to the current user.

4. In the dialog box, select All Users, and click OK. The Connection Manager is now launched, as shown in Figure 9.27.

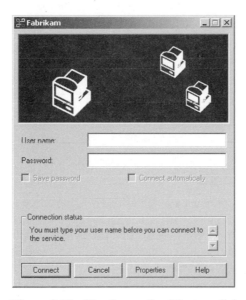

Figure 9.27   The Connection Manager dialog box

5. Specify a User Name and Password, and click Connect to make the connection.

Note   Connecting requires a telephone number. Click Properties to specify a number. You can also specify a list of telephone numbers when creating the service profile.

Lesson Review

The following questions are intended to reinforce key information in this lesson. If you are unable to answer a question, review the lesson and try the question again. Answers to the questions can be found in the appendix.

1. When RADIUS is not in use, what tool do you use to manage remote access policies?

2. If a user is connecting to an RRAS server and matches several remote access policies, which policy will be used for the connection?

3. How would you restrict the session length for a remote access policy?

4. When you answer the questions in the Connection Manager Administration Kit Wizard, where are the answers saved?

5. What happens if an incoming connection matches a remote access policy and the policy is set to deny access?

Lesson Summary

- Remote access policies are managed through the RRAS or IAS management console, depending on the authentication type selected. When users attempt to connect, the connection uses the first policy that matches the current conditions. Each policy can specify conditions to match as well as restrictions and settings in the connection's profile.

- The Connection Manager Administration Kit (CMAK) allows you to create a customized Connection Manager for use by employees, partners, or clients. The CMAK can customize aspects of the connection including phone numbers, protocols, documentation, and graphics.

- A service profile created by the CMAK can include a copy of the Connection Manager software. This can be distributed along with the service profile and provides a simply installed program for establishing an RRAS connection from a client.

Lesson 4: Securing Communications Using a VPN

A virtual private network (VPN) provides a secure transport for network services over a public network, such as the Internet. This is accomplished by using a tunneling protocol to encapsulate private data and pass it in encrypted form through the public network. VPNs provide a low-cost alternative to dedicated WAN links. Windows 2000 Server includes dedicated support for VPN networking, as do the Microsoft Windows 2000 Professional and Windows XP clients.

After this lesson, you will be able to

- Understand virtual private networking and VPN protocols
- Understand VPN protocol security
- Manage and troubleshoot VPN protocols

Estimated lesson time: 30 minutes

Understanding Virtual Private Networks

A Virtual Private Network (VPN) allows you to create an encrypted link between computers over the Internet as if the two computers were connected by a single, private link such as a dial-up connection.

There are two basic configurations for a VPN, client-to-gateway and gateway-to-gateway. A *client-to-gateway connection* is used when a traveling user connects to a private network using a VPN. This is similar to using dial-up RRAS access, but the user can connect through any dial-up provider or a separate LAN with Internet access rather than over the phone system. A *gateway-to-gateway connection* is used to form a permanent link between two RRAS servers on separate networks, each with its own Internet connectivity. Gateway-to-gateway connections are also used to connect RRAS servers to VPN devices from third-party vendors.

VPN connections use a tunneling protocol to encrypt packets of data and pass them over the public network. Windows 2000 supports two tunneling protocols:

- Point-to-Point Tunneling Protocol (PPTP)
- Layer 2 Tunneling Protocol (L2TP)

PPTP

PPTP is a tunneling protocol based on the dial-up PPP protocol. It supports the same authentication methods as PPP, such as PAP, MS-CHAP, and EAP. PPTP uses the Microsoft Point-to-Point Encryption (MPPE) protocol for encryption. PPTP is not considered as secure as L2TP.

Caution   New VPN server installations should use L2TP rather than PPTP. Microsoft provides the Microsoft L2TP/IPSec VPN client for Windows 98, Windows Me, and Windows NT 4, so there is no longer any reason to use PPTP to support clients running these operating systems. Download the client from *http://www.microsoft.com/windows2000/downloads/tools/*.

L2TP

L2TP is a more secure tunneling protocol that extends PPTP with additional features. L2TP supports the same authentication methods as PPTP. It also supports and requires Certificate Services, which are used to provide the encryption keys necessary to establish the encrypted session and ensure the identity of both parties. L2TP uses IPSec for encryption. L2TP is supported natively by Windows 2000 and Windows XP clients and by the Microsoft L2TP/IPSec VPN client for earlier versions of Windows.

Configuring VPN Protocols

Before you configure L2TP, you need to deploy machine certificates to all participanting machines (clients and servers). Refer to Chapter 6 for detailed instructions about how to deploy machine certificates. You also need to enable RRAS services as described in Lesson 1. Once you have deployed machine certificates and enabled RRAS, you're ready to configure L2TP.

Configuring VPN protocols is handled through the RRAS manager. If you are enabling RRAS to provide VPN services, you can select the VPN Server option in the RRAS Setup Wizard to configure all the required settings automatically. Otherwise, you will need to enable L2TP manually and configure L2TP filtering.

Enabling L2TP Filtering on the Server

Enabling L2TP in RRAS permits a server to answer L2TP connections, but it doesn't block other traffic from being routed by the RRAS server onto your network. Because RRAS servers must be connected to the Internet to receive L2TP connections, the RRAS server itself is vulnerable to attack by hackers who will attempt to connect using other protocols. To prevent unwanted traffic from reaching your RRAS server or being routed onto your private network, you must also enable L2TP filtering.

Enabling L2TP filtering prevents the public interface from passing traffic other than the L2TP protocol. L2TP runs over UDP port 1701. Kerberos is also required, so you will have to open UDP port 500. You'll learn how to open these ports in the exercise in this lesson.

Configuring Client VPN Settings

Windows 2000 Professional and Windows XP clients include built-in VPN clients. To create a VPN connection at a client, open the Network And Dial-up Connections window and double-click Make New Connection. In the Network Connection Wizard, select Connect To A Private Network Through The Internet, and specify the IP address or host name of the RRAS server.

Tip   You can create an automated installer to set up a VPN connection using the CMAK, described earlier in this chapter.

You can also specify VPN protocol settings on the client. Click Properties in the Connect dialog box, select Advanced on the Security tab, and click Settings. The Advanced Security Settings dialog box appears. In this dialog box, you can choose which authentication methods can be used to connect to the VPN, and whether the client will request an encrypted connection or require encryption. If the server does not offer the level of encryption required, the connection cannot continue.

Caution   If a client and server cannot negotiate a compatible set of encryption and authentication protocols for L2TP, they will subsequently attempt to establish a PPTP connection unless you disable PPTP on the RRAS server or filter the PPTP port.

After you have created a VPN connection and established an Internet connection, click the VPN entry in the Network And Dial-up Connections window and, when prompted, enter a user name and password to connect to the private network.

Practice: Configuring and Troubleshooting VPN Protocols

In this practice, you configure an RRAS server to provide L2TP VPN service to Internet clients. The RRAS server must have two network adapters to provide VPN service: one adapter for the private network and one adapter to connect to the public network. In this example, Local Area Connection is the private interface and Local Area Connection 2 is the public interface.

Exercise 1: Configuring an RRAS Server

In this exercise, you configure an RRAS server to support L2TP. This exercise builds on Lesson 3 of this chapter and shows you how to configure an L2TP server without using the Routing And Remote Access Server Setup Wizard.

Tip   If you are only configuring RRAS to create a VPN, using the Routing And Remote Access Server Setup Wizard is easier than manually configuring L2TP.

▶   **To enable routing on the RRAS server**

1. Click Start, point to Programs, point to Administrative Tools, and click Routing And Remote Access Service. The Routing And Remote Access management console appears.

2. Right-click DC01 (local), and choose Properties. The DC01 (Local) Properties dialog box appears, as shown in Figure 9.28.

Figure 9.28   The DC01 (Local) Properties dialog box

3. Select Router, ensuring that Local Area Network Routing Only and Remote Access Server remain selected.

4. Click the Security tab.

5. Click Authentication Methods to open the Authentication Methods dialog box shown in Figure 9.29.

Figure 9.29   The Authentication Methods dialog box

6. Select Extensible Authentication Protocol (EAP), and clear the other check boxes.

7. Click OK to close the Authentication Methods dialog box.

8. Click the IP tab, shown in Figure 9.30.

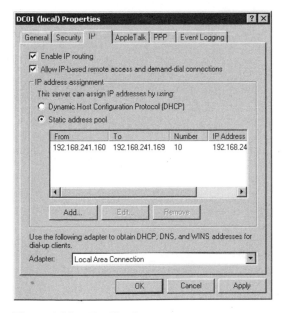

Figure 9.30   The IP tab

9. Ensure that the Enable IP Routing and Allow IP-Based Remote Access And Demand-Dial Connections check boxes are selected.

10. Select Static Address Pool.

11. Click Add. The New Address Range dialog box appears as shown in Figure 9.31.

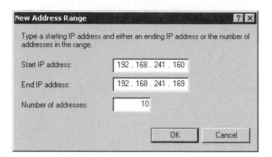

Figure 9.31   The New Address Range dialog box

12. Type **192.168.241.160** as the Start IP Address, and type **192.168.241.169** as the End IP Address.

13. Click OK to close the New Address Range dialog box.

14. Click OK to close the DC01 (Local) Properties dialog box.

15. If a message box appears asking if you want to view help, click No. L2TP is now enabled on the RRAS server.

▶ **To configure L2TP filters on the public interface**

1. In the Routing And Remote Access management console, expand DC01, IP Routing, and select General.

2. Right-click Local Area Connection 2, and choose Properties. Local Area Connection 2 is the public interface for this RRAS server.

   The Local Area Connection 2 Properties dialog box appears, as shown in Figure 9.32.

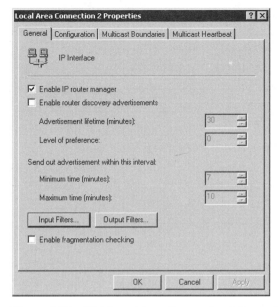

Figure 9.32   The Local Area Connection 2 Properties dialog box

3. Click Input Filters. The Input Filters dialog box appears.
4. Click Add to open the Add IP Filter dialog box, as shown in Figure 9.33.

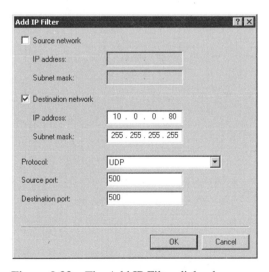

Figure 9.33   The Add IP Filter dialog box

5. Select the Destination Network check box.

6. Type **10.0.0.80** in the IP Address box and **255.255.255.255** in the Subnet Mask box. (The IP address is the IP address of the Local Area Connection 2 adapter.)

7. Select UDP in the Protocol list.

8. Type **500** in the both the Source Port and Destination Port boxes.

9. Click OK. The newly added filter appears in the filter list.

10. Click Add. The Add IP Filter dialog box appears again.

11. Select the Destination Network check box.

12. Type **10.0.0.80** in the IP Address box and **255.255.255.255** in the Subnet Mask box.

13. Select UDP in the Protocol list.

14. Type **1701** in both the Source Port and Destination Port boxes.

15. Click OK. The newly added filter appears in the filter list.

16. In the Input Filters dialog box, select Drop All Packets Except Those That Meet The Criteria Below. Your settings should appear as shown in Figure 9.34.

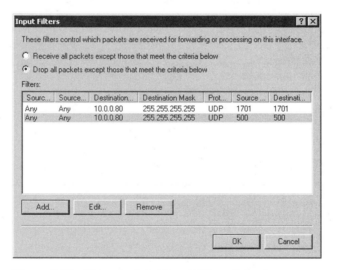

Figure 9.34   The completed Input Filters dialog box

17. Click OK to close the Input Filters dialog box.

18. Click Output Filters in the Local Area Connection 2 Properties dialog box. The Output Filters dialog box appears.

19. Click Add. The Add IP Filter dialog box appears.

20. Select the Source Network check box.

21. Type **10.0.0.80** in the IP Address box and **255.255.255.255** in the Subnet Mask box.

22. Select UDP in the Protocol list box.

23. Type **500** in the Source Port and Destination Port boxes.

24. Click OK to close the Add IP Filter dialog box.

25. Click Add in the Output Filters dialog box.

26. Select the Source Network check box.

27. Type **10.0.0.80** in the IP Address box and **255.255.255.255** in the Subnet Mask box.

28. Select UDP in the Protocol list box.

29. Type **1701** in the Source Port and Destination Port boxes. Your dialog box should appear as in Figure 9.35.

Figure 9.35   The finished source and destination ports

30. Click OK to close the Add IP Filter dialog box.

31. Select the Drop All Packets Except Those That Meet The Criteria Below option in the Output Filters dialog box. Your dialog box should appear as in Figure 9.36.

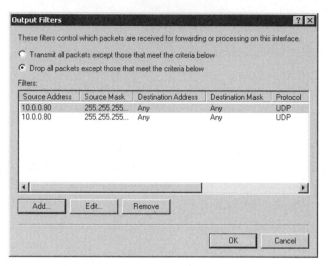

Figure 9.36   The Output Filters dialog box

32. Click OK to close the Output Filters dialog box.

33. Click OK to close the Local Area Connection 2 Properties dialog box.

    The L2TP filters are now configured.

▶ **To configure remote access VPN policy**

1. Click Start, point to Programs, point to Administrative Tools, and click Internet Authentication Service. The IAS management console appears.

2. Right-click Remote Access Policies, and choose New Remote Access Policy. The Add Remote Access Policy Wizard appears, as shown in Figure 9.37.

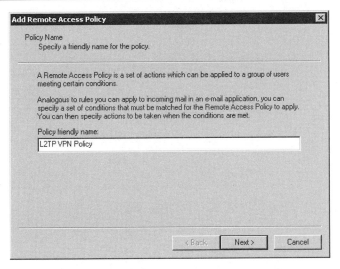

Figure 9.37   The Add Remote Access Policy Wizard

3. Type **L2TP VPN Policy** as the Policy Friendly Name, and click Next. The Conditions page appears.

4. On the Conditions page, click Add. The Select Attribute dialog box appears as shown in Figure 9.38.

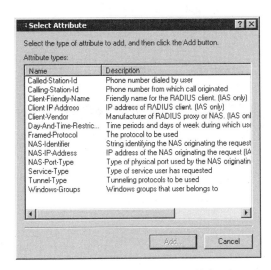

Figure 9.38   The Select Attribute dialog box

5. Double-click NAS-Port-Type. The NAS-Port-Type dialog box appears as shown in Figure 9.39.

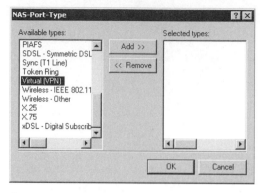

Figure 9.39   The NAS-Port-Type dialog box

6. Select Virtual (VPN) in the Available Types list, and click Add.

7. Click OK to close the NAS-Port-Types dialog box.

8. On the Conditions page of the Add Remote Access Policy Wizard, click Add. The Select Attribute dialog box appears.

9. In the Select Attribute dialog box, double-click Tunnel Type.

10. In the Tunnel-Type dialog box, select Layer Two Tunneling Protocol, and click Add.

11. Click OK to close the Tunnel-Type dialog box. The Conditions page of the Add Remote Access Policy Wizard now shows two conditions, as shown in Figure 9.40.

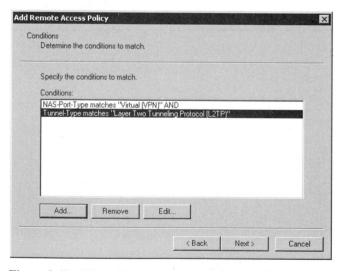

Figure 9.40   The Add Remote Access Policy page with two conditions

12. Click Next. The Permissions page appears.

13. On the Permissions page, select Grant Remote Access Permissions, and click Next. The User Profile page appears.

14. On the User Profile page, click the Edit Profile button. The Edit Dial-In Profile dialog box appears.

15. In the Edit Dial-In-Profile dialog box, click the Encryption tab. The dialog box is shown in Figure 9.41.

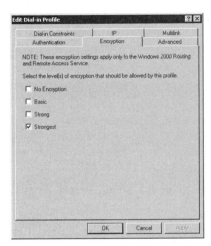

Figure 9.41   The Encryption tab of the Edit Dial-In Profile dialog box

16. Clear all the check boxes except Strongest. This specifies 3DES encryption for L2TP connections.

17. Click OK to close the Edit Dial-In Profile dialog box.

18. Click Finish to close the Add Remote Access Policy Wizard.

Exercise 2: Creating a Secure Connection to the L2TP VPN Server

In this exercise, you securely connect to the L2TP VPN server using a Windows 2000 Professional client.

▶ **To connect to the VPN from Windows 2000 Professional**

1. Right-click My Network Places, and click Properties to open the Network And Dial-up Connections window.

2. Double-click the Make New Connection icon. The Network Connection Wizard starts.

3. Click Next to continue. A list of network connection types is displayed in the Network Connection Type page, as shown in Figure 9.42.

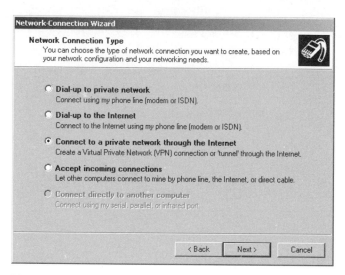

Figure 9.42   Selecting a network connection type

4. Select Connect To A Private Network Through The Internet, and click Next.

5. When prompted whether to dial an Internet connection before making the VPN link, select Do Not Dial The Initial Connection, and click Next. The Destination Address page is displayed, as shown in Figure 9.43.

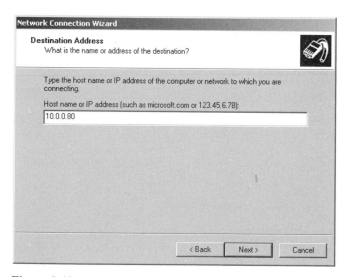

Figure 9.43   The Destination Address page

6. Type **10.0.0.80** in the Host Name Or IP Address box, and click Next.

   You are prompted whether to use a smart card.

7. Select Do Not Use My Smart Card, and click Next.

8. On the Connection Availability page, click Next to continue. The Completing The Network Connection Wizard page appears.

9. Click Finish to create the connection. The Connect Virtual Private Connection dialog box appears, as shown in Figure 9.44.

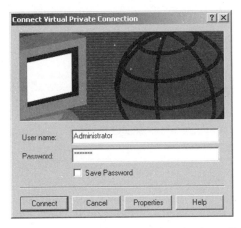

Figure 9.44   The Connect Virtual Private Connection dialog box

10. Type **Administrator** in the User Name box, type the Administrator's password in the Password box, and click Connect.

11. A message box confirms that the connection was successful. Click OK to exit.

Lesson Review

The following questions are intended to reinforce key information in this lesson. If you are unable to answer a question, review the lesson and try the question again. Answers to the questions can be found in the appendix.

1. Which of the VPN protocols supported by Windows 2000 Server is considered more secure?

2. Which utility can quickly configure an RRAS server to act as a VPN server?

3. Where do you add a VPN connection from a Windows 2000 Professional client?

4. Which VPN protocol requires certificate-based authentication?

5. What information is required from a client to connect to a remote VPN?

Lesson Summary

- A Virtual Private Network (VPN) uses a tunneling protocol to encrypt data on a private network and pass it across a public network, such as the Internet. Windows 2000 Server supports two main VPN protocols: PPTP (Point-to-Point Tunneling Protocol) and L2TP (Level 2 Tunneling Protocol).

- To quickly set up VPN access, you can specify VPN Server as the server role when you initially configure an RRAS server, or you can manually configure VPN access using the Routing And Remote Access console. An RRAS server can act as a dial-up server, VPN server, and router concurrently.

- Windows 2000 and Windows XP clients can easily connect to a VPN using the Add New Connection Wizard from the Network And Dial-up Connections window. Specify a VPN connection and the IP address of the VPN server. You need to establish an Internet connection, such as a dial-up or LAN connection, on the client before attempting to connect to a VPN.

C H A P T E R   1 0

Wireless Security

About This Chapter

The amazing usefulness of new wireless network devices has fueled their sudden and rapid widespread adoption. As with all sudden changes in the fabric of networks, the benefits of new technology often precede real security by a period of time. Wireless devices have created a new vector that allows hackers to attack private networks. Although these attacks are usually against targets of opportunity and perpetrated merely to gain Internet access, they also provide the means for malicious users to attach to your network without worrying about the physical security you employ.

Security standards for wireless protocols are still evolving, which is creating a moving target for vendors and users alike in their efforts to secure this new capability. The existing security standard for encryption in wireless devices, Wired Equivalent Privacy (WEP), is being replaced by the newer 802.1x port authentication protocol. Both technologies are discussed in detail in this chapter.

Exam Tip   Make sure you know how to secure a wireless access point by using Wired Equivalency Protocol.

Before You Begin

> **Note**   To accomplish the exercises in this chapter, you'll need relatively expensive hardware. If you don't have this hardware, you should still read through the exercises to learn how wireless devices are configured for security.

To *follow* the lessons in this chapter, you must have

- The domain.Fabrikam.com Microsoft Windows 2000 domain controller
- A wireless access point that supports the 802.1x protocol
- A laptop computer running Microsoft Windows XP with a wireless network adapter

To *complete* the lessons in this chapter exactly as written, you will need

- The domain.Fabrikam.com Windows 2000 domain controller
- An Intel PRO/Wireless 5000 LAN Access Point with the latest firmware
- A Windows XP client laptop
- A Windows 2000 client
- A Tribeca Technologies' Proxim Harmony 802.11a CardBus Card network adapter

Lesson 1: Setting Up a Wireless Network

Wireless local area networks (WLANs) allow client computers to connect to networks without physical connections. They are simple to set up and easy to use so their popularity has exploded—at the cost of security. WLANs have often been deployed without any serious consideration for the security risks that are inherent to them. Because they can allow intruders who are physically near your network to connect to your network, WLANs now represent the second greatest threat to network security after the Internet.

In this lesson, you will connect a wireless access point to your network and configure a Windows XP client to connect to it using a wireless network adapter.

To complete this lesson, you will need

- A wireless access point
- A laptop computer running Windows XP with a wireless network adapter

---

After this lesson, you will be able to

- Understand wireless technology and its security implications
- Connect a wireless access point to your network and connect to it

Estimated lesson time: 20 minutes

Understanding Wireless Technology

Wireless network technology has been around for a long time. The University of Hawaii originally developed the prototype on which Ethernet is based in the early 1970s as a wireless broadcast protocol. Until the early 1990s, the radio equipment required for wireless networking was prohibitively expensive for general purpose use and kept wireless networking from being used for anything but bridging networks over spans where cable could not be used. These early wireless networks did not include any form of security as a rule—security was not necessary because the equipment to participate in the network was too expensive.

The Institute of Electrical and Electronics Engineers (IEEE) developed the 802.11 protocol in the early 1990s to standardize a few independent efforts at creating true WLANs. The original 802.11 protocol operated at 2 Mbps in its client/server (infrastructure) mode, and 1 Mbps in its peer-to-peer (ad hoc) mode.

In infrastructure mode, client network adapters talk only to special radio bridges called wireless access points (WAPs) that are connected directly to the wired network. Creating the association between the client and WAP requires that the client use the same Service Set Identifier (SSID) that's programmed into the WAP. SSIDs are not technically secure because they can be sniffed. Also, clients can specify the special "ANY" SSID that will allow them to connect to any WAP that isn't secured.

Building an Infrastructure WLAN

To build an infrastructure WLAN, administrators need only place WAPs throughout their enterprise. WLAN users can then connect from their laptops to the nearest WAP to connect to the network. In the much less commonly used ad hoc mode, clients with network adapters simply communicate among themselves. To reach the Internet or another network, one of the peers must act as a router and be wired to the network.

The 802.11 protocol includes a data link layer private key encryption protocol called Wired Equivalent Privacy (WEP) that uses a 40-bit key and RC4 stream encryption. The idea behind WEP is that, while not perfectly secure, it is at least as secure as a wired network. The original 802.11 protocol was moderately successful in enterprises, but it was prohibitively expensive so it was never widely deployed in the mass market.

More Info   WEP encryption is discussed in detail in Lesson 2.

That situation suddenly changed in 1999 with the release of the 802.11b protocol that operated at 11 Mbps. The much higher speed of 802.11b for basically the same price resonated with users, and 802.11b equipment sold very well even early in its product life cycle. Manufacturers were surprised at the adoption rate of 802.11b— so much so that many manufacturers and OEMs began producing equipment. Competition drove down prices, and with lower prices the adoption rate increased dramatically. Within two years, wireless networking went from relative obscurity to very widespread adoption. It is used in the majority of large businesses today, and in a significant percentage of homes and small businesses.

Early in the life cycle of 802.11b, researchers discovered that the 40-bit WEP encryption was deeply flawed. The key exchange protocol could be easily spoofed, allowing anyone with the right hacking software to connect to a WLAN. But because attaching to the network required physical proximity to the network, threats from wireless intrusion did not concern users nearly as much as threats from Internet attack, and the security flaws of wireless networks did not slow the rate of adoption. This means that a large number of non-secure wireless networks are currently deployed.

Another fundamental security problem is caused by wireless networking technology: anyone who has physical access to your network can connect a hidden WAP to it and broadcast access outside your facilities. Even if you don't implement wireless networking in your network (especially if you don't), an intruder who has access to a wired port on your network can place a low-cost 802.11b WAP on your network, and then connect to it from outside your facilities at any time. This is a potential security problem whether you use wireless networking or not, and it's an extraordinarily difficult problem to solve.

Solutions to these problems are now becoming available along with the newer 802.11a protocol, which increases speeds to 54 Mbps and introduces support for the 802.1x port authentication protocol. Many 802.11b devices as well have been retrofitted with 802.1x compatibility through firmware upgrades. The 802.1x protocol is the topic of Lesson 3.

Common Attacks on Wireless Networks

Due to the popularity of wireless networks, even ethical computer users have begun the practice of "wardriving"—searching for unsecured wireless networks that can be used for surfing the Web. In most downtown areas, users can find an unsecured wireless network within a few minutes, just by watching the signal strength meter in the Wireless Network Connections window.

The typical solution to wireless security has been to treat WAPs as if they were the Internet—unsecured. By placing them outside network firewalls, you force valid users to authenticate with the firewall or use VPN connections to reach the interior of the network. This doesn't prevent unauthorized users from exploiting the WAP for Internet access, but it does prevent the internal network from being exploited. Treating WAPs as if they were the Internet is a baseline security requirement for using WAPs and should be used along with all other security measures you might implement.

Tip   Prevent hackers from stealing your Internet access through WAPs by placing the WAPs in their own perimeter network that does not have Internet access. Valid users who can authenticate with the VPN can then go through the private network to reach the Internet if necessary. When hackers can't reach the Internet and can't get to the internal network, they won't bother staying attached to your wireless networks.

Other clever tactics administrators use to secure wireless networks include

- **Closed networks.**   Some WAPs support a "closed network" mode in which the WAP does not broadcast its SSID. Users have to know the SSID or they won't know that the wireless network exists. Closed networks can go a long way towards defeating wardrivers.
- **SSID spoofing.**   Special software that generates numerous WAP packets advertising bogus SSIDs causes hackers to receive so many SSIDs when they scan for a wireless network that they can't separate the one valid SSID from the many bogus ones.
- **MAC address filtering.**   Most WAPs support MAC address restrictions that limit the clients that the WAP will communicate with by their media access control address. This works well in smaller environments, but creates excessive administrative overhead in larger environments.

Practice: Connecting a WAP and Client to the Network

In this practice, you connect a WAP to your test network and connect a client to it. These exercises set the stage for Lessons 2 and 3.

Exercise 1: Configuring a Wireless Access Point

For purposes of illustration, this exercise configures an Intel PRO/Wireless 5000 LAN Access Point. Follow the manufacturer's instructions for configuring your specific wireless access point. Begin this exercise after you have connected the WAP to the network and powered it on.

▶ **To configure a workstation to manage a new WAP**

Perform this procedure on a workstation connected to the network. You need to change your workstation's IP address so it's in the same IP network range as the WAP's default IP address so that you can connect to it to change it. If you are using a different brand of WAP, make sure you use an IP address that is close to that WAP's default IP address. If your WAP has already been configured with an IP address, you can skip this procedure.

Important   After you've changed the WAP IP address in the next procedure, repeat this exercise to restore the workstation's original TCP/IP address.

1. Log on to the workstation using any local or domain computer account.
2. Right-click My Network Places, and click Properties. The Network And Dial-up Connections window appears, as shown in Figure 10.1.

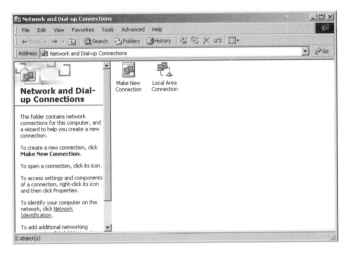

Figure 10.1   The Network And Dial-up Connections window

3. Right-click Local Area Connection, and click Properties. The Local Area Connection Propertics dialog box appears, as shown in Figure 10.2.

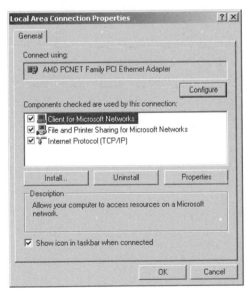

Figure 10.2   The Local Area Connection Properties dialog box

4. Double-click Internet Protocol (TCP/IP). The Internet Protocol (TCP/IP) Properties dialog box appears, as shown in Figure 10.3.

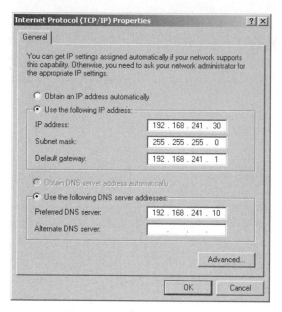

Figure 10.3 The Internet Protocol (TCP/IP) Properties dialog box

5. Record the computer's current IP address settings so that you can restore them after you've configured the WAP.

6. Type **192.0.2.2** in the IP Address box. Leave the Subnet Mask as 255.255.255.0.

7. Clear the Default Gateway address box.

8. Click OK to close the Internet Protocol (TCP/IP) Properties dialog box.

9. Click OK to close the Local Area Connection Properties dialog box.

10. Close the Network And Dial-Up Connections window.

▶   **To configure a WAP device**

1. Open Internet Explorer, and browse to *http://192.0.2.1*, the address of the Intel PRO/Wireless 5000 management Web site, as shown in Figure 10.4.

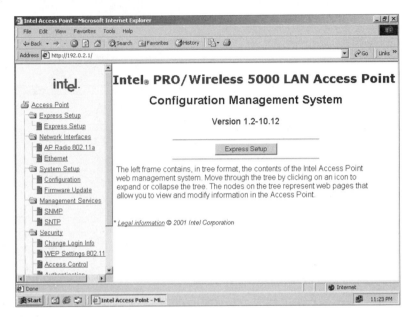

Figure 10.4   The management Web site for a typical WAP

2. Click Express Setup. The Enter Network Password dialog box appears.

3. Type **Intel** in both the User Name and the Password boxes, and click OK. The Express Setup page appears.

> **Important**   "Intel" is the preconfigured user name and password that you must enter before you can choose a new user name and password. Always ensure that you use secure passwords in your work environment.

4. Type **192.168.241.254** as the Default IP Address, or any other free valid IP address in your network range.

5. Type **255.255.255.0** as the Default Subnet Mask.

6. Type **192.168.241.1** as the Default Gateway or enter the default gateway for your network.

7. Type **TestWLAN** in the SSID 11A box. The Express Setup page now looks like Figure 10.5.

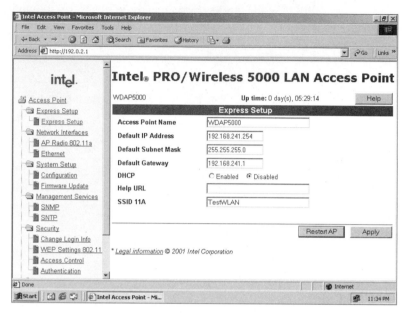

Figure 10.5   The Intel WAP Express Setup page

8. Click Apply.

9. In the approval message box, click OK.

10. Click Restart AP to re-initialize the access point using the new settings. The access point is now configured for non-secure wireless networking.

Exercise 2: Configuring a Client Computer to Connect to the Wireless Network

In this exercise, you configure a laptop computer and attach it to the network.

▶ **To configure a client computer to connect to the wireless network**

1. Log on to the Windows XP Professional laptop as an administrator.

2. Insert your WLAN adapter into the laptop. The Found New Hardware Wizard appears.

3. Follow the steps of the wizard, as directed by the hardware's documentation, to install the driver for the adapter.

4. When the Completing The Found New Hardware Wizard page appears, click Finish. A Wireless Network Connection balloon appears, as shown in Figure 10.6.

Figure 10.6   The Wireless Network Connection

5. Click the network icon in the system tray indicated by the balloon. The Wireless Network Connection dialog box appears.

6. Select Allow Me To Connect To The Selected Wireless Network Even Though It Is Not Secure, and click Connect. A Wireless Network Connection balloon appears indicating that a wireless signal has been found, as shown in Figure 10.7.

Tip   If you cannot connect to a wireless access point, move closer to the active device until a connection balloon appears.

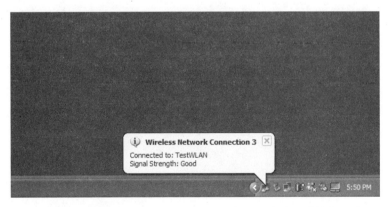

Figure 10.7   A balloon appears indicating that a wireless link is active

7. Your network adapter should now receive an IP address if your network has a DHCP server. Otherwise, manually assign an IP address in your network range and configure the default gateway and Domain Name System (DNS) server according to the values set on the other computers in your network.

   The laptop computer is now attached to the network and can operate as if it were physically wired.

Lesson Review

The following questions are intended to reinforce key information in this lesson. If you are unable to answer a question, review the lesson and try the question again. Answers to the questions can be found in the appendix.

1. What is the most common variant of the 802.11 protocol?

2. How does adding wireless capability to your network affect security?

3. What is WEP?

4. What is the most common method used to prevent WLANs from allowing access to a private network?

5. What is wardriving?

Lesson Summary

- The 802.11 protocol is the IEEE standard for wireless networks. The 11 Mbps 802.11b variant is the most commonly used, and the new 802.11a protocol offers higher speed and improved security.
- Security in 802.11 is implemented through the Wired Equivalent Privacy protocol, and through 802.1x port authentication.
- It is common for administrators to place WAPs outside firewalls and treat them as Internet clients. This prevents access to the interior of the network, but allows hackers to exploit the WLAN to gain access to the Internet or to attempt to exploit the firewall.
- Closed networks do not advertise the WAP's SSID, so clients must know what it is to authenticate with the WAP. This eliminates the ability of casual hackers to find the network and it can dramatically improve security.

Lesson 2: Securing Wireless Networks

To combat the obvious security problem associated with allowing unencrypted, unauthenticated communications with the network, the IEEE designed the Wired Equivalent Privacy (WEP) encryption protocol for use in 802.11 networks. This lesson discusses WEP and its appropriate use, and teaches you how to configure it in Windows XP clients.

Note   Windows XP is the first operating system to include support for wireless networks and protocols such as WEP and 802.1x. To use these protocols in earlier operating systems, you must use vendor-supplied drivers.

To complete this lesson, you will need

- A wireless access point
- A laptop computer running Windows XP with a wireless network adapter

---

After this lesson, you will be able to

- Understand the capabilities and limitations of WEP
- Configure WEP to prevent illicit attachment to your wireless networks

Estimated lesson time: 20 minutes

Understanding Wired Equivalent Privacy

Wired Equivalent Privacy (WEP) is the original security protocol for 802.11b WLANs. There are two components to WEP:

- *Authentication*, which can be Open (all clients accepted) or Shared Key (only clients possessing a valid key can attach to the WLAN).
- *Encryption*, which uses RC4 stream encryption to encrypt the data portion of the packets.

Authentication in WEP is simple to configure:

- If you want to allow any client to attach, select Open authentication.
- If you want to control which clients can attach, select Shared Key authentication.

  In Shared Key authentication mode, the WAP and the client go through a challenge response cycle very similar to NTLM authentication using the WEP encryption key as the shared secret key.

Note   WEP is simply secret key–based RC4 stream encryption at the data-link layer using a fixed key length of 40, 128, 154, or 256 bits. (Supported key lengths vary somewhat among manufacturers, but these are the most common).

To establish WEP, you need to install the same secret key in each WAP throughout your enterprise, either individually or by using some manufacturer-supplied management software, and then install that key in each client. There is no standard mechanism for distributing secret WEP keys to clients or WAPs.

When you configure WEP for shared secret key authentication, WAPs automatically deny access to any client that does not have the correct secret key. This prevents unauthorized users from connecting to the wireless network.

Security Problems with WEP

WEP is vulnerable to brute-force attacks at shorter key lengths, and it is also vulnerable to differential cryptanalysis attacks. *Differential cryptanalysis* is the process of comparing an encrypted text with a known portion of the plaintext and deriving the key by computing the difference between them. This isn't as easy as it sounds, and it requires an attacker to know that an encrypted text matches a specific portion of a plaintext. Because WEP encrypts TCP headers, hackers know what the headers should contain in many cases, and they can attempt to find patterns in a large body of collected WEP communications in order to decrypt the key. The attack is complex and difficult to automate, so it is unlikely to occur for most networks, especially at key lengths greater than 128 bits.

Note   A new WEP protocol is in development that will support automatic re-keying, which limits the lifetime of a WEP key, thus defeating brute-force attacks.

Nothing about WEP prevents someone from attaching a hidden WAP on the network somewhere and using it to exploit the network. While it's unlikely that an intruder would do this, it's likely that an employee might do it without understanding the security implications. To defeat this attack requires 802.1x, which is discussed in Lesson 3.

There's nothing technically complicated about establishing WEP on small networks. However, you must individually key most WAP devices and clients with WEP keys. Keeping shared secret keys private in a large enterprise requires rigorous IT procedures and can dramatically increase the workload on IT workers. Managing WEP encryption on a device-by-device basis can be daunting.

Wide-scale deployment of WEP encryption can be made simple only by selecting wireless equipment designed for enterprise environments, which includes management utilities to automatically deploy WEP secret keys. These utilities are proprietary and vary widely from one vendor to another.

Managing WEP on the Client

Prior to Windows XP, modifying the wireless adapter's driver configuration configured WEP encryption. Windows XP allows these properties to be managed directly by the operating system through the Network Connections control panel.

The device's driver must conform to the operating system's requirements to be properly managed. A number of devices do not conform and can be configured only by setting driver properties directly, or by making the required configuration settings both in the driver configuration and in the Wireless Networks tab of the Network Connections Properties dialog box. If you find you have problems getting WEP encryption working correctly using Windows configuration, and you know you've set the shared key correctly, follow the manufacturer's instructions to configure driver settings directly.

Practice: Establishing WEP Encryption

In this practice, you configure WEP encryption and authentication on the WAP and in a Windows XP client. In this example, a Proxim Harmony 802.11a CardBus adapter is used, but the same procedure should work with any wireless adapter that has passed Windows XP logo requirements.

Exercise 1: Configuring Security on the Wireless Access Point

The first step towards securing wireless access is controlling administrative access to the WAP. This is normally done on a device-by-device basis using a Web-based management console.

Once access to the WAP has been secured, you can enable WAP encryption. In this exercise, you use Shared Key authentication and configure WAP for 128-bit encryption, the largest size supported by both the card and the WAP in this case.

▶ **To change the user name and password**

1. On the wireless client computer, open Internet Explorer and browse to *http://192.168.241.254* or the IP address of your WAP. The WAP management page appears.

2. Expand Access Point and Security.

3. Click Change Logon Info. The logon prompt appears.

4. Type **Intel** as the Name and Password. The Change Login Info page appears, as shown in Figure 10.8.

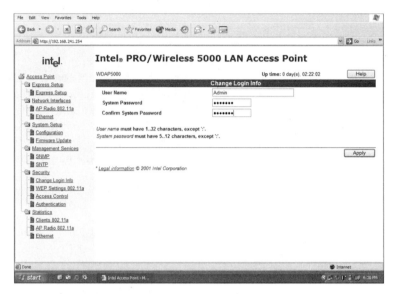

Figure 10.8   Changing the default account name and password on the WAP

5. Type **Admin** as the User Name, and type the same password in the System Password and Confirm System Password boxes.

6. Click Apply.

▶   **To configure WEP settings**

1. Click WEP Settings 802.11a. The logon prompt appears.

2. Type **Admin** and your password, and click OK. The WEP Settings 802.11a page appears, as shown in Figure 10.9.

Figure 10.9   Configuring Wired Equivalent Privacy in a WAP

3. For the Authentication Type, select Shared.

4. Select Enabled in the WEP (Privacy) list box.

5. In the WEP Key 1 list box, type a 26-character random key that's hexadecimal (0..9, a..f).

6. Click Apply.

7. When the approval message box appears, click OK.

8. Click Restart AP.

9. When a Restart Access Point message appears, click OK.

    You will find that you are unable to reload the management page. Why?

10. Close Internet Explorer.

Exercise 2: Configuring WEP on the Client

A Wireless Network Unavailable balloon should appear in the system tray. This exercise walks you through configuring the WEP.

▶ **To configure WEP on the client**

1. Right-click My Network Places, and click Properties. The Network Connections window appears, as shown in Figure 10.10.

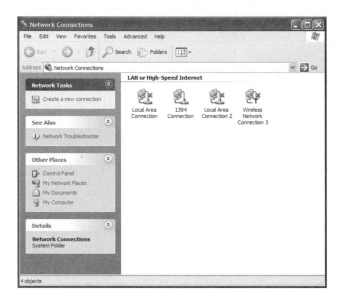

Figure 10.10   The Network Connections window in Windows XP

2. Right-click Wireless Network Connection 3, and click Properties. The Wireless Network Connections 3 Properties dialog box appears.

3. Click the Wireless Networks tab as shown in Figure 10.11.

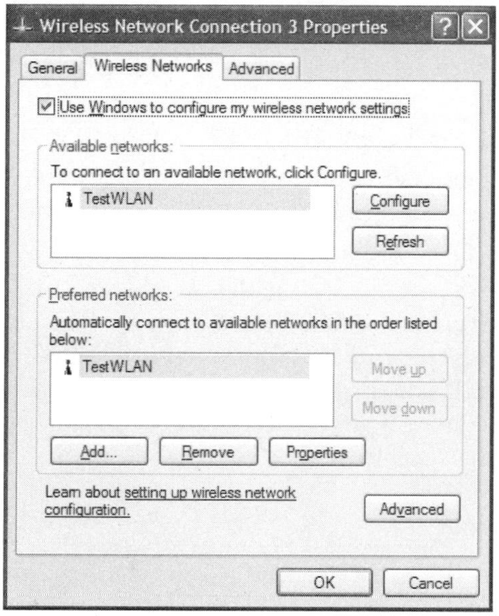

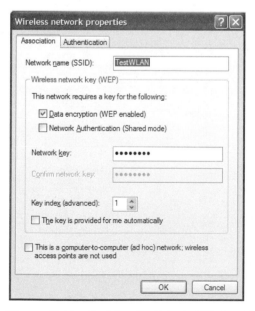

Figure 10.11   The Windows XP Wireless Network Connection 3 Properties
dialog box

4. Click Configure. The Wireless Network Properties dialog box appears as shown
in Figure 10.12.

Figure 10.12   Enabling WEP in the Wireless Network Properties dialog box

5. Select the Data Encryption (WEP Enabled) and Network Authentication (Shared Mode) check boxes.

6. Type the same WEP encryption key into both the Network Key box and the Confirm Network Key box as you typed into the WAP in step 5 of the previous procedure.

7. Click OK to close the Wireless Network Properties dialog box.

8. Click OK to close the Wireless Network Connection 3 Properties dialog box. A balloon appears indicating the TestWLAN network is available and showing the signal strength, as previously shown in Figure 10.7.

9. If the balloon appears indicating that wireless networks are available, in the Network Connections window, right-click the Wireless Network Connection 3, and click Disabled. After the connection is disabled, right-click it again, and click Enabled. If you do not see a balloon indicating that the network is available, you need to re-type your WEP encryption key and ensure that shared authentication is enabled.

Lesson Review

The following questions are intended to reinforce key information in this lesson. If you are unable to answer a question, review the lesson and try the question again. Answers to the questions can be found in the appendix.

1. What does WEP stand for, and why was that name chosen?

2. What types of authentication are supported?

3. What encryption algorithm is used to encrypt WEP payloads?

4. What common key lengths are available for use with WEP?

5. Is there a standard protocol used to establish WEP secret keys among all WAPs in an enterprise?

Lesson Summary

- WEP provides security for wireless connections through data payload encryption and optional authentication using RC4 stream encryption in 40-bit, 128-bit, 154-bit, 256-bit, and various other less common bit key lengths.

- WEP has a number of security vulnerabilities, especially at shorter key lengths where brute force attacks are useful. WEP validates only the computer, not the user, and has no support for automatic re-keying.

- In Windows XP, wireless client settings can be managed by Windows rather than requiring the user to directly modify variables in the driver configuration. This allows the operating system to control security for the client.

Lesson 3: Configuring Clients for Wireless Security

Configuring encryption can prevent hackers from attaching to your valid wireless devices. However, encryption doesn't prevent hackers who have gained physical access to your facilities from placing their own unsecured WAPs on your network. These devices, once placed, can go undiscovered, because you can't find them without expensive wireless test equipment.

Preventing illicit attachment of wireless devices to an existing network requires reconsidering whether to allow devices to connect to the network without authentication. Fixing the problem, once it occurs, requires major changes to your network devices. The problem doesn't go away just because you don't use wireless in your network; wireless equipment doesn't cause the problem—hackers cause the problem.

This lesson discusses the 802.1x port authentication protocol, which is the future of data-link layer port authentication. Essentially, this protocol requires users to authenticate before they are granted access to the network even at the most basic level.

After this lesson, you will be able to

- Understand the need for data-link layer access control and authentication
- Configure the 802.1x authentication protocol
- Secure wireless access using certificates

Estimated lesson time: 40 minutes

Ensuring Secure Access

No form of simple encryption or authentication can solve the most vexing problem with wireless security: the attachment of an illicit WAP to your network that provides unauthorized access.

Preventing illicit WAPs requires controlling access to the network at the data-link physical port level. No client computer, hub, or other device should be given access to a bridge, hub, or switch unless the device can authenticate successfully with an authentication server. To function, a protocol that could provide this level of security would have to control access to every data link port connected to the network—wired ports as well as wireless. If access to any port on the network is provided without authentication, a WAP could be connected to the unsecured ports to compromise network security.

Securing ports is the theory behind 802.1x authentication. While 802.1x was developed as a response to the security problems caused by wireless networking, it is not only an authentication protocol for wireless ports—it must be supported by every data-link layer hub, switch, and bridge in your network infrastructure to effectively prevent unauthorized access to your network.

The 802.1x authentication protocol challenges clients to provide machine authentication when they attach to the network, and then again to provide user authentication when a user logs on. If either phase of authentication fails, the data-link layer access device (WAP, bridge, or switch) will not forward packets from the device onto the network. This prevents an attacker from exploiting the network layer or reaching other servers or clients on the network.

The 802.1x protocol must be supported at three places in the network: on the client, on the data-link device, and on an authentication server. The data-link device (WAP or switch) is responsible for detecting new clients, passing their authentication to an authentication server, and locking the client out if the server reports that the authentication failed. The authentication server is responsible for checking the clients' credentials and reporting the authentication status back to the data-link device.

Because data-link devices are simple, they do not maintain the sort of processing power necessary to perform complex cryptographic authentication for a large number of users.

Important   Authentication should be centralized and not distributed to numerous individual devices.

In Windows 2000, the existing Internet Authentication Service (IAS) is used to provide Remote Authentication Dial-In User Service (RADIUS) remote user authentication based on either Message Digest version 5 (MD5) secret key encryption protocol or user and machine certificates. The data-link device opens the UDP port for authentication to all clients that connect, but blocks all other ports until the authentication server reports that the client's authentication has been successful. Once the client authenticates with the IAS server, the data-link device lifts the restriction and allows the client open access to the network.

Important   Remember that 802.1x cannot prevent surreptitious attachment of WAPs to your network unless every data-link device in your network supports 802.1x. For most enterprises, this means that there's little reason to implement 802.1x until you've upgraded your entire network to the next generation of Ethernet switches.

Even if you can't enable 802.1x throughout your network, 802.1x can be used to perform machine authentication. But WEP, which is required to use 802.1x in Windows, already does that in a manner that provides a similar level of security. In addition, while it's true that 802.1x can also perform per-user authentication, your domain logon process provides that function automatically, so there's little reason to duplicate that functionality, either. The 802.1x protocol was designed to prevent illicit attachment of devices to the network. Its complexity is warranted for that purpose alone in high-security environments.

Identifying Security Problems with 802.1x Implementation

The most important problem with 802.1x is that it's an all-or-nothing proposition. Unless every network attachment port on your network, wired or wireless, supports 802.1x, there's little point in deploying the protocol at all, because WEP can be used to prevent unauthorized clients from attaching to the network.

Another major problem is the chicken-and-egg dilemma that comes with new computers. A computer requires a domain association, a machine certificate, and a user certificate before it can authenticate on the network, but it can't be joined to the domain or have certificates installed securely unless it's able to connect to the network. This means that all clients must be configured on a non-802.1x network port before they're deployed to users. Technically, this violates the all-or-nothing premise of 802.1x. In the real world, machines are usually configured in an access-controlled IT room and then deployed to end users, but this might not be an option in large enterprises with many hundreds of computers to roll out.

Finally, flaws in the 802.1x protocol have already been exploited by security researchers. While somewhat esoteric, this attack is easy to perpetrate and hackers are likely to generate programs to completely automate it. To perpetrate the attack, the attacker listens on the wireless network for a client to authenticate. Once it has located a client, the attacker sends the client an 802.11"disassociate" packet, which causes the client to drop off the network. The attacker then assumes the MAC address of the dropped client and participates on the network until the next connection timeout, which is usually hourly.

WEP encryption, which is required in the Windows 2000 implementation of 802.1x, makes this attack much more difficult—the attacker must first crack the WEP encryption key before the 802.1x protocol weakness can be exploited. As you learned in the lesson on WEP, a determined attack against WEP will succeed within a few weeks and, because WEP keys are not automatically refreshed (in reality, they are usually never changed), determined attackers will eventually succeed in exploiting any existing wireless protocol.

Other weaknesses exist in 802.1x. Because implementing 802.1x requires complex configuration and the complete replacement of existing infrastructure, 802.1x is likely to be superseded by the next generation of 802.11b security protocols before it is ever widely implemented.

Note   The measures described in this section are intended to keep casual hackers from exploiting your network. Other methods can be used to determine if hackers are attacking the network for the length of time that would be required to perpetrate these attacks. Exploiting the weaknesses of 802.1x requires a serious effort and is attempted only by hackers who are specifically trying to attack your network.

Troubleshooting 802.1x Connections

The 802.1x protocol relies on many services of Windows 2000, which makes configuring it correctly difficult to achieve and subject to a wide range of possible failures. 802.1x can fail for any one of the following reasons:

■ There is a general connectivity problem with the client, WAP, or network. Ensure that all participants in the network can communicate correctly without any form of encryption or authentication enabled. Ensure that the client can log on to the domain and that DNS is correctly configured on the client and server.

■ WEP is not correctly configured between the client and the WEP. Ensure that WEP encryption is working correctly before attempting to enable 802.1x.

■ IAS is not installed correctly or has not been activated correctly in the domain. Ensure that IAS is correctly installed and enabled in the domain.

■ The IAS policy is incorrect. Study the example in this lesson and ensure that IAS policy is configured similarly.

■ IAS and the WAP are not pointing to each other properly with a correctly configured shared secret key. You must add the WAP as a client to the IAS server, and you must point the WAP to the server in the WAP's authentication configuration settings.

■ The 802.1x client does not have a valid machine certificate. Use the certificates console on the client to request a machine certificate, or use Group Policy to automatically distribute certificates to domain members.

■ The user attempting to log on does not have a valid user certificate on the client. Use the Certificates management console or the Certificate Services Web site to request a valid user certificate.

■ The user does not have dial-in permissions configured in the domain. Use the Active Directory Users And Computers management console to allow dial-in permissions for the user in question.

Practice: Configuring Your Network for 802.1x Authentication

In this practice, you configure the domain controller to authenticate wireless clients, configure the WAP to pass authentication requests to the domain controller, and configure the client computer to authenticate using 802.1x.

Exercise 1: Installing Internet Authentication Server

In this exercise, you configure the domain.Fabrikam.com domain controller to authenticate 802.1x clients. The server-side configuration is somewhat complex. Be certain that you go through the steps carefully. If you already have Service Pack 3 installed, you can skip the first procedure.

▶ **To install Windows 2000 Service Pack 3**

1. Log on to the Windows 2000 domain controller as the administrator.

2. Open Internet Explorer, and browse to *http://windowsupdate.microsoft.com*. The Security Warning dialog box appears asking to install Windows Update Control, as shown in Figure 10.13.

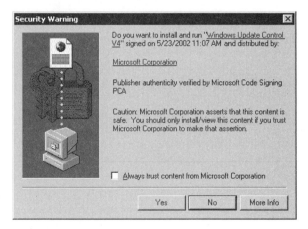

Figure 10.13   Downloading the Windows Update Active-X control

3. Click Yes. After a moment, the Welcome to Windows Update page appears, as shown in Figure 10.14.

4. Click Scan For Updates.

5. In the left pane, click Review And Install Updates. A list of updates will appear.

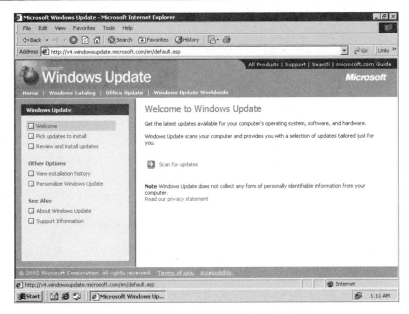

Figure 10.14   The Welcome To Windows Update Web page

6. Click Remove for every item *except* Windows 2000 Service Pack 3. Your screen should appear as shown in Figure 10.15.

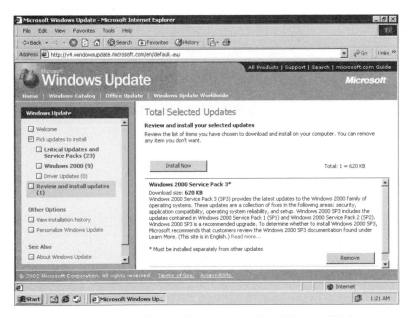

Figure 10.15   Selecting Service Pack 3 on the Total Selected Updates page

7. Click Install Now.

8. When the Microsoft Windows Update EULA dialog box appears, click Accept to continue.

9. When the Welcome To Windows 2000 Service Pack Setup Wizard appears, click Next.

10. On the License Agreement page, select I Agree, and click Next.

11. On the Select Options page, when the wizard asks if you want to archive files for un-installation, select Archive Files, and click Next.

    The wizard will inspect your configuration and begin downloading files. The process may take a considerable amount of time, depending upon your Internet connection speed.

12. When the Wizard finishes, click Finish to restart you computer.

► **To install Internet Authentication Service**

1. Click Start, point to Settings, and click Control Panel. Control Panel appears.

2. Double-click Add/Remove Programs, and click Add/Remove Windows Components. The Windows Components Wizard appears.

3. In the Components list, double-click Networking Services. The Networking Services dialog box appears.

4. Select the Internet Authentication Service check box, as shown in Figure 10.16, and click OK.

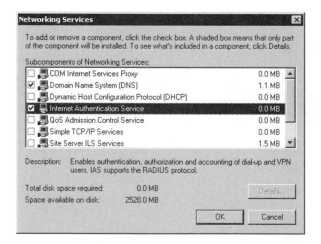

Figure 10.16   Selecting Internet Authentication Service for installation

5. In the Windows Components Wizard, click Next, and click Finish.

6. In the Add/Remove Programs window, click Close.

7. Close Control Panel.

▶ **To enable IAS authentication**

1. Click Start, point to Programs, point to Administrative Tools, and click Internet Authentication Service.

   The Internet Authentication Service management console appears, as shown in Figure 10.17.

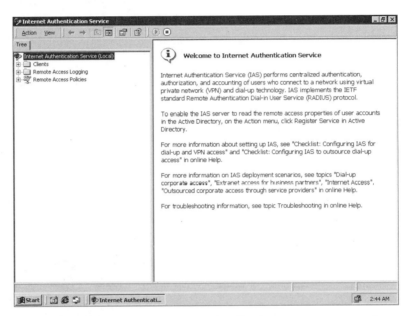

Figure 10.17   The Internet Authentication Service management console

2. Right-click Internet Authentication Service (Local), and click Register Service in Active Directory. The Register Internet Authentication Service In Active Directory dialog box appears.

3. Click OK to register the service. The Service Registered dialog box appears.

4. Click OK to enable IAS.

► **To add the WAP as an IAS client**

1. Right-click the clients folder in the IAS management console, and click New Client. The Add Client dialog box appears as shown in Figure 10.18.

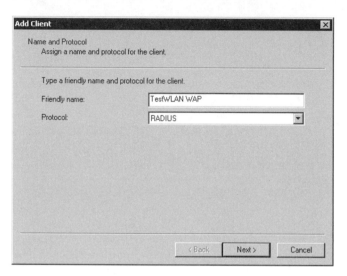

Figure 10.18   Adding the WAP as an IAS client

2. On the Name And Protocol page, type **TestWLAN WAP** as the Friendly Name for the client, and click Next.

   The Client Information page appears, as shown in Figure 10.19.

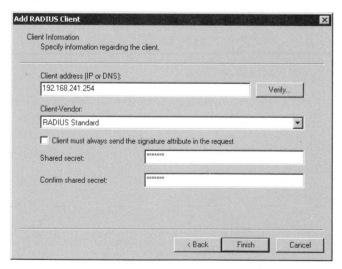

Figure 10.19   The Add RADIUS Client page with information about an 802.1x client

3. On the Client Information page, type **192.168.241.254** or the IP address of your WAP in the Client Address box.

4. Type the same password in both the Shared Secret and Confirm Shared Secret boxes. Remember this password for later use when configuring the WAP. The longer the password is, the more secure it will be.

5. Click Finish. The TestWLAN WAP client now appears in the list of clients in the IAS management console, as shown in Figure 10.20.

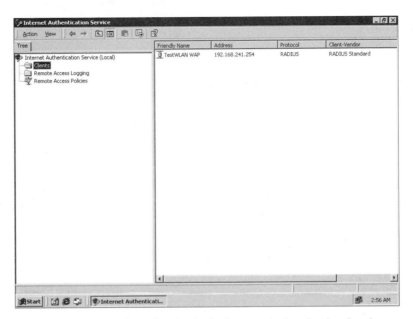

Figure 10.20   The client showing in the Internet Authentication Service management console

▶ **To create a wireless remote access policy**

1. In the Internet Authentication Service management console, right-click Remote Access Policies, and click New Remote Access Policy. The Add Remote Access Policy Wizard appears, as shown in Figure 10.21.

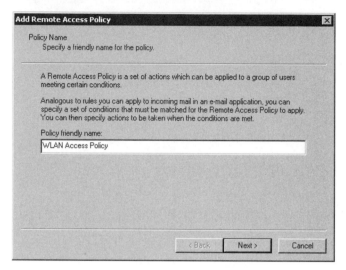

Figure 10.21   Adding a Remote Access Policy

2. Type **WLAN Access Policy** in the Policy Friendly Name box, and click Next. The Conditions page appears, with no conditions showing.

3. On the Conditions page, click Add. The Select Attribute dialog box appears, as shown in Figure 10.22.

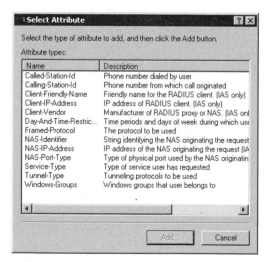

Figure 10.22   The Select Attribute dialog box shows the available policy attributes

4. Select Windows-Groups, and click Add. The Groups dialog box appears.

5. In the Groups dialog box, click Add. The Select Groups dialog box appears, as shown in Figure 10.23.

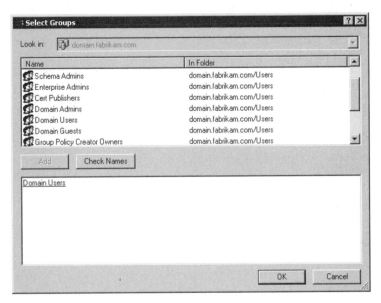

Figure 10.23   Selecting Groups to allow for RADIUS authentication

6. In the Select Groups dialog box, double-click Domain Users, and click OK.

7. Click OK to close the Groups dialog box. The Conditions page in the Add Remote Access Policy Wizard shows the new condition.

8. On the Conditions page, click Add. The Select Attribute dialog box appears.

9. Select NAS-Port-Type, and click Add. The NAS-Port-Type dialog box appears, as shown in Figure 10.24.

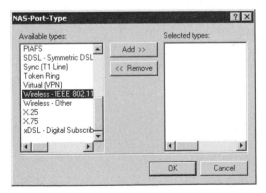

Figure 10.24   Selecting the NAS Port Type for RADIUS authentication

10. Select Wireless - IEEE 802.11 in the Available Types list, click Add, and click OK.

11. On the Conditions page in the Add Remote Access Policy Wizard, click Next. The Permissions page appears.

12. On the Permissions page, select Grant Remote Access Permission, and click Next. The User Profile page appears.

13. On the User Profile page, click the Edit Profile button. The Edit Dial-In Profile dialog box appears as shown in Figure 10.25.

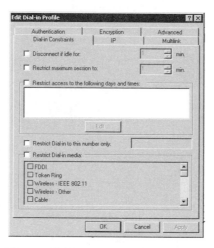

Figure 10.25 The Edit Dial-In Profile dialog box

14. Click the Authentication tab.

15. Select Extensible Authentication Protocol, and clear all the other check boxes. The dialog box should appear as in Figure 10.26.

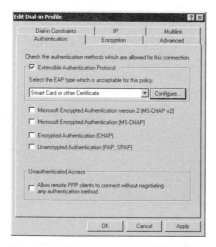

Figure 10.26 Enabling Extensible Authentication Protocol for 802.1x authentication

16. Click Apply.

17. Click the Encryption tab.

18. Clear all check boxes except Strongest. The dialog box should appear as shown in Figure 10.27.

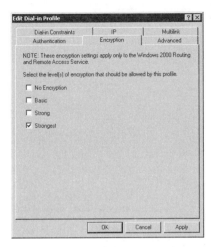

Figure 10.27   Selecting an encryption level

19. Click OK. Click No if a message box asks if you want to view help.

20. In the Add Remote Policy Wizard, click Finish.

21. Select Remote Access Policies in the console tree of the Internet Authentication Service management console.

22. Right-click the Allow Access If Dial-In Permission Is Enabled policy, and click Delete. The Delete Policy dialog box appears.

23. Click Yes, and close the Internet Authentication Service management console.

▶ **To allow dial-in access for the administrator**

1. Open the Active Directory Users And Computers management console.

2. Expand domain.Fabrikam.com, and click the Users folder.

3. Double-click the Administrator account. The Administrator Properties dialog box appears.

4. Click the Dial-In tab as shown in Figure 10.28.

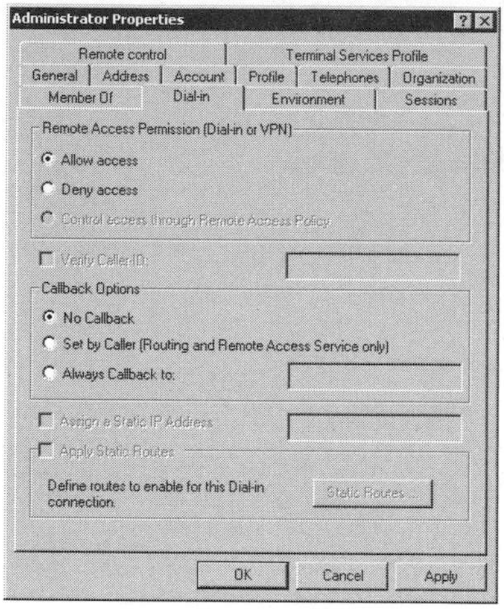

Figure 10.28   Enabling dial-in permission for the Administrator

5. Click Allow Access.

6. Click OK to close the Administrator Properties dialog box.

7. Close the Active Directory Users And Computers management console.

Exercise 2: Configuring the WAP for 802.1x

In this exercise, you enable the 802.1x protocol in the WAP by configuring it to relay authentication requests to a RADIUS server. Your equipment might vary, so be sure to follow the instructions provided by the manufacturer of your devices, using these procedures as a guide.

▶   **To configure the WAP to relay authentication requests**

1. Open Internet Explorer, and browse to *http://192.168.241.254* or the IP address of your WAP.

2. In the left pane in Internet Explorer, expand Access Point, and expand Security.

3. Click Authentication. The logon prompt appears.

4. Type **Admin** and the WAP password, and click OK. The Authentication page appears.

5. Type **192.168.241.10** or your domain controller's IP address in the Server IP Address box.

6. Type the shared secret key you entered in the previous exercise in the Shared Secret box.

7. Type **1812** in the Port box.

8. For Enable Authentication, select Yes.

9. Click Apply. The Add Server dialog box appears. Click OK.

10. Click Restart AP. The Restart AP dialog box appears. Click OK.

Exercise 3: Configuring Windows XP for 802.1x

The final component in an 802.1x configuration is the client. Clients must have a certificate installed that grants them access to the network, and they must be configured to request authentication from the RADIUS server to participate on the network.

▶ **To prepare the client for 802.1x**

1. Connect the wireless laptop client to the network with a network cable.

2. Join the computer to the domain.

3. Ensure that the computer has a computer certificate. Chapter 6, "Managing a Public Key Infrastructure," has detailed instructions on how to verify the presence of a computer certificate.

4. Log on as the domain administrator.

5. Ensure that the administrator has a user certificate on the computer.

▶ **To enable 802.1x authentication on the client**

1. Right-click My Network Places, and click Properties. The Network Connections window appears.

2. Right-click Wireless Network Connection, and click Properties. The Wireless Network Connections 3 Properties dialog box appears.

3. Click the Wireless Networks tab. The Wireless Networks tab appears, as shown in Figure 10.29.

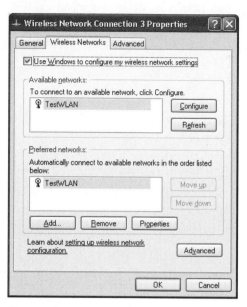

Figure 10.29   The Windows XP Wireless Networks tab

4. Click Configure. The Wireless Network Properties dialog box appears.

5. Click Authentication. The Authentication tab appears, as shown in Figure 10.30.

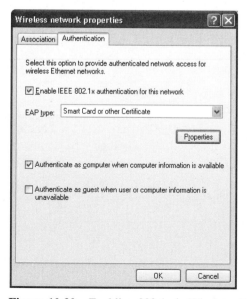

Figure 10.30   Enabling 802.1x in Windows XP

6. Select Enable IEEE 802.1x Authentication For This Network.

7. Click OK to close the Wireless Network Properties dialog box.

8. Click OK to close the Wireless Network Connection 3 Properties dialog box.

▶ **To negotiate authentication and enable secure wireless access**

1. In the Network Connections window, right-click Wireless Network Connection 3, and click Disable. The Wireless Network Connection icon will appear dimmed, indicating that it is not available.

2. Right-click Wireless Network Connection 3 again, and click Enable. The icon will indicate the enabling and authenticating status. When the authentication succeeds, the Network Connections window will appear as shown in Figure 10.31. If the authentication fails for any reason, the network connection will be disconnected, and a red X will appear on the icon.

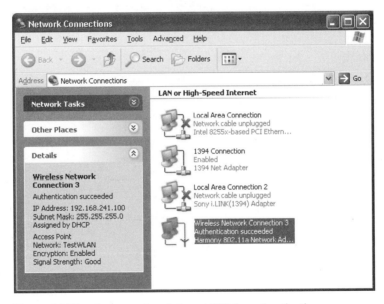

Figure 10.31   A connection that uses 802.1x authentication

Lesson Review

The following questions are intended to reinforce key information in this lesson. If you are unable to answer a question, review the lesson and try the question again. Answers to the questions can be found in the appendix.

1. What is the most difficult security problem that wireless networks cause?

2. What security measure is required to prevent the illicit attachment of uncontrolled wireless equipment, and what protocol was developed to solve it?

3. How does 802.1x work?

4. Which component of Windows 2000 is used to implement authentication for 802.1x?

5. What is the primary problem with 802.1x that will prevent its adoption in the near term?

Lesson Summary

- The 802.1x protocol was developed to solve the problem of users or hackers illicitly attaching WLAN devices to the network in an unsecure manner.
- The 802.1x protocol works by blocking traffic from a client until an authentication server has informed the WAP that the client has successfully authenticated.
- The 802.1x protocol must be supported by clients, data-link equipment, and an authentication server. Support is built into Windows XP for client-side authentication and into IAS for Windows 2000.
- The 802.1x protocol performs both machine authentication and user authentication using certificates or MD5 shared secrets.

C H A P T E R   1 1

Public Application Server Security

About This Chapter

Protecting servers that provide public services might be the most daunting security problem you face. Web and e-mail servers must be open to access from the Internet while still protected from anonymous attack. To accomplish this goal, you use a firewall that, when properly configured, protects your private network at the same time as it provides access to your public servers. Using a firewall is the most important step you can take to keep your network secure.

Exam Tip   Using a firewall to protect your network is a major component of security that you must be familiar with to pass the exam. Make sure you understand the security perimeter architecture and how to protect servers with ISA Server.

This chapter details the types of attacks you can expect to encounter and the methods for defending against them. You'll create a secure Internet services infrastructure by using firewalls, properly securing e-mail servers, and protecting the database servers that frequently provide back-end data for Web servers.

More Info   Securing Web servers is discussed in Chapter 12, "Web Service Security." Research methods for protecting your network in Chapter 13, "Intrusion Detection and Event Monitoring."

Before You Begin

To complete the lessons in this chapter, you will need

- A domain controller for the domain.fabrikam.com domain
- A member server in the domain
- A workstation in the domain

Lesson 1: Providing Internet Security

Securing computers that will provide service on the Internet is one of the most challenging security problems you are likely to encounter. When you face accidents or malicious acts by logged on users, you can use auditing to identify the culprit, and use training or legal action to prevent the act from happening again. However, attacks from the Internet are always anonymous, making it very difficult to pinpoint a perpetrator who might easily come from a part of the world that is beyond the reach of local law. These acts cannot be eliminated, so you must harden your network security to prevent them from affecting you.

To complete this lesson exactly as written, you will need

- A Microsoft Windows 2000 server configured as the domain controller for domain.Fabrikam.com
- A Windows 2000 server to configure as a firewall
- A Windows 2000 Professional workstation
- An evaluation edition of Microsoft Internet Security and Acceleration (ISA) Server

Note   If you are using another type of firewall, you will need to adjust the steps.

After this lesson, you will be able to
- Understand the fundamental problems of Internet security
- Understand the requirements of a secure network architecture
- Configure a firewall to protect a private network

Estimated lesson time: 45 minutes

Understanding the Requirements for Internet Security

Securing public Internet servers is very difficult because you are inviting the public to use your computers in a specific context. The goal of Internet security is to ensure that the public cannot use your servers in any manner that you don't specifically invite. To keep your public servers secure, you need to follow these four security practices:

- Restrict access to all protocols except public protocols that you intend to serve.
- Harden public protocols so that they cannot be exploited.
- Ensure that legitimate remote users cannot be impersonated.
- Monitor all access to determine that the first three practices are successful.

In this chapter, you learn to use firewalls and proper network architecture to prevent hacking that originates from outside your network.

What Is the Threat?

To prepare and protect your network, you need to understand the multiple types of attacks.

Types of Attack

The seriousness of a hacking event is determined mostly by whether you are a random target of opportunity or you have been specifically targeted.

- A *random attack* does not indicate a specific, malicious intent against your company and it is unlikely to result in a sustained hacking effort. Therefore, there is little reason to respond to these types of hacking events once you've identified them as such.

- A *targeted attack* is perpetrated specifically against your organization. It requires vigilance to prevent and research to determine who is (or might be) perpetrating the attack.

Specifically, you need to prepare for the following three types of attacks:

- **Automated attacks.** Also referred to as "worms," automated attacks are perpetrated by virus-like software that exploits a known weakness in specific Internet service software, such as a Web server or an e-mail server. This type of attack has been around since the very early days of the Internet and affects all major operating systems. Because Windows is a popular operating system, it's a major target for these types of attacks. Once your service software is patched to be invulnerable to a specific worm, you can safely ignore further warnings from your firewall about it.

- **Target of opportunity attacks.** Random target-of-opportunity attacks are the typical "hacking" events that occur on the Internet. Novice hackers who have little to lose generally perpetrate these attacks. Hackers typically attempt to exploit only one or two vulnerabilities that they have recently learned about. This type of attack is easily defended against by using firewalls and security proxies, and by updating services that are exposed to the Internet with the latest security patches. Random attacks don't require serious research or follow-up because they occur routinely and are perpetrated against all Internet participants equally.

- **Targeted attacks.** Attacks specifically targeted against your organization are very rare and far more serious. These attacks are unlikely to happen to most businesses, but attackers who carry them out are more persistent and likely to use any means possible to gain access or cause a denial of service. These attacks are always very serious and are most often perpetrated by disgruntled employees, ideological activists, illicit competitors, or extortionists. In exceptionally rare cases, these attacks might be perpetrated by an experienced hacker looking for a technical challenge.

Methods of Attack

There are three primary ways attacks might be perpetrated against you:

- **Denial of Service (DoS) attacks.**   These attacks exploit the nature of Internet protocols to prevent valid users from reaching a service. These attacks do not attempt to gain access to a system; they seek only to prevent others from using it. Typical methods include flooding a service with information to use up available bandwidth (called flooding), creating a large number of bogus connection attempts to use up server resources (similar to prank phone calling), or transmitting a specifically malformed request to trigger a bug that will crash the server. Either ideological hackers or extortionists almost always perpetrate doS attacks.

- **Exploitation attacks.**   Frequently referred to as "buffer overruns," this type of attack seeks to connect anonymously to a service and then elevate the attacker's privileges on the system to that of a valid user or an administrator. This type of attack exploits a weakness in the server code allowing attackers to execute arbitrary code that they've sent to the service. The code elevates their privileges and allows them to gain direct access. When they are on the system as an administrator, they can take measures to further compromise the system. This type of attack is exploited by worms so it automatically propagates through vulnerable systems, and it is also performed by target-of-opportunity hackers whenever new exploits are discovered.

- **Impersonation attacks.**   These attacks occur when a user without valid access uses a valid user account to gain access by either discovering a password or performing a brute-force password attack that reveals an account password. Disgruntled former employees or illicit competitors typically perpetrate these attacks, but hackers looking for a challenge might perpetrate them. These attacks are very serious because they indicate specific, malicious intent directed against your company.

Vectors for Attack

Computers are not vulnerable to random attacks from any source—there are only a few ways an attacker can reach a computer.

- **Direct attack.**   A direct attack occurs when a hacker attempts to exploit a computer directly from the computer's console. These attacks are exceptionally rare and are typically performed only by disgruntled employees or employees performing pranks on others who leave their computers logged on. Modern logon systems are hardened against these sorts of attacks, and with little administrative effort, administrators can eliminate them as a serious concern.

- **Wireless.** These attacks occur when hackers directly connect to the interior of the network using wireless services intended for legitimate users and begin attacking from inside the perimeter of the network. Once rare, wireless technology has brought these attacks to the fore as hackers are able to exploit wireless access points to gain access to networks.

Tip   Defeating these types of attacks can be very difficult. The most effective methods are to put wireless access points outside the firewall and treat them as Internet connections, and then use technology like the 802.1x protocol to prevent unauthorized users from attaching. Chapter 10, "Wireless Security," explains how to secure wireless access to your network.

- **Dial-up.** Dial-up attacks were the original method that hackers exploited to connect remotely to networks. These attacks have become rare as the technology is being replaced by Internet connectivity, and they can be prevented by placing Routing and Remote Access Service (RRAS) servers outside the perimeter and treating dial-up connections as Internet connections.
- **Internet.** The Internet is the most common vector for attacks. The vast majority of businesses and many consumers worldwide have Internet access. This level of connectivity and the anonymous nature of lower-level Internet protocols create the perfect environment for hacking and invite abuse. Because direct attacks are rare, and wireless and dial-up vectors can be placed outside a firewall so that they can be treated as Internet attacks, attacks from the Internet are the only type of attack from outsiders that you need to be concerned about in a properly constructed network infrastructure.

Securing Public Services

The first step to securing your network is controlling the intrusion vectors by narrowing them down to the fewest possible intrusion points. Listed below are methods of control for the four possible intrusion vectors:

- *Direct access* attacks must be prevented by implementing strong physical security, such as security guards and identification badges for valid users. Implementing a smart card infrastructure can prevent user credentials from being exploited by hackers.
- The *wireless* security problem is most often solved by placing wireless devices outside your firewall and using strong authentication protocols like 802.1x or a combination of media access control (MAC) address filtering and disabling Service Set Identifier (SSID) broadcast to prevent hackers from finding your wireless access points.

- *Dial-up* attacks are a serious concern you can eliminate by placing remote access servers outside your Internet firewall. Even if hackers are able to exploit the remote access server, they still won't be inside your network. Keep Remote Authentication Dial-In User Service (RADIUS) servers inside your network, and create a firewall policy that allows public remote access servers to connect to the internal RADIUS servers on the RADIUS port only to authenticate users. Consider creating a separate domain for user accounts on the RADIUS server so that externally used account credentials are not valid on the interior of your network.

- Secure *Internet* access requires virtual private network (VPN) connections so that remote users can get through your interior firewall, even if they've already authenticated with a dial-up or wireless access point. VPN provides strong encryption that will keep data secure in transit, and it provides machine authentication, which prevents hackers from reaching the interior of your network if they don't have valid machine certificates for your VPN.

Caution   Remember that you must secure all clients that connect through your VPN. Use the same level of security you use for the interior of your network to prevent hackers from exploiting a VPN-connected client and then traveling through the VPN to attack the network.

Establishing Firewall Security

Once you have three of the four vectors handled by your firewalls and the direct attack vector handled by strong physical security, you can use firewall policy to secure your network against attack from all public sources. Firewalls are essential in creating a secure network architecture.

If you provide public services, you must have at least three security zones:

- The public Internet (untrusted)
- The perimeter network (semi-trusted)
- The private network (trusted)

This three-zone infrastructure creates two borders: the border between the public and the perimeter network, and the border between the perimeter network and the private network. Each of these two borders must have a separate policy to allow data to flow through it. Perimeter security is usually accomplished using a two-stage firewall system: one stage allows access to public servers, and another stage prevents all access to the interior of your network.

The network between the public and private networks is called a *perimeter network* or a demilitarized zone (DMZ). The public side of the perimeter network is protected by a firewall that allows public access to the services you intend to provide, such as Web access. The private side of the perimeter network is protected by another firewall that allows only encrypted and authenticated protocols required for remote access and to allow public servers to exchange data with private servers. Figure 11.1 shows a diagram of a secure network architecture.

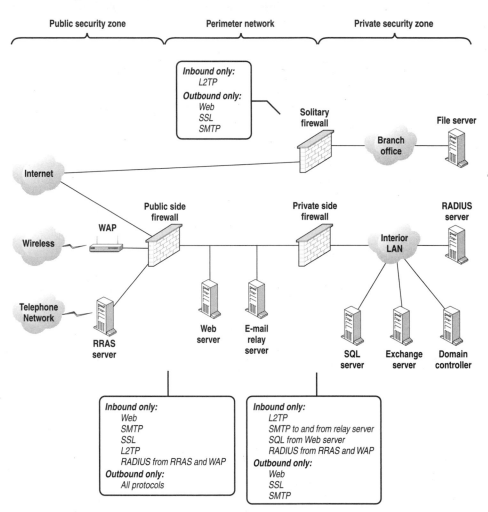

Figure 11.1   Providing public services requires three firewall policy zones

In Figure 11.1, you'll notice that the branch office does not require two firewalls. This is because the branch office provides no public services and therefore does not require a separate policy to allow access to public servers that would have to be enforced using a separate firewall.

The private network must be strongly blocked against servers in the perimeter network—it is not enough to protect perimeter network servers and then create policies that allow these servers wide access to the private network, because it's likely that servers in the perimeter network will someday be exploited by hackers who are able to gain administrative access to them. If your private-side firewall policy allows those servers wide access to your private network, hackers will be able to bounce through the perimeter network to the private side of the network. Policies that allow access on the private side of the firewall should be restricted to the specific protocols and machines that the public servers actually require access to. Servers in the perimeter network should never be linked to the domain, so that domain account information cannot be gleaned from them if they are exploited.

Some firewalls, including Microsoft Internet Security and Acceleration (ISA) Server, allow you to create a virtual perimeter network by employing a third network adapter in the firewall with its own policy. The Internet is attached to one adapter, the private network to another, and the perimeter network to the third. These firewalls are frequently referred to as being tri-homed or as having DMZ support. These firewalls are just as effective as using two firewalls to enforce your public security policy as long as they are correctly configured. Some software-based firewalls such as ISA Server have no inherent limit to the number of interfaces you can use. However, because policy can be configured strictly based on IP addresses, it is usually not necessary to use more than three network interfaces in a single firewall. Figure 11.2 shows the same security problem as shown in Figure 11.1, but with configuration managed using a single perimeter network-based firewall.

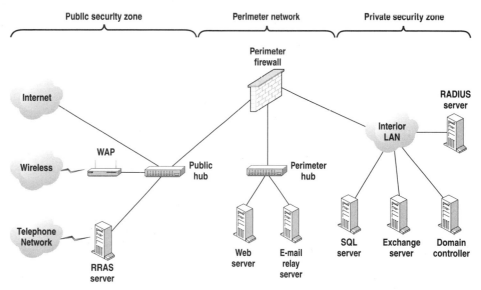

Figure 11.2   Creating three security zones using a firewall with perimeter network support

Because the Internet doesn't require a log on, wireless access points located in a typical perimeter network can be exploited to gain Internet access. It has recently become popular for hackers to connect to wireless devices for a free Internet connection rather than attempting to break into the network that they serve.

To prevent this type of use, place RRAS dial-in servers and wireless access points in a fourth security zone that blocks both Internet access and private network access to users who have not established a VPN connection. Once hackers find that they can't easily reach the Internet, they'll stop using your resources and go elsewhere.

Important Even though exploiting dial-in and wireless servers for free Internet access is relatively harmless for your network, it doesn't mean that it's not a security issue. If hackers used your Internet connection to perpetrate an illegal attack against a third party, your IP addresses and network would appear in the audit logs of the attacked party and could make you or your company liable for the damages incurred.

What Are the Types of Firewall?

Firewalls come in two primary types: firewall routers and security proxies.

Firewall Routers

Firewall routers (also called device-based firewalls) provide a TCP/IP network-layer firewall by inspecting packets at the IP and TCP layers. Packets that don't conform to the protocol rules configured in the firewall are dropped. Because network-layer filtering is relatively simple, firewall routers typically do not include hard disk drives and are not based on general-purpose server computers. Cisco Systems routers with the firewall option are good examples of *device firewalls* (also called router-based firewalls).

Besides packet filtering, firewall routers typically provide Network Address Translation (NAT), which converts the IP addresses of packets from public addresses to private addresses that are unknown outside the private network as the packets flow through the router. While NAT does translate packet headers, it does not otherwise modify or regenerate the packets. Therefore, maliciously deformed packets designed by hackers to exploit some weakness in the TCP/IP protocol on interior machines might still get through NAT routers. NAT routers also modify packet headers, which is incompatible with Internet Protocol Security (IPSec) Authenticated Headers (AH) because the AH checksum will no longer match, meaning that IPSec cannot be used through firewalls that perform NAT. See Chapter 8, "IP Security" for more information about IPSec.

Security Proxies

Security proxies work by receiving client connections and interpreting them at the application layer, such as HTTP or SMTP. The proxy "stands in" for the server and receives the client's Web request as if it were the target Web server. It then regenerates the request on the Internet as if it were the client. When the real Web server returns the Web page, the proxy subsequently returns the page to the requesting client.

Because requests are regenerated on the security proxy, the proxy can filter the higher-level protocol for dangerous content and hacking exploits. For example, a security proxy can scrub characters usually exploited by hackers but rarely found in valid URLs, to ensure that buffer overruns are not being sent to the client from the Web server (or vice versa—security proxies can stand in front of Web servers to protect them as well). Also, because the TCP connections are completely regenerated, any malformed TCP/IP packets will be stopped at the security proxy and not passed to the interior of the private network.

Circuit-layer generic proxies (also called Socket, Windows Sockets or Winsock, or SOCKS proxies) are similar to application-specific proxies, except that they can proxy any TCP layer protocol without knowing what is contained within the TCP packets. These proxies work by receiving the TCP/IP stream on one interface and regenerating it on the other, rather than routing it through the TCP/IP stack. Unlike filtering or NAT firewalls, no original network-layer packets flow through, and the proxy itself must be configured as the destination. For example, to reach a Web server behind a filter, you would use the Web server's actual IP address, and the filtering router would inspect packets flowing through it, whereas with a circuit-layer proxy, the client would specify the proxy itself as the destination Web server, and the proxy would be configured to forward all traffic received on port 80 to an interior Web server.

Circuit-layer proxies are configured exactly like port forwarding on NAT firewalls, and the differences between them can be confusing. Circuit-layer proxies regenerate the TCP/IP packets completely, forwarding only the interior application-layer protocol intact. NAT firewalls, even when they are configured to forward ports, translate only IP addresses and ports numbers in the packet header, so they don't eliminate network-layer malformation attacks.

Modern security proxies often include the functionality of device-based firewall routers and can be configured as either network-layer or application-layer firewalls—in fact, most allow you to configure either circuit-layer proxying or NAT, two ways to achieve the same functionality at different layers. If routing is enabled on the security proxy (which is required for NAT), it can operate as a network-layer firewall. Microsoft ISA Server and Symantec Enterprise Firewall are good examples of security proxies.

Important If you configure a security proxy to act as a network-layer firewall, you might unintentionally reduce the security of the firewall by allowing malformed TCP/IP packets through. Always proxy protocols at the application or circuit layer if possible, and if you run into protocols that must be routed through at the network layer, consider replacing them rather than reducing your security posture.

In the two-stage firewall system, network-layer firewalls are appropriate for the public-side firewall system, where their simplicity and speed provide a strong defense against most denial of service attacks. Security proxies are a good choice for private-side firewalls for two reasons: They can perform much more rigorous security checking on protocols, and their network interface can be protected by the public-side firewalls, although it is not as secure against attack as a firewall router because it is the standard protocol stack for a general purpose operating system.

More Info It is also common to use the private-side firewall as the endpoint for VPN connections originating on the Internet. VPNs are discussed in Chapter 9, "Remote Access and VPN."

Using ISA Server

Microsoft ISA Server is an excellent example of a security proxy and a strong Internet firewall. As with all firewalls designed to run on general-purpose computers, you must ensure that the firewall is configured correctly and does not expose any services that could be exploited to take control of the firewall. The setup wizard does a good job of performing this function, as you will see in the practice for this lesson.

The default configuration of ISA Server (suggested by the setup wizard) is to allow all outbound access. While this default setting is common to most firewalls, it allows considerably more access than you will probably need and could allow Trojan horses embedded in viruses or downloaded executables to connect back to hackers from the interior of your network.

Tip You should treat outbound connections just like inbound connections— scrutinize the need for the protocol and allow only those protocols that have a valid purpose. This can be done easily in ISA Server by disabling routing and using application-layer proxy services to move protocols through the firewall.

ISA Server can be configured as a protocol proxy for HTTP, SMTP, POP3, and FTP, and as a circuit-layer proxy for almost any other TCP protocol. Furthermore, ISA Server can be configured as a firewall router with packet filtering and NAT. However, as with all security proxies, ISA Server is most secure when routing is disabled and circuit-layer proxying is used to forward protocols through it.

Practice: Configuring a Firewall

In this practice, you configure a private-side firewall to protect a private network. This practice presumes that a public-side firewall already exists to keep network-layer hacking attempts at bay, creating a perimeter network between the public-side firewall and the private-side firewall that will be used to secure public servers in subsequent lessons.

You will implement the following specific policy:

- All inbound connection attempts should be dropped.
- All outbound connection attempts should be allowed.

This policy is very typical of a baseline firewall policy and is a good starting point for most businesses. For organizations that have unusually strict security policies, consider starting with all connections dropped both ways and loosening outbound restrictions on a per-protocol basis. You will extend this policy in later lessons to provide connectivity through the firewall for perimeter network servers.

Exercise 1: Installing and Configuring ISA Server

In this exercise, you install ISA Server on a newly installed Windows 2000 Server computer named ISA, which is not a member of the domain. The computer has two network adapters, named Public (with an IP address of 10.0.0.90) and Private (with an address of 192.168.241.90).

▶ **To install Microsoft ISA Server**

1. Start the ISA Server 2000 setup program.

   The setup program will unpack numerous files. The ISA Server installation screen appears, as shown in Figure 11.3.

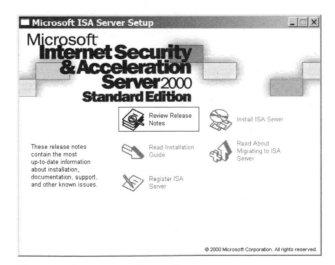

Figure 11.3   The ISA Server Setup screen

2. Click Install ISA Server. Microsoft Internet Security And Acceleration Server Enterprise Edition Setup dialog box appears.

3. In the Microsoft ISA Setup dialog box, click Continue.

4. When the Microsoft Internet Security And Acceleration dialog box requests a CD Key, type in your ISA Server key. If you have downloaded the evaluation edition, the key is provided during step 5 of the download process.

5. Click OK. The Microsoft ISA Server Setup dialog box shows your product key.

6. Click OK. The Microsoft ISA Server Setup dialog box presents the EULA.

7. Click I Agree. The Microsoft ISA Server Setup dialog box appears.

8. Click Typical Installation. The Microsoft ISA Server Setup mode dialog box appears, as shown in Figure 11.4.

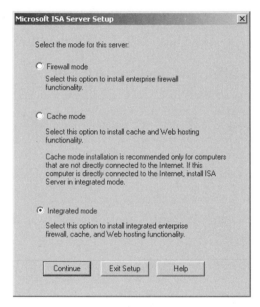

Figure 11.4   The ISA mode page sets the fundamental operating mode of the firewall

9. Select Integrated Mode, and click Continue. The Microsoft Internet Security And Acceleration Server Setup drive cache dialog box appears.

10. Click the C Drive, type **100** in the Cache Size box, click Set, and click OK.

Tip   If you have other physical drives, you might want to place the cache on them to improve system performance.

The Microsoft Internet Security And Acceleration Server Setup dialog box appears asking you to enter the IP range of the Internal network.

11. Type **192.168.241.0** in the From box, and **192.168.241.255** in the To box. Click Add; the dialog box will look like Figure 11.5.

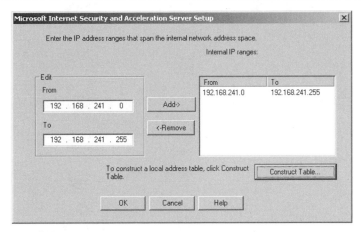

Figure 11.5   Configuring the Private Network range allows ISA Server to automatically determine security zones

12. Click OK. A setup progress indicator appears, showing the file installation progress.

13. When file installation finishes, the Launch ISA Management Tool dialog box appears. Click OK.

14. The Microsoft ISA Server Setup dialog box indicates that setup completed successfully. Click OK.

15. The ISA Management console displays the Getting Started page as shown in Figure 11.6.

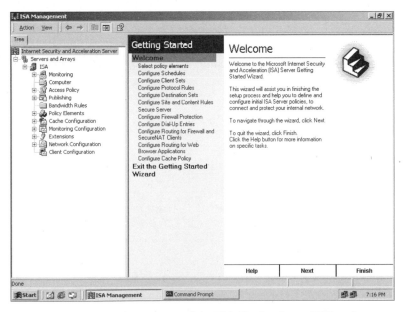

Figure 11.6   The Welcome page of the ISA Getting Started Wizard

► **To configure ISA Server**

1. In the Welcome page of the ISA Management console Getting Started Wizard, click Configure Protocol Rules. The Configure Protocol Rules page appears, as shown in Figure 11.7.

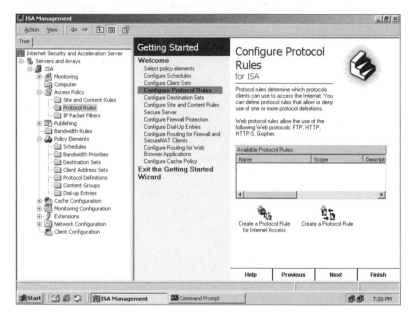

Figure 11.7   Configuring protocol rules

2. Click Create A Protocol Rule For Internet Access. The New Protocol Rule Wizard appears as shown in Figure 11.8.

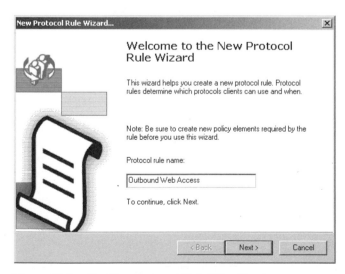

Figure 11.8   The New Protocol Rule Wizard

3. Type **Outbound Web Access** in the Protocol Rule Name box, and click Next. The Protocols page appears.

4. In the Protocols list, select HTTP and HTTPS, and clear FTP, FTP Download Only, and Gopher. These settings restrict which protocols you allow to pass through the firewall. Click Next. The Schedule page appears.

5. In the Use This Schedule box, select Always, and click Next. The Client Type page appears.

6. Select Any Request under Apply The Rule To Requests From, and click Next.

7. Click Finish to close the New Protocol Rule Wizard. A protocol rule appears in the Available Protocol Rules list box.

8. In the right-hand pane of the ISA Management console, click Secure Server. The Secure Server page appears as shown in Figure 11.9. You use this page to create appropriate host security for various roles.

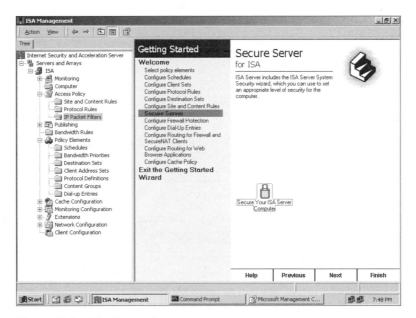

Figure 11.9 The Secure Server page

9. Click Secure Your ISA Server Computer. The ISA Server Security Configuration Wizard appears.

10. Click Next. The Select System Security Level page appears.

11. Select Dedicated, and click Next.

12. On the Congratulations page, click Finish. The ISA Security Configuration page will appear, and it might take several minutes to configure security on the server.

13. The ISA Server message appears informing you that the server must be restarted for the new security settings to take effect. Click OK to continue.

14. In the ISA Management console, click Configure Firewall Protection. The Configure Firewall Protection page appears, as shown in Figure 11.10. Use this page to configure firewall protection to strengthen the ISA server against network-layer attacks.

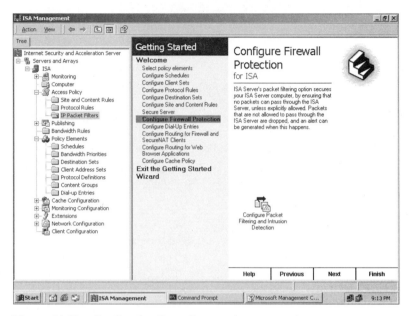

Figure 11.10   Configuring firewall protection

15. Click Configure Packet Filtering And Intrusion Detection. The IP Filters Properties dialog box appears.

16. In the dialog box, select both the Enable Packet Filtering check box and the Enable Intrusion Detection check box.

17. In the dialog box, click the Packet Filters tab, and select the Enable Filtering Of IP Fragments check box.

18. Click the Intrusion Detection tab, as shown in Figure 11.11.

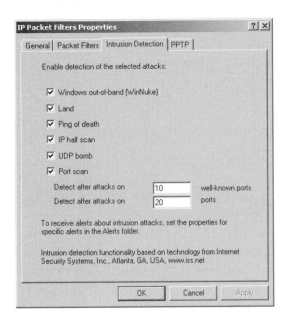

Figure 11.11   Configuring Intrusion Detection options

19. Select all of the available options, and click OK.

20. In the ISA Management console, click Finish. The ISA Welcome page appears.

21. Restart the server to allow the security settings to take effect.

Lesson Review

The following questions are intended to reinforce key information in this lesson.
If you are unable to answer a question, review the lesson and try the question again.
Answers to the questions can be found in the appendix.

1. Why is it difficult to protect public servers?

2. Are all hacking attempts serious?

3. What is the most important attack vector to defend against and why?

4. What is a perimeter network?

5. What are the primary types of firewalls that are available?

Lesson Summary

- Internet security basics are similar to any security problem:
  - Reduce the scope of the problem as much as possible by restricting access to only what is necessary to meet requirements.
  - Strengthen security for those services that must be provided, authenticate all participants, and vigilantly monitor activities to ensure that attacks are detected as early as possible.
- Attacks are common and constant on the Internet. The real problem is determining which attacks are merely random and which indicate a serious attempt to access your network in a manner that would be damaging.
- There are three primary types of attacks: denial of service attacks that interrupt service but do not compromise information, exploitation attacks that gain access by exploiting bugs, and impersonation attacks that gain access by masquerading as legitimate users.
- There are four primary vectors for attack: direct intrusion through physical access, through dial-up, through wireless connection, and through the Internet. When you've implemented strong physical security and placed wireless and dial-up access points outside your firewall, you need to concern yourself only with Internet security. Firewalls are used to protect against attacks stemming from the Internet.
- For those who must provide public Web server and e-mail server access, Internet security is not simple. You must establish three zones of security: the untrusted Internet, the semi-trusted public server zone, referred to as a perimeter network, and the trusted private network. A firewall is required at the boundaries between each of these networks, by using either two physical firewalls or a single, tri-homed perimeter network firewall.
- Firewalls come in two primary types: device-based firewall routers that inspect packets at the TPC/IP layer, and security proxies that inspect data at the application (Web, e-mail) layer. VPN endpoints are frequently configured on firewalls to connect networks together securely at their borders.

Lesson 2: Configuring Microsoft SQL Server for Internet Security

Public services like Web sites are often designed to communicate with database servers, and databases are often used to collect sensitive data from public Internet users, such as credit card information. Because this data must eventually reach the interior of the network, a connection from the Internet through to the private network must exist. Determining how to secure necessary connections between public servers and sensitive private servers is the most difficult aspect of implementing Internet security.

To complete this lesson, you will need

- The dc01.domain.Fabrikam.com certificate authority
- The ISA server configured in Lesson 1
- A newly installed Microsoft SQL Server configured in the private network on address 192.168.241.130

Tip   You can download an evaluation version of Microsoft SQL Server 2000 at *www.microsoft.com/sql*.

- A workstation or server running Windows 2000 configured in the 10.0.0.0 perimeter network

---

After this lesson, you will be able to

- ˙ Understand the proper place for public servers in your network
- Configure SQL Server for protocol encryption
- Configure a firewall to allow SQL data to pass through

Estimated lesson time: 45 minutes

Protecting Public Database Servers

Protecting servers that actually store critical data, such as e-mail and database servers, is vital. Protecting Web servers is somewhat less important if the Web service has been properly separated from other services so that the Web server does not store sensitive information. A server that provides only the Web service will be running from a relatively static set of Web pages or Web applications that connect to dynamic data on a database server. If the Web server is somehow exploited or destroyed, it can be quickly replaced from a backup or another member of a Web service cluster, so the only real security concern is ensuring that the data is not compromised.

Important   As long as a successful attack on a Web server does not allow further attacks to the interior of the private network, your data will remain secure. Remember to secure your database servers against your own front-line Web servers when you implement security, under the assumption that the Web servers might someday be exploited.

The Proper Place for Database Servers

Because data servers require strong security and communicate closely with other enterprise systems, it is normal practice to place them inside the private network and provide access to them through a proxy server like ISA Server. The firewall or proxy is then configured to allow only Web servers in the perimeter network to connect to the database servers, and only on the service port required for data connectivity, such as the SQL Server TCP port. Furthermore, the connection should be encrypted for maximum security, to prevent hackers who might have exploited another Web server inside the perimeter network from sniffing the network to determine passwords that will allow access to private machines.

This configuration prevents any computers on the Internet from connecting to the database servers, and it prevents even the perimeter network-based Web servers from connecting using any method other than the SQL Service port. In addition, by using certificate-based data encryption, you can make it impossible for other machines to impersonate the Web servers to gain access to the SQL server. The only possible exploit with these levels of security in place would be to compromise the Web server itself, and then install software to query the database directly to retrieve data. The database is still protected by logon authentication, which could possibly be determined by examining the source code of applications that run on the Web server and connect to the database server.

By strongly securing Web servers and monitoring them for intrusion attempts, you practically eliminate an attacker's ability to exploit them and bounce through the perimeter network to the database server. However, because a connection must exist for the service to function, you can never completely eliminate the possibility of attack.

Securing Microsoft SQL Server

Microsoft SQL Server supports the ability to encrypt communications over TCP/IP connections to the server using Secure Sockets Layer (SSL), which is based on machine SSL certificates. By installing an SSL certificate on a SQL server and configuring the server to require encryption, you can prevent all computers that do not have valid machine certificates from the same root certificate authority (CA) from being able to connect to the SQL data service. By using a firewall to eliminate access to other ports, you can prevent exploitation of the machine by any untrusted machine. This feature allows you to establish the strongest level of database server security possible.

When you proxy connections through an ISA server on a single TCP port, you must configure the SQL server and the client to communicate using the TCP/IP network library rather than the traditional named pipes network library. Because all other ports are closed, you will find that Windows integrated authentication is not available—it runs on a separate service port. To connect to a SQL server securely through the SQL Server port alone, you must use SQL Server authentication.

Warning   Always change the default SA (system administrator) password in SQL Server. By default, the password is empty and anyone can use it to connect to a database server. There is currently a worm released on the Internet that exploits that fact to gain access to SQL servers, and an empty password would be an open invitation to any hacker who exploited a Web server connected to a database server.

SQL Server supports encryption over the SQL Server protocol by using SSL. SSL is used to encrypt the data stream before the stream is transmitted, so it can be correctly proxied by ISA Server, unlike IPSec connections, which cannot be proxied or network address translated. You should always use SSL encryption on SQL data streams that flow over the Internet to protect data and SQL authentication information from exposure.

Practice: Establishing SQL Server Security for the Internet

In this practice, you use ISA Server to proxy connections between the perimeter network and an internal SQL server, in preparation for establishing a perimeter Web server that will use data stored on the private SQL server.

In this practice, you will place a SQL server inside the private network, publish it to the perimeter network using Microsoft ISA Server, and then configure the SQL server to accept only encrypted connections. This will prevent any computer that does not have a valid certificate from your root CA from establishing a connection to the SQL server.

This exercise requires three computers: the ISA server configured in Lesson 1, a Windows 2000 workstation or server located in the perimeter network (10.0.0.0 network), and a Windows 2000 server running Microsoft SQL Server 2000.

Before you perform these exercises, perform a default installation of Microsoft SQL Server 2000 and configure it to use both Windows integrated and SQL authentication. In this exercise, the SQL server is named SQL.domain.Fabrikam.com and it has an IP address of 192.168.241.130.

Note   In production environments, once you test connectivity between the perimeter network machine and the SQL server, you are ready to deploy the Web application on the perimeter network machine that requires access to the database server.

Exercise 1: Publishing the SQL Server

In this exercise, with the SQL server inside the private network, you publish it to the perimeter network using ISA Server.

► **To publish the SQL Server to the perimeter network**

1. Log on to the ISA Server as the administrator.
2. Click Start, point to Programs, point to Microsoft ISA Server, and then click ISA Management.
3. In the console tree, click Publishing. The Configure Publishing Policy page appears, as shown in Figure 11.12.

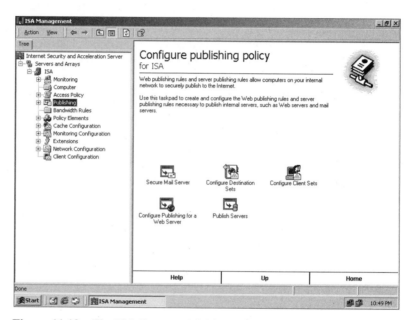

Figure 11.12   The ISA Server publishing policy page

4. Click Publish Servers. The Publish Servers page appears.

5. Click Publish A Server. The New Server Publishing Rule Wizard appears, as shown in Figure 11.13.

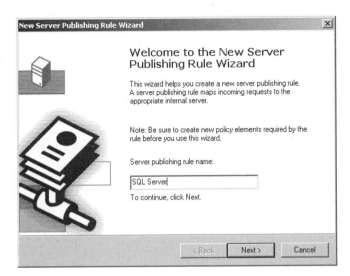

Figure 11.13   The New Server Publishing Rule Wizard

6. Type SQL Server in the Server Publishing Rule Name box, and click Next.

7. The Address mapping page appears. Type the internal IP address of the SQL server, **192.168.241.130**, in the IP Address Of Internal Server box.

8. Click Browse, and then click OK to select the External IP Address On ISA Server.

9. Click Next. The Protocol Settings page appears.

10. Select Microsoft SQL Server in the Apply The Rule To This Protocol drop-down list, and click Next.

11. In the Client Type page, select Any Request, and click Next.

12. Click Finish to close the wizard. A new server will appear in the published servers list.

Exercise 2: Enabling SSL Encryption on the SQL Server

In this exercise, you configure the SQL server to accept only encrypted connections by requiring protocol encryption and then installing an SSL encryption certificate.

▶ **To force encryption on the SQL server**

1. Click Start, point to Programs, point to Microsoft SQL Server, and click Server Network Utility. The SQL Server Network Utility dialog box appears as shown in Figure 11.14.

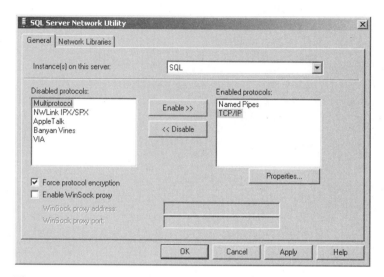

Figure 11.14   The SQL Server Network Utility dialog box

2. Select the Force Protocol Encryption check box.
3. Click OK to close the Network Server Utility dialog box.
4. Click OK when a message box appears informing you that changes will not take effect until the SQL Server service is restarted.
5. Right-click the SQL Server icon in the system tray, and click Stop.
6. When a message appears asking if you're sure, click Yes.

   The System Tray icon appears with a red stop icon, indicating that the service is stopped.

7. Right-click the SQL Server icon in the system tray, and click Start.

   Notice that you cannot start the service. This occurs because no valid SSL Encryption certificate for the server exists in the certificate store.

▶   **To install an SSL encryption certificate for the SQL server**

1. Open Internet Explorer and browse to *http://dc01/certsrv*. The Microsoft Certificate Services Web page appears.

2. Select Request a Certificate, and click Next. The Choose Request Type page appears.

3. Select Advanced Request, and click Next. The Advanced Certificate Request page appears.

4. Select Submit a Certificate Request To This CA Using A Form, and click Next. The Advanced Certificate Request page appears.

5. In the Certificate Template list box, select Web Server. The page changes to the Advanced Certificate Request page, as shown in Figure 11.15.

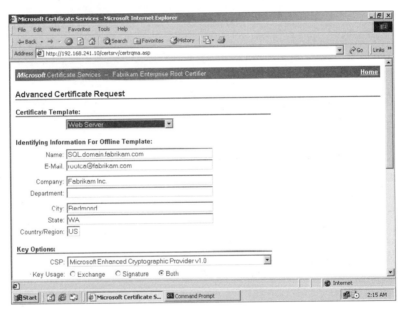

Figure 11.15   Requesting a SQL certificate

6. Type **SQL.domain.fabrikam.com** in the Name box.

Caution   The name you type in the Name box must exactly match the server's fully qualified domain name for the SSL Certificate to be recognized by the SQL Server service. To find out exactly what your server's fully qualified domain name is, open a command prompt on the SQL server, and ping local-host. The name returned is your server's fully qualified domain name.

7. Type **rootca@Fabrikam.com** in the E-Mail box.

8. Select Microsoft Enhanced Cryptographic Provider in the CSP list box.

9. Select Use Local Machine Store.

10. Click Submit. After a moment, the Certificate Issued page appears.

11. Click Install This Certificate. The Certificate Installed page appears.

12. Close Internet Explorer.

13. Right-click the SQL Server system tray icon, and click Start. The SQL Service starts.

    All SQL communications with this server will now be encrypted for all clients. Clients must have a valid machine certificate from the same root CA installed to communicate with this server.

Exercise 3: Verifying SQL Connectivity Through the Firewall

In this exercise, you use SQL management tools to verify that SQL is connected through the firewall. First, you install the tools, and then you test connectivity through the ISA server using SSL encryption from the perimeter network.

If the query analyzer is already installed on your Windows 2000 client machine, you can skip this procedure.

▶ **To install SQL management tools**

1. Log on to a Windows 2000 client machine in the perimeter network.

2. Insert the SQL Server CD, or unpack the SQLEVAL file.

3. Browse to the root of the CD or *c:\sqleval*.

4. Double-click Autorun. The Microsoft SQL Server 2000 installer screen appears.

5. Click SQL Server 2000 Components. The components screen appears.

6. Click Install Database Server. Microsoft SQL Server 2000 installation wizard appears.

7. Click Next. The Computer Name page appears.

8. Ensure that Local Computer is selected, and click Next. The Installation Selection page appears.

9. Ensure that Create A New Instance Of SQL Server, Or Install Client Tools is selected, and click Next. The User Information page appears.

10. Type **Administrator** in the Name box and **Fabrikam** in the Company box, and then click Next.

11. When the Software License Agreement page appears, click Yes.

12. On the Installation Definition page, select Client Tools Only, and click Next.

13. In the Select Components page, clear the Books Online and Development Tools check boxes.

14. Select Management Tools. Clear Enterprise Manager, Profiler, DTC Client Support, and Conflict Viewer.

You should have only Query Analyzer selected in the Sub-Components list, and Management Tools and Client Connectivity selected in the Components list, as shown in Figure 11.16.

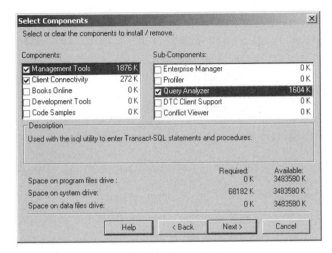

Figure 11.16   Installing the Query Analyzer

15. Click Next. The Start Copying Files page appears.

16. Click Next. Setup installs the Query Analyzer.

17. When the Query Analyzer is installed, the Setup Complete message appears. Click Finish to close the installer.

▶ **To test connectivity through the ISA server using SSL encryption**

1. Click Start, point to Programs, point to Microsoft SQL Server, and click Query Analyzer. The Query Analyzer, which allows you to check SQL connections, appears as shown in Figure 11.17.

Figure 11.17   The Microsoft Query Analyzer

2. In the SQL Server box, type **10.0.0.90**.

   Why do you enter the IP address of the ISA server rather than the IP Address of the SQL server in the SQL Server box?

3. Ensure that SQL Server Authentication is selected and that the Login Name is **sa**. Type the sa password in the Password box, and then click OK.

   The SQL Query Analyzer Object Browser, shown in Figure 11.18, appears showing the SQL server and the list of default databases configured. Notice that you can browse through the objects on the database server by expanding the databases in the Object Browser.

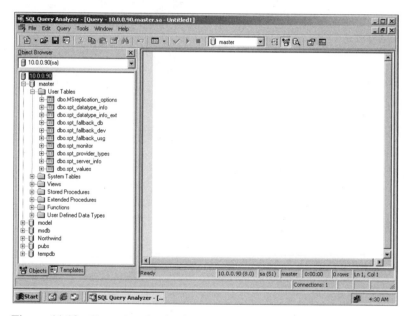

Figure 11.18   Browsing the database through an encrypted connection

4. Close the SQL Query Analyzer.

Lesson Review

The following questions are intended to reinforce key information in this lesson. If you are unable to answer a question, review the lesson and try the question again. Answers to the questions can be found in the appendix.

1. Which public security problem represents more risk for most businesses: the exploitation of a Web server or the exploitation of a database server?

2. What is the proper security zone for a database server in a typical network architecture?

3. How does ISA Server secure Microsoft SQL Server database servers?

4. How does SQL Server ensure that only specific clients can connect to it?

Lesson Summary

- Database servers that communicate with Web servers are a dangerous security problem because they can be exploited if the Web servers they communicate with are exploited. Successful attacks against Web servers are common, and subsequent attacks against database servers are common as well. Web servers do not usually store crucial data, but database servers usually do, so their security is actually far more important.

- Because of the requirement to communicate closely with other enterprise systems and to be as protected as possible, database servers are normally placed inside private networks even when they have to communicate with Web servers in the perimeter network. Special security measures such as protocol proxying and encryption can help prevent attacks against database servers.

- Microsoft SQL Server can by proxied securely by Microsoft ISA Server. As with all proxy connections, the TCP/IP layer is broken at the proxy and regenerated, so TCP/IP layer attacks will not reach the database server.

- Microsoft SQL Server supports SSL encryption of the TCP/IP SQL protocol, so that attackers cannot observe communications and so that the client and server can authenticate one another using certificates, which prevents unauthorized computers from connecting to the server.

Lesson 3: Securing Microsoft Exchange Server for the Internet

E-mail is one of the two primary reasons people use the Internet, so interoperability among different e-mail server applications was originally more important than security. Competing vendors either did not implement any form of security or chose different security standards rather than developing and adopting widely accepted cross-platform standards for security. Therefore, two primary security problems affect e-mail delivery on the Internet:

- The lack of a standard authentication protocol to determine who is a valid mail sender. Any unauthorized user can send e-mail through your mail servers. Any e-mail server can attach to your e-mail server and send e-mail to it with no specific form of authentication.
- The lack of a standard encryption standard for exchanging credentials securely. The only standard method for users to log on to an e-mail server is to pass plaintext user names and passwords.

Microsoft products like Exchange Server and Outlook 2000 use existing Internet standards like SSL to provide strong security. By deploying these products together, you can completely avoid the security problems that plague other systems.

To complete this lesson, you will need

- The dc01.domain.Fabrikam.com domain controller and certificate authority
- The Microsoft ISA Server private-side firewall set up in Lesson 1
- A new Exchange server named exchange.domain.Fabrikam.com on IP address 192.168.241.11 installed using all default options
- A Microsoft Windows 2000 Professional computer configured on an IP address outside the firewall

After this lesson, you will be able to

- Understand the security problems inherent in providing Internet e-mail service
- Configure Exchange Server to encrypt e-mail communications to clients
- Configure Microsoft Outlook Express to support encrypted communication

Estimated lesson time: 30 minutes

Exploiting Open Relays

Spammers, those who send unsolicited e-mail to Internet consumers, frequently try to exploit mail servers on high-capacity Internet connections to send more e-mail than they would normally be able to send. This attack works because the SMTP protocol, in its standardized form, does not include any type of authentication so anyone can connect to it and send mail, which the server dutifully delivers to the intended recipient.

The solution to preventing *spam* from being sent through a server in your domain is to prevent e-mail from being forwarded unless it originates within, or is destined for, a valid domain on your network. In other words, as long as the "from" or "to" address is the local domain, the mail should be sent. This type of mail server is known as a *closed relay*.

Note   In the context of e-mail servers, "domain" refers to the DNS domain such as "Fabrikam.com," not the windows security domain.

To prevent spammers from simply claiming to be on the local domain, local source restrictions are typically enforced by checking the source IP address of the mail sender or by requiring the user to log on to the mail server using a protocol such as the UNIX AUTH protocol, POP3, or Windows authentication. Microsoft Exchange Server uses normal Windows authentication to determine whether a user can send mail out through the server.

Note   In its default configuration, Microsoft Exchange Server 2000 is immune to open relay attacks and cannot be exploited to relay spam. Earlier versions of Microsoft Exchange Server are not secure by default. You can find instructions on securing these versions against open relay attacks on the Microsoft Web site. Search for article 324059 at *http://support.microsoft.com* for information about how to close an Exchange 5.5 open relay. Earlier versions of Exchange cannot be closed and must be upgraded to Exchange 5.5 SP1 or later to prevent spammers from exploiting them.

Properly Protecting an Exchange Server

The strong support for authentication in Exchange Server comes at a price: Exchange Server must be closely integrated into a Windows domain to work correctly, which makes it dangerous to place Exchange 2000 servers in the public or perimeter network security zones. This danger arises because a large number of protocols must be exchanged through the firewall (each of which could be a potential vector for attack) and because confidential domain user account information could be sent through the firewall into the perimeter network.

As a rule, you should never have computers that are domain members sitting outside your private network. Because Exchange 2000 must participate in Active Directory, it is not a good candidate for deployment in a perimeter network. However, because it's a public server, it shouldn't be placed inside a private network. If hackers were able to exploit a public server inside a private network, they would have open access inside that unprotected private network

The solution to the Exchange Server dilemma is either to use an SMTP relay server inside the perimeter network that filters mail and forwards it securely to the Exchange Server, or to use a strong security proxy such as ISA Server to protect the Exchange Server.

Protecting Exchange Server with a Relay Mail Server

An SMTP relay server is a server whose only purpose is to receive e-mail from the Internet and then relay it to another server inside a private network. In this case, the relay sits inside the perimeter network to receive e-mail and then relays it securely to an Exchange server inside the network through some secure connection such as an SSL or IPSec tunnel, depending upon what the firewall is capable of forwarding. This solution is complex to configure and requires a third-party SMTP relay, because Exchange Server is not well suited to the task.

Protecting Exchange Server with a Strong Security Proxy

The simpler solution for Exchange 2000 is to rely on ISA Server to examine the mail protocols at the border and proxy them to an Exchange server. This solution is simple, as it requires merely using publication wizards built into ISA Server that are configured correctly for Exchange Server by default. Configuring other strong security proxies is similar in complexity.

You can install ISA Server directly on, and configure it to work in conjunction with, an Exchange server. While this configuration is not specifically covered in this chapter, it is not difficult to set up, because ISA's installation process handles it as a standard case. It is wise to use ISA Server in this mode to protect any server that is reachable from the Internet, because ISA can be configured to trap hackers who have exploited a server, preventing them from bouncing through the server to exploit the rest of your network. However, installing ISA Server should be a secondary measure after e-mail protocols have been forwarded through a private-side security proxy, not a replacement for it.

Securing Credentials with SSL

After you secure your e-mail server from attack by correctly locating it in your network and ensuring that it is not configured to relay mail without authorization, you need to consider how users will securely access their e-mail from the Internet. Internal users can simply rely on Exchange 2000 and Outlook support for integrated

Windows Authentication to make security transparent on the interior of your network, but the Messaging Application Programming Interface (MAPI) protocol used natively by Exchange to transfer e-mail to clients and Integrated Windows authentication are both too complex to operate securely over the Internet.

The standard POP3 e-mail client protocol is simple enough to securely forward, network address translate, and proxy easily, but it does not meet security requirements because logon names and passwords (as well as e-mail text) are not encrypted and could be revealed to any attacker who could sniff the network.

Exchange 2000 and Outlook solve this problem by enabling SSL encryption of POP3 data between the client and the server, beginning before credentials are exchanged. This ensures that passwords and e-mail body text remain secure between the client and the server. Enabling SSL for POP3 (to receive e-mail messages) and SMTP (to securely send e-mail messages) requires only a standard encryption certificate; Exchange System Manager can walk you through requesting a standard encryption certificate from your own enterprise CA.

Caution   Certificates do not need to be deployed to clients, so end users can reach your e-mail server from their own clients as long as they know a valid user name and password. SSL is used only for encryption in Exchange Server, not for client computer authentication.

Practice: Securing Microsoft Exchange for the Internet

In this practice, you configure an ISA private-side firewall to forward e-mail service to an interior Exchange server that is a member of the domain and that is Active Directory integrated. You also configure the server to use Secure Password Authentication to protect the passwords of clients that use POP3 from the Internet. Finally, you test the configuration by configuring a client on the Internet to connect securely using Outlook Express.

This exercise requires the following

- The dc01.domain.Fabrikam.com domain controller
- An Exchange server installed in default mode named exchange.domain.Fabrikam.com, operating on IP address 192.168.241.11
- The ISA private-side firewall configured in Lesson 1

Tip   You can download an evaluation version of Microsoft Exchange 2000 at *www.microsoft.com/exchange*.

Exercise 1: Forwarding Ports to Exchange

In this exercise, you configure ISA Server to publish a Microsoft Exchange Server located inside the private network.

▶ **To configure ISA Server**

1. Log on to the ISA server as the administrator.
2. Click Start, point to Programs, point to Microsoft ISA Server, and click ISA Management. The ISA Management console appears as shown in Figure 11.19.

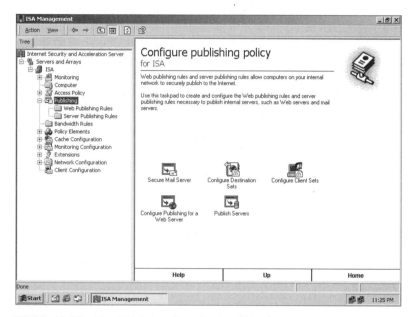

Figure 11.19   The ISA Management console

3. Expand Servers And Arrays, ISA, and Publishing.
4. Click Publishing, and then click Secure Mail Server. The Mail Server Security Wizard appears.
5. Click Next. The Mail Services Selection page appears.
6. Select the Default Authentication check boxes for Incoming SMTP and Outgoing SMTP.
7. Under Incoming SMTP, select Apply Content Filtering.

8. Select the SSL Authentication check boxes for Incoming SMTP, Outgoing SMTP, and Incoming POP3.

   Your Mail Services Selection page should look like Figure 11.20.

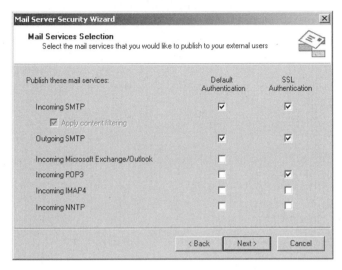

Figure 11.20   Selecting secure mail protocols

9. Click Next. The ISA Server's External Address page appears.

10. Click Browse, click the external IP address entry in the IP Address list, and click OK.

11. Click Next. The Internal Mail Server address page appears.

12. Click Find. The Find Internal IP Address dialog box appears as shown in Figure 11.21.

Figure 11.21   Selecting the inside IP address for the mail server

13. Type **EXCHANGE** in the Server Name box, and click Find.

    The Server's IP Address appears in the IP Addresses list box, as shown in Figure 11.21.

14. Click OK to close the Find Internal IP Address dialog box, and then click Next. The Completing The Mail Server Security Wizard appears.

15. Click Finish, and then close the ISA server. The internal Exchange server is now available to public servers and clients.

Exercise 2: Configuring Secure Password Authentication

In this exercise, you configure a default Exchange Server installation to require SSL and install an SSL certificate to accomplish that goal.

▶ **To obtain an SSL encryption certificate for the Exchange server**

1. Log on to the Exchange server as the domain administrator.

2. Click Start, point to Programs, point to Microsoft Exchange, and click System Manager.

3. Expand First Organization (Exchange), Servers, EXCHANGE, Protocols, POP3, and Default POP3 Virtual Server. The screen will appear like Figure 11.22.

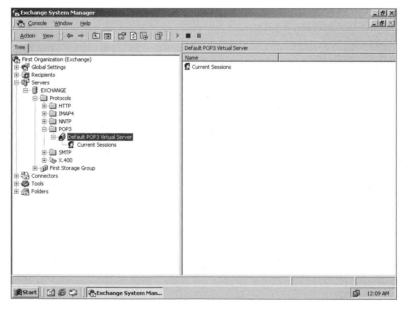

Figure 11.22 The Exchange System Manager showing the POP3 protocol service

4. Right-click Default POP3 Virtual Server, and click Properties. The Default POP3 Virtual Server Properties dialog box appears.

5. Click the Access tab, as shown in Figure 11.23.

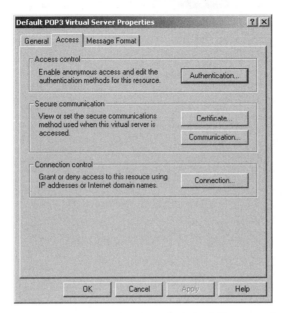

Figure 11.23   Configuring POP3 for SSL encryption

6. Click the Certificate button. The IIS Certificate Wizard appears.

7. Click Next. The Server Certificate page appears.

8. Select Create A New Certificate, and click Next. The Delayed Or Immediate Request page appears.

9. Select Send The Request Immediately To An Online Certificate Authority, and click Next.

10. The Name And Security Settings page appears, as shown in Figure 11.24, to set the certificate name and bit length.

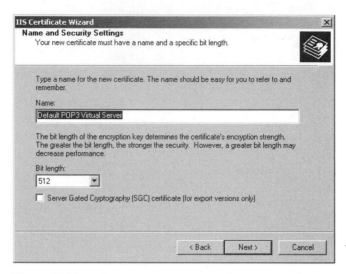

Figure 11.24   The POP3 SSL Certificate name

11. Accept the defaults, and click Next. The Organization Information page appears.

12. Type **Fabrikam** in the Organization box and **Headquarters** in the Organizational Unit box.

13. When the Your Site's Common Name box appears, type **10.0.0.90**, and click Next.

Important   The content of the Your Site's Common Name box is crucial to the proper operation of POP3 and SMTP over SSL. The information in this box must match the server name entered into every client e-mail application's account server name box, or the SSL connection will fail. In this exercise, you are using an IP address because it is not feasible to register the IP address of a test machine with an Internet Domain Name registrar for a lesson, but you would normally use the fully qualified domain name of the server (in this case, exchange.domain.fabrikam.com) in this box for a production server.

---

14. When the Geographical Information page appears, select US in the Country/Region box, type **WA** in the State/Province box, and type **Redmond** in the City/Locality box.

15. Click Next. The Choose A Certificate Authority page appears. The dc01.domain.Fabrikam.com\Fabrikam Enterprise Root Certifier should appear in the box.

16. Click Next. The Certificate Request Submission page appears as shown in Figure 11.25.

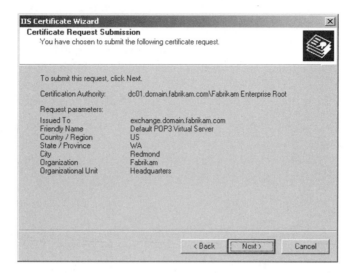

Figure 11.25   The elements of a completed certificate form

17. Click Next. The completion page appears. Click Finish.

▶ **To establish SSL encryption for POP3 connections**

1. On the Access tab of the Default POP3 Virtual Server Properties dialog box, click the Communication button.

2. The Security dialog box appears as shown in Figure 11.26.

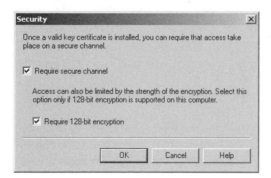

Figure 11.26   Configuring POP3 for SSL

3. Select the Require Secure Channel and Require 128-bit Encryption check boxes.

4. Click OK to close the Security dialog box.

5. Click OK to close the Default POP3 Virtual Server Properties dialog box.

6. Click the stop icon in the toolbar to stop the POP3 service.

7. Click the start icon in the toolbar to start the POP3 service.

▶ **To configure the Exchange server e-mail address policy**

1. Under Recipients in the Exchange Systems Manager console, click Recipient Policies.

2. Double-click Default Policy. The Default Policy Properties dialog box appears.

3. Click the E-Mail Addresses tab. The dialog box now appears as shown in Figure 11.27.

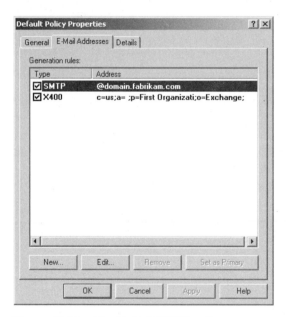

Figure 11.27   The Default SMTP policy

4. Double-click SMTP. The SMTP Address Properties dialog box appears.

5. Replace the @domain.fabrikam.com text in the Address box with **@fabrikam.com**, as shown in Figure 11.28.

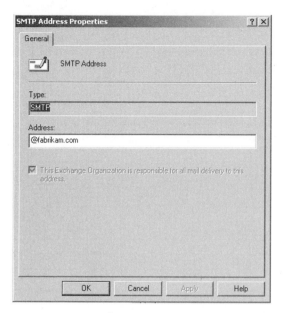

Figure 11.28   Changing the default SMTP domain

6. Click OK to close the SMTP Address Properties dialog box.

7. Click OK to close the Default Policy Properties.

8. Click Yes when the Exchange System Manager console asks if you want to update all corresponding recipient e-mail addresses to match the new address.

9. Close the Exchange System Manager console.

Exercise 3: Testing Exchange Server Security

In this exercise, you test the Exchange Server and ISA Server configuration by configuring a machine in the perimeter network to connect through the ISA server to the Exchange server using POP3/SSL. For the purposes of this exercise, the perimeter network is essentially the same as the Internet.

▶ **To configure an e-mail account in the domain**

1. Log on to the EXCHANGE server as the administrator.

2. Open the Active Directory Users And Computers management console.

3. Expand domain.Fabrikam.com and Departments.

4. Click Design.

5. Right-click Syed Abbas, and click Exchange Tasks. The Exchange Task Wizard appears.

6. Click Next.

7. Verify that Create Mailbox is selected, and click Next. The Create Mailbox page appears as shown in Figure 11.29.

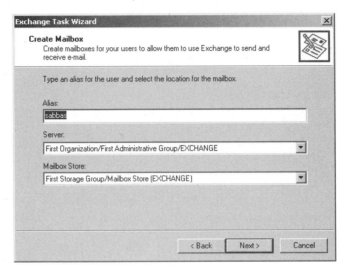

Figure 11.29   Creating a user's mailbox in Active Directory

8. Click Next. The wizard creates the mailbox.

9. Click Finish, and close the Active Directory Users And Computers management console.

▶ **To connect securely to an Exchange server from the Internet**

1. Log on to the Windows 2000 workstation located in the perimeter network.

2. Start Outlook Express.

   Outlook Express appears, and the Internet Connection Wizard opens to help you configure an e-mail account the first time you use Outlook Express.

3. In the Display Name box, type **Kevin Kennedy,** and click Next.

4. In the E-mail Address box, type **kkennedy@Fabrikam.com,** and click Next.

5. In the Incoming Mail Server and Outgoing Mail Server boxes, type **10.0.0.90**, and click Next.

6. Click Finish to close the Internet Connection Wizard.

7. The Outlook Express e-mail client appears as shown in Figure 11.30.

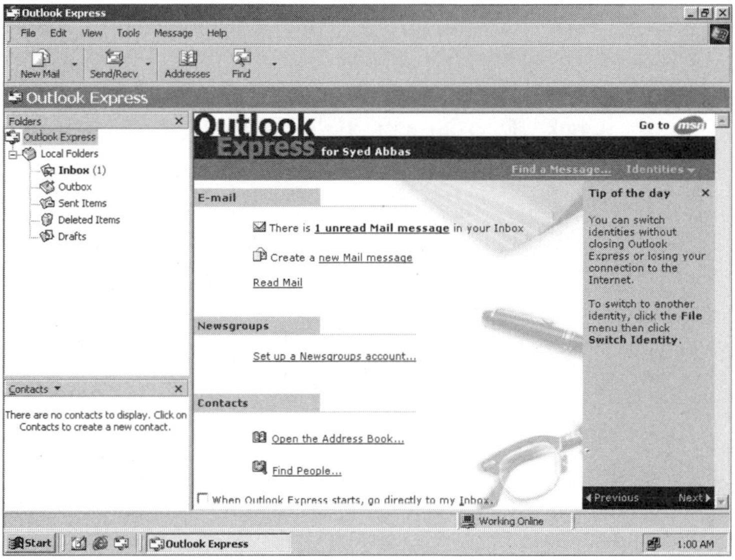

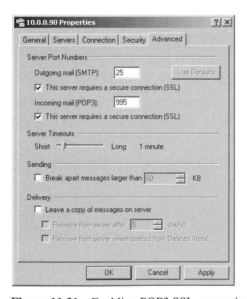

Figure 11.30   Outlook Express

8. From the Tools menu, choose Accounts. The Internet Accounts dialog box appears with account 10.0.0.90 selected.

9. Click Properties. The 10.0.0.90 Properties dialog box appears.

10. Click the Advanced tab. The Advanced tab appears as shown in Figure 11.31.

Figure 11.31   Enabling POP3 SSL encryption on the client side

11. Under Outgoing Mail (SMTP), select the This Server Requires A Secure Connection (SSL) check box.

12. Under Incoming Mail (POP3), select the This Server Requires A Secure Connection (SSL) check box. The displayed TCP port will change from 110 to 995.

13. Click OK to close the 10.0.0.90 Properties dialog box.

14. Click Close to close the Internet Accounts dialog box.

15. Click the Send/Rcv button in the toolbar. Exchange will use the SSL connection to check for e-mail on the Exchange server mapped through the ISA server and report that the exchange was successfully completed, as shown in Figure 11.32.

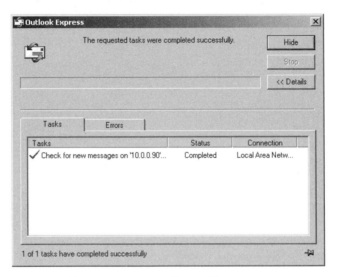

Figure 11.32   Exchanging mail over SSL

Lesson Review

The following questions are intended to reinforce key information in this lesson. If you are unable to answer a question, review the lesson and try the question again. Answers to the questions can be found in the appendix.

1. What are the two primary problems affecting e-mail on the Internet?

2. How does Exchange Server solve these problems?

3. Why is it unwise to place an Exchange server in the perimeter network?

4. What are common methods used to secure an Exchange 2000 server inside a private network?

5. What method of encryption does Exchange Server support for passing credentials?

Lesson Summary

- Traditional e-mail protocols lack standards for authenticating other mail servers and for protecting and authenticating e-mail clients. Microsoft Exchange implements these two functions using SSL for encryption and certificates.

- Open Relays allow spammers to send bulk e-mail through them. Microsoft Exchange 2000 is immune to bulk spamming because it requires authentication from e-mail clients in order to transmit e-mail.

- Exchange 2000 servers should remain on the interior of private networks because they interact heavily with the Active Directory database and store sensitive information. A strong security proxy or a relay SMTP server should be used to transmit e-mail through the perimeter network to the Exchange server.

- For clients on the Internet, POP3 with SSL is the preferred method of authenticating securely with Exchange Server. The default MAPI protocol used with Exchange Server is difficult to get working correctly through a firewall and difficult to encrypt.

C H A P T E R   1 2

Web Service Security

About This Chapter

Web servers, which have become as ubiquitous in private networks as they are on the Internet, are used for so many different purposes that no single security method is appropriate for all of them. Because a Web server must be available to a large number of clients whose identities might not be known, configuring it for maximum security in its specific environment (such as on the Internet or as an intranet or extranet server) is vital.

Microsoft Windows 2000 Server includes Internet Information Services (IIS), a set of services that enables a Windows 2000 server to function as a Web server. IIS supports a number of security features, including basic user authentication, certificates, and Secure Sockets Layer (SSL) encryption. By configuring these security features correctly, you can make your Web servers as secure as possible.

Before You Begin

To complete this chapter, you must have

- A domain controller for the domain.fabrikam.com domain
- An enterprise or standalone certificate authority as configured in Chapter 5, "Certificate Authorities"
- A Windows 2000 Server computer running IIS
- A Windows 2000 or Microsoft Windows XP client computer on the domain
- A Web browser that supports SSL connections

IIS is installed by default on Windows 2000 Server. If the computer was upgraded from an earlier operating system, you might need to install IIS separately.

Lesson 1: Securing Public Web Servers

Windows 2000 Server includes IIS and a management console that allows you to control the IIS settings, including its security options. This lesson covers the basics of security for Windows 2000 Web servers.

After this lesson, you will be able to
- Understand IIS and its security features
- Configure basic IIS security settings
- Restrict connections by IP address or domain name

Estimated lesson time: 10 minutes

Understanding Internet Information Services

Microsoft Internet Information Services (IIS) is a full-featured Web server that you use to publish Internet or intranet Web pages. IIS 5.0 is included with Windows 2000 Server. A single installation of IIS can manage multiple Web sites. IIS supports a variety of security features, including user authentication and SSL encryption.

Important   IIS security does not replace other security features—it enhances them. Make sure you use the security features specific to IIS in addition to the other security features of Windows 2000, such as IP filtering and NTFS file system security.

IIS serves Web documents using HTTP and the secure HTTPS version. In addition, it supports FTP, SMTP, and NNTP.

Tip   When IIS is installed on a server, it includes an online copy of the IIS documentation. You can access this documentation with the URL *http://localhost/iisHelp* on the IIS computer.

Implementing IIS Security

Security for IIS Web sites can be managed separately for the following:

- Globally for all Web sites and directories on the server
- Per Web site
- Per virtual directory

To manage security at these different levels, right-click the server, the Web site, or the virtual directory that you want to configure, click Properties, and then click the Directory Security tab in the Properties dialog box. All three levels present the same set of security options.

IIS Web servers provide Web sites in three primary security contexts:

- *Intranets* are private Web sites that operate inside private networks.
- *Extranets* are Web sites that connect a specific group of users from multiple organizations.
- *Internet* Web sites provide Web pages to anonymous users from the public.

Each security context has dramatically different security requirements, and IIS is designed to handle all of them. However, not all security features are appropriate for every security context. For example, authenticated access is not designed for public use because you can't create a user account for every member of the public.

Establishing Security Settings

The security settings in IIS are designed primarily to protect IIS services in intranets and extranets. You must use a strong security proxy such as Microsoft Internet Security and Acceleration (ISA) Server to protect public Web servers, and your security restrictions for public servers should be implemented on the proxy server rather than on the IIS server. You also must use NTFS permissions to restrict access to critical files on public Web servers.

For each Web site, the security settings in IIS allow you to choose one of the following types of authentication:

- *Anonymous access* for the Internet or when authentication is not necessary
- *Basic authentication* for extranets that serve clients other than Windows computers when you can't use digest authentication or certificate mapping
- *Integrated Windows authentication* for intranets where users will be using Microsoft Windows computers with Internet Explorer
- *Digest authentication* for extranets where you can't deploy certificates to all users and all browsers support digest authentication
- *Certificate mapping* for extranet use when you can deploy certificates to all users

Managing Directory Security Properties

To access most of the security properties for a Web site, select a Web site in the Internet Information Services management console, choose Properties from the Action menu, and click the Directory Security tab in the Properties dialog box that appears. You'll find these security options on the Directory Security tab:

- Allow anonymous access and control authentication methods
- Restrict access based on domain name or IP address
- Manage Web server and client certificate settings

The properties for a folder or virtual directory also include a Directory Security tab. For purposes of security, you can think of a virtual directory as a "Web site within a Web site"—it's a collection of Web content that has its own security settings. Virtual directories also allow you to store Web site files anywhere you want and make them appear to be within the directory structure of your Web site. You can use virtual directories to enable security features for a section of a site if the main portion of the site allows anonymous access.

Using IP Address and Domain Name Restrictions

To prevent access to a Web site from specific computers or to make a private Web site available only to specific machines, you can grant or deny access in IIS to a Web site based on the IP address or domain name of the user.

Note   Restricting access by domain name requires a reverse Domain Name System (DNS) lookup for each page access. This can slow down the server and is not recommended in most cases.

To manage these settings, click the Edit button within the IP Address And Domain Name Restriction area of the Directory Security tab in the Properties dialog box. You can choose to either grant or deny access to the server by default and then add a list of exceptions to this rule. For each exception, you can specify a single IP address, a range of addresses, or a domain name.

Caution   Restricting access to Web sites using IIS is not as secure as restricting access using Windows IP filtering in the TCP/IP configuration properties, ISA Server, or a dedicated firewall. Before using IIS to restrict access to a site, ensure that you want to restrict only Web protocols. In most cases, you are better off restricting all TCP/IP protocols using IP filtering or your firewall.

Keeping IIS Secure

Hackers target IIS because it is the most public of all services provided by Windows 2000. For this reason, more bug exploit attacks are perpetrated against IIS than any other service. Servers that run IIS should not be considered secure, regardless of the IIS security settings described here.

Make all of your security decisions for Web servers with the understanding that all public Web servers are subjected to an extraordinary amount of hacking activity. Data you can't afford to lose should never be stored on public Web servers. Never activate IIS on servers that don't require it to function unless those servers are protected from the Internet by a strong firewall.

Carefully consider the security ramifications of hosting multiple Web sites on a single Web server. Do not put secure Web sites on public Web servers and rely on Web authentication for security, because hackers who gain access to the public server will have access to the secure site on the same public Web server. Hosting multiple Web sites on a single server is a convenience feature, not a security feature. Keep Internet sites on public Web servers and intranet sites on private servers. Use certificate mapping (see Lesson 3) for extranet servers.

Maintaining IIS security is an ongoing process. When using IIS as a public Web server:

- Use the most secure authentication, and use SSL certificates for critical transactions. Secure authentication is described in Lesson 2 of this chapter; SSL certificates are described in Lesson 3.
- Turn off non-Web services such as FTP and SMTP that you are not currently using. (Select the service from the Internet Information Services management console and, from the Action menu, choose Stop to stop a service, or Delete to remove it entirely.)
- Keep IIS updated with the latest security patches, and implement a policy to ensure regular updates. See Chapter 14, "Software Maintenance," for information about automatic update services.

Practice: Configuring IIS Security

In this practice, you configure basic security properties for IIS. To complete this practice, you need a Windows 2000 Server computer with IIS installed. If your server was upgraded from an earlier version of Windows, you might need to install IIS using Add/Remove Programs in Control Panel.

Exercise 1: Configuring IIS Security Options

In this exercise, you configure basic IIS security options, including setting up IP address restrictions for a private Web site.

▶ **To configure IP address and domain name restrictions**

1. Log on as the administrator.
2. From the Administrative Tools menu, select Internet Services Manager. The Internet Information Services management console appears, as shown in Figure 12.1.

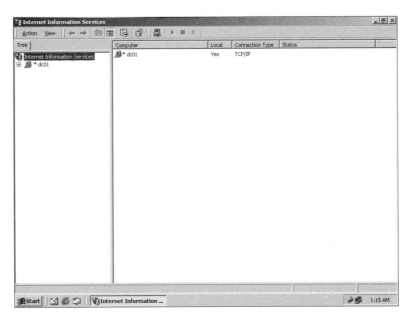

Figure 12.1   The Internet Information Services management console

3. Expand DC01 and select Default Web Site in the console tree.

4. From the Action menu, choose Properties. The Default Web Site Properties dialog box is displayed, as shown in Figure 12.2.

Figure 12.2   Default Web Site Properties

5. Select the Directory Security tab. The Directory Security properties are displayed, as shown in Figure 12.3.

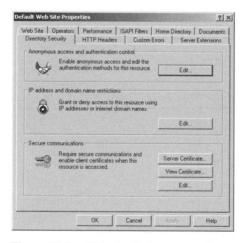

Figure 12.3   Web site directory security properties

6. In the IP Address And Domain Name Restrictions area, click Edit. The IP Address And Domain Name Restrictions dialog box is displayed, as shown in Figure 12.4.

Figure 12.4   IP Address And Domain Name Restrictions dialog box

7. Select the Denied Access option.

8. Click Add to add an IP address range. The Grant Access On dialog box is displayed, as shown in Figure 12.5.

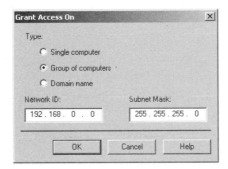

Figure 12.5   Granting access to an IP address range

9. Select the Group Of Computers option.

10. Type **192.168.0.0** in the Network ID box, and **255.255.255.0** in the Subnet Mask box.

11. Click OK. The range you entered is now included in the list in the IP Address And Domain Name Restrictions dialog box.

12. Click OK, and then click OK in the Properties dialog box.

   The Web server is now limited to access from computers in the 192.168.0 address range.

Lesson Review

The following questions are intended to reinforce key information in this lesson. If you are unable to answer a question, review the lesson and try the question again. Answers to the questions can be found in the appendix.

1. What component provides Web services in Windows 2000 Server?

2. What type of authentication is normally used for public Internet Web sites?

3. Which tab in the Properties dialog box for a Web site includes most security options?

4. What additional mechanisms should you use to enhance security besides IIS service-specific security options?

5. Which services can IIS provide along with HTTP?

Lesson Summary

- Internet Information Services (IIS) is included with Windows 2000 Server and provides Web services as well as basic support for FTP and other network services. IIS can support any number of Web sites using the HTTP and HTTPS (secure HTTP) protocols.

- You manage IIS using the settings in the Internet Information Services management console, available from the Administrative Tools menu. This console lists Web sites and other services and allows you to manage their properties.

- The Directory Security property page for a Web site provides options with which you can manage most of the security aspects of IIS. This includes authentication methods, IP address and domain name restrictions, and certificate options.

- The IP address and domain restrictions settings provide simple IP-based security for IIS. You can configure these settings to either grant or deny access by default, and you can add as exceptions to the default rule one or more IP addresses, address ranges, or domain names.

Lesson 2: Web Authentication

A Web server cannot determine the identity of an Internet user. Although this is not an issue for most Internet Web sites, private areas of a Web site need a way to authenticate users. IIS supports a variety of authentication methods for this purpose. This lesson explains these authentication methods and their advantages and disadvantages.

Exam Tip   Understanding the different authentication methods available for Web access is crucial to securing Web servers.

After this lesson, you will be able to

- Understand IIS authentication methods
- Enable and configure anonymous access
- Manage IIS authentication settings

Estimated lesson time: 30 minutes

Understanding Web Authentication

IIS supports several different authentication methods, ranging from simple password-based authentication to authentication using SSL certificates.

When users connect to a Web server, the server creates a browsing session using the default Web service account, which is typically named IUSR_*computername*. This account is created when IIS is installed. As with all accounts, this user account is a member of the Everyone group.

When a Web browser connects to a Web server, the server creates a new thread of execution and attaches to it the access token for the IUSR_*computername* account. This session remains connected to the Web browser based on the browser's IP address and connecting port until the Web browser closes the session or the server destroys the thread because it is inactive (typically about 20 minutes).

When Web pages are requested by a browser, the browsing session reads the file containing the page using the user account security context just as if the user were logged on to the domain and reading files from a file server. Whenever a file is requested that the anonymous user account does not have access to, IIS checks for user credentials and creates a new thread using those credentials according to the following rules:

- If the user's Web browser provides a certificate that is mapped to a certificate on the Web server, the user is logged on using the mapped certificate (see Lesson 3).

- If the Web browser can provide credentials automatically using the user's computer logon information, the server automatically logs the user on using those credentials.

- If these two methods don't succeed, the Web server requests authentication and displays a logon prompt for the user.

Tip   You can force users to authenticate with the Web server. Change the NTFS security permissions of the Web page files so that they exclude the IUSR_*computername* account and the Everyone group, and include those users or groups to whom you want to grant access.

Anonymous Access

Basic, unsecured Web pages do not authenticate the user at all. This is called anonymous authentication. When IIS is first installed, it creates a user account called IUSR_*computername*, where *computername* is the name of the IIS computer. This user account is configured as a member of the Guests user group and, as with all accounts, is also a member of the Everyone group.

By changing the NTFS permissions for the IUSR_*computername* account or Guest group, you can control which areas anonymous users can access. You can also specify a different user account for anonymous access in the Web site's properties. This allows you to configure separate user accounts for each site and manage their permissions individually rather than by using the permissions of the Guests group.

To change the user account that will be used to represent anonymous users, open the Properties dialog box for a server, Web site, or virtual directory. Click the Directory Security tab, and then click Edit in the Anonymous Access And Authentication Control area. In the Authentication Methods dialog box, ensure that the Anonymous Access check box is selected, and click Edit to change the user account used for anonymous access. If you want to create a new account for the purpose of representing anonymous users, create the account in the Active Directory Users And Computers management console, and then assign its access properties in the authentication control properties for IIS.

Important   If you disable the Anonymous Access option, you must configure one of the authentication methods described below, or users will be unable to access the Web site.

Basic Authentication

Basic authentication, a part of the HTTP standard, is a simple method of authentication that provides minimum security. You should use basic authentication only when security is not critical, because basic authentication requests are not encrypted. To enable basic authentication, select the Basic Authentication check box in the Authentication Methods properties for a Web site.

Basic authentication uses existing user names and passwords in a domain. When you create accounts for basic authentication, you must assign each account the Log On Locally user right.

Users can specify a domain when they authenticate. A default domain is used for users who do not specify a domain. You can specify this default domain by clicking Edit next to the Basic Authentication check box.

Basic authentication should be used only for private areas of otherwise public Web sites when the purpose for its use isn't as much to provide security as it is to restrict access, such as for members-only sites.

Important   Basic authentication sends passwords across the network as plaintext, and it is vulnerable to network snooping. It should be used only to meet low-level security needs.

Digest Authentication

Digest authentication is an HTTP 1.1 standard that provides a more secure authentication method. In digest authentication, the client sends a one-way encryption calculated from the user name, password, and information received from the server to authenticate the user. This avoids sending plaintext passwords over the network.

Like basic authentication, digest authentication uses user names and passwords from a domain. While it is more secure than basic authentication, it requires the storage of plaintext versions of the passwords and therefore is not an ideal solution. Digest authentication is less widely supported than basic authentication by third-party Web browsers, but more widely supported than Integrated Windows authentication.

Digest authentication is appropriate for use in extranets, where Web browser requirements are easy to enforce and medium-level security is appropriate.

Integrated Windows Authentication

Integrated Windows authentication is a more secure authentication method than basic or digest authentication. It takes advantage of the security features of Windows clients and servers. If the client is currently logged on and using Microsoft Internet Explorer 2.0 or later, an authenticated connection is established without prompting the user for logon information. If the user is not logged on or is using a different browser, the server prompts for a user name and password.

Integrated Windows authentication relies on Internet Explorer and does not work over HTTP proxies. Therefore, it is best suited for use in intranets where clients are all within a domain.

Certificates

Certificate-based authentication is appropriate for extranets or members-only sites where security is a strong concern. It provides a stronger key for encryption than digest authentication and does not send passwords in plaintext that can be intercepted by hackers. It's easier to control the distribution of certificates than it is to control who might have heard a Web site password. The Secure Sockets Layer (SSL) protocol provides a way to exchange certificates over HTTP connections. It is typically used to publish a server certificate, authenticating the Web site and enabling encryption. Additionally, SSL supports client certificates, which can be used to authenticate users on a site. The SSL features of IIS are explained in Lesson 3 of this chapter.

Configuring Web Authentication

You can configure the authentication settings of IIS using the Internet Information Services management console. You can enable a single method or several methods. IIS will attempt to use the most secure method first. If the most secure method isn't available, it attempts to use a less secure method. IIS will refuse connections if the client does not support one of the available authentication methods.

To configure authentication methods, open the Properties dialog box for a server, Web site, or virtual directory. Click the Directory Security tab, and then click Edit in the Anonymous Access And Authentication Control area of the tab. This opens the Authentication Methods dialog box. In this dialog box, clear the Anonymous Access check box to require authentication for the current resource.

The bottom portion of the dialog box allows you to enable basic authentication, digest authentication, and Integrated Windows authentication. A warning about plaintext passwords will be displayed if you enable basic or digest authentication.

Tip   You can enable SSL authentication using the Secure Communications property dialog box, described in Lesson 3.

Practice: Selecting Authentication Methods

In this practice, you configure anonymous access and authentication methods for an IIS Web site. You can use the default Web site on a new installation of IIS for this practice.

Exercise 1: Configuring Anonymous Access

In this exercise, you configure and manage anonymous access for an IIS Web site.

▶ **To enable anonymous access for a site**

1. From the Administrative Tools menu, choose Internet Services Manager. The Internet Information Services management console appears.

2. Open the server (DC01) container in the console tree, and select Default Web site. The components of the Web site are displayed.

3. From the Action menu, choose Properties. The Web Site Properties dialog box appears.

4. Click the Directory Security tab to display the Directory Security properties.

5. Click Edit in the Anonymous Access And Authentication Control area. The Authentication Methods dialog box is displayed, as shown in Figure 12.6.

Figure 12.6   Authentication Methods dialog box

6. Select the Anonymous Access check box, and click OK.

7. Click OK to close the Properties dialog box.

Important   This enables anonymous access to the Web site. User authentication is not used.

▶ **To change the anonymous access user account**

1. In the Internet Information Services management console, select Default Web Site in the console tree.

2. From the Action menu, choose Properties. The Web Site Properties dialog box is displayed.

3. Click the Directory Security tab.

4. Click Edit in the Anonymous Access And Authentication Control area. The Authentication Methods dialog box is displayed.

5. Click Edit in the Anonymous Access area. The Anonymous User Account dialog box is displayed.

6. Click Browse. The Select User dialog box is displayed, as shown in Figure 12.7. This dialog box contains a list of user accounts and their associated folders.

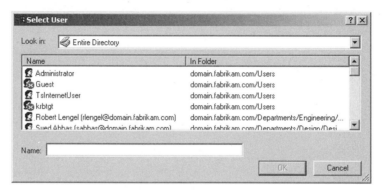

Figure 12.7   Selecting an anonymous user account

7. Select IUSR_DC01 from the user account list.

8. Click OK, and then click OK in the Anonymous User Account dialog box.

9. Click OK in the Authentication Methods dialog box, and then click OK to close the Properties dialog box.

Exercise 2: Configuring Authentication Methods

In this exercise, you select and configure IIS authentication methods to allow authorized users to access a Web site.

▶ **To select authentication methods**

1. In the Internet Information Services management console, select Default Web Site in the console tree, and choose Properties from the Action menu.

2. Click the Directory Security tab.

3. Click Edit in the Anonymous Access And Authentication Control area to open the Authentication Methods dialog box.

4. Select the Digest Authentication For Windows Domain Servers check box. A warning message is displayed, indicating that digest authentication works with Windows 2000 domain accounts only and that passwords are stored as encrypted clear text.

5. Click Yes to enable digest authentication.

   Digest Authentication is now enabled in the Authentication Methods dialog box, as shown in Figure 12.8.

Figure 12.8   Digest authentication is enabled

6. Click OK to close the Authentication Methods dialog box.

7. Click OK to close the Properties dialog box.

   You have now enabled digest authentication.

▶ **To configure basic authentication**

1. In the Internet Information Services management console, select Default Web Site in the console tree, and choose Properties from the Action menu.

2. Click the Directory Security tab.

3. Click Edit in the Anonymous Access And Authentication Control area to open the Authentication Methods dialog box.

4. Select the Basic Authentication option. A warning about plaintext passwords is displayed, as shown in Figure 12.9.

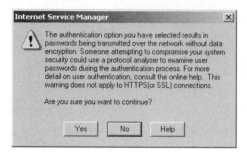

Figure 12.9   Enabling basic authentication

5. Click Yes to continue.

6. Click Edit next to the Basic Authentication check box. The Basic Authentication Domain dialog box is displayed, as shown in Figure 12.10.

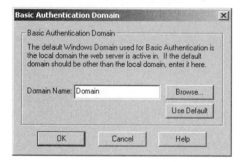

Figure 12.10   Selecting a basic authentication domain

7. Type **Domain** in the Domain Name box, and click OK.

8. Click OK to close the Authentication Methods dialog box.

9. Click OK to close the Properties dialog box.

Important   You have now enabled basic authentication. If you are using a public server, you should disable basic authentication and digest authentication unless clients require them.

Lesson Review

The following questions are intended to reinforce key information in this lesson. If you are unable to answer a question, review the lesson and try the question again. Answers to the questions can be found in the appendix.

1. Which are the two least secure authentication methods?

2. Which authentication method uses Windows user accounts?

3. Which authentication method supports client and server certificates?

4. Which dialog box includes options to enable authentication methods and anonymous access?

5. For which IIS resources can you select authentication methods?

Lesson Summary

- You can configure anonymous access to a Web site. IIS uses a user account to access resources requested by anonymous users. You can change the user account or use different accounts for different resources, and manage the files the accounts can access with NTFS permissions.

- Basic authentication is an HTTP 1.0 standard for simple authentication. It sends plaintext passwords over the network and is vulnerable to network interception, so it should be used only when security needs are minimal.

- Digest authentication is an HTTP 1.1 standard that uses a one-way encryption to authenticate a user name and password. Because the password is not sent directly over the network, it is more secure than basic authentication, but it requires the storage of plaintext passwords.

- Integrated Windows authentication uses domain user names and passwords to authenticate users. For users using Internet Explorer 2.0 or later on Windows clients logged on to the domain, Integrated Windows authentication does not prompt for a user name and password.

- You can enable and configure these authentication methods using the Authentication Methods properties, available from the Directory Security tab in the Properties dialog box for a Web site or virtual directory.

Lesson 3: Using Secure Sockets Layer

While authentication methods like Integrated Windows authentication can reliably provide access to a page only to authorized users, the information sent between the client and server after authentication is still sent in plaintext in an easily intercepted form. IIS supports Secure Sockets Layer (SSL), a standard for encryption of data over an HTTP connection. SSL can authenticate the server with a certificate and encrypt the data sent in both directions, and it also supports optional client certificates for user authentication.

After this lesson, you will be able to

- Understand SSL and its support in IIS
- Obtain, install, and renew SSL certificates
- Configure SSL encryption and authentication

Estimated lesson time: 30 minutes

Understanding SSL

SSL uses a public-key encryption system, described in Chapter 5, "Certificate Authorities," to transmit encryption keys over the network and establish a secure connection. SSL is often used on Web sites when dealing with confidential information, such as credit card transactions.

SSL uses a 40-bit encryption key by default. Because 40-bit security is no longer considered secure, you should enable 128-bit encryption keys. This requires that browsers support 128-bit encryption. Encryption laws have recently been relaxed, allowing 128-bit encryption to be exported widely. Most current versions of Web browsers now support 128-bit encryption by default.

Obtaining and Installing SSL Certificates

Before you can enable SSL in IIS, you must request and install an SSL certificate. You can obtain an SSL certificate from a certificate authority (CA), either a CA within a private network or an external trusted CA. The Internet Information Services management console includes a wizard that can package a certificate request and send it to a CA to be signed.

Caution   If you install a certificate from your own CA, users who do not have your CA in their certificate trust lists will receive a warning message when they connect to your site. To proceed, they will be required to click the Accept button to indicate they trust your certificate. This process can be very confusing to public Internet users. Consider obtaining a Web server certificate from a commercial root CA to avoid interrupting users with this message.

Installing Server Certificates

If you have an online CA, you can request, obtain, and install a server certificate from the IIS Certificate Wizard. To start this wizard, open the Properties dialog box for a Web site, folder, or virtual directory. Click the Directory Security tab, and click the Server Certificate button. The wizard includes three main functions:

- Create A New Certificate
- Assign An Existing Certificate
- Import A Certificate From A Key Manager Backup File

Select the Create A New Certificate option to request a new certificate. You can then choose to prepare a request to be sent later if you are sending the request to a third party, or to send the request immediately if you're transmitting it to a CA that you control. If you send the request immediately, you are prompted for the CA that you want to send the request to.

To obtain a certificate, you will need to specify information that will be stored in the certificate about the site. This includes a site name, organization, organizational unit, domain name, and geographical location information. If any of this information changes later, you will need to request a new certificate.

Requesting Certificates from an External CA

If you are requesting a certificate from a third-party CA, you usually need to save the request as a text file and send it to the CA. To do this, select the Prepare The Request Now, But Send It Later option in the IIS Certificate Wizard. You are prompted for the same information as when requesting from an online CA, and the request is saved to the text file you specify. You can then forward this request file to the Certificate Authority using e-mail or however else the CA tells you to send it.

Once you have received the certificate from the CA, you can install it from the IIS Certificate Wizard. Select the Process The Pending Request And Install The Certificate option, and then locate the CA response, which should be saved in a file with the .cer extension. The certificate is then installed for the site.

Important   Be sure to install the certificate for the same site you used when requesting it. Otherwise the certificate will not be valid.

Managing Server Certificates

Once you have installed a server certificate, you need to configure the SSL settings correctly to require SSL for access. You can also view the contents of a certificate or renew an existing certificate.

Configuring SSL Options

To edit SSL options, open the Properties dialog box for a site or virtual directory. Click the Directory Security tab, and click Edit in the Secure Communications area. The first option in the Secure Communications dialog box allows you to require SSL communications for the site. You can also require 128-bit encryption, although it might not be supported by all clients.

This dialog box also includes options to enable client certificates, client certificate mapping, and certificate trust lists. These are described later in this lesson.

When you have configured the server to require SSL, clients must use *https:* instead of *http:* in URLs to access the server, and each client must support SSL at the level of encryption you have specified.

Viewing Certificate Details

You can view three types of information about any installed server certificate:

- To view *basic certificate information*, click the View Certificate button on the Directory Security tab in the Properties dialog box. The basic certificate information includes the purpose of the certificate, the server it was issued to, the issuing CA, the dates the certificate is valid, and whether it includes a private key.
- To view more *details* about the certificate, click the Details tab. The details include serial number, the algorithm the CA used to sign the certificate, the bit length, and other attributes.
- To view the *chain of authority* for the certificate, click the Certification Path tab. You can select a CA in the list and click the View Certificate button to view other certificates. The bottom portion of the dialog box displays a brief status message indicating whether the certificate has any errors, such as its being expired.

Renewing or Removing Certificates

If you click Server Certificate to launch the IIS Certificate Wizard after an existing certificate is installed, the wizard includes an option to renew the certificate, remove it from the server, or replace it with a new certificate.

If you choose to renew the certificate, you are prompted to confirm the identification information. As with creating a certificate, you can either renew directly using an online CA or package a request to send to an external authority.

Authenticating Clients

You can also use SSL to authenticate clients. When SSL is used, you can enable or require client certificates that provide proof of identity for the clients. To use the client certificate features, you must first install a server certificate as described earlier in this lesson.

By using certificates to authenticate clients, you can allow large groups of users to access your system by trusting a root CA that they trust, and mapping those users to a single account based on the trusted root CA. For example, you could have all employees of a specific client mapped to a single trusted certificate and Web account, and manage their permissions on your site using that user account. This is why certificate-based authentication is the best option for extranet users.

Enabling Client Certificates

To enable client certificates, open the Properties dialog box for a Web site or virtual directory, and click the Directory Security tab. Click Edit in the Secure Communications area to open the Secure Communications dialog box. This dialog box allows you to select one of these Client Certificates options:

- **Ignore Client Certificates.**   Client certificates are not used.
- **Accept Client Certificates.**   A client certificate is used if the client has one, but the certificate is not required for access.
- **Require Client Certificates.**   A valid client certificate is required for access to the site. To use this option, you must enable the Require SSL option.

Installing a Client Certificate

When the server is configured to accept or require client certificates, you can install a client certificate on a browser. If you have a local Windows 2000 Server CA, you can do this by accessing the Certificate Services URL *http://computername/certsrv*.

From the Certificate Services page, you can request a certificate—this is a simple process. After the certificate is received from the CA, you can automatically install it on the browser.

Managing Client Certificate Settings

To configure client certificates in Internet Explorer, choose Internet Options from the Tools menu, click the Content tab, and then click Certificates. The Certificates dialog box displays a list of certificates installed on the local computer. You can filter the dialog box by the intended purpose of the certificates. For example, to view only Web client certificates, select Client Authentication from the Intended Purpose list.

To export a certificate to a file, select a certificate in the Certificates dialog box and click Export. You can use this feature with client certificate mapping, described in the next section.

Important   Internet Explorer can export certificates in several formats. To create exported certificates that can be used with IIS for client certificate mapping, select the Base-64 encoded X.509 format. (IIS might not recognize other formats as valid.)

Using Client Certificate Mapping

While client certificates serve to verify the identity of users, requiring client certificates does not restrict access to authorized users. Any user with a client certificate can access the site. You can use the client certificate-mapping feature to map their certificates to user accounts, and then use those user accounts to restrict access to resources based on their identity.

Client certificate mapping creates an association from client certificates to Windows user accounts. You can do this in one of two ways:

- **One-to-one mapping.**   Maps individual certificates to individual user accounts. Import each client certificate and choose a user account to associate it with.
- **Many-to-one mapping.**   Configures a list of rules for certificates to match. Each rule includes a user account and password that will be used with certificates that match its conditions.

To enable client certificate mapping, select the Enable Client Certificate Mapping check box in the Secure Communications dialog box. You can then use the corresponding Edit button to open the Account Mappings dialog box and create mappings. The Account Mappings dialog box includes tabbed sections for one-to-one and many-to-one mappings.

Note   To create one-to-one mappings, you need an exported copy of each client certificate.

Using a Certificate Trust List

Along with mapping certificates to user accounts, you can configure a list of trusted certification authorities called a *certificate trust list* (CTL). If a client connects to the site and has a client certificate signed by one of the CAs listed in the CTL, it is allowed access. Clients with a certificate that does not match a trusted authority will not be allowed to access the site if the Require Client Certificates option is enabled.

To enable CTLs, open the Properties dialog box for a Web site and click the Directory Security tab. Click Edit in the Secure Communications area to open the Secure Communications dialog box, and then select the Enable Certificate Trust List check box. You can then click New to create a new CTL or click Edit to edit the current CTL.

When you create a new CTL, the Certificate Trust List Wizard prompts you for certificates that should be trusted. You can add certificates to this list from the local certificate store or from an imported certificate file.

Practice: Using SSL

In this practice, you will request, obtain, and install a server certificate on an IIS server, view SSL certificate information, renew a certificate, and manage client SSL settings. You will need access to a standalone or enterprise CA, as configured in Chapter 5, "Certificate Authorities."

Exercise 1: Configuring SSL in IIS

In this exercise, you obtain and install an SSL server certificate for IIS, view the information stored in the certificate, and renew the certificate.

▶ **To obtain and install an SSL certificate**

1. In the Internet Information Services management console, select Default Web Site in the console tree.
2. From the Action menu, choose Properties. The Web Site Properties dialog box appears.
3. Click the Directory Security tab.
4. In the Secure Communications area of the dialog box, click Server Certificate. The IIS Certificate Wizard opens and displays an introductory page.
5. Click Next to continue. The Server Certificate page appears, as shown in Figure 12.11.

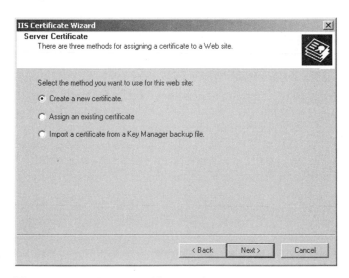

Figure 12.11   Server Certificate options

6. Select Create A New Certificate, and click Next. The Delayed Or Immediate Request page appears, as shown in Figure 12.12. You can either send the request to the CA immediately or send the request later.

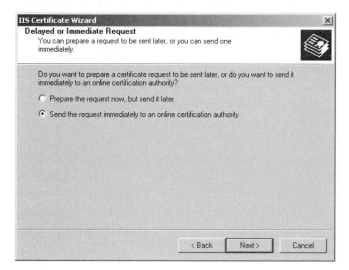

Figure 12.12   Selecting a delayed or an immediate request

7. Select Send The Request Immediately To An Online Certification Authority, and click Next. The Name And Security Settings page appears, as shown in Figure 12.13.

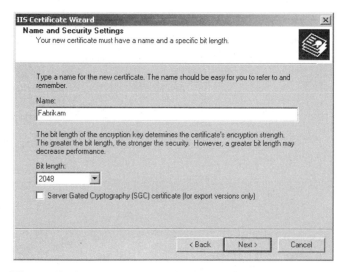

Figure 12.13   Name and security settings for a certificate

8. Type **Fabrikam** in the Name box.

9. Select 2048 for the Bit Length, and click Next. The Organization Information page appears, as shown in Figure 12.14.

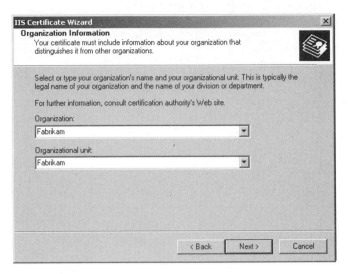

Figure 12.14   The Organization Information page

10. Type **Fabrikam** in both the Organization and Organizational Unit boxes, and click Next.

11. On the Your Site's Common Name page, type **DC01** in the Common Name box, and click Next. The Geographical Information page appears, as shown in Figure 12.15.

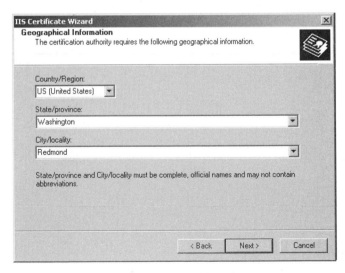

Figure 12.15   The Geographical Information page

12. Select US (United States) from the Country/Region list.

13. Type **Washington** in the State/Province box and **Redmond** in the City/Locality box.

14. Click Next to continue. You are prompted to choose a Certification Authority.

15. Select dc01.domain.fabrikam.com\Fabrikam Enterprise Root Certifier from the list, and click Next. A summary of the certificate to be requested is displayed, as shown in Figure 12.16.

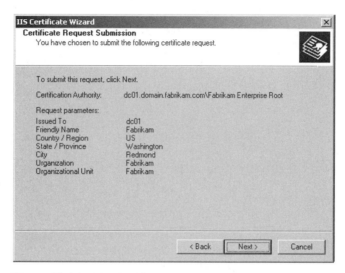

Figure 12.16   The Certificate Request Submission summary page.

16. On the Certificate Request Submission page, click Next to request the certificate. A message appears indicating the request completed successfully.

17. Click Finish to exit the IIS Certificate Wizard.

You have now installed an IIS certificate for the Web site.

▶   **To view SSL certificate information**

1. In the Internet Information Services management console, select Default Web Site in the console tree.

2. From the Action menu, choose Properties.

3. Click the Directory Security tab.

4. In the Secure Communications area of the dialog box, click View Certificate. The Certificate properties dialog box appears.

5. Click the Details tab to view a detailed list of certificate information, as shown in Figure 12.17.

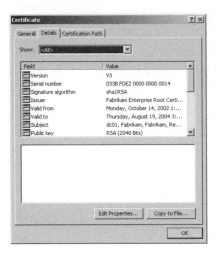

Figure 12.17   Certificate details

6. Click the Certification Path tab to view a path diagram that shows the root CA.

7. Click OK to close the Certificate properties dialog box.

8. Click OK to close the Web Site Properties dialog box.

▶ **To renew an SSL certificate**

1. In the Internet Information Services management console, select Default Web Site in the console tree.

2. From the Action menu, choose Properties.

3. Click the Directory Security tab.

4. Under Secure Communications, click Server Certificate. The IIS Certificate Wizard displays an introductory message.

5. Click Next to continue. The certificate assignment options are displayed, as shown in Figure 12.18.

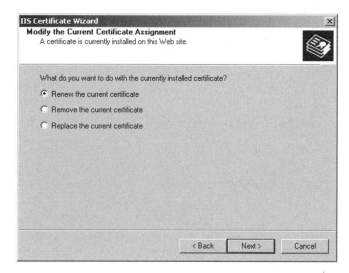

Figure 12.18   The Modify The Current Certificate Assignment page

6. On the Modify The Current Certificate Assignment page, select Renew The Current Certificate, and click Next. The Delayed Or Immediate Request page appears.

7. Select Send The Request Immediately To An Online Certification Authority, and click Next.

8. On the Choose A Certificate Authority page, select dc01.domain.fabrikam.com\Fabrikam Enterprise Root Certifier from the Certification Authorities drop-down list, and click Next. A summary of the renewal information to be sent is displayed.

9. On the Certificate Request Submission page, click Next to request the renewal.

10. Click Finish to close the wizard, and then click OK to close the Properties dialog box.

The certificate is now renewed.

▶ **To enable SSL security**

1. In the Internet Information Services management console, select Default Web Site in the console tree.

2. From the Action menu, choose Properties.

3. Click the Directory Security tab.

4. In the Secure Communications area of the dialog box, click Edit. The Secure Communications dialog box appears, as shown in Figure 12.19.

Figure 12.19   The Secure Communications options

5. Select the Require Secure Channel (SSL) check box, and click OK.

6. Click OK to close the Properties dialog box.

Important   SSL is now required for access to the site. Only browsers that support SSL connections can be used.

Exercise 2: Using Client Certificates

In this exercise, you configure IIS to enable client certificates and you install a client certificate in Internet Explorer.

▶ **To install a client certificate**

Perform this procedure from a Windows 2000 or Windows XP client logged on to the domain.

1. In Internet Explorer, browse to *https://dc01/certsrv/*. The Microsoft Certificate Services Welcome page appears, as shown in Figure 12.20.

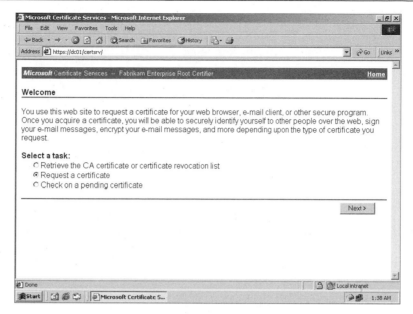

Figure 12.20   The Microsoft Certificate Services Web site

2. Select Request A Certificate, and click Next. The Choose Request Type page appears, as shown in Figure 12.21.

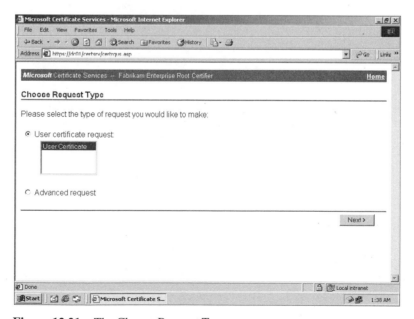

Figure 12.21   The Choose Request Type page

3. Select User Certificate, and click Next.

4. On the User Certificate – Identifying Information page, click Submit to request the certificate. The request is sent to the server.

   After the certificate is issued, the Certificate Issued page appears.

5. Click the Install This Certificate link to install the certificate on the browser.

   The certificate has now been installed.

▶ **To view client certificate settings**

Perform this procedure from the client using Internet Explorer.

1. From the Tools menu of Internet Explorer, choose Internet Options.
   The Internet Options dialog box opens.

2. Click the Content tab. The Content options are displayed, as shown in Figure 12.22.

Figure 12.22   The Content tab of the Internet Options dialog box

3. On the Content tab, click Certificates to open the Certificates dialog box.

4. Select Client Authentication in the Intended Purpose drop-down list. The installed client certificate is listed, as shown in Figure 12.23.

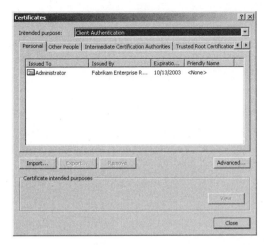

Figure 12.23   Client certificates

5. Select the certificate from the list, and click View. The Certificate dialog box appears.

6. Click OK to close the Certificate dialog box.

7. Click Close to close the Certificates dialog box.

8. Click OK to close the Internet Options dialog box.

   Basic information about the certificate is displayed. You can select the Details and Certification Path tabs of this dialog box to display additional information.

▶ **To enable client certificates**

Perform this procedure from the IIS server.

1. In the Internet Information Services management console, select Default Web Site in the console tree.

2. From the Action menu, choose Properties.

3. Click the Directory Security tab.

4. In the Secure Communications area of the dialog box, click Edit. The Secure Communications dialog box appears.

5. Select the Require Secure Channel (SSL) check box and the Require Client Certificates option. Client certificates are now enabled, as shown in Figure 12.24.

Figure 12.24   Enabling client certificates

6. Click OK.

7. Click OK to close the Properties dialog box.

Important   Client certificates are now required to access the site. You must install a client certificate, as described in the previous sections, to test the site.

▶ **To export a client certificate**

Perform this procedure from the client using Internet Explorer.

1. In Internet Explorer, choose Internet Options from the Tools menu. The Internet Options dialog box opens.

2. Select the Content tab, and then click Certificates. The Certificates dialog box appears.

3. Select Client Authentication in the Intended Purpose drop-down list. The installed client certificates are listed.

4. Select the certificate from the list, and click Export. The Certificate Export Wizard displays an introductory page.

5. Click Next to continue.

You are asked whether to export the private key, as shown in Figure 12.25. Because this certificate's key cannot be exported, the No option is selected.

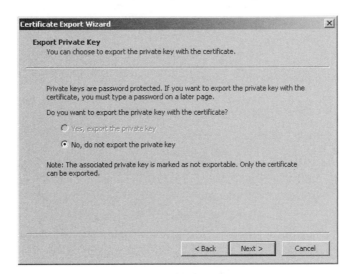

Figure 12.25   The Export Private Key page

6. On the Export Private Key page, click Next to continue. The Export File Format page appears, as shown in Figure 12.26.

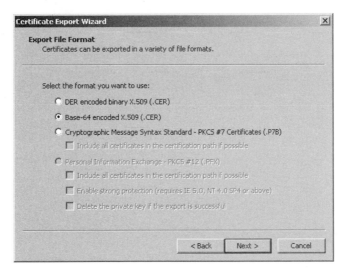

Figure 12.26   The Export File Format page

7. On the Export File Format page, select Base-64 Encoded X.509, and click Next. You are prompted for a file name for the exported certificate.

8. On File To Export page, type **c:\user.cer** in the file name box, and click Next. The Completing The Certificate Export Wizard page appears.

9. Click Finish to export the file. A message informs you that the export was successful.

10. Click Close to close the Certificates dialog box, and click OK to close the Internet Options dialog box.

▶ **To create a one-to-one client certificate mapping**

Perform this procedure from the IIS server. You will need access to the User.cer file that you exported in the previous procedure.

1. In the Internet Information Services management console, select Default Web Site from console tree.

2. From the Action menu, choose Properties.

3. Select the Directory Security tab. The Directory Security options are displayed.

4. In the Secure Communications area of the tab, click Edit. The Secure Communications dialog box appears.

5. In the Secure Communications dialog box, select the Enable Client Certificate Mapping check box.

6. Click Edit. The Account Mappings dialog box appears, as shown in Figure 12.27.

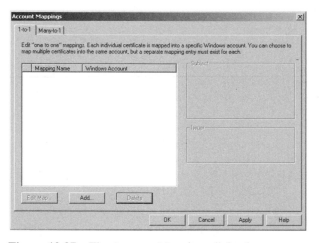

Figure 12.27   The Account Mappings dialog box

7. Click Add to add a one-to-one account mapping. The Open dialog box appears.

8. In the Open dialog box, select the User.cer file you exported in the previous procedure, and click Open. The Map To Account dialog box appears, as shown in Figure 12.28.

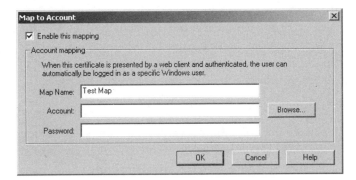

Figure 12.28   The Map To Account dialog box

9. Type **Test Map** in the Map Namc box.

10. Click Browse. The Choose Mapping Account dialog box lists the domain users, as shown in Figure 12.29.

Figure 12.29   A list of available user accounts for the mapping

11. In the Choose Mapping Account dialog box, select user packerman from the list, and click Add.

12. Click OK to return to the Map To Account dialog box.

13. Specify the password for user packerman, and click OK. The Confirm Password dialog box appears.

14. Type the password again and click OK. The new mapping has been added.

15. Click OK to close the Account Mappings dialog box.

16. Click OK to close the Secure Communications dialog box.

17. Click OK to close the Properties dialog box.

▶ **To create a many-to-one client certificate mapping**

Perform this procedure from the IIS server.

1. In the Internet Information Services management console, select Default Web Site in the console tree.

2. From the Action menu, choose Properties.

3. Click the Directory Security tab. The Directory Security options are displayed.

4. Click Edit in the Secure Communications area of the dialog box. The Secure Communications dialog box appears.

5. Click Edit next to the Enable Client Certificate Mapping check box. The Account Mappings dialog box appears.

6. Click the Many-To-1 tab. The current many-to-one mappings are displayed.

7. Make sure the Enable Wildcard Client Certificate Matching check box is selected, and click Add. As shown in Figure 12.30, the General dialog box appears in which you can describe the rule.

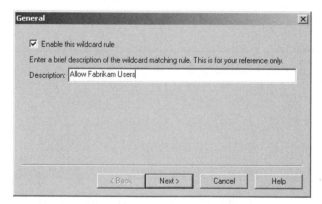

Figure 12.30   Providing a description for a new rule

8. In the General dialog box, type **Allow Fabrikam Users** in the Description box, and click Next. The Rules dialog box appears.

9. In the Rules dialog box, click New to add a match criterion. The Edit Rule Element dialog box appears, as shown in Figure 12.31.

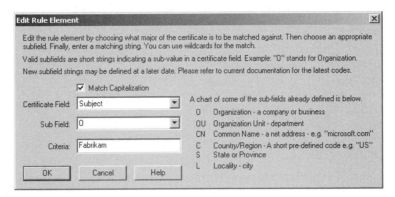

Figure 12.31   Specifying a new rule element

10. Type **Fabrikam** in the Criteria box, and click OK. You are returned to the Rules dialog box.

11. In the Rules dialog box, click Next. As shown in Figure 12.32, you are prompted to indicate whether you want the user account to be granted or denied access to the Web site based on the criteria you've established.

Figure 12.32   Specifying a user account and action

12. In the Mapping dialog box, ensure that Accept This Certificate For Logon Authentication is selected.

13. Click Browse. A list of domain users is displayed in the Choose Mapping Account dialog box.

14. In the Mapping Account dialog box, select the Guest account from the list, click Add, and then click OK.

15. In the Mapping dialog box, click Finish to complete the mapping.
16. Click OK to close the Account Mappings dialog box.
17. Click OK to close the Secure Communications dialog box.
18. Click OK to close the Properties dialog box.

This enables access for users with Fabrikam in the organization box of their client certificate.

▶ **To configure a certificate trust list**

Perform this procedure from the IIS server.

1. In the Internet Information Services management console, select Default Web Site in the console tree.
2. From the Action menu, choose Properties.
3. Click the Directory Security tab. The Directory Security options are displayed.
4. Click Edit in the Secure Communications area of the dialog box. The Secure Communications dialog box appears.
5. Select the Enable Certificate Trust List check box.
6. Click New next to the Enable Certificate Trust List check box. The Certificate Trust List Wizard displays an introductory page.
7. Click Next to continue. A blank list of trusted certificates appears, as shown in Figure 12.33.

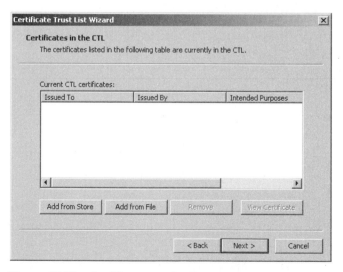

Figure 12.33   Certificates In The CTL page

8. On the Certificates In The CTL page, click Add From Store. The Select Certificate dialog box lists certificates in the server's store, as shown in Figure 12.34.

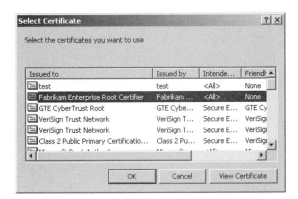

Figure 12.34   The Select Certificate dialog box

9. In the Select Certificate dialog box, select Fabrikam Enterprise Root Certifier, and click OK.

10. On the Certificates In The CTL page, click Next. You are prompted for a name and description for the CTL.

11. On the Name And Description page, type **Fabrikam** in the Friendly Name box, and click Next. The Completing The Certificate Trust List Wizard page appears.

12. Click Finish to save the CTL. A message box indicates that the wizard succeeded.

13. Click OK to close the Secure Communications dialog box.

14. Click OK to close the Properties dialog box.

Lesson Review

The following questions are intended to reinforce key information in this lesson. If you are unable to answer a question, review the lesson and try the question again. Answers to the questions can be found in the appendix.

1. What is required to enable SSL on an IIS server?

2. Which feature allows you to connect user accounts with particular client certificates?

3. When a CTL is in use, which clients are allowed access?

4. Which option do you enable to prevent clients from accessing a site without a client certificate?

5. What are the two types of client certificate mapping?

Lesson Summary

■ SSL (Secure Sockets Layer) is a standard protocol for encrypting communications between Web servers and clients using certificates issued by a certification authority. SSL can also authenticate the server's identity and authenticate clients using client certificates.

■ SSL requires a server certificate installed for the Web site on the IIS server. You can request a certificate from a local CA, or save the request to a file to be sent to an external CA.

■ Client certificates authenticate the identity of Web users. You can either optionally accept client certificates or require them. Each client must request a certificate and install it in their browser. Client certificates can also be mapped to Windows user accounts.

■ You can use a certificate trust list (CTL) to list trusted certification authorities. Clients that have certificates issued by one of the authorities in the CTL will be allowed access to the site.

C H A P T E R   1 3

Intrusion Detection and Event Monitoring

About This Chapter

Regardless of the security of your network, attacks can and do occur. These events range from malicious intrusions to denial of service attacks that inhibit your Internet servers. To respond to these events quickly, you must detect them by closely monitoring event and audit logs. In this chapter, you look at strategies for detecting network intrusions and methods of using event-monitoring features in Microsoft Windows 2000.

Before You Begin

To complete this chapter, you must have

- A domain controller for the domain.fabrikam.com domain
- A member workstation in the domain
- A workstation in the domain

Lesson 1: Establishing Intrusion Detection for Public Servers

The most vulnerable servers on your network provide Internet services, such as Web services and e-mail. To defend against intrusion into these servers, you must be aware of attacks as they occur. In this lesson, you examine the kinds of intrusion incidents you can expect to encounter on public servers, and how to detect them.

To complete this lesson, you will need

- A domain controller for the domain.fabrikam.com domain
- A Microsoft Windows 2000 Server computer to act as a decoy server

After this lesson, you will be able to

- Understand the concept of intrusion detection
- Configure Windows 2000 for strong auditing
- Configure Microsoft Internet Security and Acceleration Server (ISA Server) to forward unused services to a decoy

Estimated lesson time: 45 minutes

Common Network Intrusions

Attackers who attempt to gain access to your network without knowledge of your network architecture use a standard sequence of attacks. They start with information gathering, then attempt to exploit known vulnerabilities, and finally move on to more difficult to perpetrate impersonation attacks, which involve attempting to take on the identify of a valid user by guessing or stealing an account name and password, stealing a smart card, or appropriating a certificate.

To gain information about your organization and your public targets, most hackers who attempt a sequence of attacks against a network will

- Check your public DNS records to determine the IP addresses of your Internet servers.
- Use port scanners to scan your Internet servers and identify the services you are running.
- Probe all services found to determine which set of vulnerability attacks to use against these services.

Once they've obtained this information, they will

- Send attacks that exploit known bugs in common services to attempt to gain remote administrative access. These attacks typically send executable code along with malformed message syntax designed to execute the sent code.
- Attempt brute-force impersonation attacks.
- Perform various denial of service (DoS) attacks if they have been unable to gain access.

Knowing how hackers work is the first step towards detecting and stopping their attacks. When you understand the basic process that hackers use to attack your network, you will be able to differentiate their patterns of usage from the patterns of regular users.

Detecting Network Intrusions

Intrusion detection is the methodical process of searching for signs that hackers have attacked your network. Just as there are numerous methods for attacking a computer, there are many ways to detect attacks.

Detecting Denial of Service Attacks

Although *denial of service* (DoS) attacks aren't really intrusions, detecting them is still considered to be intrusion detection. While you might be able to detect some types of DoS attacks by examining event logs or real-time status of the performance monitor in Windows 2000, you won't be able to detect the majority of DoS attacks. Reliably detecting DoS attacks requires intrusion detection software, because Windows 2000 doesn't log every processing action that occurs so it can't match actions to specific known attacks.

To defend against DoS attacks, you use two methods: hardening the TCP/IP stack on the targeted server by implementing IP filters and opening only those ports that you need for the services, and filtering known DoS attacks with a firewall that can detect them. You should use both methods in tandem.

Any attacks that the firewall filters are attacks you don't have to consume server resources to defend against. But firewalls cannot filter all types of attacks; public servers need to be able to defend themselves against attacks that firewalls can't filter. For example, many firewalls can recognize and block synchronous idle character (SYN) floods originating from a single IP address, but if the source addresses have been randomized, there's no way to distinguish a SYN flood from a high volume of valid connections. There's certainly no way to determine which attempted connections are part of a malicious flood and which are valid users trying to reach a server.

Even if you could somehow filter out SYN floods that have random source addresses, you won't be able to defend against all types of DoS attacks, because clever DoS attacks come disguised as dramatic increases in valid traffic.

Consider what would happen if your Web site URL were posted on a very popular news outlet. If millions of readers were to click the link to your site, your Web server might not be able to service the majority of the requests. While not malicious, this certainly causes a DoS problem, which happens frequently when popular Web sites contain links to small sites. If a hacker included a link to your site on a popular Web site and misrepresented its contents to increase the appeal to the site's audience, the members of the audience would be unwitting participants in a malicious DoS attack that you would not be able to distinguish from a sudden enormous increase in traffic.

Detecting Vulnerability Attacks

Vulnerabilities are bugs in public services that hackers can exploit to cause some behavior that the software is not supposed to perform, such as crashing servers or gaining access to them as an administrator. Vulnerabilities exist in all software, but hackers concentrate on finding them in public services, such as those on Web and e-mail servers, that they can reach from the Internet.

It is not possible for a server to specifically detect vulnerability attacks. If the affected service could detect the problem, it would not be vulnerable to it.

Important   You will have no warning of effective vulnerability attacks and there is very little that you can do about them except to keep your security fixes up to date. The only other potential solution is to use a security proxy to scan the protocol for malformation before delivering it to the intended service, but there is no guarantee that proxies will detect the malformation that causes the vulnerability to be exposed.

However, attempted vulnerability attacks are sometimes recognizable as strange characters sent in a URL or in FTP upload file names that contain characters that are not valid. While the server might not recognize which bug the characters represent, it can be configured to drop connections that make suspicious-looking requests. This is exactly how the IIS Lockdown tool and the URLScan tool recognize malicious attempts to exploit Internet Information Services (IIS) Server and drop the connection before the attack can succeed. When properly configured, URLScan is able to prevent many of the attacks against IIS without being specific to the attack. You can find these tools at *http://www.microsoft.com/technet* by searching on their names.

Caution   Even though a tool like URLScan can protect an unpatched IIS server against vulnerabilities, you must keep your security fixes up to date. URLScan and similar tools can't guarantee effectiveness against all types of exploits in the future.

Detecting Impersonation Attacks

There is no way to detect a hacker who is logging on using a valid user account name and password. However, truly public servers should be configured to process only anonymous requests for public services. An attempt by a specific user to log on from the Internet could then be detected as an attack.

Tip   For services that necessitate a log on, such as Microsoft Outlook Web Access or extranet access, require Secure Sockets Layer (SSL) and certificate authentication to ensure that only valid users can connect to the public service. This prevents hackers from using brute-force attacks to determine account names and passwords and simplifies and automates authentication for valid users.

If an attacker authenticates against a machine that normally processes only anonymous requests by using a user account, the logon attempt can be logged, and the user's activity in the system can be tracked. By separating public systems into different domains or workgroups from those of the interior private systems, you can keep hackers from being able to use account names that are valid in the interior of your network to attack public servers.

Windows 2000 can detect all impersonation attacks if hackers do not know account passwords. Auditing logon events and configuring logon policy will log the occurrence of brute-force password-guessing attempts in the security event log and will stop most attacks—except against the administrator account, which cannot be locked out and should therefore be renamed.

Tip   Because brute-force attacks against the administrator account cannot be stopped, rename the administrator account to something that is not obvious, and create a new limited user account with the name "administrator." This way you can detect attempts to log on as administrator and lock the account after a few attempts. Remember that domain member servers have two administrator accounts— the domain administrator account and the local machine administrator account. Make sure you rename both the local administrator account on public servers and the domain administrator account for domains in which they are members.

Using a Decoy Server

Detecting intrusions into a Windows 2000 test machine is easy: you enable auditing to record every access of every account, file, object, and use of rights by every user account. Then monitor the security logs, and trigger an alert any time a file is accessed that isn't being explicitly served. Unfortunately, this level of auditing cannot be performed on a production server because the processing and logging overhead is extreme and would prevent the server from processing valid requests.

Detecting intrusion into a production Windows 2000 server is extremely difficult. All three types of attacks (exploiting vulnerabilities, impersonation, and DoS) can be crafted to simulate typical usage that cannot be distinguished from routine valid access, and busy production servers don't have the resources to enable the types of auditing that would be required to reliably detect intrusion.

The solution to this load problem is to use a decoy machine to detect intrusion and use a production machine to service valid requests. This can be accomplished using any modern firewall or security proxy to create a *decoy server*.

A decoy server (also called a *honeypot server*) is simply a server running an unsecured (or lightly secured) version of the same operating system as your production server. The theory is simple: all types of access are forwarded to the decoy except those that you want to serve publicly, which are forwarded to the actual server. To an outsider, the two machines look like a single machine, but all extraneous services go to the decoy rather than the real server.

Creating a decoy is simple, but it requires a firewall or a proxy server. On your firewall or security proxy, you can forward to this decoy machine the TCP ports of incidental services that you don't use but that are commonly available on unsecured servers. The decoy machine would be located in the DMZ but configured to block outbound connections. The point of this machine is to be attacked and exploited—and to alert you to any access at all. Simultaneously, you can use your firewall or security proxy to forward the TCP ports of your actual public services to your production machines in the perimeter network. Figure 13.1 shows how this configuration works.

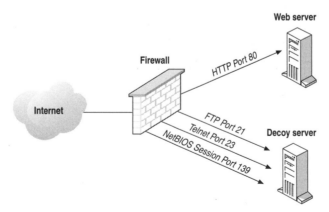

Figure 13.1   Using a decoy to detect intrusion

A hacker who scans your public IP addresses will see what appears to be a single unprotected server. The valid service port forwarded to the actual server will appear among all the service ports forwarded to the decoy server. Architecture probes that attempt to determine which operating system and types of services are running will reveal no difference between the machines because the decoy and the production server use the same operating system. Using common identification methods that are forwarded to the decoy, hackers are lured to the decoy server by easier exploits than those that can be perpetrated against your actual service ports. Because the decoy server alerts you to any access attempt, the intrusion attempt is revealed immediately.

Valid users of the public service will not reach the decoy server at all, and their requests will be processed with no additional overhead. The intensive auditing and intrusion processing on the decoy server do not affect the ability of valid servers to function and do not affect valid users.

The Psychology of Decoy Intrusion Detection

For a decoy to be effective, hackers must believe that the decoy is a valid server. This means that the combined list of ports from the decoy and the valid server should be similar to those a hacker would see when attacking a regular server. Most servers aren't completely unprotected, but they might have unprotected services that hackers can exploit. This means that you don't want your decoy servers to seem completely unprotected. However, you should add unprotected services that are forwarded to the decoy server to attract hackers away from attacking the valid service ports. For example, you might want to forward ports 135, 139, and 445 (which provide file sharing) to the decoy while forwarding port 80 to your valid Web server. Hackers who want to attack your Web server will be attracted to the file-sharing ports because they provide numerous ways for hackers to get in.

Hackers expect public servers to be protected by a firewall, so they will expect to see only those services that an administrator has explicitly made public, and they will expect ping responses to be blocked. What a hacker hopes to find is a protocol that administrators use for remote administration or to transfer files, such as FTP or the RDP protocol used by Terminal Services.

There are a number of services in Windows 2000 that are so tempting to hackers that the detection of their presence in a port scan invites attack. These services are almost certain to be attacked by any hacker who finds them, because they can provide easy administrative access if the administrator has not been careful. Commonly attacked ports include

- The NetBIOS session port (139)
- SMB over TCP port (445)

- FTP (21)
- Telnet (23)
- SMTP (25)
- POP3 (110)
- PPTP (1723)
- L2TP (1701)
- RDP (3389)

By configuring your decoy to alert you when these services are accessed, you'll catch any hackers who don't know you're running a decoy. Even if they know you are running a decoy, to avoid immediate detection, they would have to know which services are really serviced and which are trapped by the decoy, and they would not be able to run a port scan.

Clever administrators will even include an offline copy of their Web site host files on the decoy server, so the hackers will find what they expect to find if they are able to compromise the decoy system. This keeps the hackers online longer, lengthening the audit trail and creating a stronger body of evidence.

Determining Which Service Ports to Decoy

The best way to create a decoy is to mimic standard services on the server using standard services on the decoy. If you want to mimic an Exchange server, install Exchange on the decoy, along with other services that hackers like to exploit, such as IIS and Telnet. Then forward to the actual server only the mail service ports you need to use, and forward the remainder to the decoy.

Tip   It's common to decoy an e-mail server. But the only service port you need to make public for an Exchange server is port 25 SMTP. Hackers will expect to see POP3 and IMAP4 on a mail server as well, so you can forward those ports to the decoy.

If you use SSL to secure public services such as Web, POP3, and SMTP, you gain an additional decoy advantage: SSL secured services don't run on the same ports as their traditional counterparts, so you can forward the SSL ports to the real server and forward the non-secure ports to the decoy.

Determining Where to Place a Decoy in Your Network Architecture

The ideal place for a decoy server is on a network segment of its own, if you have a firewall that can support four zones (public, private, perimeter, and decoy). ISA Server can be configured to support four zones, but the configuration is very complex. The reason for this four-zone methodology is to prevent hackers from gaining a foothold inside your network once they exploit the decoy.

Important   Your network must block access from the decoy as if it were a hacker's machine, because the decoy is designed to be exploited.

To simplify configuration, reduce hardware costs, and remain compatible with firewalls that do not support additional network segments, you can place decoy servers in the perimeter network with public servers. If you do this, you should ensure that all of your public servers are configured to filter and drop packets from the decoy server and that your private-side firewall drops any packets from your decoy server.

Warning   You should never place decoy servers inside your private network, because an exploited decoy would allow hackers inside your network.

The Hole in Decoy Intrusion Detection

Decoy intrusion detection is not perfect. It cannot detect attacks against your valid services because it does not see them—those attacks are forwarded to your valid public servers. On the other hand, your public servers cannot be exploited using any protocol they do not specifically serve. If a server serves only Web pages, it can only be attacked by Web server–specific vulnerability and DoS attacks that are specific to HTTP. Everything else goes to the decoy.

This means that you must use a strong security proxy to scrub the protocols going to your public server, and you should use any additional security tools that will increase the security of your public services. The URLScan tool from Microsoft is an excellent example of this type of security tool—it allows you to block suspicious URLs and malformed HTTP requests, and it logs them so that you can preserve evidence of them. All of your public service protocols need to be hardened using similar tools. Once hackers find that they cannot exploit the public protocols, they'll move to other protocols that are actually served by your decoy, and you'll be alerted when they do.

Performing Event Analysis and Preserving Evidence

When all auditing measures are enabled, the security log creates a strong body of evidence. The complete set of events that occur during an attack is called an *audit trail*. By examining the audit trail, you can reconstruct the hacker's activities with a considerable degree of precision. Your study might reveal attacks you were not aware of, or actual statistics you can use to justify new security policies.

Planning   When you initially configure your decoy server, and before you deploy it, create an image of the configuration and store it offline. You will use this image to refresh the decoy after each time that it is exploited.

The key to discovering hacking methods and eventually holding hackers responsible for their actions is preserving evidence. To do this requires that you preserve the entire state of the decoy server's hard disk, by removing it at the time you stop the attack.

As soon as your decoy server alerts you to an attack in progress, watch the event logs and open the event monitor to reveal the attack as it progresses. Allow the hackers to continue working as long as you can be certain that they are not able to use the decoy system to perpetrate further attacks against your network.

When you are no longer comfortable allowing the hacker to continue, and before the hacker is able to begin destroying evidence to cover his tracks (such as by deleting event logs), power off the server (without a shutdown), remove the decoy's hard disk and replace it with a new disk containing a fresh image of the decoy server's operating system and configuration. Then configure your firewall to block the hacker's IP address before it reaches the decoy or any services on your network.

The removed drive can be retained and analyzed for evidence by booting it in a recovery machine that is not attached to any network. Retain the full audit logs, changed files, and copies of anything the hacker placed on the computer. This hard disk can be turned over to law enforcement officials or examined by computer forensics experts to determine as much as possible about the identity of the hacker.

Practice: Detecting Intruders

In this practice, you configure an ISA server to protect an Exchange server by using a decoy server. In this case, you configure the decoy to run Telnet and IIS, and forward all e-mail protocols to the decoy. You will use the ISA server and the Exchange server configured in Chapter 11, "Public Application Server Security," along with a decoy server installed in this chapter.

To perform this practice, you must start with a default installation of Windows 2000 including IIS named exchange01, without membership in the domain and with an IP address of 192.168.241.160. For the purpose of this exercise, you should consider the 10.0.0.0 network to be the public Internet and the 192.168.241 network to be the perimeter network to minimize the amount of configuration you need to perform on the existing ISA server. This configuration will have the effect of changing the ISA server's role from being the private-side firewall to being the public-side firewall, and placing the decoy server inside the perimeter network instead of the private network. In an actual deployment, you would configure your public-side firewall to forward ports to the decoy server using the firewall's management interface.

Exercise 1: Configuring a Decoy Server

In this exercise, you create a decoy server to attract traffic destined for an interior server. The decoy will be configured to retain security log information until the log is cleared manually, and to shut down if the security log becomes full. This guarantees that the decoy server will shut down under a sustained attack, which will alert you to the attack in progress.

▶ **To configure an ISA server to forward ports to a decoy**

1. Log on to the ISA server as the administrator.
2. Click Start, point to Programs, point to Microsoft ISA Server, and click ISA Management. The ISA Management console appears.
3. Expand Servers And Arrays, ISA, Publishing, and then click Web Publishing Rules, as shown in Figure 13.2.

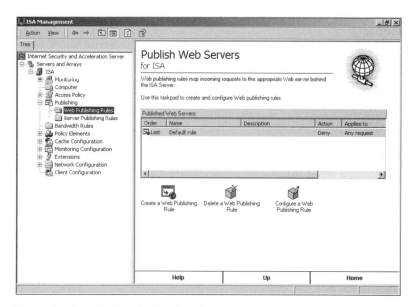

Figure 13.2   ISA Web Publishing Rules

4. Click the Create A Web Publishing Rule icon. The New Web Publishing Rule Wizard appears.

5. Type **Decoy Server** in the Server Publishing Rules Name box, and click Next. The Destination Sets page appears.

6. Select All Destinations, and click Next. The Client Type page appears.

7. Select Any Request, and click Next. The Rule Action page appears, as shown in Figure 13.3.

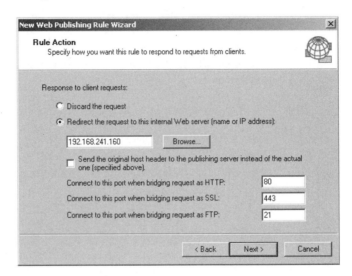

Figure 13.3   The Rule Action page

8. Select Redirect The Request To This Internal Web Server.

9. Type **192.168.241.160** in the IP address box, and click Next.

10. Click Finish to close the New Web Publishing Rule Wizard.

11. Close the management console, and restart the server.

▶   **To configure a decoy for audits and alerts**

1. Log on to the decoy server as the administrator.

2. Click Start, point to Programs, point to Administrative Tools, and click Local Security Policy. The Local Security Settings management console appears.

3. Expand Security Settings, Local Policies, and click Audit Policy. The Local Security Settings management console appears, as shown in Figure 13.4.

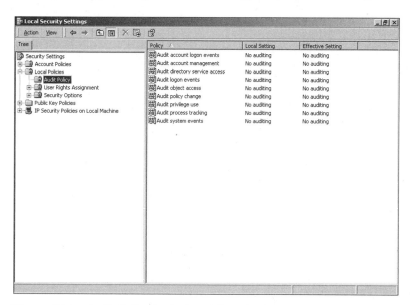

Figure 13.4   Audit Policy in the Local Security Settings management console

4. Double-click Audit Account Logon Events. The Local Security Policy Setting dialog box appears.

5. Select Success, and select Failure in the Audit These Attempts group, and then click OK.

6. Repeat steps 4 and 5 for each of the policies listed.

7. Select Security Options in the console tree.

8. Double-click Shut Down System Immediately If Unable To Log Security Events. The Local Security Policy Setting dialog box appears, as shown in Figure 13.5.

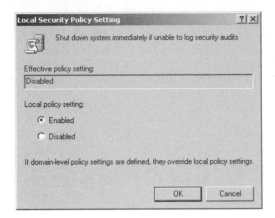

Figure 13.5   Local Security Policy Setting dialog box

9. Select Enabled, and click OK to close the dialog box.

10. Close the Local Security Settings management console.

▶ **To manage log retention for the decoy**

1. Click Start, point to Programs, point to Administrative Tools, and click Event Viewer. The Event Viewer appears, as shown in Figure 13.6.

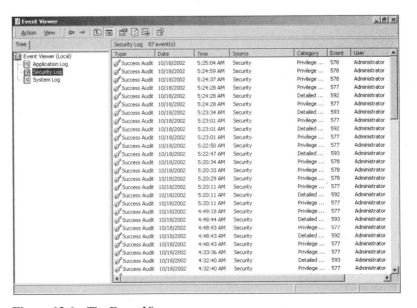

Figure 13.6   The Event Viewer

2. Right-click Security Log, and click Properties. The Security Log Properties dialog box appears as shown in Figure 13.7.

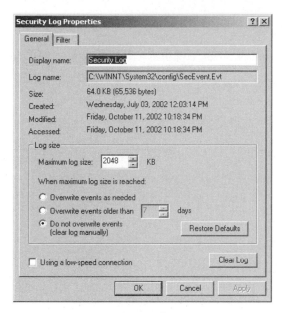

Figure 13.7   The Security Log Properties dialog box

3. Select Do Not Overwrite Events (Clear Log Manually).
4. Type **2048** in the Maximum Log Size box.
5. Click OK to close the Security Log Properties dialog box.
6. Close the Event Viewer.

Lesson Review

The following questions are intended to reinforce key information in this lesson. If you are unable to answer a question, review the lesson and try the question again. Answers to the questions can be found in the appendix.

1. Which type of attack attempts to log on with a user's password?

2. What type of attacks cannot be detected using a decoy server?

3. What is the purpose of saving event logs after an attack?

4. Where in the network should a decoy server be placed?

5. What tool recognizes intrusion attempts through URLs on a Web server?

Lesson Summary

- Denial of service (DoS) attacks attempt to slow down, stop, or damage a server, usually by overloading it with requests. Some DoS attacks cannot be detected until service is disrupted. You can prevent most of them by keeping software up to date, hardening the TCP/IP stack on the server, and using a firewall to detect known types of attacks.

- Vulnerability attacks take advantage of vulnerabilities in the operating system or software services. New exploits might be impossible to detect, but known exploits can be prevented by installing security fixes. Tools like URLScan can recognize suspicious requests that might indicate this type of attack.

- Impersonation attacks attempt to access the system using a valid user's password. The Windows 2000 password policy and auditing features can detect and prevent attempts to guess passwords. If an attacker knows a user's password, it might be impossible to distinguish the attacker from the actual user.

- You can use a decoy server to detect intrusion attempts. This tactic provides services strictly for the purpose of logging intrusion attempts, using a server that can be easily replaced and that contains no important data. This tactic can also help you to both detect attacks early and preserve evidence when they do occur.

Lesson 2: Event Monitoring in the Private Network

Security breaches are just as likely to come from users with valid credentials as they are to come from hackers, but the effects of security breaches by insiders can be far more serious. Users have wide access to the network and they know exactly where valuable information is stored.

Because insider security breaches can be so serious, you must preserve the event logs, which document these breaches. This lesson shows you how to preserve event logs as evidence in case of a serious breach of security by internal users. It also shows you how to search through event logs across your network for security breaches. To complete this lesson, you need a domain controller for the domain.fabrikam.com domain.

Exam Tip   Be certain you understand how to detect internal security violations and how to preserve evidence when security events occur.

After this lesson, you will be able to
- Manage event log retention to preserve evidence
- Configure auditing to detect internal security breaches
- Search for security events across a number of servers simultaneously

Estimated lesson time: 30 minutes

Establishing Intrusion Detection in Private Networks

Intrusion detection in private networks is performed through strong auditing. By enabling auditing for files and objects that are critical to security, you can track exactly which users have accessed sensitive objects and in what manner.

The major difference between anonymous hacking from the Internet and abuse by valid users is that you can easily determine the identity of valid users and hold them legally accountable for their behavior.

Intrusion detection in production private computers is simpler but less effective than intrusion detection in public sites. Internal users won't be fooled by decoys—they know the network architecture. They also have no need for the signature attacks like port scanners used by hackers, because they know exactly where servers are and what they service. In Chapter 3, "Restricting Accounts, Users, and Groups," you learned how Windows 2000 provides strong support for interior intrusion detection through object access auditing. In this lesson, you learn to use an additional tool—logging—to detect intrusions by valid users.

Detecting Attack

You probably examine the system and application logs on your servers routinely, looking for evidence of services that are malfunctioning or improperly configured. It's a simple process—you scan through the log looking for red-flagged events, read them, research the cause, and fix them or determine that they're not important.

Examining audit logs is fundamentally different. Success and failure notices both routinely appear for a variety of reasons—a mistyped user name is not an indication of hacking, nor is a document that a user is denied access to once. Isolated security events are routine and not cause for serious examination.

When you examine audit logs, look for patterns rather than isolated incidents. A few mistyped passwords for a single user account don't indicate an attack, but a single mistyped password for a number of accounts does, and so do a number of mistyped passwords for a single account. Certain user accounts are also immediate indicators of attack—for example, even a few failed attempts to log on using administrative accounts are indicative of attack.

Tip   When you look at audit logs, look for long chains of failure operations. Automated brute-force password attacks appear as long chains of logon failures in audit logs. Be especially vigilant about examining the account logon audit logs of machines in your perimeter network, because these machines are highly likely to be attacked in this manner. Remember to look at the success entry at the end of every chain of failure event—it might indicate that a password was successfully guessed!

An attempt by one user to open a restricted document is something to analyze, but it could simply be accidental. If the same user tries to open numerous secure documents, or if a number of user accounts attempt to open the same document, you have evidence of inappropriate behavior.

Consider extensively auditing delete activity on file servers. File servers usually have excess computing power that can be used for stronger auditing than you would be able to perform on resource-limited machines like SQL servers or mail servers. If you track deletion, you'll be able to see whether a user has (accidentally or otherwise) initiated a mass deletion of files that the user shouldn't be deleting.

Tip   Rename the Administrator accounts for your domain and local computers, and then create a user account named "Administrator" that is not a member of any group. Set up strong auditing on this user account to identify any attempt to use it to log on to the network. Because it's not a real account, no valid administrator would use it. Any attempt to use it is an immediate indication of a serious attack against your network.

The Worst-Case Scenario

The worst-case scenario for attack on a network is a disgruntled network administrator. These attacks are extremely rare, but when they occur they are the most damaging form of attack that can be perpetrated against a network. Network administrators typically have extremely wide access to the network, they know what sort of security measures are in place, and they can take steps to disable the auditing measures designed to track their activities.

The best way to prevent attacks by disgruntled administrators is to create separate administrative accounts for each administrator and leave the password to the built-in administrative account in the hands of non-administrative executives of the organization. The built-in accounts should be used only to create subordinate administrative accounts and change their passwords. Restrict the rights of subordinate administrative accounts so that they can perform only administrative tasks within their purview, such as creating user accounts, changing passwords, and installing drivers. You can perform this by assigning user rights for these accounts.

Tip   By having separate administrator accounts for each administrator and maintaining secrecy about administrative passwords, you can at least retain the ability to audit use by administrators.

You should realize that it's not possible to prevent damage by administrators who have wide access to your systems if they don't care about being identified. You will have to use rigorous hiring procedures and be extremely selective about the individuals to whom you entrust your network in order to avoid these types of problems.

You can also limit the scope of damage by treating attacks by administrators as natural disasters that cannot otherwise be prevented. By handling administrator attack like an earthquake or fire, you focus on restoration rather than prevention as a method of security. The best way to do this is to separate backup and archiving from all other administrative functions, and have a separate group of people handle these processes. Establish a role whose only administrative function is to handle changing backup tapes and moving backup sets off site. This process eliminates an administrator's ability to destroy backup sets as well as online data, and backup operators can't destroy online systems or offsite backups. It is typical to have a clerical worker or executive handle offsite tape backup rotation, or to use an outsourced firm to collect and store backup tapes on a daily basis.

Administrators and Passwords

Administrators usually know the passwords of non-administrative co-workers and even their administrative peers because the passwords have been given out for the sake of convenience to trusted administrators. Most users assume that administrators can access their passwords anyway, so telling it to them to solve a problem is not a big deal.

While it's true that administrators usually have wide access to systems, you should instill a culture of secrecy about passwords. To cause malicious damage to the system, a disgruntled administrator could log on using other people's user accounts. The audit logs would point to those user accounts rather than to the administrator's account. Even if you suspected an administrator was to blame, you'd have no solid evidence to support your conclusion.

Unfortunately, administrators often must log on as users to perform certain tasks such as modifying a user's profile. To cover these cases, establish a policy that administrators will not ask for the user's password—rather, they will change the password to one known to them, and then assist the user in changing the password back when they're finished. This way, administrators don't need to know a user's password, and users always know if an administrator has logged on using their account.

Caution   Beware of using remote control software such as pcAnywhere or VNC that allows an administrator (or hacker) to connect to a user's computer and remotely control it. Be sure that users know that they should watch the on-screen activity any time anyone is controlling their user account, because it's their account that will show up in audit logs if anything happens.

Preserving the Evidence

Evidence preservation is key when you suspect that an internal security violation has occurred, because the burden of proof is on the IT staff. You also want to eliminate the possibility of error.

If the problem is minor, you should make backup copies of the Event log files located in the C:\WINNT\System32\config directory. If you are logged on as the administrator, you can copy the files using any normal file copy method. Table 13.1 lists the files.

Table 13.1   Event Log Files

File name	Log file
AppEvent.evt	Application Log
SysEvent.evt	System Log
SecEvent.evt	Security Log

If the event has caused damage to the system, shut down the server and make an image of the hard disk drives. If the computer has mirrored disks, you can remove the mirror, replace it with new blank disks, and reboot the server to regenerate the mirror. Otherwise, you will have to use a third-party imaging utility to copy the disks. The reason for using images rather than a backup is to retain the sectors that contain deleted data, which could be used to prove exactly what has happened using third-party information forensics tools.

Searching Audit Logs with EventComb

While the Event Viewer console provides easy access to logs on a single computer, you will often need to examine log files on a number of servers. The EventComb utility allows you to search log files on one or more servers in a domain simultaneously for the events of your choice.

Obtaining and Installing EventComb

The current version of EventComb supports multiple threads for a more efficient search, and is called EventCombMT. This tool is distributed with the *Security Operations Guide for Windows 2000 Server*.

More Info   The text of the *Security Operations Guide for Windows 2000 Server* provides more details about EventComb's features. It is available for download from the Microsoft TechNet Web site at *http://www.microsoft.com/technet*.

EventComb is distributed as a self-extracting executable file with other Security Operations Guide tools. Double-click the downloaded .exe file to extract the tools to a folder.

Using EventComb

EventComb does not require any special installation process. Simply launch the Eventcombmt.exe file included in the extracted folder to start EventComb. The first time EventComb is run, it displays a set of instructions. To search for events with this tool, enter the domain name for the search, as shown in Figure 13.8.

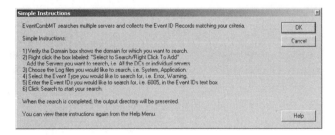

Figure 13.8   The EventComb tool

If you run EventComb on a domain controller or member server, the current domain will be selected by default. You can then specify the following search criteria:

- The log files (System, Application, Security, and other logs installed by specific applications such as the DNS service.)
- The events (Error, Informational, Warning, Success, and Audit events)
- The event types (ID numbers)
- The source (service or protocol) of events

Once you have selected these items, click the Search button to begin the search, which might take several minutes. The events found are stored in a text file, which is displayed on the desktop after the search has completed. Once you have successfully defined a search, you can choose Save This Search from the Searches menu to save it for later use.

Tip   EventComb also includes a number of predefined searches on the Searches menu, such as searches for disk errors and account lockouts.

Configuring Event Logs to Support Using EventComb

Configure the logs to a size large enough to capture a significant amount of data but small enough to make reasonable searches; 2048 KB is a reasonable value.

Ensure that events are retained long enough that they will not expire and be removed from the log before you see them. For example, if you intend to search through events once per month, set your log maximum age to a reasonable value such as 30 days.

Practice: Managing Event Logs

In this practice, you configure event-logging settings and practice using the EventComb tool to search for events in logs.

Exercise 1: Configuring Event Logs

In this exercise, you configure event logging using Group Policy.

▶   **To configure event logs**

1. Log on to the domain controller as the administrator.
2. Click Start, point to Programs, point to Administrative Tools, and click Active Directory Users And Computers. The Active Directory Users And Computers management console appears.
3. Right-click domain.Fabrikam.com, and click Properties.
   The domain.Fabrikam.com Properties dialog box appears.
4. Click the Group Policy tab.
5. Double-click Domain Group Policy. The Group Policy editor appears.

6. Expand Computer Configuration, Windows Settings, Security Settings, and Event Log.

7. Select Settings For Event Logs. The management console appears as shown in Figure 13.9.

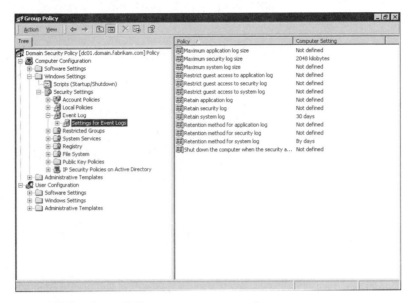

Figure 13.9   Group Policy management console

8. Double-click Maximum Security Log Size.

9. Select Define This Policy Setting, type **2048** in the Kilobytes box, and click OK.

10. Double-click Retain System Log.

11. Select Define This Policy Setting, type **30** in the Days box, and click OK. The Suggested Value Change dialog box appears.

12. Click OK to accept the suggested change to Retention Method For System Log.

13. Close the Group Policy editor.

14. Click OK to close the domain.Fabrikam.com Properties dialog box.

15. Close the Active Directory Users And Computers management console.

Exercise 2: Using EventComb

In this exercise, you use the EventComb tool to search for events matching specified criteria. Perform this exercise from the domain controller.

▶ **To search for events using EventComb**

1. Double-click the Eventcombmt.exe file. The first time you run EventComb, it displays a Help screen, shown in Figure 13.10.

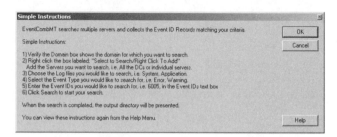

Figure 13.10   EventComb instructions

2. Click OK. The main EventComb dialog box is displayed, as shown in Figure 13.11.

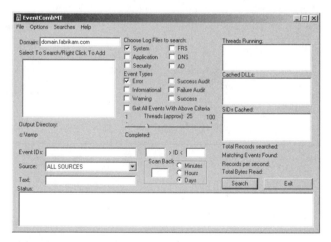

Figure 13.11   The EventComb utility

3. Verify that domain.fabrikam.com is specified in the Domain box.

4. Right-click in the box labeled Select To Search/Right Click To Add, and click Add Single Server. The Add Server dialog box appears, as shown in Figure 13.12.

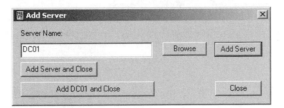

Figure 13.12 Adding a server

5. Type **DC01** in the Server Name box, and click Add Server And Close.

6. Click on DC01 in the Select To Search box to select it.

7. Select both System and Security under Choose Log Files To Search.

8. Select both Error and Warning under Event Types, and select the Get All Events With Above Criteria check box.

9. Click Search to begin the search.

   The search can take several minutes. Statistics are displayed after the search completes, as shown in Figure 13.13.

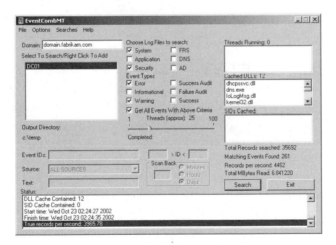

Figure 13.13 Eventcomb search completed

10. Click Exit to close the application.

Lesson Review

The following questions are intended to reinforce key information in this lesson. If you are unable to answer a question, review the lesson and try the question again. Answers to the questions can be found in the appendix.

1. What should you do after detecting intrusion on a system?

2. What are the three basic log files used in Windows 2000?

3. Where can you manage log retention settings?

4. Which utility allows you to search for events in logs across a network?

5. Where does EventComb store its results?

Lesson Summary

- You can use the Windows 2000 auditing and logging features to detect intrusions by valid users of the system and preserve evidence of the attacks.
- After an intrusion occurs, it is important to make backup copies of the log files on the compromised system and create an image of the hard disks if files have been damaged or modified.
- The EventComb utility, available for download from TechNet, provides a simple way to search for events in the log files of multiple servers in a domain. You can search for particular events or event types in the system, application, and security logs with this tool.

C H A P T E R   1 4

Software Maintenance

About This Chapter

To keep a network secure, you must ensure that clients and servers have the latest
updates to the installed operating system. Microsoft Windows 2000 Server includes
a number of ways to accomplish this, including service packs, hotfixes, automatic
updates, and Group Policy features. In this chapter, you will learn about the various
tools you can use to update client and server computers.

Exam Tip   Be sure you know how to configure and use all of the service pack,
hotfix, and update tools for Microsoft Windows 2000. You also need to know how
to perform updates on computers that are not connected to the Internet.

Before You Begin

To complete the exercises in this chapter, you will need

- A domain controller for the domain.fabrikam.com domain
- A member server in the domain
- An Internet connection for obtaining software updates

You also need a Windows 2000 Server computer to install Remote Installation
Services (RIS). This can be the domain controller. However, you will need an
NTFS file system volume on this computer, separate from the system volume,
with about 1 GB of storage space.

Lesson 1: Working with Service Packs and Hotfixes

Between operating system version releases, Microsoft releases regular updates to correct bugs and security vulnerabilities. Updates are distributed in two basic forms:

- *Service packs* are packages that contain a large number of updates.
- *Hotfixes* are small, incremental updates released between service packs.

In this lesson, you will use Windows 2000 tools to install service packs and hotfixes, manage existing updates, and create an integrated installation of Windows 2000 that includes all updates.

After completing this lesson, you will be able to

- Install service packs and hotfixes
- Determine current hotfix status
- Combine hotfixes with Windows 2000 installation

Estimated lesson time: 30 minutes

Understanding Service Packs and Hotfixes

A service pack contains all of the updates for an operating system over a period of time, and all the updates found in previously released hotfixes. Service packs are eventually rolled into the distribution of the operating system; for example, Microsoft Windows 2000 is currently available with Service Pack 3.

Service packs become a stable part of the operating system. Fixes in service packs continue to work as you uninstall and reinstall other components, unless you uninstall the service pack. Hotfixes, on the other hand, can be overridden by the installation of new software. If you install a hotfix and then later update a component affected by the hotfix, you will need to reinstall the hotfix.

Note   You can easily install both service packs and hotfixes on a single machine using an executable file. You can also combine them with a network installation share and automatically install them when clients are installed from that share. This process is known as *slipstreaming*.

Checking Service Pack and Hotfix Status

To check the current service pack and hotfix status of a computer, you can use the Qfecheck.exe program, available for download from the Microsoft support Web site. Go to *http://support.microsoft.com/* and search for Knowledge Base Article Q282784. Qfecheck.exe is delivered in the form of a hotfix. Once you have downloaded the .exe file, run it to install Qfecheck.

Note   Versions of Qfecheck are available for all versions of Microsoft Windows 2000 and Windows XP.

The Qfecheck utility reads the information about installed hotfixes that Windows 2000 and Windows XP store in the Windows registry. You can also examine this information directly at the registry key HKEY_LOCAL_MACHINE\SOFTWARE\Microsoft\Updates.

Qfecheck.exe Options

To display a Qfecheck report, run Qfecheck.exe from the command prompt. The report includes the current service pack level of the operating system and a list of installed hotfixes. Qfecheck indicates whether each hotfix is current on the system or needs to be reinstalled. You can use the command-line parameters listed in Table 14.1 to modify the report output.

Table 14.1   Qfecheck.exe Options

Option	Purpose
/v	Use verbose output.
/q	Use quiet mode (no output).
/l	Save output to default file.
/l:*file*	Save output to specified file.
/?	Display a list of options.

If you use the /l option to save the report output to a file, Qfecheck uses the name of the local computer and a .log extension as the file name. You can also specify a file name for the report, which can be a UNC path to a network share.

Managing Service Packs and Hotfixes

To upgrade computers on a small network, you can manually install service packs and hotfixes when you download them, or install them from a CD or downloaded file source.

Installing a Service Pack

Download the latest service packs for your operating system from the Microsoft Web site. Service packs are typically distributed in two downloadable forms:

- **Express Installation.**   Use this option when you do not need the software for additional computers. Download and install the service pack on a single computer. This option scans the computer and downloads only the updates needed.
- **Network Installation.**   Use this option when you need to install the service pack on other computers or deploy it across a network. This option includes the entire service pack in a single .exe file.

For enterprise deployment of service packs, you need the network installation download or a service pack CD. The service pack is distributed in the form of an .exe file. For example, the distribution file for Windows 2000 Service Pack 3 is W2ksp3.exe. You can execute this file directly to install the service pack on the current computer. This extracts the files to a temporary directory and runs the Update.exe program, which performs the update.

Extracting a Service Pack

Instead of installing a downloaded service pack on the local computer, you can extract the files to a directory. This allows you to make the service pack available over the network or to specify options to Update.exe (for example, to expand the service pack into a slipstream installation share), as described later in this lesson.

To extract the files from a service pack executable, use the -x option following the .exe file at a command prompt. For example, type **w2ksp3.exe -x** to extract the Windows 2000 Service Pack 3 files. When you use this option, you are prompted for a destination directory for the service pack files.

Installing a Hotfix

Hotfixes are distributed as .exe files, similar to service packs, but they are typically smaller in size. Microsoft uses a standard naming convention for hotfixes:

```
Q######_XXX_YYY_ZZZ_LL.exe
```

In this system, *Q######* is the Microsoft Knowledge Base article number describing the hotfix:

- *XXX* is the operating system.
- *YYY* is the service pack level required for the hotfix.
- *ZZZ* is the hardware platform.
- *LL* is the language.

To install a hotfix on a local computer, run the executable file. Because the changes made by hotfixes are usually rolled into a service pack, the hotfix verifies that you have the correct service pack level. If you have a newer service pack, the hotfix is not required, and the installer exits without making any changes.

The hotfix installation is actually performed by an Update.exe program located within the self-extracting archive. As with service pack distributions, you can use the -x option with a hotfix to extract its files into a directory for later use.

Important   Most hotfixes require you to reboot the computer to complete the installation. If you are installing multiple hotfixes, you must reboot after each one and before installing the next. You can avoid this by using the Qchain utility, described in Lesson 3.

Removing a Service Pack or Hotfix

If a service pack or hotfix causes incompatibilities with software or causes other issues, you can remove it. The current service pack and any installed hotfixes are listed with other installed software in the Add/Remove programs control panel. Hotfixes are listed with the Q###### number that uniquely identifies each hotfix. To uninstall a service pack or hotfix, select its entry from the list and click the Change/Remove button.

Important   You cannot remove service packs or hotfixes that were installed from an integrated (or slipstream) installation of the operating system with fixes. Also keep in mind that uninstalling a service pack may affect any software that was installed after the service pack.

Slipstreaming Service Packs and Hotfixes

When you are deploying operating systems on multiple computers, it can be cumbersome to install numerous service packs and hotfixes after each installation. Windows 2000 and Windows XP support *slipstreaming* to solve this problem. You can update a network installation share with a service pack and any number of hotfixes, which will then be transparently installed with the operating system.

If you do not already have a network installation share, create one by copying the I386 folder of the operating system CD to a shared folder. This process is described in the "Practice: Managing Service Packs and Hotfixes" section of this lesson.

Adding a Service Pack to a Network Installation Share

The Update.exe program included with each service pack includes an option to update a network installation share with the service pack files. To use this option, you must first extract the service pack files to a folder using the -x option on the distributed .exe file.

After the files are extracted, you can update the network share. From the I386\Update directory of the service pack files, execute the following command:

```
update.exe -s:folder
```

For *folder*, specify the folder where the installation files were extracted. This should be the parent folder to the I386 folder containing the installation files.

Adding Hotfixes to a Network Installation Share

Adding a hotfix to a network installation share is a more complex process. You should do this only with critical hotfixes released after the most recent service pack. To add a hotfix, extract its files using the -x option to the .exe file, and then perform these basic steps:

1. Copy the .cat (catalog) file and the .exe file for the hotfix into the I386\svcpack directory. Create this directory if it does not exist.
2. Copy the hotfix binary files into the network installation folder.
3. Create a Svcpack.inf file describing the additional hotfix to be installed.

The details of these steps are described in the "Practice: Managing Service Packs and Hotfixes" section of this lesson.

Tip Especially when installing multiple hotfixes, you might find it easier to use Group Policy to install the updates after installation, as described in Lesson 3, or use RIS to create an image, as described in the next section.

Working with Remote Installation Services

Remote Installation Services (RIS) provides an automated way to manage the installation of client operating systems. The RIS server stores an operating system installation image. Clients can connect using a network computer with a pre-execution environment (PXE) boot ROM or using a network installation floppy disk.

Installing RIS

RIS is included with Windows 2000 Server. The installation process for RIS is described in the "Practice: Managing Service Packs and Hotfixes" section of this lesson. RIS requires the following components and services to work:

- Access to a Domain Name System (DNS) server.
- Access to a Dynamic Host Configuration Protocol (DHCP) server.
- Access to Active Directory. This means RIS should be installed on a domain controller or member server.
- An NTFS-formatted disk for storage of operating system images. This must not be the same disk as the system drive (usually C).

After RIS is installed, you must authorize it in Active Directory. You can do this using the DHCP management console.

Creating a RIS Installation Image

For RIS to work, you need to create an installation image. This will provide the necessary installation files to clients when the operating system is installed. There are two ways to create the installation image:

- From an installed system, use the Riprep.exe utility, located in the \RemoteInstall\Admin\I386 folder on the RIS server. This utility scans an existing Windows 2000 Professional system and creates a remote installation image to match it, including any installed hotfixes, service packs, and applications.
- From an installation CD or network share, use the Risetup.exe utility. This method does not require an existing system. If you use a network share that has been updated with slipstreamed hotfixes or service packs, installed clients will be configured with the updated system.

To create the installation image you will need an NTFS volume with at least as much space requied by the installation CD or network share files. The drive cannot be the system volume, so you might need to install a new drive or partition a drive to support RIS.

Important   RIS supports the installation of client operating systems only, currently including Windows 2000 Professional. It cannot be used to deploy server operating systems.

Installing Clients with RIS

You can install an operating system on a client with RIS if it has a network card with a PXE boot ROM, or using a remote installation boot disk. To create a boot disk, use the Rbfg.exe program, located in the \RemoteInstall\Admin\I386 folder on the RIS server.

Practice: Managing Service Packs and Hotfixes

In this practice, you install hotfixes and service packs manually and using slipstreaming, check service pack status, and use RIS to remotely install an operating system with updates.

Exercise 1: Manually Installing a Service Pack and a Hotfix

In this exercise, you use the Qfecheck.exe program to check a computer's current service pack and hotfix status, and practice manually installing a service pack and hotfix.

▶ **To check hotfix and service pack status**

Perform this procedure on any Windows 2000 or Windows XP computer. You should have already downloaded the appropriate .exe hotfix file for your operating system, as described in this lesson.

1. Double-click the downloaded .exe file to install the Qfecheck.exe file.
2. Open a command prompt.
3. From the command prompt, type **qfecheck** and press ENTER. A summary of hotfix status is displayed, as shown in Figure 14.1.

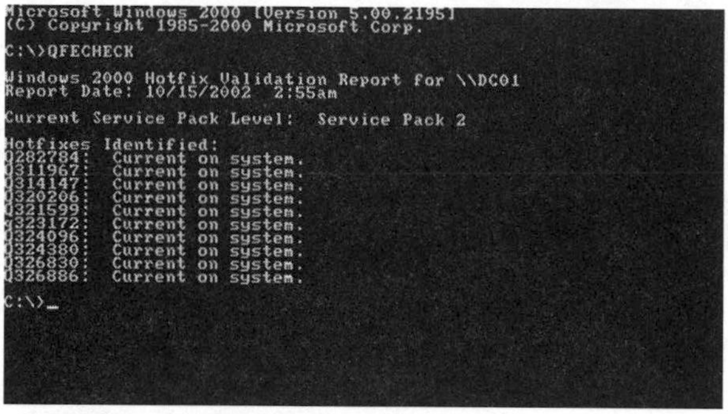

Figure 14.1   Qfecheck.exe output

▶ **To install a service pack**

Perform this procedure on a Windows 2000 computer.

Important   The service pack installation program may vary slightly with each service pack. Follow the specific instructions available with the service pack.

1. Download the service pack .exe file (network installation) from the Microsoft Web site.
2. Launch the .exe file (for example, W2ksp3.exe) from the command prompt or the Run dialog box.

   The installer extracts the files and begins the installation. This might take several minutes. The setup wizard then displays an introductory page.
3. Click Next to continue. The license agreement for the service pack appears.

4. Select the I Agree option, and click Next to continue. On the Select Options page, you are prompted to indicate whether to archive replaced files for later removal, as shown in Figure 14.2.

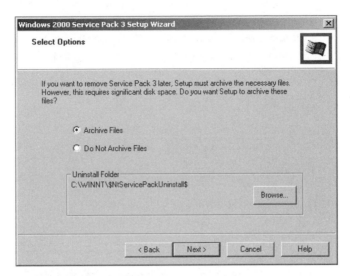

Figure 14.2   Archiving options

5. Select the Archive Files option, and click Next.

The wizard now updates the computer with the service pack components. This might take several minutes. After the installation, a completion message appears, as shown in Figure 14.3.

Figure 14.3   Completing the service pack installation

6. Click Finish to restart the computer and apply the service pack.

▶   **To install a hotfix**

1. Download the hotfix .exe file.
2. Launch the .exe file from the command prompt or Run dialog box.

   In most cases, you are not prompted for any information. Some hotfixes have a more complex installation procedure and might display one or more dialog boxes. When the installation is finished, a message appears indicating that the update was successful, as shown in Figure 14.4.

Figure 14.4   The hotfix is now installed

Important   Restart the computer after the hotfix is installed.

Exercise 2: Slipstreaming Service Packs and Hotfixes

In this exercise, you add a service pack and hotfix to a network installation share using the Windows 2000 slipstreaming features.

▶   **To add a service pack to a network installation share**

Perform this procedure from a Windows 2000 Server computer.

1. Download or transfer the service pack .exe file to the C drive.
2. Create a directory called c:\Win2000\I386 and copy the contents of the I386 directory on the Windows 2000 Professional installation CD to it. If you already have a network installation share, you can skip this step.
3. From the command prompt or Run dialog box, type **c:\w2ksp3.exe /x**.

   Note   If you have a service pack later than service pack 3 (SP3), use the appropriate file name instead.

   The service pack installation program extracts the files and then prompts you for an installation directory.
4. Type **C:\SP3** and click OK.

   The service pack installation files are now extracted to C:\SP3\I386. This might take several minutes.
5. Click OK to exit.

6. From the command prompt or Run dialog box, type
C:\SP3\I386\Update\Update.exe -s:C:\Win2000 and then press ENTER.

The Windows 2000 Service Pack Setup progress window displays a progress
indicator, shown in Figure 14.5, and the service pack changes are applied to the
installation files.

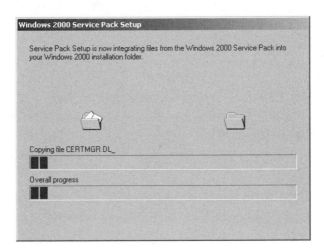

Figure 14.5   Applying the service pack to the installation files

7. Click OK to exit the update program.

Installations using the updated installation share will now automatically include
the service pack.

▶ **To add a hotfix to a network installation share**

Perform this procedure from the Windows 2000 Server computer that holds the
network installation share you created in the previous procedure.

1. Download the hotfix file to the hard drive.

In this example, the file is C:\Q322842_W2K_SP4_X86_EN.exe.

2. From the command line, type **md c:\Win2000\I386\svcpack** and press ENTER.

This creates a svcpack directory under the network installation folder.

3. Type **copy /b C:\Q322842*.exe C:\Win2000\I386\svcpack\Q322842.exe**
and press ENTER.

This copies the service pack to the installation folder using an 8-character
file name.

4. Type **md c:\hotfix** to create a temporary location to extract the hotfix files.

5. Type **C:\Win2000\I386\svcpack\Q322842 /x** and press ENTER.

    You are prompted for a location for the hotfix files, as shown in Figure 14.6.

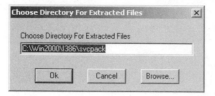

Figure 14.6   Extracting the hotfix files

6. Type **c:\hotfix** and click OK. The hotfix files are now extracted.

7. From the command prompt, type these commands to copy the catalog file and binary files:

```
copy c:\hotfix\update\Q322842.cat c:\Win2000\I386\svcpack

copy c:\hotfix\*.dll c:\Win2000\I386

copy c:\hotfix\*.exe c:\Win2000\I386

copy c:\hotfix\*.sys c:\Win2000\I386

copy c:\hotfix\uniproc\*.* c:\Win2000\I386\uniproc\*.*
```

8. Create a new text file at *c:\Win2000\I386\Svcpack.inf*, and add the following contents:

```
[Version]

Signature="$Windows NT$"

MajorVersion=5

MinorVersion=0

BuildNumber=2195

[SetupData]

CatalogSubDir="\i386\svcpack"

[ProductCatalogsToInstall]

Q322842.cat

[SetupHotfixesToRun]

Q322842.exe /q /n /z
```

The hotfix is now integrated into the installation files. To include additional hotfixes, add the appropriate lines to the ProductCatalogsToInstall and SetupHotfixesToRun sections.

Exercise 3: Using Remote Installation Services

In this exercise, you install RIS, create an installation image from a network installation share, and use RIS to install Windows 2000 Professional on a client computer.

▶   **To install RIS**

Perform this procedure from a domain controller or member server.

1. In Control Panel, double-click Add/Remove Programs.
2. Click Add/Remove Windows Components. The Windows Components Wizard displays a list of currently installed components, as shown in Figure 14.7.

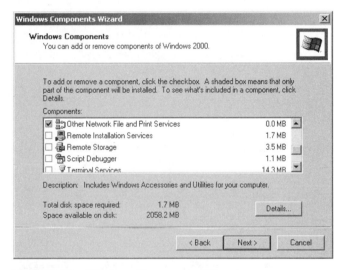

Figure 14.7   Windows Components Wizard

3. Select the Remote Installation Services check box, and click Next. The RIS server software is installed, which can take several minutes.

    After the installation, the Windows Components Wizard displays a completion message.

4. Click Finish to exit the wizard.

    You are prompted to restart the computer. You must restart before using RIS.

▶   **To create the RIS operating system image**

Perform this procedure on the computer that has RIS installed. You will need an NTFS disk other than the system volume.

1. From the command prompt or Run dialog box, type **risetup.exe**. The Remote Installation Services Setup Wizard displays an introductory page.

2. Click Next to continue. You are prompted for a folder to serve as the root location for remote installation files, as shown in Figure 14.8.

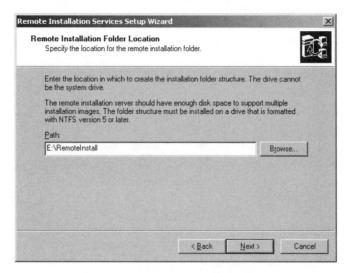

Figure 14.8   Specify a remote installation folder

3. Type **E:\RemoteInstall** in the Path box and click Next.

Important   Substitute the drive letter of your non-system NTFS volume above.

The Initial Settings page appears, as shown in Figure 14.9.

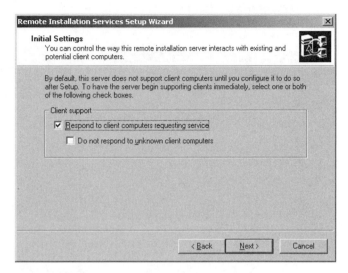

Figure 14.9   RIS Initial Settings page

4. Select the Respond To Client Computers Requesting Service check box, and click Next.

   You are prompted for the location of the source installation files.

5. Specify the network installation folder. If you used the instructions in Exercise 1, this will be C:\Win2000.

   You are prompted for a name for the OS installation image folder, as shown in Figure 14.10.

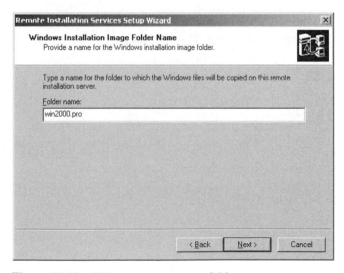

Figure 14.10   RIS installation image folder page

6. Accept the default setting of win2000.pro, and click Next.

   You are prompted for a description and help text for the operating system image, as shown in Figure 14.11.

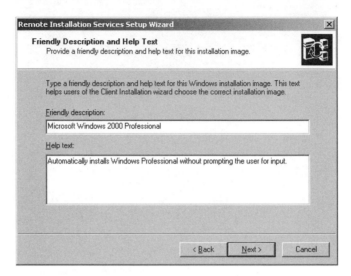

Figure 14.11 RIS description and help text boxes

7. Click Next to continue. The Review Settings page summarizes the settings you specified.

8. Click Finish to create the installation image.

   The remote installation image is now created. This process will take at least a few minutes to complete.

9. Click Done to exit the setup wizard.

▶ **To authorize RIS in Active Directory**

Perform this procedure from a domain controller.

Tip You do not need to perform this step if you installed RIS on the same machine as the DHCP server.

---

1. Click Start, point to Settings, point to Administrative Tools, and then click DHCP to launch the DHCP management console.

2. Select DHCP in the console tree.

3. From the Action menu, choose Manage Authorized Servers. The Manage Authorized Servers dialog box appears, as shown in Figure 14.12.

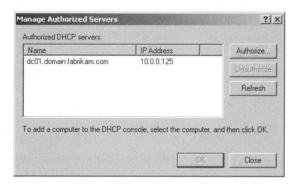

Figure 14.12   Manage Authorized Servers dialog box

4. Click Authorize. You are prompted for the name or IP address of the server to authorize.

5. In the Name Or IP Address box, type the IP address of the computer running RIS, and click OK.

6. Click the Close button to exit the dialog box.

Lesson Review

The following questions are intended to reinforce key information in this lesson. If you are unable to answer a question, review the lesson and try the question again. Answers to the questions can be found in the appendix.

1. Which utility displays a summary of service pack and hotfix levels for a computer?

2. Which type of update is not affected by other software updates?

3. What is the name for the process of adding updates to a set of operating system installation files?

4. From what two sources can Remote Installation Services (RIS) create an installation image?

5. What are the requirements for the disk used to store a RIS installation image?

Lesson Summary

- Service packs are major updates to an operating system. You can install a service pack using a downloaded .exe file, or from a CD. More recent versions of the operating system often include service packs.

- Hotfixes are simple updates released after a service pack and integrated into the next service pack. A hotfix is distributed as an .exe file. You can install hotfixes at any time, as long as they are newer than the currently installed service pack.

- The Qfecheck.exe utility displays the service pack level for a computer and a list of hotfixes that have been installed after the service pack. This information is useful for determining which upgrades are needed on a computer.

- Service packs and hotfixes can be slipstreamed, or integrated into a set of installation files for the operating system. When the operating system is then installed, it will include the updates.

- Remote Installation Services (RIS) is a Windows 2000 Server component that allows you to store an installation image for a client operating system. You can then install the operating system on clients using PXE boot ROMs or a network installation floppy disk.

Lesson 2: Automating Updates with Microsoft Software Update Services

While you can download and install hotfixes and service packs manually, Windows 2000 also supports automated methods to simplify this process. These include the following methods:

- *Windows Update* is a Web-based interface that displays updates for a computer and allows users to install their choice of updates.
- *Automatic Updates* is a feature of Windows Update that notifies users of critical updates and optionally installs updates automatically.
- *Software Update Services (SUS)* provides a service similar to Windows Update for enterprises and allows administrators to manage the installation of available updates.

After completing this lesson, you will be able to

- Update computers using Windows Update and Automatic Updates
- Install and manage Software Update Services
- Configure clients to update through Software Update Services

Estimated lesson time: 30 minutes

Using Windows Update

Windows Update is a Web-based service that scans the local computer, determines which updates have not been installed, and then displays potential updates and provides a convenient interface for installing them.

Accessing Windows Update

You can access the Windows Update site with the shortcut installed by default in the Start menu, or by going to the Windows Update site at *http://windowsupdate.microsoft.com/*. Once the site is displayed, you click the Scan For Updates link to scan the computer.

After the scan completes, Windows Update displays a list of available updates. Critical updates and new service packs are listed first, followed by non-critical operating system updates and updated hardware drivers. Click the Add button next to an update description to add the update to the list of updates to install. After you are finished adding items, click the Review And Install Updates link to install the updates.

Note   Some updates have special installation needs. In particular, some updates must be installed separately. Windows Update will inform you in these cases, so you can install the update and restart the computer before installing additional updates.

Using the Windows Update Catalog

While Windows Update is a convenient service for computers that have Internet connections, it is not useful for a computer that does not have an Internet connection. To service computers that are not connected to the Internet, you can use the Windows Update Catalog, which provides local copies of the available updates.

Once you have local copies of the updates on a computer that is connected to the Internet, you can distribute those updates to computers that are not connected to the Internet by using a local network or removable media such as CD-R. The Windows Update Catalog can then be configured on those machines to use the local sources for installation rather than connect to the Internet.

You can enable the Windows Update Catalog from the Windows Update page. Click Personalize Windows Update and then select the Display The Link To The Windows Update Catalog check box to enable the catalog.

After you choose an operating system and hardware device from the Windows Update Catalog, the catalog displays a complete list of available updates. You can customize the display of updates to include only certain categories of updates or you can search for updates by keyword.

Using the catalog, you can add updates to a basket, as you do in the standard Windows Update, enter a download location, and download all of the updates in a single operation. You can then distribute the updates to the appropriate computers.

Unlike Windows Update, the catalog does not determine whether an update is needed or is compatible with the destination computer. Ensure that you, as administrator, install only the appropriate updates for each computer and that you install using a user account with the permissions required to overwrite operating system files.

Tip   You can use the Qfecheck.exe utility, described in Lesson 1, to determine which updates have already been installed on a computer.

Using Automatic Updates

In computers with Windows 2000 Service Pack 3 or Windows XP Service Pack 1 installed, Critical Update Notification, a utility that periodically checked the Windows Update Web site for critical updates to a computer, has been replaced by Automatic Updates. This service expands the original concept of the Critical Update Notification utility by not only notifying users of updates, but also downloading and installing them automatically if desired.

Automatic Updates downloads updates directly from *http://www.microsoft.com* and stores them in a temporary directory on each computer until they are installed. For large enterprises or for those that do not have a direct connection to the Internet, this default behavior is not always desirable. Automatic Updates can also act as a client for Microsoft Software Update Services (SUS), described later in this lesson, which allows administrators to establish a local server that can distribute updates.

Installing Automatic Updates

To obtain Automatic Updates, either install the Windows 2000 Service Pack 3, Windows XP Service Pack 1, or install the Automatic Updates feature separately using Windows Update.

Configuring the Automatic Updates Client

After the Automatic Updates feature is installed on a computer, an Automatic Updates option is added to Control Panel. This provides access to the Automatic Updates dialog box. To enable automatic updates, select the Keep My Computer Up To Date option within this dialog box. You can also choose one of three notification options:

- Notify before downloading any updates and before installing them. Use this option if controlling connections to the Internet is required.
- Download automatically, then notify before installing updates. Use this option if you want to retain administrative control over which updates are installed.
- Download automatically, and install updates automatically at the selected daily or weekly interval. Use this option for completely automatic updating.

You can also control the update policies of Automatic Updates by using Group Policy, which is detailed in the next section.

Installing and Configuring Software Update Services

Microsoft Software Update Services (SUS) provides the same benefit on local servers as the Windows Update servers provide on the Internet. It allows you to make your choice of updates available to clients using Automatic Updates. The SUS server synchronizes with the Windows Update server to obtain the latest updates, and multiple SUS servers can synchronize with each other.

Installing Software Update Services

SUS has complex requirements, and Microsoft recommends dedicating a server to it. SUS requires a Windows 2000 Server computer configured as a stand-alone server or member server. It cannot be installed on a domain controller. It also requires Internet Information Services (IIS).

To install SUS, first download the server software from the Microsoft Web site. SUS is provided as a file, Sussetup.msi, that uses the Windows Installer to install the service. Run this program to begin the installation. A wizard guides you through the installation process.

Configuring Software Update Services

Once you have installed SUS, you can use its Web-based configuration system. To access this system, browse to the *http://localhost/SUSAdmin/* page in Internet Explorer. Click the Options link to set up the basic SUS options. At a minimum, you must specify whether to use a proxy server for Internet access, and whether to synchronize updates from the Microsoft Windows Update servers or from another SUS server.

Synchronizing Updates

To synchronize SUS with Windows Update, click the Synchronize option in the SUS administration page, and then click the Synchronize Now button. The first synchronization may take a few minutes (or even longer on a slow Internet connection) because it must download the current catalog of updates and all pending updates. You can also click the Synchronization Schedule button to configure a schedule for regular synchronization.

Approving Updates

Once updates have been downloaded, you must approve them before they will be made available to clients. This approval process allows you to pre-test updates before deploying them across the enterprise. To approve updates, click the Approve Updates option in the SUS administration page. The list of downloaded updates is displayed, and you can choose the updates to approve. The updates you approve will be installed by clients running Automatic Updates on their next scheduled connection to the SUS server.

Note   You can also remove approval from updates that have been previously approved. However, this does not remove them from any clients that have already installed the update. You would do this to prevent an update from being installed on new computers if that update conflicts with third-party software that is essential.

Configuring Automatic Updates Clients

For clients to poll the local SUS server rather than the Windows Update servers, you must configure each client to use the SUS server. You configure clients across the network using Group Policy. The Automatic Updates installation includes a template, Wuau.adm, that you can configure and deploy to configure Automatic Updates settings. The template is stored in the \inf folder within the Windows directory. To use the template, create a new Group Policy for the organizational unit (OU) that contains the computers that require automatic update settings. Add the template to the policy's Administrative Templates section. This adds two new policies under the Windows Update heading:

- **Configure Automatic Updates.**   Allows you to set Automatic Updates options, as described earlier in this lesson, for all computers in the OU.
- **Specify Intranet Windows Update Server Location.**   Allows you to specify a server name for Automatic Updates to contact. Specify the SUS server here.

Tip   You can also use the Wuau.adm template and Group Policy to automatically configure Automatic Updates without installing an SUS server if you don't mind having clients directly download updates from *http://www.microsoft.com*. To do this, install the Wuau.adm template and configure the GPO options without installing or specifying an intranet SUS server.

Practice: Using Software Update Services

In this practice, you test the Windows Update and Windows Update Catalog features and configure Automatic Updates settings. You can perform these tasks from any Windows 2000 computer with Service Pack 3 or the Automatic Updates add-on installed.

Exercise 1: Managing Automatic Updates

In this exercise, you use Windows Update and the Windows Update Catalog to download and manage updates, and configure a computer to use the Automatic Updates feature.

▶   **To install updates with Windows Update**

Perform this procedure on any Windows 2000 computer.

1. Choose Windows Update from the Start menu, or browse to *http://windowsupdate.microsoft.com*. The Windows Update page appears, as shown in Figure 14.13.

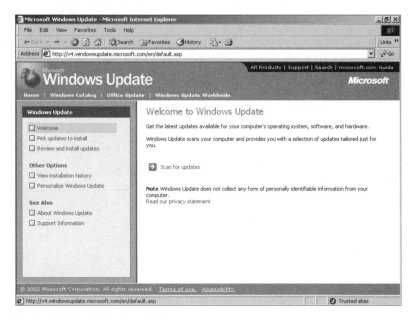

Figure 14.13   Windows Update

2. Click the Scan For Updates link to begin the scan.

3. Click the Review And Install Updates link. A list of available critical updates appears, as shown in Figure 14.14.

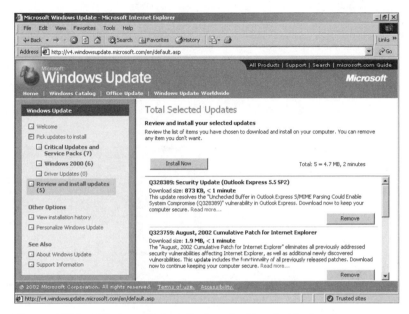

Figure 14.14   Windows Update displays the list of critical updates

4. By default, all critical updates are selected to be installed. Click the Remove button to remove any update you do not want to install.

5. Click the Install Now button to begin the installation. The license agreement for the updates appears.

6. Click Accept to begin downloading and installing the updates.

   The updates are installed. This might take several minutes and depends on the speed of the Internet connection.

7. Click OK to restart the computer and complete the installation.

▶   **To download updates with the Windows Update Catalog**

Perform this procedure from any Windows 2000 computer connected to the Internet.

1. Choose Windows Update from the Start menu, or browse to *http://windowsupdate.microsoft.com*. The Windows Update page appears.

2. Select the Personalize Windows Update link in the left column. The Windows Update options are displayed, as shown in Figure 14.15.

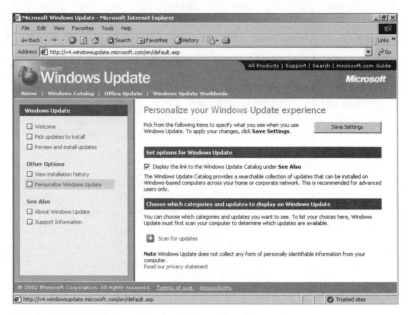

Figure 14.15   Windows Update personalization options

3. Select the Display The Link To The Windows Update Catalog Under See Also check box, and click Save Settings. Your settings are saved, and the Windows Update Catalog link appears in the left column.

4. Click the Windows Update Catalog link in the left column. The Windows Update Catalog page appears.

5. Click the Find Updates For Microsoft Windows Operating Systems link. A list of operating systems appears, as shown in Figure 14.16.

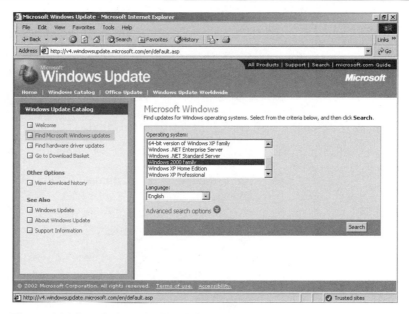

Figure 14.16   Windows Update Catalog

6. Select Windows 2000 Family from the list, and click Search. A list of categories appears.

7. Click the Critical Updates And Service Packs link. A list of updates appears, as shown in Figure 14.17.

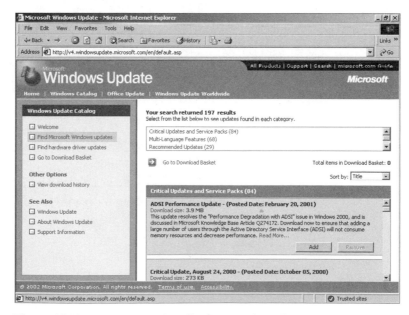

Figure 14.17   Windows Update Catalog search results

8. Click Add to add one or more updates to the basket.

9. Click the Go To Download Basket link. The updates you selected are listed.

10. Click Browse, and select a destination for the downloaded files.

11. Click Download Now.

The updates are now downloaded to your selected location.

▶ **To enable and configure Automatic Updates**

Perform this procedure from a Windows 2000 computer with Service Pack 3 installed.

1. In Control Panel, double-click Automatic Updates. The Automatic Updates dialog box appears, as shown in Figure 14.18.

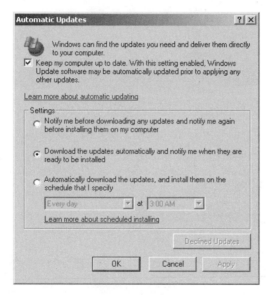

Figure 14.18 Automatic Updates

2. Select the Keep My Computer Up To Date check box.

3. Select the Download The Updates Automatically And Notify Me When They Are Ready To Be Installed option.

4. Click OK to exit the Automatic Updates dialog box.

Automatic Updates are now enabled for the local computer.

Exercise 2: Using Software Update Services

In this exercise, you install SUS on a server, configure its settings, and configure a group of clients to access the server for updates.

▶ **To install Software Update Services**

1. Perform this procedure from a member server.

1. Click the Sussetup.msi file to launch the installer. The Microsoft Software Update Services Setup Wizard displays an introductory page.

2. Click Next to continue.

3. Accept the license agreement, and click Next. The Choose Setup Type page appears, as shown in Figure 14.19.

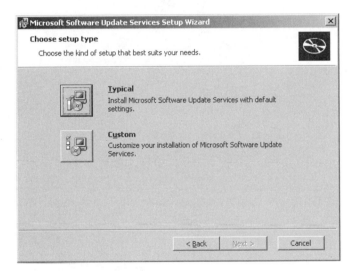

Figure 14.19   Choose the installation type

4. Click the Typical button, and click Next.

5. Click Next to begin the installation.

   SUS is installed. The installation might take several minutes. During the installation, the Internet Information Services Lockdown Wizard runs to set up secure IIS settings, as shown in Figure 14.20.

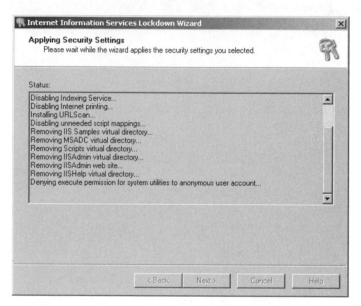

Figure 14.20   The Internet Information Services Lockdown Wizard

6. When the completion screen appears, click Finish to exit the installer.

▶ **To configure Software Update Services**

Perform this procedure from the SUS server.

1. Browse to *http://localhost/SUSAdmin/*. The SUS administration pages are displayed, as shown in Figure 14.21.

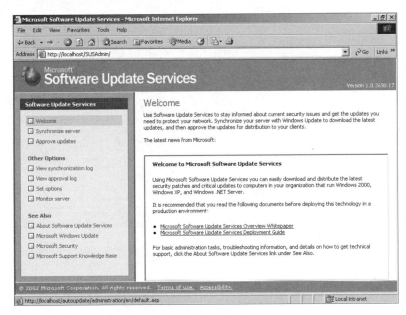

Figure 14.21   Software Update Services configuration

2. Select whether to use a proxy server for Internet access, and specify the server if necessary.

3. Click Set Options. A scrollable list of options appears.

4. Specify the name that clients use to contact the server. The default choice is the NetBIOS name of the server, which is usually sufficient.

5. Choose the server from which to synchronize content. Select the Synchronize Directly From The Microsoft Windows Update Servers option, as shown in Figure 14.22.

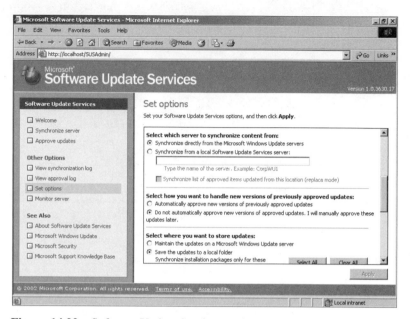

Figure 14.22   Software Update Services options

6. Select whether to automatically approve new versions of updates you previously approved.

7. Choose a location to store the updates, and select the languages for which you want to synchronize updates.

8. Click Apply to save the settings.

9. Click the Synchronize Server link in the left column. The Synchronize Server page appears, as shown in Figure 14.23.

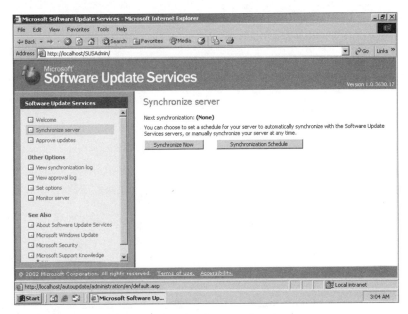

Figure 14.23   Software Update Services synchronization

10. Click the Synchronize Now button to begin synchronization.

The catalog is downloaded, followed by the latest updates. The download process can take several minutes.

▶ **To configure clients using Group Policy**

Perform this procedure from the domain controller.

1. Click Start, point to Programs, point to Administrative Tools, and click Active Directory Users And Computers. The Active Directory Users And Computers management console appears.

2. Select the Information Technology organizational unit under Departments in the console tree.

3. From the Action menu, choose Properties. The Information Technology Properties dialog box appears.

4. Select the Group Policy tab. The Group Policy properties dialog box is displayed, as shown in Figure 14.24.

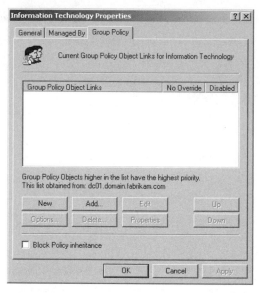

Figure 14.24   Group Policy properties dialog box

5. Click New, and name the new policy Automatic Updates.
6. Click Edit to edit the new GPO. The Group Policy management console appears, as shown in Figure 14.25.

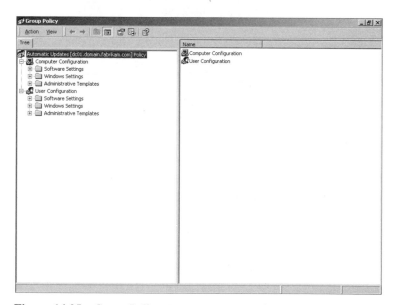

Figure 14.25   Group Policy management console

7. In the console tree, select Administrative Templates under Computer Configuration.

8. From the Action menu, choose Add/Remove Templates. The Add/Remove Templates dialog box appears.

9. Click Add. A list of available templates appears, as shown in Figure 14.26.

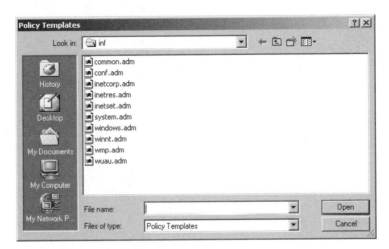

Figure 14.26   Adding a template to the policy

10. Select wuau.adm from the list, and click Open.

11. Click Close to close the Add/Remove Templates dialog box.

12. In the console tree, expand Administrative Templates, Windows Components, and select Windows Update.

13. Double-click the Specify Intranet Microsoft Update Service Location policy. The policy settings are displayed, as shown in Figure 14.27.

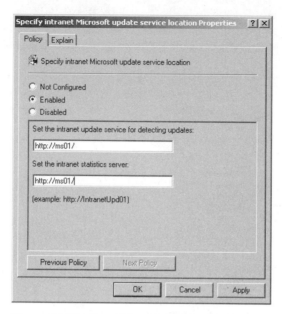

Figure 14.27   Specifying the service location

14. Select the Enabled option, and then type **http://** followed by the name of the server running SUS in the update service and statistics server boxes, and click OK.

15. Click Close to close the Properties dialog box.

16. Close the Group Policy console, and then click Close to close the Information Technology Properties dialog box.

    The new settings will be configured as each client refreshes its Group Policy.

Lesson Review

The following questions are intended to reinforce key information in this lesson. If you are unable to answer a question, review the lesson and try the question again. Answers to the questions can be found in the appendix.

1. Which Windows Update feature notifies users of critical updates and optionally installs updates automatically?

2. What two sources can be used to obtain the latest updates using Automatic Updates?

3. What service provides a local version of the Windows Update service?

4. How can clients be configured to update using an SUS server?

5. Where are notification settings for Automatic Updates managed?

Lesson Summary

- Windows Update is a Web-based service provided by Microsoft that scans a computer's installed software, determines needed or available updates, and optionally allows you to install them.
- The Windows Update Catalog allows you to display the complete list of available updates for operating systems. This is useful for obtaining updates for a computer that doesn't have Internet connectivity.
- The Automatic Updates feature is available in Windows 2000 Service Pack 3 and Windows XP. This service automatically contacts the Windows Update servers to determine needed updates, notifies the user when updates are available, and can install updates automatically.
- Microsoft Software Update Services (SUS) is a server component for Windows 2000 Server that locally provides the same service as Windows Update. Clients can be configured to use the local SUS server for Automatic Updates.

Lesson 3: Deploying Updates in the Enterprise

Along with RIS, you can use Group Policy to deploy software updates, including service packs. You can also create custom scripts to install hotfixes or other updates. In this lesson, you look at how Group Policy can simplify software deployment and use the Qchain.exe utility to simplify the installation of multiple hotfixes.

After completing this lesson, you will be able to

- Understand the software installation features of Group Policy
- Deploy a service pack using Group Policy
- Use Qchain.exe to install multiple hotfixes

Estimated lesson time: 30 minutes

Using Group Policy to Deploy Software

Windows 2000 Group Policy includes features for deploying software updates. You can use this feature to deploy a service pack or other installation package across an OU or other Active Directory container.

To make effective use of this feature, you should place computers with identical operating systems and service pack levels in the same OU. If computers within the OU contain a different operating system or incompatible software, the installation process might cause errors. For the same reason, you should use computer policy rather than user policy to deploy software because a user might log on to an incompatible computer.

More Info   Group Policy is explained in detail in Chapter 1, "Group Policy."

Understanding .msi Installation Packages

Windows 2000 includes Windows Installer, a standard utility for installing software updates and other software packages. Windows Installer uses files with the .msi extension to control each installation. The distribution for each service pack includes an Update.msi file for use with the installer. Group Policy features for software installation also use .msi files. After you apply the policy to a group of computers, Windows Installer installs the file on each computer.

Tip   Windows 2000 Server also includes tools for creating custom .msi files, so you can install third-party software using Group Policy.

Creating the GPO

You can deploy a service pack using a user policy or a computer policy. A computer policy is the logical choice because it is not dependent on the logon process and automatically installs the service pack when the computer is booted and connects to the domain.

To create the Group Policy Object (GPO), right-click the OU containing the computers to be updated. Click Properties, and then click the Group Policy tab. Create a new policy, open its Computer Configuration node, and select Software Settings. You can then add the Update.msi package to the policy. This process is detailed in the "Practice: Deploying Multiple Hotfixes in the Enterprise" section.

Installing Multiple Hotfixes

When a large number of hotfixes have been released, especially critical security updates, you might find it inconvenient to install multiple hotfixes at each computer in the network, especially when a reboot is required after each installation. You can use a batch file to simplify this process and install several hotfixes at once.

Using Qchain.exe

Normally, you must reboot a computer after installing each hotfix. Microsoft provides the Qchain.exe utility to simplify this process. This utility configures the system after you install several hotfixes so that a single reboot can correctly install all the hotfixes. You can obtain Qchain.exe from the *http://support.microsoft.com/* Web site. Search for Knowledge Base article #Q296861.

To use Qchain, first run the .exe file for each hotfix, as described in Lesson 1. Use the -z option to prevent the hotfix from rebooting the computer after installation, as in this example:

```
Q123456_w2k_sp4_x86.exe -z
```

After you have installed all of the hotfixes, run the Qchain.exe utility, and then reboot the computer. This ensures that the hotfixes do not conflict with each other.

Important   The Qchain functionality is built into hotfixes for Windows 2000 after Service Pack 3 and into all Windows XP hotfixes. You do not need to use Qchain unless you are installing older hotfixes.

Using Batch Files

You can combine several hotfixes and the Qchain.exe program, if necessary, into a batch file to install multiple hotfixes in a single operation. Use the -m option with each hotfix .exe file to suppress its output, along with the -z option to prevent rebooting. If Qchain.exe is required, include it as the last command in the batch file. The following is a simple example of a batch file to install two hotfixes:

```
Q123456_w2k_sp4_x86.exe -m -z

Q234567_w2k_sp4_x86.exe -m -z

qchain.exe
```

Create the batch file as a text file with the .bat extension. You can then execute this file at each computer that requires the hotfixes.

Using Tools for Security Management

Depending on the size of the network you manage and your particular security concerns, you might find several other tools useful for checking update status and managing software updates across the enterprise. Tools available from Microsoft include the following:

- Microsoft Baseline Security Analyzer (MBSA)
- The HFNetChk command-line utility
- Systems Management Server (SMS)

Microsoft Baseline Security Analyzer

MBSA is a graphical tool that can analyze the security of one or more systems and produce a report. MBSA can check for hotfixes or updates that have not been installed, similar to the Qfecheck.exe tool described earlier in this chapter. It also checks for common security issues, such as misconfigured Guest or Administrator accounts. MBSA can perform checks on the following server components:

- Windows 2000, Windows XP, and Windows NT 4
- Internet Information Services (IIS)
- Internet Explorer
- SQL Server 7.0 or SQL Server 2000
- Exchange Server 5.5 or Exchange Server 2000

You can download MBSA from the Microsoft Technet Web site. It is distributed as a .MSI file and installed by the Windows Installer. Once you start MBSA, you can choose to scan a single computer or multiple computers across the network.

After the scan has completed, MBSA stores its results in an XML (extensible markup language) file and displays it in a graphical interface.

Important   To download MBSA or view its detailed documentation, visit the Technet Web site at *http://www.microsoft.com/technet*, and select Security, Tools And Checklists from the navigation tree.

HFNetChk

HFNetChk is a command-line tool that checks the patch status of one or more machines across the network. Formerly a separate command-line utility, the latest version of HFNetChk is built into MBSA version 1.1, and is used by MBSA to display information in a graphical format.

You can manually run the HFNetChk utility using the Mbsacli.exe /hf command. The Mbsacli.exe program is installed as part of MBSA. You can also use the options described in Table 14.2 on the command line.

Table 14.2   Basic HFNetChk Options

Option	Description
-v	Display detailed information about patches that are not installed.
-u	Specify a user name to access remote computers.
-p	Specify a password to access remote computers.
-h	Specify the host (NetBIOS) names of computers to scan, separated by commas.
-i	Specify the IP addresses of computers to scan, separated by commas.

Important   For more information about HFNetChk including a complete list of command-line options, visit *http://support.microsoft.com* and search for Knowledge Base article #303215.

SMS

Microsoft Systems Management Server (SMS) is a comprehensive tool that can manage the distribution of operating systems, applications, and software updates across the enterprise. It also includes tools for remote troubleshooting and asset management. You can use SMS to deploy updates to a large number of computers and track which computers have been updated.

SMS is a separate product available from Microsoft, and is licensed based on the number of users. For more information about SMS and to learn where to obtain licenses, visit *http://www.microsoft.com/smserver*.

Practice: Deploying Multiple Hotfixes in the Enterprise

In this practice, you create a GPO to deploy a Windows 2000 service pack and create a batch file to install multiple hotfixes. Because the service pack and hotfix levels on your computer can vary, be sure to use only updates you have not already installed instead of those shown in this practice.

Exercise 1: Deploying Updates with Group Policy

In this exercise, you deploy a Windows 2000 service pack by creating a GPO and adding the Update.msi file to the policy.

▶ **To deploy a service pack using Group Policy**

Perform this procedure from the domain controller.

1. Click Start, point to Programs, point to Administrative Tools, and click Active Directory Users And Computers. The Active Directory Users And Computers management console appears.

2. In the console tree, select the Information Technology organizational unit under Department.

3. From the Action menu, choose Properties. The Information Technology Properties dialog box appears.

4. Select the Group Policy tab. The Group Policy Properties are displayed.

5. Click New, and name the new policy Service Pack 3.

6. Click Edit to edit the GPO. The Group Policy management console appears.

7. In the console tree, expand Computer Configuration, Software Settings, and select the Software Installation.

8. From the Action menu, point to New and then choose Package. The Open dialog box is displayed, as shown in Figure 14.28.

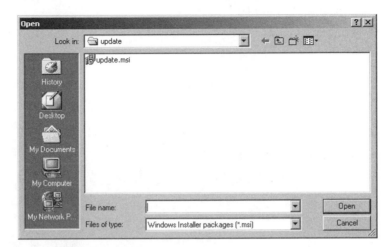

Figure 14.28   Selecting a package file

9. Select the C:\SP3\I386\Update\Update.msi file, and click Open.

Important   This requires that you have extracted the service pack files to C:\SP3, as described in Lesson 1, Exercise 2.

The Deploy Software dialog box appears.

10. Select the Assigned option, and click OK.

The service pack will now be deployed to each computer in the OU when the computer is next booted.

11. Close the Group Policy console.

12. Click OK to close the Information Technology Properties dialog box.

13. Close the Active Directory Users And Computers management console.

Exercise 2: Using Qchain and Batch Files

In this exercise, you create a batch file to install multiple hotfixes using the Qchain.exe utility.

▶ **To create a batch file to install multiple hotfixes**

1. From the command prompt, type **edit fix.bat**. The text editor is displayed, as shown in Figure 14.29.

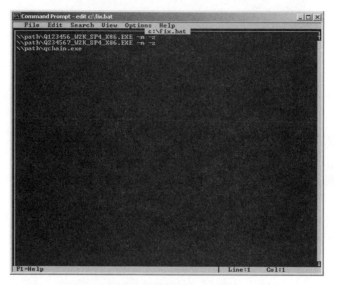

Figure 14.29   Creating a batch file

2. Type two or more hotfix .exe file names in the batch file. Be sure to include the correct path to the location of the hotfixes.

3. Type **Qchain.exe** as the last line.

4. From the File menu, choose Exit.

5. Select Yes to save the batch file.

   After you have created the batch file, you can run it by typing its name at the command prompt or in the Run dialog box, or run it on multiple computers using Group Policy.

Lesson Review

The following questions are intended to reinforce key information in this lesson. If you are unable to answer a question, review the lesson and try the question again. Answers to the questions can be found in the appendix.

1. Which file format does Group Policy support for installation files?

2. What is the package file name for a service pack?

3. Are user or computer policies better for deploying service packs?

4. What is the purpose of the Qchain.exe utility?

5. For which hotfixes is Qchain.exe required?

Lesson Summary

- You can use Group Policy to deploy a service pack or other software updates. This allows you to update all of the computers within an Active Directory container object. To accomplish this, you create a new policy and assign the package to its Software Installation node.

- Group Policy deploys software in Windows Installer .msi packages. Each service pack includes an Update.msi package for this purpose, and other software is also available in this format.

- You can use a batch file to deploy multiple hotfixes. With older hotfixes, the Qchain.exe utility is required to enable the hotfixes to be installed without rebooting after each one.

A P P E N D I X

Questions and Answers

Chapter 1: Group Policy
Lesson 1: Active Directory and Group Policy

Page 7

▶ **Lesson Review Questions**

1. To what must you link GPOs for them to take effect?

   GPOs must be linked to Active Directory objects to take effect.

2. What are the types of Active Directory containers?

   Domains, OUs, and sites are all Active Directory containers.

3. What does an Active Directory hierarchy usually model?

   A business's organizational structure.

4. What are the two reasons for a business to use more than one domain?

   Businesses use more than one domain if they are extremely large (more than 100,000 employees) or if they need especially strong security enforcement between business units.

Lesson 2: Configuring Group Policy

Page 17

▶ **Exercise Question**
Exercise 1: Creating GPOs

8. Type **Domain Standard Desktop** as the name of the GPO. Two GPOs have now been created.

   Why would you want to create a separate GPO to manage settings at the same Active Directory level as an existing GPO, rather than simply modifying the existing object?

   While it is good practice to minimize the number of GPOs, it is more important to separate GPOs by widely separated themes such as security and convenience, because you are highly like to change where these types of GPOs will be linked into the directory in the future.

Page 26   ▶ **Lesson Review Questions**

1. From what management tool can you create GPOs?

   From both the Active Directory Users And Computers management console and the Active Directory Sites And Services management console.

2. When you create a GPO, what is automatically created along with it?

   A link to the Active Directory container from which you created the GPO.

3. What is the default application order for GPOs?

   Local, site, domain, OU.

4. Group Policy is implemented by distinct components called what?

   Group Policy client-side extensions.

Lesson 3: Configuring Client Computer Security Policy

Page 43   ▶ **Lesson Review Questions**

1. What is the most important security feature of Group Policy?

   The ability to restrict users to an allowed set of executables.

2. What is the easiest way to test how Group Policy will affect a class of users?

   Create a test user account that is located in the same Active Directory container as the users you want to test.

3. What security component is required to truly secure users and computers from potentially harmful Internet content?

   A security proxy server.

4. What should users be restricted from using to prevent them from mis-configuring their computers?

   The MMC.

5. Why would you delete drive mappings prior to establishing them in a logon script?

   Because mappings will be ignored if a drive mapping already exists with the same drive letter.

Lesson 4: Troubleshooting Group Policy Application

Page 51   ▶ **Lesson Review Questions**

1. To which file does Windows log Group Policy application errors?

   %systemroot%\Debug\userenv.log.

2. If a new Windows 2000 client computer can log on to the local domain controller, but no Group Policy is applied for the machine or user configurations, what is the most likely problem?

   DNS is not configured correctly on the client.

3. If you log on to a Windows 2000 domain from a Windows NT 4 computer using a user account managed by Active Directory, how will Group Policy be applied?

The user configuration will come from Group Policy, and the machine configuration will come from system policy.

Lesson 5: Security Limitations

Page 55   ▶   **Lesson Review Questions**

1. What are some of the ways that users could interfere with the application of Group Policy on their computers?

By changing DNS settings or by unplugging their computer's network cable during the logon phase.

2. If you disable access to the C drive in a Group Policy, what methods might a user use to regain access to it?

Using the command prompt or a third-party file manager, by connecting to the default share through the Network Neighborhood, or by using the DOS Subst command to map a different drive letter to it.

3. If you limit a client computer to running just a single program, how might a hacker run the program of their choice?

By renaming the program to have the same name as the allowed program.

Chapter 2: User Accounts and Security Groups
Lesson 1: Creating Local User Accounts and Security Groups

Page 72   ▶   **Lesson Review Questions**

1. If a user account has been deleted, can you restore it by creating a user with the same name? Why or why not?

No, because the system identifies accounts by their SID, which would not be the same.

2. What happens to local accounts when a computer is joined to a domain?

Nothing. They remain available and active. However, local accounts are destroyed when a server is upgraded to domain controller status by installing Active Directory.

3. What is the difference between workgroup background authentication and domain authentication when a user accesses a resource on a remote computer?

Workgroup background authentication passes the user's account name and password to the remote computer, while domain authentication passes the user's SIDs between the computers involved.

Lesson 2: Working with Active Directory Domain Accounts and Security Groups

Page 89   ▶ **Lesson Review Questions**

1. What is the difference between a global group and a domain local group?

   Domain local groups are not added to a user's TGT or session tickets. They are added to access tokens when the access tokens are created by the server on which the session is established.

2. Are access tokens ever transmitted across the network?

   No. Access tokens are created for each unique session on every server to which a client attaches. Security identifiers are transmitted over the network in TGT and session tickets.

3. What are universal groups?

   Universal groups are security groups that are valid throughout the Active Directory forest for very common security group categories.

4. What is the purpose of separating groups into user groups and resource groups, when you can use the same groups for both purposes?

   The purpose is to reduce the amount of network traffic required to create an access token. By securing a resource only with groups that are local to the domain, servers do not need to create extra inter-domain network traffic to check permissions.

Chapter 3: Restricting Accounts, Users, and Groups
Lesson 1: Understanding Account Policies

Page 103   ▶ **Lesson Review Questions**

1. How many logon attempts can hackers perpetrate against a Windows 2000 server in one hour?

   Over 4 million.

2. What is the shortest recommended length for a password for a network connected to the Internet?

   At least 12 characters.

3. What is the default maximum time difference between a client and a server before Kerberos tickets can no longer be decrypted?

   Five minutes.

Lesson 2: Managing User Rights

Page 108 ▶ **Lesson Review Questions**

1. How are user rights managed?

   Through Group Policy Objects linked to Active Directory containers.

2. At what level in the Active Directory are user rights applied?

   User rights can be linked to any Group Policy container.

3. What is the typical use of user rights?

   Applications typically modify the user rights of their service accounts during installation to properly perform their function.

4. How often do user rights need to be modified by administrators?

   Administrators rarely need to modify user rights directly.

Lesson 3: Controlling Access Through Restricted Groups

Page 112 ▶ **Lesson Review Questions**

1. What is the primary purpose of restricted groups?

   To enforce control over group membership in large domains where administrative authority has been delegated widely.

2. What subtle difference exists between the way that restricted groups handle members and the way they handle being members of another group?

   The restricted groups feature adds and removes members, and creates memberships in other groups for the restricted group, but it does not remove the restricted group from the membership of other groups.

3. How should you create members of a restricted group?

   Add the group to the membership list of the restricted group and let Group Policy make the membership change.

Lesson 4: Administering Security Templates

Page 126 ▶ **Exercise Question**
Exercise 6: Using the Security Configuration and Analysis Management Console

8. In the management console, expand Security Configuration and Analysis, Account Policy, Password Policy, and select Maximum Password Age.

   Notice that the effective setting does not match the policy that was just applied.

   Why have the settings on this domain controller not taken effect?

   Because the local GPO settings have been overriden by the domain GPO, which has different settings.

Page 127   ▶   **Exercise Question**
Exercise 8: Using SecEdit.exe

11. Click OK to close the User Defined Templates Properties dialog box.

   Why does this exercise specify reducing security and using the Everyone group, rather than using a more secure group such as Domain Users?

   Because the security templates in this share will be accessed by startup scripts. Startup scripts run in the user context of a computer's local system account, so they are not a part of any typical security group. Everyone access is required to allow these types of machine accounts to access files prior to a user log on.

Page 129   ▶   **Lesson Review Questions**

1. What is the easiest way to deploy security templates?

   By importing them into Group Policy Objects.

2. What is the primary purpose of the Security Configuration And Analysis snap-in?

   To compare a computer's effective security configuration to a security template baseline.

3. When would it be appropriate to use the SecEdit.exe tool?

   Whenever you cannot accomplish your deployment goals using Group Policy Objects.

4. In what format are security templates stored?

   As text files.

Chapter 4: Account-Based Security
Lesson 1: Managing File System Permissions

Page 151   ▶   **Lesson Review Questions**

1. What does Windows attach to a secured resource to manage permissions?

   A security descriptor containing an access control list.

2. What is an access control list?

   A list of access control entries that specifies the actions that security principals are allowed to take on the secured resource.

3. If a user has Read and Write permission because of a membership in one group, has Full Control because of membership in a second group, and has a Deny Write ACE because of membership in a third group, what are the user's effective permissions?

   All actions except Write will be allowed for this user.

4. If a resource has no ACL, what are the effective permissions?

   Full Control for all users; resources without ACLs cannot be secured.

Lesson 2: Implementing Share Service Security

Page 160   ▶   **Exercise Question**
Exercise 2: Managing Share Security

5. In the Allow column, clear the Change permission check box.

What is the effective difference between clearing the Allow check box and selecting the Deny check box?

Clearing the Allow check box doesn't permit Information Technology users to change files, but membership in another group may allow the same user Change access. The Deny check box will prevent any member of Information Technology Users from changing files in this share, regardless of their membership in other groups.

Page 160   ▶   **Lesson Review Questions**

1. If you set NTFS permissions on a shared folder that allow Full Control to the Domain Admins group and no other permissions, but the share security settings allow Full Control to the Everyone group, what are the effective permissions for the folder?

The effective permissions would be Full Control for the Domain Admins group. The most restrictive permissions are the effective permissions when NTFS and share permissions conflict.

2. Why is it important to rely on NTFS permissions for share security?

Because there are many ways to circumvent share security by accessing files through other mechanisms, such as FTP or local disk access.

3. Why should you set share permissions when NTFS permissions can perform the same security function on an NTFS volume?

Because the additional security might prevent unauthorized access in the event that NTFS permissions are incorrectly set.

Lesson 3: Using Audit Policies

Page 170   ▶   **Lesson Review Questions**

1. Why should you be judicious in your use of auditing rather than audit all possible events?

Excessive auditing puts the system under unnecessary load and creates numerous unimportant security log entries that can make it difficult to find high-priority activities.

2. How would you use auditing to determine if hackers are attempting to run a password list against the administrative account of a computer attached to the Internet?

By enabling the account logon audit policy and searching the security log for numerous failed logon events in a short period of time.

3. How would you use auditing to determine if an employee has been changing the reported hours worked in a Microsoft Excel spreadsheet after the accounting department has left at 5:00 P.M.?

By enabling object access auditing, creating an SACL entry on the work hours spreadsheet to record successful write and append operations on the file, and then searching for audit events associated with the user's account that occur after 5:00 P.M.

4. How does auditing prevent users from damaging files to which they have access?

Auditing does not prevent users from damaging files to which they have access. It can only record that the activity occurred.

Lesson 4: Including Registry Security

Page 176   ▶   **Lesson Review Questions**

1. What security mechanism is used to provide security for registry keys?
ACL-based permissions.

2. How are registry permissions problems in Windows 2000 normally dealt with?
Through the hotfixes and service packs developed by Microsoft.

3. What tool is used to modify registry permissions in Windows?
RegEdt32.

Chapter 5: Certificate Authorities
Lesson 1: Understanding Certificates

Page 187   ▶   **Lesson Review Questions**

1. What is the difference between a symmetrical algorithm and an asymmetrical algorithm?

Symmetrical algorithms use the same key for encryption and decryption, whereas asymmetrical algorithms use different keys for each purpose.

2. How does a digital signature system differ from a public key cryptosystem?

In a public key system, the encryption key is made public. In a digital signature system, the decryption key is made public.

3. How does a certificate authority sign a document?

By performing a checksum operation on the document and embedding the result in an encrypted digital signature that is appended to the document.

4. How does a CA certify another CA?

By digitally signing that CA's certificate.

Lesson 2: Installing Windows 2000 Certificate Services

Page 201   ▶   **Lesson Review Questions**

1. What is the strongest standard CSP provided by Microsoft?

    Microsoft Enhanced CSP.

2. How are certificates normally requested from a stand-alone CA?

    Through the Web service at *http://localhost/certsrv*.

3. What is the primary difference between an enterprise CA and a stand-alone CA?

    Enterprise CAs can issue Windows 2000 domain-specific certificates.

4. How many certificate authorities can a single server host?

    One.

Lesson 3: Maintaining Certificate Authorities

Page 208   ▶   **Exercise Question**
Exercise 2: Managing the CRL

5. When the Certificate Revocation List dialog box appears, click the Revocation List tab. Verify that the CRL is empty.

    Why does the CRL appear to be empty when certificates have been revoked?

    Because the CRL publication interval has not yet expired, so changes the CRL have not yet been published.

Page 211   ▶   **Lesson Review Questions**

1. What are the two mechanisms through which a certificate can be rendered invalid?

    Expiration and certificate revocation.

2. What are the two methods by which the CRL is published in Windows 2000?

    In the Active Directory database and in a text file stored in a shared file.

3. What is the best way to back up a CA?

    By using the standard Windows 2000 Backup tool or a third-party server backup solution.

Chapter 6: Managing a Public Key Infrastructure
Lesson 1: Working with Computer Certificates

Page 223   ▶   **Lesson Review Questions**

1. What is the primary purpose for computer certificates in Windows 2000?

   Computer certificates are used primarily for encrypting communications using IPSec.

2. When would you choose to use manual computer certificate deployment?

   When you have a limited number of computers that require certificates and you don't want to encumber your certificate authority with requests from numerous computers.

3. When would you choose to use automatic computer certificate deployment?

   When you want to deploy computer certificates throughout your organization.

4. What tool do you use to perform manual deployment?

   The Certificates management console.

5. What tool do you use to perform automatic deployment?

   Group Policy.

Lesson 2: Deploying User Certificates

Page 235   ▶   **Lesson Review Questions**

1. Can administrators create user certificates on behalf of users without knowing their account user name and password?

   No. User certificates are designed to be individually requested by the user.

2. For which purposes can user certificates be used?

   To encrypt files, authenticate with Web sites, and secure e-mail.

3. Where is a user's certificate store permanently stored?

   In the user's profile.

4. What is the recommended method for moving certificate stores when a user changes workstations?

   Enable roaming profiles to allow the profile to move with the user.

5. Which certificate format is used to export and import user certificates?

   PKCS #12.

6. Which type of certificates can be exported without being explicitly marked as exportable?

   Certificates automatically generated for EFS.

Lesson 3: Using Smart Card Certificates

Page 251 ▶ **Lesson Review Questions**

1. What is a smart card?

   A device containing a microprocessor and permanent memory, some of which is designated as a private store and is available only to the onboard microprocessor.

2. Are there any types of computers that cannot support smart card readers?

   No. All computers contain the necessary hardware to support smart card readers.

3. For what purposes are smart cards used in Windows 2000?

   For log on, e-mail security, and disk encryption.

4. What does an administrator do to authorize a smart card to function in the domain?

   Sign it with an enrollment agent certificate.

5. What program is used to deploy smart cards?

   Smart cards are deployed by using the Smart Card Enrollment Station page on the CertSrv Web site.

Lesson 4: Deploying S/MIME Certificates

Page 258 ▶ **Lesson Review Questions**

1. Why can't you use user certificates in many e-mail clients to sign and encrypt e-mail?

   Because they don't contain the user's e-mail address in the Identity field.

2. Why is an e-mail address usually required in the Identity field of an S/MIME certificate?

   To guarantee that mail is being delivered from the e-mail address claimed in the certificate. The mail client program can ensure that the address in the certificate is the same as the address configured in the client, so there's no possibility of fraudulently stating a different e-mail address than the certificate specifies.

3. Why don't user certificates contain e-mail addresses?

   Because e-mail addresses are not necessarily entered in Active Directory, and user certificates are optimized for automatic issuance.

4. Why does Outlook accept user certificates if they don't contain an e-mail address?

   Because it trusts that the certificate was generated by an enterprise CA, which required a legitimate domain log on to authenticate the user.

Chapter 7: Increasing Authentication Security
Lesson 1: Supporting Earlier Versions of Windows Clients

Page 268 ▶ **Lesson Review Questions**

1. What are the four types of authentication supported by Windows 2000 to support current and earlier versions of Windows clients?

   LAN Manager, NTLM, NTLM version 2, and Kerberos.

2. Which two authentication protocols are considered the most secure?

   NTLM version 2 and Kerberos.

3. What components must be installed in Windows 98 to use NTLM version 2?

   The latest version of Internet Explorer and the Directory Services client.

4. What encryption strength is used to secure NTLM version 2 passwords?

   128-bit encryption.

Lesson 2: Supporting Macintosh Clients

Page 277 ▶ **Lesson Review Questions**

1. What server component is used to provide the Apple File Service?

   Services for Macintosh.

2. Is AppleTalk required to provide service to Macintosh clients?

   No. All recent versions of the Mac OS can use TCP/IP as their network layer transport.

3. What client component provides NTLM version 2 authentication for Macintosh computers?

   The Microsoft User Authentication Module (UAM).

4. Does the NTLM version 2 compatible Microsoft UAM require reversible encryption to support Macintosh clients?

   No. Reversible encryption is required for earlier UAMs and plaintext passwords only.

Lesson 3: Trust Relationships

Page 284 ▶ **Exercise Question**
Exercise: Establishing a Trust Relationship

4. Type **\\GDI-DC1-01\Fabrikam** as the name of the network place, and click Next.

   What would you type as the name of the server if the two servers were not on the same network?

   Gdi-dc1-01.extranet.graphicdesigninstitute.com or the server's IP address.

Page 284   ▶   **Lesson Review Questions**

1. What are the three reasons why you would explicitly modify trust relationships?

   To establish trust with a Windows NT 4 server, to establish trust with an external server, and to create a trust shortcut in a complex forest.

2. What is the difference between transitive and non-transitive trust?

   Transitive trust stipulates that if domain A trusts domain B, and domain B trusts domain C, then domain A trusts domain C.

3. What is the difference between one-way and two-way trust relationships?

   One-way trust relationships allow one domain to trust accounts in another, but not vice versa. Two-way trust relationships are reciprocal.

4. What type of trust relationship results when you manually create a trust relationship?

   A one-way non-transitive trust relationship.

5. What type of trust relationship is automatically created when a domain is added to a forest?

   A two-way transitive trust relationship.

Chapter 8: IP Security
Lesson 1: Configuring IPSec Within a Domain

Page 301   ▶   **Lesson Review Questions**

1. What are the two primary methods IPSec uses to authenticate and encrypt IP packets?

   Authenticated Headers (AH) and Encapsulating Security Payload (ESP).

2. What are the two encrypted payload modes that IPSec supports?

   Transport mode and tunnel mode.

3. Explain the difference between transport mode and tunnel mode.

   Transport mode encrypts the packet payload. Tunnel mode encrypts the entire packet and creates a new header to transport it.

4. How does IKE determine whether to trust the participants when it establishes a security association?

   By the presence of the same shared secret on both systems.

5. How is IPSec managed in Windows 2000?

   By using Group Policy.

6. What mechanism would you use to distribute secret keys automatically in a domain?

   Kerberos secret keys can be used with minimal administrative effort.

Lesson 2: Configuring IPSec Between Untrusted Networks

Page 319   ▶   **Lesson Review Questions**

1. Which methods are available to distribute IKE secret keys in Windows 2000?

    Kerberos, manual keying, and certificates.

2. When would you use manual keying rather than Kerberos or certificates?

    When servers do not participate in a domain trust relationship and do not have an IPSec compatible certificate from the same certificate authority in common.

3. How is IPSec policy defined in Windows 2000?

    By using filter lists containing filters that specify the hosts, networks, or ports that should trigger filter actions.

4. Name the types of traffic that are never secured by IPSec.

    Broadcast, multicast, IKE, Kerberos, or QOS.

Lesson 3: Configuring IPSec on Internet Servers

Page 329   ▶   **Lesson Review Questions**

1. When would it be appropriate to use certificates to distribute IKE secrets?

    Whenever no domain trust relationship exists and certificates are available for use.

2. What are the two requirements for certificates to work correctly for IKE negotiation?

    They must be rooted in the same trusted CA, and they must contain a private key.

3. What two portions of a GPO apply to certificate deployment?

    The IP Security portion allows you to create and apply IPSec policies, and the Automatic Certificate Request portion allows you to automatically create and deploy certificates that are compatible with IPSec to computers in a domain or OU.

Lesson 4: Troubleshooting IPSec Configuration

Page 336   ▶   **Lesson Review Questions**

1. What IPSec problem could have the most serious consequences?

    Thinking that data flowing between end systems is secured when it isn't.

2. What utility is used to refresh Group Policy on a computer that receives its IPSec configuration from a domain GPO?

    Secedit.

3. What utility is used to enable IKE logging?

    The Registry Editor.

4. What's the easiest way to eliminate IKE as a potential problem source?

Use manual keying.

5. What problems might cause certificate-based IKE negotiations to fail?

Certificates lack a private key or are not rooted in the same certificate authority.

Chapter 9: Remote Access and VPN
Lesson 1: Securing RRAS Servers

Page 350   ▶   **Lesson Review Questions**

1. Which utility do you use to manage most of Windows 2000's RRAS settings?

The Routing And Remote Access management console.

2. If you select automatic IP address assignment for an RRAS server, where do IP addresses come from?

From a DHCP server if available, otherwise from the RRAS server's static address pool.

3. What is the easiest way to set up an RRAS server on a Windows 2000 Server computer?

Using the Routing And Remote Access Server Setup Wizard.

4. How can you change the settings of a server, such as its IP addressing, after configuring RRAS?

Using the server Properties dialog box in the Routing And Remote Access management console.

5. How can you allow a user to connect to RRAS without using remote access policies?

Using the dial-in properties for the user account.

Lesson 2: Managing RRAS Authentication

Page 357   ▶   **Exercise Question**
Exercise 1: Selecting Windows Authentication Methods

4. Select the MS-CHAP v2 check box, and clear the other check boxes.

Why would you limit authentication options rather than simply select them all?

To prevent users from authenticating with less secure protocols that could present their credentials in a form that is easy to intercept.

Page 363   ▶ **Lesson Review Questions**

1. Which RRAS authentication type can be used with an RRAS server to provide centralized authentication?

   RADIUS authentication.

2. Which Windows authentication method uses completely unencrypted passwords?

   PAP (Password Authentication Protocol).

3. What Windows authentication method would you use to support smart card authentication?

   EAP (Extensible Authentication Protocol).

4. How do you manage authentication and security policy settings for an RRAS server when RADIUS authentication is in use?

   Using the Internet Authentication Service (IAS) management console.

5. In a network using an IAS server to provide centralized management of dial-in authentication for several RRAS servers, to which machine do dial-up clients send authentication requests?

   Their local RRAS server, which then sends a request to the IAS server for authentication.

Lesson 3: Securing Remote Clients

Page 380   ▶ **Lesson Review Questions**

1. When RADIUS is not in use, what tool do you use to manage remote access policies?

   The Routing And Remote Access management console.

2. If a user is connecting to an RRAS server and matches several remote access policies, which policy will be used for the connection?

   The first policy that matches, based on the order set in the console.

3. How would you restrict the session length for a remote access policy?

   From the Edit Dial-In Profile dialog box in the policy Properties dialog box.

4. When you answer the questions in the Connection Manager Administration Kit Wizard, where are the answers saved?

   In a service profile, stored in a .cms file.

5. What happens if an incoming connection matches a remote access policy and the policy is set to deny access?

   The user is denied access, unless the user account is explicitly granted permission in its properties.

Lesson 4: Securing Communications Using a VPN

Page 395 ▶ **Lesson Review Questions**

1. Which of the VPN protocols supported by Windows 2000 Server is considered more secure?

   L2TP (using IPsec encryption).

2. Which utility can quickly configure an RRAS server to act as a VPN server?

   The Routing And Remote Access Server Setup Wizard.

3. Where do you add a VPN connection from a Windows 2000 Professional client?

   From the Network And Dial-up Connections window.

4. Which VPN protocol requires certificate-based authentication?

   L2TP.

5. What information is required from a client to connect to a remote VPN?

   The VPN server's IP address, and possibly specific protocols or encryption levels.

Chapter 10: Wireless Security
Lesson 1: Setting Up a Wireless Network

Page 408 ▶ **Lesson Review Questions**

1. What is the most common variant of the 802.11 protocol?

   802.11b.

2. How does adding wireless capability to your network affect security?

   Wireless capability significantly degrades security unless strict compensating measures are taken.

3. What is WEP?

   Wired Equivalent Privacy (WEP), a data link layer encryption protocol used to prevent snooping and unauthorized access.

4. What is the most common method used to prevent WLANs from allowing access to a private network?

   Placing WAPs outside the firewall boundary and treating them as if they were Internet clients.

5. What is wardriving?

   The practice of searching for unsecured WLANs that provide Internet access.

Lesson 2: Securing Wireless Networks

Page 413
▶ **Exercise Question**
Exercise 1: Configuring Security on a Wireless Access Point

9. When a Restart Access Point message appears, click OK.

You will find that you are unable to reload the management page. Why?

Because the WAP now requires WEP encryption to connect.

Page 416
▶ **Lesson Review Questions**

1. What does WEP stand for, and why was that name chosen?

Wired Equivalent Privacy, because the security was intended to be as good as the security of a typical wired network.

2. What types of authentication are supported?

Open, which is not authenticated, and Shared Key, which implements shared secret key authentication.

3. What encryption algorithm is used to encrypt WEP payloads?

RC4 stream encryption.

4. What common key lengths are available for use with WEP?

40-bit, 128-bit, 154-bit, and 256-bit key lengths.

5. Is there a standard protocol used to establish WEP secret keys among all WAPs in an enterprise?

No standard method exists.

Lesson 3: Configuring Clients for Wireless Security

Page 436
▶ **Lesson Review Questions**

1. What is the most difficult security problem that wireless networks cause?

The illicit attachment of uncontrolled wireless equipment to your network.

2. What security measure is required to prevent the illicit attachment of uncontrolled wireless equipment, and what protocol was developed to solve it?

Authentication of attached equipment at the data-link layer, 802.1x.

3. How does 802.1x work?

It blocks all but authentication traffic from clients until an authentication server informs the WAP that the client has been authenticated.

4. Which component of Windows 2000 is used to implement authentication for 802.1x?

Internet Authentication Server (IAS).

5. What is the primary problem with 802.1x that will prevent its adoption in the near term?

All data-link layer infrastructure equipment must support the protocol for it to solve the illicit WAP attachment problem.

Chapter 11: Public Application Server Security
Lesson 1: Providing Internet Security

Page 455   ▶   **Lesson Review Questions**

1. Why is it difficult to protect public servers?

Because you must allow anonymous users to connect to them while preventing those users from performing any activity that might damage the system.

2. Are all hacking attempts serious?

No. Automated attacks and random target-of-opportunity attacks are common. Once your network has been secured against them, they are of little consequence.

3. What is the most important attack vector to defend against and why?

The Internet, because other access points can be placed outside the network and treated like the Internet.

4. What is a perimeter network?

A security zone between the public Internet and the private network where public servers that are trusted but might be exploited are located.

5. What are the primary types of firewalls that are available?

Firewall routers and security proxies.

Lesson 2: Configuring Microsoft SQL Server for Internet Security

Page 466   ▶   **Exercise Question**
Exercise 3: Verifying SQL Connectivity Through the Firewall

2. In the SQL Server box, type **10.0.0.90**.

Why do you enter the IP address of the ISA server rather than the IP Address of the SQL server in the SQL Server box?

Because the ISA server is publishing (proxying) the SQL server's SQL Service port on its own external IP address and forwarding requests.

Page 467 ▶ **Lesson Review Questions**

1. Which public security problem represents more risk for most businesses: the exploitation of a Web server or the exploitation of a database server?

   Database server, because it stores proprietary and sensitive information.

2. What is the proper security zone for a database server in a typical network architecture?

   Inside the private network.

3. How does ISA Server secure Microsoft SQL Server database servers?

   By proxying the TCP/IP SQL protocol.

4. How does SQL Server ensure that only specific clients can connect to it?

   By requiring SSL with certificates rooted in the same certificate authority as the server.

Lesson 3: Securing Microsoft Exchange Server for the Internet

Page 482 ▶ **Lesson Review Questions**

1. What are the two primary problems affecting e-mail on the Internet?

   Lack of authentication and lack of secure communication.

2. How does Exchange Server solve these problems?

   By using SSL to secure communications.

3. Why is it unwise to place an Exchange server in the perimeter network?

   Because Exchange 2000 servers must participate heavily in Active Directory and therefore communicate a considerable amount of private information that is difficult to securely transmit through a firewall.

4. What are common methods used to secure an Exchange 2000 server inside a private network?

   Relaying mail through an SMTP relay in the perimeter network or using a strong security proxy like ISA Server to proxy e-mail protocols.

5. What method of encryption does Exchange Server support for passing credentials?

   Secure Sockets Layer (SSL).

Chapter 12: Web Service Security
Lesson 1: Securing Public Web Servers

Page 494   ▶   **Lesson Review Questions**

1. What component provides Web services in Windows 2000 Server?

   Internet Information Services (IIS).

2. What type of authentication is normally used for public Internet Web sites?

   Anonymous access.

3. Which tab in the Properties dialog box for a Web site includes most security options?

   The Directory Security tab.

4. What additional mechanisms should you use to enhance security besides IIS service-specific security options?

   IP filtering and NTFS permissions.

5. Which services can IIS provide along with HTTP?

   FTP, SMTP, and NNTP.

Lesson 2: Web Authentication

Page 503   ▶   **Lesson Review Questions**

1. Which are the two least secure authentication methods?

   Basic authentication and digest authentication.

2. Which authentication method uses Windows user accounts?

   Integrated Windows authentication.

3. Which authentication method supports client and server certificates?

   Secure Sockets Layer (SSL).

4. Which dialog box includes options to enable authentication methods and anonymous access?

   The Authentication Methods dialog box accessed from the Directory Security tab in the Web site Properties dialog box.

5. For which IIS resources can you select authentication methods?

   Web sites, folders, and virtual directories.

Lesson 3: Using Secure Sockets Layer

Page 527   ▶ **Lesson Review Questions**

1. What is required to enable SSL on an IIS server?

    A computer certificate and client browsers that support SSL.

2. Which feature allows you to connect user accounts with particular client certificates?

    Client certificate mapping.

3. When a CTL is in use, which clients are allowed access?

    Clients with a certificate issued by a trusted certificate authority (CA) on the certificate trust list (CTL).

4. Which option do you enable to prevent clients from accessing a site without a client certificate?

    Require Client Certificates.

5. What are the two types of client certificate mapping?

    One-to-one and many-to-one.

Chapter 13: Intrusion Detection and Event Monitoring
Lesson 1: Establishing Intrusion Detection for Public Servers

Page 544   ▶ **Lesson Review Questions**

1. Which type of attack attempts to log on with a user's password?

    An impersonation attack.

2. What type of attacks cannot be detected using a decoy server?

    Access to legitimate public ports and services.

3. What is the purpose of saving event logs after an attack?

    To preserve evidence of the attack.

4. Where in the network should a decoy server be placed?

    In the perimeter network, with public servers.

5. What tool recognizes intrusion attempts through URLs on a Web server?

    URLScan.

Lesson 2: Event Monitoring in the Private Network

Page 554 ▶ **Lesson Review Questions**

1. What should you do after detecting intrusion on a system?

   Back up the event logs if possible, and shut down the server if it was damaged.

2. What are the three basic log files used in Windows 2000?

   Application Log, System Log, Security Log.

3. Where can you manage log retention settings?

   In the Group Policy properties for the domain.

4. Which utility allows you to search for events in logs across a network?

   EventComb.

5. Where does EventComb store its results?

   In a text file it creates.

Chapter 14: Software Maintenance
Lesson 1: Working with Service Packs and Hotfixes

Page 571 ▶ **Lesson Review Questions**

1. Which utility displays a summary of service pack and hotfix levels for a computer?

   Qfecheck.exe.

2. Which type of update is not affected by other software updates?

   Service packs.

3. What is the name for the process of adding updates to a set of operating system installation files?

   Slipstreaming.

4. From what two sources can Remote Installation Services (RIS) create an installation image?

   A computer with the operating system installed, or a set of installation files.

5. What are the requirements for the disk used to store a RIS installation image?

   NTFS format, and must not be the system volume.

Lesson 2: Automating Updates with Microsoft Software Update Services

Page 590   ▶   **Lesson Review Questions**

1. Which Windows Update feature notifies users of critical updates and optionally installs updates automatically?

    Automatic Updates.

2. What two sources can be used to obtain the latest updates using Automatic Updates?

    Microsoft Windows Update servers or a local Software Update Services (SUS) server.

3. What service provides a local version of the Windows Update service?

    Microsoft Software Update Services (SUS).

4. How can clients be configured to update using an SUS server?

    Using Group Policy.

5. Where are notification settings for Automatic Updates managed?

    In the Automatic Updates dialog box you access through Control Panel.

Lesson 3: Deploying Updates in the Enterprise

Page 599   ▶   **Lesson Review Questions**

1. Which file format does Group Policy support for installation files?

    Windows Installer .msi packages.

2. What is the package file name for a service pack?

    Update.msi.

3. Are user or computer policies better for deploying service packs?

    Computer policies.

4. What is the purpose of the Qchain.exe utility?

    To allow the installation of multiple hotfixes without rebooting.

5. For which hotfixes is Qchain.exe required?

    For anything prior to Windows 2000 Service Pack 3 or Windows XP.

Glossary

A

Access Control Entry (ACE) An entry in an ACL that binds a Security Identifier to a specific type of access. *See* ACL, SID.

Access Control List (ACL) A list of ACEs attached to an object such as a file, a share, a registry key, or an Active Directory object. *See* ACE.

access token A data structure passed to every running program that contains all the security identifiers of the user who executed the program. The program passes its Access Token to the Security Reference Monitor each time it accesses a secured object so the SRM can compare the SIDs in the Access token to the SIDs contained in the object's ACL to determine what type of access to allow. See Security Reference Monitor, ACL.

account policies Group Policy settings that affect how user accounts can be used and set limits on passwords and other attributes.

account *See* user account.

Active Directory (1) A database of security objects such as user accounts, machine accounts, domains, organizational units, Group Policies, and the links between these objects. Active Directory services provide Single Sign-On functionality for Windows 2000 networks. (2) The Windows 2000 directory service that enables management and security for users, computers, and other resources in a single hierarchy.

Active Directory container An Active Directory object that can contain other objects.

Active Directory object A node of the Active Directory hierarchy that represents a resource or a container for organizing resources.

AH *See* Authenticated Headers.

algorithm A mathematical function implemented as computer code.

anonymous access Access to a service without authentication. Many protocols support both authenticated and anonymous access, such as HTTP, FTP, and SMB, but typically restrict the activities allowed to anonymous users.

asymmetrical An encryption algorithm that uses different keys for the encrypt and decrypt functions.

auditing The process of logging all access to a object so that activities can be reconstructed if a security event occurs.

audit trail Any evidence that can be used to reconstruct a user's activities on a system.

Authenticated Headers (AH) The process of computing a checksum of the data contained in the header of an IP packet to guarantee that the data has not been modified in transit. *See* IPSec.

authentication The process of verifying user identity prior to establishing a session with a service by providing a key.

B

Bandwidth Reservation Protocol A TCP/IP protocol used by routers to provide a guaranteed minimum amount of bandwidth to a specific protocol. Implemented by the Quality of Service protocol in Windows.

biometric authentication Authentication using the unique characteristics of a human as the key. *See* authentication.

brute-force attack An exploit in which a hacker attempts to determine a password or private key by trying all possible values.

buffer overrun attack An exploit in which a data is transmitted to a service that intentionally misrepresents its size, causing the service to allocate less storage space than the data requires, thus overrunning the end of the temporary storage buffer that the service allocated to receive the data. This changes code that the service executes, allowing the attacker to force the service to perform any activity allowed by the operating system.

bug exploit attack A network intrusion method in which a hacker attempts to take advantage of a security-compromising bug in a system, service, or protocol. See also buffer overrun attack, Denial of Service attack.

C

CA *See* certificate authority (CA).

certificate A data structure that can contain numerous public keys and digital signatures. Certificates are primarily used to perform trusted third-party authentication.

certificate authority (CA) A service that accepts and completes or revokes certificate requests.

certificate revocation list (CRL) A published list of certificates that are no longer valid.

Certificate Services A Windows 2000 tool that allows users to request and obtain encryption certificates for use by numerous security services.

Certificate Trust List (CTL) A list of root certifier certificates that a computer trusts.

challenge/response An authentication methodology that allows two parties to prove that they both know a secret without transmitting the secret.

Challenge/Response Authentication Protocol (CHAP) An obsolete but widely implemented challenge/response authentication protocol that is obsolete due to its vulnerability to replay attacks.

cipher An encryption algorithm.

circuit layer proxy A TCP layer proxy that accepts sockets on one interface and regenerates them on another. Circuit layer proxies are typically used in firewalls to prevent TCP and IP malformations from reaching the interior of a private network.

cleartext Unencrypted text used in the context of transmission. *See* plaintext.

computer account A domain account required for each computer that connects to the domain.

converged A functional IPSec connection is said to be converged when IKE is able to negotiate a compatible set of authentication and encryption protocols and successfully transmit data.

crack (n) A software patch designed to circumvent licensing or protection features. (v) To circumvent a software protection.

credentials A user account name and password or secret key. All the information required to prove identity.

cryptanalysis The process of analyzing an encrypted text to determine the key or algorithm used to encrypt it.

Cryptographic Service Provider (CSP) A set of algorithms which implement a specific type of cryptography and which are implemented and managed as a common library for Windows 2000.

cryptography The study of encryption.

D

Data Encryption Standard (DES) An early private key data encryption protocol developed under contract to the U.S. government. DES is now considered weak due to its 56-bit key length, and has been superseded by a variant called triple-DES (3DES) that uses 168-bit keys that are three times as long.

decoy server A server specifically installed and configured to attract hacking attempts and seduce hackers away from valid service machines.

decrypt To transform an obscured text into a plain text by using a mathematical function and a key.

demilitarized zone (DMZ) *See* perimeter network.

Denial of Service (DoS) attack A network intrusion method that attempts to bring a system or service down, usually by overloading it with spurious requests.

Deny ACE An ACE used to explicitly deny access to a SID that may appear in other allow ACEs in a specific ACL. *See Also* ACE, ACL.

digital signature A method of encrypting identity information, such as contact information, in such a way that anyone can decrypt the information to verify it, but only the originator can encrypt the information.

Discretionary Access Control List (DACL) An ACL used to determine whether or not to allow access. *See also* ACL, SACL.

domain A group of computers that all share the same database of security accounts.

domain account A user account that allows access to a domain.

domain controller A computer that manages a domain and stores a database of user accounts or Active Directory objects.

Downlevel Any version of software prior to the currently released and supported version.

E

Encapsulating Security Payload (ESP) An IPSec protocol used to encrypt the data portion of an IP packet. Two modes are available: Transport mode provides encryption only, and tunnel mode encrypts the entire IP packet and places it in another packet as the payload.

encrypt To transform a plain text into an obscured form by using a mathematical function and a key.

Encrypting File System (EFS) A feature of NTFS that provides the ability to encrypt files on demand using a secret key contained in a certificate.

enterprise CA A certificate authority that is part of an enterprise-wide security infrastructure and requires Active Directory.

Exchange Microsoft's e-mail and group messaging service.

Extensible Authentication Protocol (EAP) A protocol that supports various authentication libraries such as smart cards, certificates, and so on.

extranet A private member's only website that is reachable from the Internet by those authorized to do so. Typically used to describe project based web sites set up to support collaboration between business partners rather than consumer to business subscription websites.

F

factoring attack An attack against a password or key in which all possible values are factored and tested. *See* brute force attack.

File Transfer Protocol (FTP) An Internet-standard protocol for transferring files between networks.

firewall A router or server used to filter Internet connections to block unauthorized access and malicious attacks.

forensics The process of reconstructing the details of a security event based on remaining evidence such as audit logs and the damage done.

forest A hierarchy of domains stored in an Active Directory database.

G

gateway A generic term for a computer that receives requests and translates or relays them between networks, such as an e-mail gateway, a security proxy, a firewall, or a router.

Globally Unique Identifier (GUID) An ID number generated using an algorithm that guarantees uniqueness amongst all computers in the world. Sometimes referred to as a Guaranteed Unique Identifier.

GPO *See* Group Policy Object.

Group Policy The primary configuration management tool for Windows networks. Group Policy determines how users are able to work with client computers and servers in a network, which installed software is available to users, how desktops look, and what operating system features are enabled.

Group Policy Object (GPO) A directory containing all the files that are required to enact a Group Policy.

Guest A user account used across a pool of users whose identities are not important. Guest accounts are typically used in services that do not support anonymous access but where anonymous access is desired.

GUID *See* Globally Unique Identifier.

H

hacker (1) A malicious user who attempts to gain unauthorized access to a system, circumvent protections, deny access to other users, or destroy data. (2) Someone who is especially skilled at computer operation.

handshake The process of establishing a connection between a client and a server.

honeypot *See* decoy server.

hotfix A software update designed to correct a single issue and released in between service packs.

HTTP *See* Hypertext Transfer Protocol.

Hypertext Transfer Protocol (HTTP) An Internet-standard protocol used by Web servers to send requested documents, typically Web pages, to clients.

I

IAS *See* Internet Authentication Service.

ICMP *See* Internet Control Message Protocol.

IETF *See* Internet Engineering Task Force.

IIS *See* Internet Information Services.

IKE *See* Internet Key Exchange.

IMAP *See* Internet Mail Access Protocol.

impersonation attack A method of network intrusion in which an attacker attempts to use a legitimate user's username and password.

interior The private side of a firewalled network.

Internet The internetwork to which the vast majority of private networks in the world are attached.

Internet Authentication Service (IAS) The Microsoft implementation of the RADIUS standard, which provides network-wide authentication and accounting.

Internet Control Message Protocol (ICMP) An IP protocol used to pass messages between hosts and routers concerning the state of connections and hosts. ICMP is the protocol used by the ubiquitous ping and trace route utilities.

Internet Engineering Task Force (IETF) A collaborative working group of industry and academic professionals who define the standards used on the Internet.

Internet Information Services (IIS) The Web (HTTP) server included with Windows 2000.

Internet Key Exchange (IKE) The protocol used to establish IPSec connections and to exchange Security Associations.

Internet Mail Access Protocol (IMAP) A client-server mail access protocol designed to replace POP3.

Internet Protocol (IP) A packet based message passing network protocol that defines each participant by using a unique hierarchical number. The core protocol of the Internet.

Internet Protocol Security (IPSec) A suite of protocols designed to authenticate or encrypt IP packets.

Internet Security and Acceleration (ISA) Server Microsoft's firewall and proxy service software.

Internet Service Provider (ISP) A commercial provider of Internet service.

intranet A private network based on Internet protocols. Typically used to describe a private web site that is not reachable from the Internet.

IP *See* Internet Protocol.

IP Security (IPSec) An Internet Engineering Task Force (IETF) body of standards that defines a protocol for authenticating and encrypting IP traffic between hosts on the Internet or within a private IP network.

ISA *See* Internet Security and Acceleration Server.

ISP *See* Internet Service Provider.

K

KDC *See* Key Distribution Center.

Kerberos An authentication service developed for use in multi-vendor distributed networks that uses session tickets and keys to exchange authentication information.

key A number (sometimes expressed as text or as a password) that is used by an encryption algorithm to transform a plain text into an encrypted text or vice versa.

Key Distribution Center (KDC) An authentication server for Kerberos. In Windows 2000, Domain Controllers perform the KDC role.

L

LAN Manager The original password authentication protocol used by Microsoft file sharing systems. LAN Manager password encryption is weak because it reduces the set of characters to uppercase only and encrypts passwords in two 7-character chunks rather than a single 14-character chunk.

Layer 2 Tunneling Protocol (L2TP) A modern host-to-gateway VPN protocol used to establish encrypted connections to networks from remote users. L2TP uses IPSec for encryption. The Windows 2000 RRAS service receives L2TP connections.

local account A user account that allows access to a local computer only.

Local Group Policy The Group Policy objects stored on a local computer and used when a domain policy does not apply.

Local Security Authority (LSA) The component of Windows 2000 that authenticates all access to secured objects on each machine. *See* Security Reference Monitor.

log A list of recorded events.

logon authentication The process of authenticating with a user interactive service.

M

Mail Application Programming Interface (MAPI) The Microsoft client/server e-mail protocol. Outlook communicates with Exchange using MAPI.

member server A server that is a member of a domain but is not a domain controller.

Message Digest Protocol version 5 (MD5) A popular protocol used for hashing passwords and creating checksums.

Microsoft Challenge Authentication Protocol (MS-CHAP) The Microsoft improved version of CHAP.

Microsoft Management Console (MMC) The standard user interface for service management in Windows 2000. Snap-in modules for MMC provide management consoles for Active Directory and other services.

Microsoft User Authentication Module (MS-UAM)
An authentication module for Macintoshes that provides NTLM version 2 support for encrypted passwords.

MMC *See* Microsoft Management Console.

MS-CHAP *See* Microsoft Challenge Authentication Protocol.

N

NAT *See* Network Address Translation.

NetBIOS The Microsoft client server session control protocol used to support file and print sharing. NetBIOS is widely supported but no longer necessary in Windows 2000.

Network Address Translation (NAT) A service that allows multiple computers on a local network to share a public IP address by translating between public and private addresses.

nonce A random number that is encrypted with an encrypted password to ensure that the encrypted password is not revealed during transit over a network.

NTLM A strengthened version of the LAN Manager authentication protocol that hashes pass-words using the full 14-character length supported by Windows NT.

O

organizational unit (OU) A container object in Active Directory that can be used to group users or other resources.

Outlook The Microsoft popular e-mail and personal information management application. Outlook can operate as a client to standard Internet e-mail servers as well as Microsoft Exchange.

P

passthrough authentication The process of a server re-using a clients encrypted credentials to establish a connection to a third server. Passthrough authentication allows sessions to be established in the proper user context rather than in the context of the server performing the connection.

password A secret key memorized by a human.

patching The process of applying changes to a program to fix bugs.

perimeter network A security zone created by firewalls between the public Internet and a private network where machines that must be protected but must also serve public protocols are placed.

permissions The access control mechanism used in Windows 2000 to secure access to various types of resources, such as files and Active Directory objects.

Personal Identification Number (PIN) A short numerical password used to unlock credentials stored on a smart card. PINs are used to confirm that the person using a smart card is the owner and that the smart card has not been stolen.

PKI *See* public key infrastructure.

plaintext An unencrypted file.

Point-to-Point Tunneling Protocol (PPTP) An obso-lete protocol used to create Host-to-Gateway VPN connections for remote users. PPTP is essentially an encrypted extension of PPP, and has been replaced by L2TP which uses much stronger authentication and encryption.

policy A set of rules that define how a system can be used.

port A number that identifies which service a specific TCP or UDP packet

Post Office Protocol version 3 (POP3) The most commonly used client/server mail delivery protocol on the Internet.

proxy server A gateway designed to terminate and reestablish connections forwarded through it so that it can filter each protocol specifically for inappropriate content.

public key encryption An encryption method that uses two keys, a publicly distributed encryption key and a private held decryption key.

public key infrastructure (PKI) The system of certificate authorities and certificate-based services that provide secure trust throughout an enterprise.

Q

Qchain A utility available from Microsoft that allows multiple hotfixes to be installed on a computer without rebooting. Qchain is not required for newer hotfixes since they have this functionality built in.

R

RADIUS *See* Remote Authentication Dial-In User Service.

realm A group of computers that share the same Kerberos KDC. Analogous to a domain in Windows.

registry The central configuration database for Windows and most software installed on a Windows-based computer. Internally, the registry is viewed as a hierarchical structure of keys and values.

Remote Authentication Dial-In User Service (RADIUS) A standard for servers that provide network-wide authentication and accounting services. IAS (Internet Authentication Service) is the RADIUS server included with Windows 2000 Server.

Remote Desktop Protocol (RDP) A Microsoft protocol designed to transport the desktop image to remote users and return their keystrokes and mouse clicks. RDP is implemented by Terminal Services in Windows 2000.

Remote Installation Services (RIS) A Windows 2000 service that stores an operating system

image and allows the installation of a client's operating system across the network.

replay attack An impersonation attack in which encrypted credentials are not decrypted, but are simply recorded and then re-used later to gain access to a server. Challenge/Response protocols were developed to counter replay attacks.

RDP *See* Remote Desktop Protocol.

Resource Reservation Setup Protocol (RSVP) *See* Bandwidth Reservation Protocol

RIS *See* Remote Installation Services

Rivest's Cipher #2 (RC2) A common block encryption protocol typically used for encrypting files and originally designed as a drop-in replacement for DES.

Rivest's Cipher #4 (RC4) A common stream encryption protocol typically used for encrypting network sessions. SSL uses RC4 as it's encryption cipher.

Root CA The topmost certificate authority in a certification hierarchy.

router A special purpose computer designed to forward packets, especially IP packets. Firewalls are routers that filter IP packets.

Routing and Remote Access (RRAS) Service The Windows 2000 component that manages routing between networks and remote access to networks.

RRAS *See* Routing and Remote Access Service.

RSVP. Resource Reservation Setup Protocol *See* Bandwidth Reservation Protocol

S

SACL *See* System Access Control List

Samba A UNIX implementation of the SMB file sharing protocol that is compatible with Windows file sharing. Samba source code is the basis of a number of Unix based attack programs that attempt to exploit the windows file sharing mechanism.

secret key encryption A reversible method of encryption that uses an algorithm on the original text and a key to create an encrypted message.

Secure Hash Algorithm (SHA1) A United States and IETF standard hashing algorithm that is less common but more secure than MD5.

S/MIME *See* Secure Multimedia Internet Mail Extensions

Secure Multimedia Internet Mail Extensions (S/MIME) The IETF standard for encrypting e-mail based on public key cryptography.

SSL *See* Secure Sockets Layer

Secure Sockets Layer (SSL) A standard for encryption of data over a secure HTTP connection using certificates. SSL has also been adapted for use with other common protocols such as FTP, POP3, and IMAP.

SAM *See* Security Accounts Manager

Security Accounts Manager (SAM) A secure database of user accounts stored in each computer's registry

SA *See* Security Association

Security Assocation (SA) An IPSec data structure that contains all the information necessary to establish a secure connection to another IPSec enabled host.

security group An object that combines a number of users into a single unit for security management.

SID *See* security identifier

security identifier (SID) A numeric code that uniquely identifies a security principal throughout the system.

security principal Any Active Directory object, such as a user account, a computer account, or a security group, that can be assigned permissions and rights.

Security Reference Monitor (SRM) The component of the LSA that compares a requesting program's Access Token to a secured object's DACL. See also LSA, Access Token, DACL.

security template A text file that contains numerous policy settings pertaining to computer security, such as password policy and account policy. Templates can be imported and exported to distribute security settings.

self-certified A certificate authority that is not rooted in another certificate authority. All who trust the CA must trust that the CA has authenticated every certificate that it issues.

Server Message Block (SMB) The Windows file sharing protocol. Also referred to as the Common Internet File Service (CIFS) in some documents.

service pack A major software update that includes a large number of bug fixes and enhancements.

session A connection between a client and server that provides continuity of authentication from the original logon until the session is terminated by serializing packets in a manner that is difficult or impossible to spoof.

share A folder that an administrator has published on a network in which users can store and retrieve files.

Shiva Password Authentication Protocol (SPAP) Shiva's extension of the obsolete Password Authentication Protocol. SPAP is slightly more secure, but still vulnerable to replay attacks.

Service Set Identifier (SSID) A unique identifier for a WAP that is used to control which WAPs wireless clients will associate with.

signed Any file that has a digital signature attached to it.

Simple Mail Transfer Protocol (SMTP) The Internet standard for server to server e-mail transmission.

Simple Network Management Protocol (SNMP) The Internet protocol used to query and control network attached devices and computers.

Single Sign-On (SSO) A set of authentication services that allow users to logon once and have that authentication follow them to every device they use, thus providing the illusion of having logged onto the entire network. In Windows, SSO is provided by Kerberos.

slipstreaming The process of including patched files in a Windows installation set so that subsequent installations will be patched up to date upon installation.

Smart Card A device in the form-factor of a credit card containing a microprocessor and nonvolatile memory that is used to create and store public/private key pairs. The private key is held irretrievably within the memory of the device, and the device's microprocessor is used to decrypt content using the key. Smart cards are often used to authenticate users and encrypt data.

SMB *See* Server Message Block.

SMTP *See* Simple Mail Transfer Protocol.

sniffer A computer (or device) used to receive all traffic on a network segment, rather than just the traffic addressed to it. Sniffers allow administrators to confirm that network protocols are operating correctly and to troubleshoot them. Sniffers are also used by hackers to inspect information and glean passwords. The Network Monitor in Windows is an example of a sniffer built into Windows 2000, but it is limited to inspecting traffic on the local machine unless you use the version included in SMS Server.

SNMP *See* Simple Network Management Protocol.

spam Unwanted un-requested e-mail, usually a commercial offer.

SPAP *See* Shiva Password Authentication Protocol.

SRM *See* Security Reference Monitor

SSID *See* Service Set Identifier.

SSO *See* Single-Sign On.

stand-alone CA A certificate authority that is separate from Active Directory and can issue certificates for intranet or extranet use.

subordinate CA A certificate authority that requires a CA certificate from a root CA.

symmetric encryption Any encryption algorithm which uses the same key for both the encrypt and decrypt functions.

SYN Flood A common type of Denial of Service attack wherein a large number of connection requests are transmitted to a server and immediately abandoned, causing the server to allocate resources waiting for replies from clients.

System Access Control List (SACL) An ACL that determines whether attempts to access an object are recorded in the audit log.

T

target-of-opportunity A victim discovered by chance rather than specifically searched for.

TGS *See* ticket granting service.

TGT *See* ticket granting ticket.

ticket An encrypted set of credentials used to prove to a server that the client has been authenticated by a KDC and has the right to access the server. In Windows 2000, Tickets contain the user's SID and the global security group SIDs that the user belongs to.

ticket granting service (TGS) The service in Kerberos that issues tickets.

ticket granting ticket (TGT) A special type of ticket that proves that the client has authenticated with the Kerberos authentication service, which is used to request subsequent tickets for use on other servers.

Trojan horse A program designed to trick users into installing it and then invisibly listen for connections from hackers.

trust The decision to place confidence in an entity to authenticate third parties.

trust relationship A defined relationship for permissions management between two domains. Security principals from a trusted domain can be given permissions for objects in a trusting domain.

tunnel A session established between routers through which typical network layer TCP/IP traffic is sent. Tunnels are typically encrypted to create a VPN.

U

UAM *See* User Authentication Module.

UDP *See* User Datagram Protocol.

user account A combination of username, password, and other attributes that define a single user's access to the network. User accounts are stored in Active Directory.

user authentication The process of determining the identity of the person accessing the computer so that the operating system can enforce security restrictions appropriate for that person.

User Authentication Module (UAM) A Macintosh operating system component written by Microsoft which enables Macintoshes to authenticate with a Windows domain using encrypted passwords. The latest version supports NTLM version 2.

User Datagram Protocol (UDP) A peer protocol to TCP that does not provide sessions, guaranteed delivery, or ordering of packets. UDP is used for simple single packet messages or protocols where reliability is less important than timing.

user rights Properties that control a user's ability to perform operations that affect the system as a whole, such as shutting the computer down.

V

Virtual Private Network (VPN) A method for connecting nodes of a private network over a public network such as the Internet by using a tunneling protocol to encapsulate private data.

W

WAN *See* Wide Area Network.

WAP *See* Wireless Access Point.

war driving The attempt to locate unsecured wireless access points by driving around with a wireless receiver.

WEP *See* Wired Equivalency Protocol.

Wide Area Network (WAN) A private internetwork that is connected by long-distance circuits or a VPN.

Windows Internet Name Service (WINS) An obsolete windows-name to IP address lookup service.

Wired Equivalency Protocol (WEP) A security protocol that encrypts wireless data using a fixed secret key.

Wireless Access Point (WAP) A bridge between a wired network and wireless clients.

Wireless Local Area Network (WLAN) A network constructed using radio transceivers rather than cables for each client.

worm A combination of a virus and a Trojan horse that is capable of automatically exploiting a host using a common vulnerability, and then using that host to propagate itself to others. Successful worms cause more damage than any other type of hacking activity due to their wide and rapid spread.

X

X.509 An IETF standard that specifies the data structure of certificates.

Index

A

Padlock and Hasp

A **padlock** is a detachable lock with a movable semicircular bar at the top, the free end of which is passed through a *hasp* and then locked shut. A **hasp** is a hinged metal fastening that fits over another semicircular metal bar called a *staple*. A *key*—a small, shaped cut of metal—is inserted into the padlock to release it so the hasp can swing open.*

At Microsoft Press, we use tools to illustrate our books for software developers and IT professionals. Tools very simply and powerfully symbolize human inventiveness. They're a metaphor for people extending their capabilities, precision, and reach. From simple calipers and pliers to digital micrometers and lasers, these stylized illustrations give each book a visual identity, and a personality to the series. With tools and knowledge, there's no limit to creativity and innovation. Our tag line says it all: *the tools you need to put technology to work*.

* **Microsoft Encarta Reference Library 2002.** © 1993-2001 Microsoft Corporation. All rights reserved.

In-depth technical information
for Microsoft Windows Server 2003

Windows Server 2003 TECHNICAL REFERENCE series is designed for IT professionals who need in-depth information but specific topics such as TCP/IP protocols and services supported by Windows Server 2003, Internet Information vices security, Active Directory Services, and Virtual Private Networks. Written by leading technical experts, these oks include hands-on examples, best practices, and technical tips. Topics are discussed by presenting real-world narios and practical how-to information to help IT professionals deploy, support, maintain, optimize, and ubleshoot Microsoft products and technologies. You start with the fundamentals and build comprehension layer by er until you understand the subject completely.

icrosoft® Windows® Server 2003 TCP/IP Protocols and rvices Technical Reference
3N: 0-7356-1291-9
S.A. $49.99
nada $76.99

icrosoft Internet Information Services Security chnical Reference
3N: 0-7356-1572-1
S.A. $49.99
nada $72.99

Active Directory® Services for Microsoft Windows Server 2003 Technical Reference
ISBN: 0-7356-1577-2
U.S.A. $49.99
Canada $76.99

Deploying Virtual Private Networks with Microsoft Windows Server 2003 Technical Reference
ISBN: 0-7356-1576-4
U.S.A. $49.99
Canada $76.99

To learn more about the full line of Microsoft Press® products for IT professionals, please visit:

microsoft.com/mspress/IT

Get a **Free**
e-mail newsletter, updates, special offers, links to related books, and more when you
register on line!

Register your Microsoft Press® title on our Web site and you'll get a FREE subscription to our e-mail newsletter, *Microsoft Press Book Connections.* You'll find out about newly released and upcoming books and learning tools, online events, software downloads, special offers and coupons for Microsoft Press customers, and information about major Microsoft® product releases. You can also read useful additional information about all the titles we publish, such as detailed book descriptions, tables of contents and indexes, sample chapters, links to related books and book series, author biographies, and reviews by other customers.

Registration is easy. Just visit this Web page and fill in your information:

http://www.microsoft.com/mspress/register

Microsoft®

Proof of Purchase

Use this page as proof of purchase if participating in a promotion or rebate offer on this title. Proof of purchase must be used in conjunction with other proof(s) of payment such as your dated sales receipt—see offer details.

MCSA/MCSE Self-Paced Training Kit: Implementing and Administering Security in a Microsoft® Windows® 2000 Network, Exam 70-214
0-7356-1878-X

CUSTOMER NAME

Microsoft Press, PO Box 97017, Redmond, WA 98073-9830

MICROSOFT LICENSE AGREEMENT

Book Companion CD

IMPORTANT—READ CAREFULLY: This Microsoft End-User License Agreement ("EULA") is a legal agreement between you (either an individual or an entity) and Microsoft Corporation for the Microsoft product identified above, which includes computer software and may include associated media, printed materials, and "online" or electronic documentation ("SOFTWARE PRODUCT"). Any component included within the SOFTWARE PRODUCT that is accompanied by a separate End-User License Agreement shall be governed by such agreement and not the terms set forth below. By installing, copying, or otherwise using the SOFTWARE PRODUCT, you agree to be bound by the terms of this EULA. If you do not agree to the terms of this EULA, you are not authorized to install, copy, or otherwise use the SOFTWARE PRODUCT; you may, however, return the SOFTWARE PRODUCT, along with all printed materials and other items that form a part of the Microsoft product that includes the SOFTWARE PRODUCT, to the place you obtained them for a full refund.

SOFTWARE PRODUCT LICENSE

The SOFTWARE PRODUCT is protected by United States copyright laws and international copyright treaties, as well as other intellectual property laws and treaties. The SOFTWARE PRODUCT is licensed, not sold.

1. **GRANT OF LICENSE.** This EULA grants you the following rights:

    a. **Software Product.** You may install and use one copy of the SOFTWARE PRODUCT on a single computer. The primary user of the computer on which the SOFTWARE PRODUCT is installed may make a second copy for his or her exclusive use on a portable computer.

    b. **Storage/Network Use.** You may also store or install a copy of the SOFTWARE PRODUCT on a storage device, such as a network server, used only to install or run the SOFTWARE PRODUCT on your other computers over an internal network; however, you must acquire and dedicate a license for each separate computer on which the SOFTWARE PRODUCT is installed or run from the storage device. A license for the SOFTWARE PRODUCT may not be shared or used concurrently on different computers.

    c. **License Pak.** If you have acquired this EULA in a Microsoft License Pak, you may make the number of additional copies of the computer software portion of the SOFTWARE PRODUCT authorized on the printed copy of this EULA, and you may use each copy in the manner specified above. You are also entitled to make a corresponding number of secondary copies for portable computer use as specified above.

    d. **Sample Code.** Solely with respect to portions, if any, of the SOFTWARE PRODUCT that are identified within the SOFTWARE PRODUCT as sample code (the "SAMPLE CODE"):

    i. **Use and Modification.** Microsoft grants you the right to use and modify the source code version of the SAMPLE CODE, *provided* you comply with subsection (d)(iii) below. You may not distribute the SAMPLE CODE, or any modified version of the SAMPLE CODE, in source code form.

    ii. **Redistributable Files.** Provided you comply with subsection (d)(iii) below, Microsoft grants you a nonexclusive, royalty-free right to reproduce and distribute the object code version of the SAMPLE CODE and of any modified SAMPLE CODE, other than SAMPLE CODE, or any modified version thereof, designated as not redistributable in the Readme file that forms a part of the SOFTWARE PRODUCT (the "Non-Redistributable Sample Code"). All SAMPLE CODE other than the Non-Redistributable Sample Code is collectively referred to as the "REDISTRIBUTABLES."

    iii. **Redistribution Requirements.** If you redistribute the REDISTRIBUTABLES, you agree to: (i) distribute the REDISTRIBUTABLES in object code form only in conjunction with and as a part of your software application product; (ii) not use Microsoft's name, logo, or trademarks to market your software application product; (iii) include a valid copyright notice on your software application product; (iv) indemnify, hold harmless, and defend Microsoft from and against any claims or lawsuits, including attorney's fees, that arise or result from the use or distribution of your software application product; and (v) not permit further distribution of the REDISTRIBUTABLES by your end user. Contact Microsoft for the applicable royalties due and other licensing terms for all other uses and/or distribution of the REDISTRIBUTABLES.

2. **DESCRIPTION OF OTHER RIGHTS AND LIMITATIONS.**

    - **Limitations on Reverse Engineering, Decompilation, and Disassembly.** You may not reverse engineer, decompile, or disassemble the SOFTWARE PRODUCT, except and only to the extent that such activity is expressly permitted by applicable law notwithstanding this limitation.

    - **Separation of Components.** The SOFTWARE PRODUCT is licensed as a single product. Its component parts may not be separated for use on more than one computer.

    - **Rental.** You may not rent, lease, or lend the SOFTWARE PRODUCT.

- **Support Services.** Microsoft may, but is not obligated to, provide you with support services related to the SOFTWARE PRODUCT ("Support Services"). Use of Support Services is governed by the Microsoft policies and programs described in the user manual, in "online" documentation, and/or in other Microsoft-provided materials. Any supplemental software code provided to you as part of the Support Services shall be considered part of the SOFTWARE PRODUCT and subject to the terms and conditions of this EULA. With respect to technical information you provide to Microsoft as part of the Support Services, Microsoft may use such information for its business purposes, including for product support and development. Microsoft will not utilize such technical information in a form that personally identifies you.

- **Software Transfer.** You may permanently transfer all of your rights under this EULA, provided you retain no copies, you transfer all of the SOFTWARE PRODUCT (including all component parts, the media and printed materials, any upgrades, this EULA, and, if applicable, the Certificate of Authenticity), **and** the recipient agrees to the terms of this EULA.

- **Termination.** Without prejudice to any other rights, Microsoft may terminate this EULA if you fail to comply with the terms and conditions of this EULA. In such event, you must destroy all copies of the SOFTWARE PRODUCT and all of its component parts.

3. COPYRIGHT. All title and copyrights in and to the SOFTWARE PRODUCT (including but not limited to any images, photographs, animations, video, audio, music, text, SAMPLE CODE, REDISTRIBUTABLES, and "applets" incorporated into the SOFTWARE PRODUCT) and any copies of the SOFTWARE PRODUCT are owned by Microsoft or its suppliers. The SOFT-WARE PRODUCT is protected by copyright laws and international treaty provisions. Therefore, you must treat the SOFTWARE PRODUCT like any other copyrighted material **except** that you may install the SOFTWARE PRODUCT on a single computer provided you keep the original solely for backup or archival purposes. You may not copy the printed materials accompanying the SOFTWARE PRODUCT.

4. U.S. GOVERNMENT RESTRICTED RIGHTS. The SOFTWARE PRODUCT and documentation are provided with RESTRICTED RIGHTS. Use, duplication, or disclosure by the Government is subject to restrictions as set forth in subparagraph (c)(1)(ii) of the Rights in Technical Data and Computer Software clause at DFARS 252.227-7013 or subparagraphs (c)(1) and (2) of the Commercial Computer Software—Restricted Rights at 48 CFR 52.227-19, as applicable. Manufacturer is Microsoft Corporation/One Microsoft Way/Redmond, WA 98052-6399.

5. EXPORT RESTRICTIONS. You agree that you will not export or re-export the SOFTWARE PRODUCT, any part thereof, or any process or service that is the direct product of the SOFTWARE PRODUCT (the foregoing collectively referred to as the "Restricted Components"), to any country, person, entity, or end user subject to U.S. export restrictions. You specifically agree not to export or re-export any of the Restricted Components (i) to any country to which the U.S. has embargoed or restricted the export of goods or services, which currently include, but are not necessarily limited to, Cuba, Iran, Iraq, Libya, North Korea, Sudan, and Syria, or to any national of any such country, wherever located, who intends to transmit or transport the Restricted Components back to such country; (ii) to any end user who you know or have reason to know will utilize the Restricted Components in the design, development, or production of nuclear, chemical, or biological weapons; or (iii) to any end user who has been prohibited from participating in U.S. export transactions by any federal agency of the U.S. government. You warrant and represent that neither the BXA nor any other U.S. federal agency has suspended, revoked, or denied your export privileges.

DISCLAIMER OF WARRANTY

NO WARRANTIES OR CONDITIONS. MICROSOFT EXPRESSLY DISCLAIMS ANY WARRANTY OR CONDITION FOR THE SOFTWARE PRODUCT. THE SOFTWARE PRODUCT AND ANY RELATED DOCUMENTATION ARE PROVIDED "AS IS" WITHOUT WARRANTY OR CONDITION OF ANY KIND, EITHER EXPRESS OR IMPLIED, INCLUDING, WITHOUT LIMITA-TION, THE IMPLIED WARRANTIES OF MERCHANTABILITY, FITNESS FOR A PARTICULAR PURPOSE, OR NONINFRINGEMENT. THE ENTIRE RISK ARISING OUT OF USE OR PERFORMANCE OF THE SOFTWARE PRODUCT REMAINS WITH YOU.

LIMITATION OF LIABILITY. TO THE MAXIMUM EXTENT PERMITTED BY APPLICABLE LAW, IN NO EVENT SHALL MICROSOFT OR ITS SUPPLIERS BE LIABLE FOR ANY SPECIAL, INCIDENTAL, INDIRECT, OR CONSEQUENTIAL DAM-AGES WHATSOEVER (INCLUDING, WITHOUT LIMITATION, DAMAGES FOR LOSS OF BUSINESS PROFITS, BUSINESS INTERRUPTION, LOSS OF BUSINESS INFORMATION, OR ANY OTHER PECUNIARY LOSS) ARISING OUT OF THE USE OF OR INABILITY TO USE THE SOFTWARE PRODUCT OR THE PROVISION OF OR FAILURE TO PROVIDE SUPPORT SERVICES, EVEN IF MICROSOFT HAS BEEN ADVISED OF THE POSSIBILITY OF SUCH DAMAGES. IN ANY CASE, MICROSOFT'S ENTIRE LIABILITY UNDER ANY PROVISION OF THIS EULA SHALL BE LIMITED TO THE GREATER OF THE AMOUNT ACTUALLY PAID BY YOU FOR THE SOFTWARE PRODUCT OR US$5.00; PROVIDED, HOWEVER, IF YOU HAVE ENTERED INTO A MICROSOFT SUPPORT SERVICES AGREEMENT, MICROSOFT'S ENTIRE LIABILITY REGARDING SUPPORT SERVICES SHALL BE GOVERNED BY THE TERMS OF THAT AGREEMENT. BECAUSE SOME STATES AND JURISDICTIONS DO NOT ALLOW THE EXCLUSION OR LIMITATION OF LIABILITY, THE ABOVE LIMITATION MAY NOT APPLY TO YOU.

MISCELLANEOUS

This EULA is governed by the laws of the State of Washington USA, except and only to the extent that applicable law mandates govern-ing law of a different jurisdiction.

Should you have any questions concerning this EULA, or if you desire to contact Microsoft for any reason, please contact the Microsoft subsidiary serving your country, or write: Microsoft Sales Information Center/One Microsoft Way/Redmond, WA 98052-6399.

System Requirements

To get the most out of this training kit and the Supplemental Course Materials CD-ROM, you will need a computer equipped with the following minimum configuration:

- Windows 2000 Server (a 120-day Evaluation Edition is included)

- Windows 2000 Professional

- Intel-based Pentium II or later processor

- 128 MB RAM

- 2 GB hard disk drive

- 100 Mbps network interface adapter

- CD-ROM drive

- Microsoft Mouse or compatible pointing device

- Display system capable of 800 x 600 resolution or better

- An Apple Macintosh computer that meets the minimum requirements for OS X 10.1

- An 802.1x-compliant Wireless Access Point with a compatible wireless network adapter

The following software is required to complete optional exercises that cover security issues specific to the software:

- Microsoft Windows 98

- Microsoft ISA Server

- Microsoft SQL Server 2000

- Microsoft Exchange Server

- Apple Macintosh OS X 10.1 or later